WILSON FAMILIES

Descendants of
Colonel Benjamin Wilson
1733-1814

Patti Sue McCrary

HERITAGE BOOKS
2007

HERITAGE BOOKS
AN IMPRINT OF HERITAGE BOOKS, INC.

Books, CDs, and more—Worldwide

For our listing of thousands of titles see our website
at
www.HeritageBooks.com

Published 2007 by
HERITAGE BOOKS, INC.
Publishing Division
65 East Main Street
Westminster, Maryland 21157-5026

International Standard Book Number: 978-0-7884-3199-4

Dedication

To my cousins by the dozens

TABLE OF CONTENTS

Introduction

In 1950 Harry Herndon McLean published the book *The Wilson Family - Somerset and Barter Hill Branch* which was based on research done by his mother's first husband, William Henry Wilson (1859-1904), a descendant of Colonel Benjamin Wilson of Cumberland Co., Virginia, or Col. Ben as he was affectionately called. As stated by McLean in his preface, there are errors, as there will surely be in this effort, and I apologize, as he did, for any misspelling of names. He contacted many people to add to the original research, giving leads to many sources of additional information. My mother, Annette (Wilson) Thomas, who seldom refused an opportunity to buy a book, purchased his publication. As a child, I was thrilled to see my name in print, spelled correctly.

This project was originally planned as a corrected version of the McLean book with documentation, when available. My research has greatly expanded several lines to Col. Ben, so I chose to organize the new findings and the data in the McLean book using the computer software, PAF (Personal Ancestral File from the Church of Jesus Christ of Latter-day Saints in Salt Lake City). The PAF data was used by GenBook (copyrighted by Rex Clement), which produced a word processing document that could be modified by WordPerfect (Corel Corporation).

GenBook numbers descendants using the line of the eldest child. When marriages of cousins resulted in a deviation of the line from the surname "Wilson", I have adjusted the order, copying the children to the Wilson line, giving details of the descendants under the Wilson name. The most obvious example of this is Ann Seay Wilson, daughter of James Wilson, who married John Meredith. Two of their daughters married sons of Goodridge Wilson. I hope the cross references show the multiple lines to Col. Ben.

I have removed some redundant place names, cross reference markers, and text generated by the software. In subsequent reformatting, some cross references are missing when the entry is on the following page. Some entries that were generated as step-children have been deleted; some data was deleted because of descendants' requests not to be named or not to be included in this book.

I want to acknowledge the members of the Wilson Round Robin who provided me with supplementary and background material, old correspondence, and insight - Maurice D. Leach, Jr., of Lexington, Virginia, Eloise Wilson (1912-2003) of Longview, Texas, John C. Reid of Peculiar,

Missouri, John M. Finley of Austin, Texas, Mary Carolyn (Steger) Mitton of Salem, Indiana, Mary Jean (Brown) Reece of Versailles, Kentucky, Williams Wilson of Charleston, South Carolina, Suzanne (Greene) Seyfried of Midvale, Utah, Virginia (Glenn) Horsman of Austin, Texas, and O. Douglas Wilson of Del Mar, California.

Other cousins who were very generous with corrections, additions, and supporting documents were Nancy (Whitman) Santheson of Roswell, New Mexico, who also provided the copy of the "hand painting on ivory" of Col. Ben, Eric S. Chamberlain of Natchez, Mississippi, Marguerite F. (Morton) Blackwood of Clearwater, Florida, Julia and Sally Watson of Kirkwood, Missouri, Martha (Watson) Hornberger of Missouri, and Martha (Witten) Johnson of Benbrook, Texas, who also helped refine the picture of Col. Ben. The sources of other corrections of the original McLean publication and additions to family groups are cited with the family.

I especially want to thank my brother Dick Thomas for proofing the manuscript.

Some information in this book has already been published in my book *Wilson Families in Cumberland County, Virginia and Woodford County, Kentucky with Correspondence and Other Papers, 1785-1849* and the article by Maurice D. Leach and Patti Sue McCrary, "The Colonel Benjamin Wilson Family, 1754-1814" published in *Cumberland County Virginia and its people*, Fourth Supplement, 1999, by the Cumberland County Historical Society.

Some marriage dates refer to the date of the marriage bond. Generation superscripts are in bold. Footnote superscripts are in italics. In most cases, the references in the footnotes are in shortened form with the full citation in the Bibliography. Since census indexes are widely available, only the year, county and state are given in the text when referring to census data. Old home place names are shown in quotes. Some additional detail is given for several of the homes in the appendix.

I hope I will be forgiven for giving more text information on my three direct lines to Col. Ben, to his sons James and Goodrich/Goodridge, and his daughter Mason.

Patti Sue (Thomas) McCrary
P. O. Box 2953
Gulf Shores AL 36547

Reading This Book

(The following is an extraction of the article which is generated, along with index and cross reference markers, by the software, GenBook. PSM)

If, while reading the following pages of this book, the reader will keep these few facts in mind, a much clearer understanding of the contents will result. The format or style used in this book is known as the **Modified Register System,** which has been refined by the National Genealogical Society.

Three types of numbers are used: one to uniquely identify the individual, one to indicate the generation into which that person falls, and one to denote his or her birth-order within the nuclear family. The identification numbering system used in this book is called **By Descendants, in Sequential Order.** The starting person is 1, his first child is 2, his first child's first child is 3, and so on. After all the descendants of the first child are listed, then the descendants of the second child are listed, and so on until 11 generations. The ID numbers are in sequential order.

When an individual is introduced in his/her separate sketch, the name appears in boldface letters. The name is preceded by the identification number. The last given name is followed immediately by a superscript number indicating the number of generations from the starting individual in this book. In parentheses following the name is a list of direct ancestors back to the starting individual. Only the given name is listed, preceded by his/her ID number, and followed by the generation number in superscript.

When the list of children is presented, the plus (+) sign indicates that more about this child will be presented in his/her separate sketch. The ID number is printed, followed by M/F indicating the sex. Next a small roman numeral in front of the name designates birth-order. Next the name is followed by the birth and death dates.

The index is arranged alphabetically by surname. Under each surname, the given names are alphabetically arranged. The name is followed by the year of birth and death in square brackets. The number to the right indicates the page where this name appears. The wife appears under her maiden name and under her married names with her maiden name in parentheses.

Colonel Benjamin Wilson (1733-1814)

CHAPTER 1

Descendants of Colonel Benjamin Wilson (1733-1814)

1. Benjamin¹ Wilson, Sr. was born 6 Jan 1733 in James City Co., Virginia. He was the son of **Willis Wilson** and **Elizabeth Goodrich.**¹ Benjamin, Sr. died 27 Oct 1814 at "Somerset", Cumberland Co., Virginia.² The marriage bond for Benjamin and **Anne Seay** is dated 25 Mar 1754 in Cumberland Co., Virginia.³ She was born 6 Mar 1735 probably in King William Co., Virginia, the daughter of **James Seay, Sr.**⁴ Anne died 25 Apr 1814 at "Somerset", Cumberland Co., Virginia.

ISSUE:⁵

+ 2. f   i.   **Mary Wilson**, born 23 Dec 1754, died 1787 <See pg. 6>.

57. f   ii.   **Elizabeth Wilson**, born 17 Oct 1756 at "Somerset", Cumberland Co., Virginia, and died there 1808.⁶

+ 58. m   iii.   **Willis Wilson**, born 22 Apr 1758, died 10 Feb 1822 <See pg. 12>.

+ 232. m   iv.   **Benjamin Wilson, Jr.**, born 24 Oct 1759, died 8 Sep 1839 <See pg. 34>.

430. f   v.   **Anne Wilson**, born 10 Sep 1762 at "Somerset", Cumberland Co., Virginia, and died there 1786.

+ 431. m   vi.   **James Wilson**, born 6 Feb 1765, died 5 Jun 1847 <See pg. 62>.

+ 1235. f   vii.   **Mason Wilson**, born 21 Dec 1768, died 1837 <See pg. 108>.

---

¹ 7 Jun 1728 Willis Wilson and Elizabeth Goodrich, Norfolk Co. VA Marriage Bonds 1706 - 1768, Library of Virginia, Richmond. Boddie, *Historical Southern Families*, 3:62-63.

² Information from the family Bible of his son Willis Wilson, "Wilson Family", *VA Mag. Hist.*, 25:199-200. A transcription of a similar version is in the Appendix. A letter written by Willis about his father's health and mother's death is in McCrary, *Wilson Families ... Correspondence .... 1785-1849*, 167.

³ Cumberland Co. VA Marriage Bonds 1749-1788, Library of Virginia, Richmond. Elliott, *Marriages, Cumberland Co. VA*, 139.

⁴ Will of James Seay, LVA. Research so far has not shown any Huguenot ancestry for his Seay line.

⁵ Woodson Family, *Papers, 1740-1945*, Accession 29437-41, LVA. Will of Benjamin Wilson, LVA. Transcriptions of Anne (Seay) Wilson's "Prayer Book" and Benjamin Wilson's will are in the Appendix.

⁶ Death dates for Elizabeth and Anne are taken from a query, by Dr. **John Meredith Kenney**. *William and Mary Quarterly*, 20 (2)433. They were not named in their father's 1812 will.

1252. m viii.   **Samuel Wilson**, born 30 Mar 1770 at "Somerset",
Cumberland Co., Virginia. He earned his medical degree at
the University of Edinburgh in Scotland in 1792.[7] From a
letter he wrote to his brother on his return from school in
Scotland, he sounds like a homesick young man, who
probably had better memories after reflection. "After a long
& disagreeable absence I three weeks ago again arrived to
my own Country, and if you can form any idea of the
feelings of a man who had been banished to one of the most
barren, stiff, formal & ceremonious Countries in the world
and then to return to one where the most copious profusion
of all things good for the body together with a free open
liberal independancy of manner displayed itself in the
countenance of every man you meet, you may then judge
how I am delighted."[8]   Later letters written by his brothers
show the respect all held for him and his medical
knowledge. He served as a justice at the county court as
early as 1805 and in 1819 received his commission from the
governor to be high sheriff.[9] At his father's death, he
became the owner of "Somerset" leaving it to nephews at
his death.[10] He died before 24 Jan 1842 and was buried at
"Somerset".[11]

+ 1253. m ix.   **Matthew Wilson**, born 25 Mar 1772, died before 18 Nov
1833 <See pg. 112>.

1706. m x.   **Alexander Wilson**, born 1 Apr 1774 at "Somerset",
Cumberland Co., Virginia. He is described in a 1798 letter
as "the least thrifty but ... the most happy" of his brothers.
Alexander describes his adventures on a river trip to St.
Louis, Missouri in 1817, "we were in a fine pickle to face it
having all our clothes wet & having swam at least 10
different creeks the preceeding five days .... I have not layn
on a feather Bed since I crossed the Ohia more than once or
twice."[12] He died probably in Woodford Co., Kentucky,
after 1850 when he is shown, age 76, in the census with his
nephew.

---

[7] "List of the American Graduates", *NEHGR*, 42:159, 162.

[8] McCrary, *Wilson Families ... Correspondence .... 1785-1849*, 46.

[9] Cumberland Co. VA Order Books 1803-1807:145, 1818-1821:231.

[10] Cumberland Co. VA Deed Book 13:148-9, Will Book 10:319.

[11] Littleton Parish, Accession 29330, LVA.

[12] McCrary, *Wilson Families ... Correspondence .... 1785-1849*, 72, 183-4.

+ 1707. m xi. **Goodridge Wilson**, born 26 Mar 1776, died 30 Sep 1849
<See pg. 176>.
+ 2138. f xii. **Martha Wilson**, born 1 Jun 1778, died before 22 Apr 1849
<See pg. 287>.
2148. f xiii. **Unita Wilson**, born 22 Feb 1783 at "Somerset",
Cumberland Co., Virginia. She is mentioned, as "Hetty", in
family letters from 1792 to 1809.[13] In 1827 she is shown
with her sister, Martha, and brother-in-law applying for a
"certificate of membership and dismission" from the
Cumberland Presbyterian Church. [14] In the 1830 census she
is probably one of the two females age 40-50 in their
household in Rockingham Co., North Carolina. Her will,
written 19 Sep 1851 and proved Feb 1852, named the
families of her niece and nephew in North Carolina.[15]

Benjamin Sr. was born in James City Co., Virginia, near the junction of the
Chickahominy and James Rivers where his grandfather **Benjamin
Goodrich** had settled.[16] His father died in 1740 when Benjamin was 7
years old; his mother probably remarried.

By 25 Mar 1754, the date of his marriage bond, he had settled in
Cumberland Co., and in 1755 he bought 200 acres on the north side of the
Willis River, the beginning of his plantation home "Somerset", adding to it
in 1765 and 1784.[17]

Benjamin was active in local affairs, serving on juries, serving as executor
of several estates and frequently as guardian.[18] He was appointed
processioner of Southam Parish from 1755-1771 and as vestryman in 1771.
Littleton Parish was formed in 1772 from Southam Parish, when Benjamin

---

[13] McCrary, *Wilson Families ... Correspondence .... 1785-1849*, 47, 63, 81, 144.

[14] Cumberland Presbyterian Church, Accession 20080, LVA, 122.

[15] Webster, *Rockingham Co NC Will Abstracts*, 61 (C:131).

[16] In 1732 his parents "of Chickohominey" sold land that Willis had inherited from
his grandfather, **James Wilson**. Norfolk Co. VA Deed Books 9:220, 11:15-16.
Benjamin assigned 200 acres in James City Co. to **Cary Wilkinson** in 1766 which
had been assigned to **Leonard Keeling** in 1763, Lee Family, *Papers, 1638-1867.*
In a *Virginia Gazette* article, 4 Dec 1766, Benjamin was shown as executor of the
estate of Leonard Keeling, (Misc. Reel 162, LVA).

[17] Cumberland Co. VA Deed Books 2:260, 4:82-3, 6:204-5. McCrary,
Cumberland County ... Historical Inventory, 47.

[18] Cumberland Co. VA Order Books 1752-1758:345, 525, OB 1767-1770: 273,
376. Reynolds, *Cumberland Co VA Will Books 1 & 2*, 22, 50, 62, 67, 83.

Wilson was again named as vestryman.[19]

In 1775 Benjamin was on a committee that wrote to delegates of the
Continental Congress "Resolved, ... we shall be ready to risk our lives and
fortunes", then later, "Resolved, ...members of the committee ... will give
..... three shillings per pound to ... persons ... who ... produce to the said
committee ... fifty pounds weight of good gunpowder, manufactured in
America ...", also that "whenever a suspicion shall arise of any merchant in
this county having infringed the association of the late Continental
Congress, ... do make information thereof ....to ... the committee."[20]
Benjamin served on the Committee of Safety, was appointed Lt. Colonel in
1781, and was a commissioner of public claims after the war.[21] He signed
a petition dated 10 November 1780 which asked the House of Delegates to
reject a bill forbidding the use of depreciated currency in payment of
debts.[22]

Benjamin was appointed coroner of Cumberland Co. in 1784 and sheriff in
1788. He served as a justice in the county court from 1777 to as late as
1807.[23] He was appointed as a trustee for the improvement of navigation
on the Willis River in 1787. In 1797 he was a member of the group of the
county court given the task of working to establish public schools, and in
the same year, he was named a county commissioner to inspect tobacco.[24]

The closeness and affection shared in the family is shown in the collection
of letters the father and brothers wrote to their son/brother, Benjamin Jr., in
Kentucky, the father showing typical parental concern, "I am desirous that
you wou'd be more frequent in your Letters; for I suppose it is a part of the
Infirmities of age to be more desirous to hear of the wellfare of those we are
nearly bound to."

James wrote in 1808, "Our parents settled at this place, poor strangers, little
improved and unsupported by connections; their acquaintance and

[19] Blomquist, *Vestry Book of Southam Parish*, 82, 214, 217. *Today and Yesterday*, 230.

[20] *Virginia Gazette* 25 Mar 1775, page 1, Film 11 Reel 5, LVA.

[21] McIlwaine, *Committee of Safety Cumberland Co.*, 7-30. Cumberland Co. VA Order Books 1779-1784:152-3, 183, 197, 204-5, 216.

[22] Hall, "Legislative Petitions", *Mag. VA Gen.*, 30:88.

[23] Virginia, Council of State. *Journals*, 3:378, 4:286. Cumberland Co. VA Order Books 1774-1778:408, 1801-1807:467.

[24] Hening, *Statutes*, 12:583, 586. Trout, *Slate and Willis Rivers*, 32. *Cumb. Co. VA and Its People*, 7. *Calendar of Virginia State Papers*, 8:452.

friendship with the Rev. Mr. McRae was certainly the most lucky occurrence in life; from his attention have their sons become learned and pious, possessing correct knowledge of both men and things."

As the parents aged, the sons spoke of their declining health. "Our parents are not much amiss but always complaining - the father is too apt to fret, our mother is very tranquil, resigned & devout, the only fit & adequate support for decaying man."[25]

Both were probably buried at "Somerset" where their son Samuel was buried.[26]

---

[25] McCrary, *Wilson Families ... Correspondence .... 1785-1849*, 93, 130, 146.
Rev. Christopher McRae of Littleton Parish was attacked for praying for the King of England in 1779, but he was defended by most citizens in the county and **Patrick Henry**. Meade, *Old Churches*, 2:35-8. *Today and Yesterday*, 235, 241.

[26] Littleton Parish, Accession 29330, LVA.

CHAPTER 2

Descendants of Mary Wilson (1754-1787)

2. Mary² Wilson <See pg. 1> (1.Benjamin, Sr.¹) was born 23 Dec 1754 at "Somerset", Cumberland Co., Virginia, the daughter of **Benjamin Wilson, Sr.** and **Anne Seay**.[27] Mary died 1787 in Amelia Co., Virginia, and was buried at Grubb Hill Church in Amelia Co. She married **Thomas Mumford, Jr.** He was born about 1755 in Amelia Co., the son of **Thomas Mumford, Sr.** and **Sarah Booker**. Thomas, Jr., died before 25 Jan 1787 in Richmond, Virginia, and was buried at Grubb Hill Church.[28] The will of Thomas Mumford was proved 25 Jan 1787; he left his estate to his daughter Mary Mumford.[29]

ISSUE:

+ 3. f   i.   **Mary Thomas Mumford**, born 20 Dec 1786, died 19 May 1860.

- - - - - - - - - - -

3. Mary Thomas³ Mumford (2.Mary², 1.Benjamin, Sr.¹) was born 20 Dec 1786 at "Cedar Grove", Amelia Co., Virginia,[30] the daughter of **Thomas Mumford, Jr.** and **Mary Wilson**. Mary died 19 May 1860 at "Blenheim", Powhatan Co., Virginia. She married **Joseph Hobson** 2 Oct 1806 at "Bonbrook", Cumberland Co., Virginia.[31] He was born 9 Aug 1780 in Cumberland Co., Virginia, the son of **Caleb Hobson** and **Phoebe Brackett**. Joseph died 22 Sep 1832 in Powhatan Co.[32]

ISSUE:[33]

+ 4. m   i.   **Thomas Ludwell Hobson**, born 4 Jul 1807.

---

[27] Woodson Family, *Papers, 1740-1945*, Accession 29437-41, LVA.

[28] DAR - Hobson Family Bible.

[29] The will, not dated but proved 25 Jan 1787 in Raleigh Parish, named daughter Mary Mumford, sister Ann executor along with friend Willis Wilson. Wise, *Amelia Co. VA Will Book 4*, 3 (WB 4:21). *Genealogies, Tyler's Quarterly*, 2:736-7.

[30] DAR - Hobson Bible. Evidently there is an error giving Mary's birth as 1782. In the Bible it is written that she was born 6 weeks before her mother's death, her father's death occurring soon after. When she married in 1806, consent was given by her guardian, W. Wilson, which indicates that she was not yet 21 years of age.

[31] Elliott, *Marriages, Cumberland Co. VA*, 68.

[32] DAR - Hobson Family Bible.

[33] "Wilson Family", *VA Mag. Hist.*, 25:200. Beck, Ancestral File, descendants chart giving birth dates and places. DAR - Hobson Bible.

+ 13. f   ii.   **Phoebe Anne Hobson**, born 27 Dec 1808 <See pg. 8>.

 25. m   iii.   **Joseph Virginius Hobson**, born 11 Nov 1810 in
                 Cumberland Co., Virginia. He married (1) **Sarah M.
                 Norvell** 18 Oct 1842. Joseph married (2) **Mary E. Bullock**
                 Sep 1853.[34] Joseph died 10 Oct 1895 in Lynchburg,
                 Virginia.[35]

+ 26. f   iv.   **Mary Mumford Hobson**, born 28 Feb 1812 <See pg. 9>.

 33. m   v.   **William Hobson**, born 1 Nov 1813.

+ 34. m   vi.   **John Caleb Hobson**, born 27 Dec 1814 <See pg. 9>.

 41. m   vii.   **Infant Hobson**, born 22 Jan 1817, died 2 Feb 1817.

 42. f viii.   **Maria Willis Hobson**, born 31 Mar 1818 in Cumberland
                 Co., Virginia, died 26 Nov 1823.

 43. f   ix.   **Lavinia Wilson Hobson**, born 16 Sep 1820 in Cumberland
                 Co. She married **William Lewis Booker** 4 Oct 1838 in
                 Powhatan Co., Virginia. Lavinia died 26 Jun 1908.[36]

 44. f   x.   **Sarah Booker Hobson**, born 20 Aug 1824 in Cumberland
                 Co. She married **David Edley Spence** 12 Jun 1869 at
                 "Blenheim", Powhatan Co., Virginia. David died 1892.[37]

+ 45. m   xi.   **Willis Wilson Hobson**, born 30 Dec 1826, died 23 Mar
                 1917 <See pg. 9>.

After Mary's parents died, she lived with her uncle **Willis Wilson**. She is
mentioned frequently in the letters that Willis and others wrote to their
brother in Kentucky, especially dealing with land in Kentucky that Mary
inherited from her father, who bought 200 acres with others in 1784.[38]
Mary appeared in the 1850 census of Powhatan Co. with her son, Willis
Wilson Hobson and his wife Arabella.

- - - - - - - - - - -

4. Thomas Ludwell[4] Hobson (3.Mary[3], 2.Mary[2], 1.Benjamin, Sr.[1]) was
born 4 Jul 1807 in Cumberland Co., Virginia, the son of **Joseph Hobson**
and **Mary Thomas Mumford**.[39] He married **Virginia Randolph Page**
27 Nov 1833 in Cumberland Co., Virginia.[40] She was born 19 Aug 1813 in
Powhatan Co., Virginia, the daughter of **John Cary Page** and **Mary Anna**

---

[34] DAR - Hobson Bible.

[35] Bradford, *Homœopathy in Virginia*, (accessed 29 Mar 2006).

[36] Vogt, *Powhatan Co. Marriages*, 102.

[37] Vogt, *Powhatan Co. Marriages*, 102.

[38] McCrary, *Wilson Families ... Correspondence .... 1785-1849*, 165.

[39] DAR - Hobson Bible.

[40] Elliott, *Marriages, Cumberland Co. VA*, 68.

Trent. Their first 4 children were baptized in 1841 in Littleton Parish.[41]

ISSUE:[42]

5. f   i.   **Mary Anna Hobson**, born 12 Dec 1834 in Powhatan Co.,
              Virginia. She married **Mann Page**. He was born about 1834
              in Albemarle Co., Virginia.

6. f   ii.   **Caroline Eppes Hobson**, born 27 Mar 1836 in Powhatan
              Co.

7. m iii. **Joseph Hobson**, born 26 Aug 1837 in Powhatan Co.

8. f   iv. **Virginia Page Hobson**, born 1840 in Powhatan Co.

9. m v.   **Thomas M. Hobson**, born 27 Nov 1842 in Powhatan Co.

10. f vi. **Ellen Cary Hobson**, born 26 Jun 1846 in Powhatan Co.
              She married **George N. Gutherie**. He was born about 1846
              in Cumberland Co., Virginia.

11. f vii. **Clara Hobson**, born 1848 in Powhatan Co. She married
              William Nash. He was born 26 Jun 1853 in Powhatan Co.

12. m viii. **Alexander Trent Hobson**, born Sep 1849 in Powhatan Co.

- - - - - - - - - - -

13. Phoebe Anne[4] Hobson <See pg. 7> (3.Mary[3], 2.Mary[2], 1.Benjamin, Sr.[1])
was born 27 Dec 1808 in Cumberland Co., Virginia, the daughter of **Joseph
Hobson** and **Mary Thomas Mumford**.[43] She married **Hilary Harris**
2 Dec 1830 in Powhatan Co., Virginia.[44] He was born 1803 in Louisa Co.,
Virginia.

ISSUE:[45]

14. m i.   **Joseph Hobson Harris**, born 1831 in Powhatan Co.,
              Virginia.

15. f   ii.   **Anne Lavinia Harris**, born 1833 in Powhatan Co.

16. m iii. **John Wilson Harris**, born 1835 in Powhatan Co.

17. m iv. **Hilary Valentine Harris**, born 1839 in Powhatan Co.

18. f   v.   **Christiana Sallie Harris**, born 1841 in Powhatan Co.

19. f   vi. **Fanny Morton Harris**, born 1843 in Powhatan Co.

20. m vii. **Abner Harris**, born 1845 in Powhatan Co.

21. f viii. **Sarah Octavia Harris**, born 1847 in Powhatan Co.

22. m ix. **Willis Overton Harris**, born 1849 in Powhatan Co.

23. f   x.   **Mary Maria Harris**, born 1850 in Powhatan Co.

24. f xi. **Martha Pryor Harris**, born 1852 in Powhatan Co.

---

[41] Littleton Parish, Accession 29330, LVA, 89.

[42] Beck, Ancestral File.

[43] DAR - Hobson Bible.

[44] Vogt, *Powhatan Co. Marriages*, 102.

[45] Beck, Ancestral File. "Wilson Family", *VA Mag. Hist.*, 25:200.

- - - - - - - - - -

26. Mary Mumford⁴ Hobson <See pg. 7> (3.Mary³, 2.Mary², 1.Benjamin, Sr.¹) was born 28 Feb 1812 in Cumberland Co., Virginia, the daughter of **Joseph Hobson** and **Mary Thomas Mumford.**[46] She married **Thomas P. Nash** 21 Nov 1832 in Powhatan Co., Virginia.[47] He was born 1811 in Powhatan Co., the son of **Thomas Nash** and **Lucy Lawson Hobson.**[48]

ISSUE:[49]

27. f i.   **Lucy C. Nash**, born 1834 in Powhatan Co., Virginia.
28. m ii. **Thomas Nash**, born 1837 in Powhatan Co.
29. f iii. **Mary J. Nash**, born 1840 in Powhatan Co.
30. f iv. **Laura E. Nash**, born 1842 in Powhatan Co.
31. m v.   **Travis S. Nash**, born 1848 in Powhatan Co.
32. f vi. **Alice W. Nash**, born 1849 in Powhatan Co.

- - - - - - - - - -

34. John Caleb⁴ Hobson <See pg. 7> (3.Mary³, 2.Mary², 1.Benjamin, Sr.¹) was born 27 Dec 1814 in Cumberland Co., Virginia, the son of **Joseph Hobson** and **Mary Thomas Mumford.**[50] He married **Sally Mumford Haskins** 5 Nov 1840 in Powhatan Co., Virginia.[51] She was born 8 Jan 1817 in Powhatan Co.

ISSUE:[52]

35. f i.   **Lavinia Hobson**, born 1841 in Powhatan Co., Virginia.
36. m ii. **Samuel M. Hobson**, born 3 Mar 1843 in Powhatan Co.
37. m iii. **J. Haskins Hobson**, born 1846 in Powhatan Co. He married **Eunice Michaux**. She was born 23 Sep 1849 in Powhatan Co.
38. f iv. **Judith Hobson**, born 1847 in Powhatan Co.
39. f v.   **Sallie W. Hobson**, born 1850 in Powhatan Co.
40. m vi. **John C. Hobson**, born 20 Jan 1853 in Powhatan Co.

- - - - - - - - - -

45. Willis Wilson⁴ Hobson <See pg. 7> (3.Mary³, 2.Mary², 1.Benjamin, Sr.¹) was born 30 Dec 1826 at "Blenheim", Powhatan Co., Virginia, the son of

[46] DAR - Hobson Bible.
[47] Vogt, *Powhatan Co. Marriages*, 102.
[48] Thomas P. Nash, www.FamilySearch.org, (accessed 6 Nov 2005).
[49] Beck, Ancestral File.
[50] DAR - Hobson Bible.
[51] Vogt, *Powhatan Co. Marriages*, 36.
[52] Beck, Ancestral File.

Joseph Hobson and **Mary Thomas Mumford.**[53] Willis died 23 Mar 1917 at "Vernon", Powhatan Co., and was buried in Hobson Cemetery in Powhatan Co. He married (1) **Arabella Gilliam Bolling** 15 May 1849 in Petersburg, Virginia. She was born 12 Aug 1828 in Petersburg, Chesterfield Co., Virginia. Arabella died 28 May 1882 at "Vernon"[54] and was buried in Hobson Cemetery.[55]

ISSUE:[56]

   46. m   i. **John Peyton Hobson,** born 3 Sep 1850 in Powhatan Co., Virginia.
 + 47. m   ii. **Joseph Mumford Hobson, Sr.,** born 3 Apr 1852, died 1933 <See pg. 10>.
   50. f iii. **Anna Gilliam Hobson,** born 29 Dec 1853 in Powhatan Co.
   51. f   iv. **Lucy Bolling Hobson,** born 5 Apr 1854 in Powhatan Co.
   52. f   v. **Mary Thomas Hobson,** born 28 Jun 1857 in Powhatan Co.
   53. m   vi. **Willis Wilson Hobson,** born 13 Dec 1858 in Powhatan Co.
   54. m vii. **Bolling Hobson,** born 15 Sep 1860 in Powhatan Co.
   55. m viii. **David Spencer Hobson,** born 1 Mar 1863 in Powhatan Co.
   56. m   ix. **Valentine Harris Hobson,** born 27 Apr 1865 in Powhatan Co.

Willis married (2) **Betty Lewis Miller** 30 Sep 1885. She was born 1833. Betty died 1895 and was buried in Hobson Cemetery in Powhatan Co., Virginia.

Willis is shown with his wife and mother in the 1850 census of Powhatan Co. Around 1882, he wrote to **Dr. Werner Crenshaw** in Versailles, Kentucky, about his ancestor Willis Wilson, signing it "your cousin". The family connection has not been determined.[57]

- - - - - - - - - - -

47. Joseph Mumford⁵ Hobson, Sr. <See pg. 10> (45.Willis⁴, 3.Mary³, 2.Mary², 1.Benjamin, Sr.¹) was born 3 Apr 1852 at "Vernon", Powhatan Co., Virginia, the son of **Willis Wilson Hobson** and **Arabella Gilliam Bolling.** Joseph, Sr. died 1933 in Ballsville, Powhatan Co. He married **Jane Gilliam Jones** 25 Sep 1875. She was born 1856 in Danville, Virginia.

---

[53] DAR - Hobson Bible.

[54] McClendon, DAR application.

[55] Weisiger, "Powhatan County, Virginia Tombstone Inscriptions".

[56] Beck, Ancestral File.

[57] Benjamin Wilson Papers 1785-1916.

THE DESCENDANTS OF MARY WILSON (1754-1787)

Jane died 9 Mar 1891 in Greensboro, North Carolina.[58]

ISSUE:

+ 48. m   i.   **Joseph Mumford Hobson, Jr.**, born 22 Dec 1881, died 17 Apr 1921.

- - - - - - - - - -

48. Joseph Mumford[6] Hobson, Jr. (47.Joseph, Sr.[5], 45.Willis[4], 3.Mary[3], 2.Mary[2], 1.Benjamin, Sr.[1]) was born 22 Dec 1881 in Richmond, Virginia, the son of **Joseph Mumford Hobson, Sr.** and **Jane Gilliam Jones**. Joseph, Jr. died 17 Apr 1921 in Amarillo, Texas. He married **Katie Louise Brooks** 9 Jan 1908. She was born 22 Jul 1880 in Roane, Texas. Katie died 6 Sep 1964 in Amarillo.[59]

ISSUE:

49. f   i.   **Margaret Hobson**, born 8 May 1913 in Miami, Texas. She married **Ben S. McClendon** 17 Aug 1933 in Amarillo, Texas. He was born 25 Jul 1912.

---

[58] McClendon, DAR application.

[59] McClendon, DAR application.

CHAPTER 3

Descendants of Willis Wilson (1758-1822)

58. Willis² Wilson <See pg. 1> (1.Benjamin, Sr.¹) was born 22 Apr 1758 at "Somerset", Cumberland Co., Virginia, the son of **Benjamin Wilson, Sr.** and **Anne Seay**.[60] Willis died 10 Feb 1822 at "Bonbrook", Cumberland Co., Virginia, and was buried there.[61] He married **Elizabeth Trent** about 1788. She was born 26 Feb 1756, the daughter of **Alexander Trent, III** and **Elizabeth Woodson**. She died 5 Oct 1834.[62]

ISSUE:

+ 59. f   i.   **Maria Willis Wilson**, born 19 Dec 1793, died 6 Jan 1818 <See pg. 13>.

Elizabeth also married (1) **William Black, Jr.** 20 Apr 1778 in Chesterfield Co., Virginia,[63] the son of **William Black** and **Ann Dent**. William, Jr. died about 1783 in Chesterfield Co., Virginia.[64]

Willis served in the Revolutionary War, Lt. 11th Virginia Continental Regiment, and was injured at "Buford's Defeat", where **Banastre Tarleton** earned his reputation as "The Butcher". Willis received a pension for his service[65] and a land grant of 2666 2/3 acres in the Virginia Military District in Ohio.[66] An interesting letter he wrote to his brother mentions the help someone gave him when he was wounded during the Revolutionary War. Willis was 7th president of the Virginia Society of the Cincinnati.[67]

In 1789 Willis purchased 1500 acres on the Willis River[68] which he named

---

[60] Woodson Family, *Papers, 1740-1945*, Accession 29437-41, LVA.

[61] WPA - Bonbrook Cemetery CUM86.

[62] Trent Family Bible Record, Accession 25300, LVA. Avant, *Southern Colonial Families*, 4:749.

[63] Knorr, *Marriages Chesterfield Co VA*, 13.

[64] "British Claims". *Virginia Genealogist* 7:112.

[65] *Virginia Revolutionary War State Pensions* ,135.

[66] Kentucky Secretary of State, Land Office, (accessed 7 Apr 2006). The patent was signed by John Adams. McCrary, *Wilson Families ... Correspondence .... 1785-1849*, 87-88,162-3.

[67] Hume, *Society of the Cincinnati in the State of Virginia*, 119.

[68] Cumberland Co. VA Deed Book 7:91-2. McCrary, *Cumberland County ...*

(continued...)

"Bonbrook" for a creek that ran through the area. In his letters to his brother in Kentucky, he wrote about politics, crop conditions and prices, requesting that his brother take care of taxes, the sale of his military grant and settlement of their niece's property. Willis appears in the Cumberland Co. 1800 tax list with 10 horses, 16 slaves over the age of 16, 4 slaves age 12-16, a chariot, and 1 stud horse.[69]

Willis was active in local affairs, serving as deputy sheriff in 1786 and 1788, as trustee for establishing the towns of Cartersville and Ca Ira in 1790 and 1796, and as a justice in the court as early as 1797.[70]

The will of Willis Wilson was dated 11 Jan 1821 and proved 26 Aug 1823. He left his estate on the East side of the Willis River to his wife. At her death it was to be divided equally between his two grandsons William Willis Wilson and Willis Wilson. The land on the west side of the Willis River had been given to his son-in-law and daughter by deed some years earlier.[71]

- - - - - - - - - - -

59. Maria Willis[3] Wilson <See pg. 12> (58.Willis[2], 1.Benjamin, Sr.[1]) was born 19 Dec 1793 at "Bonbrook", Cumberland Co., Virginia, the daughter of **Willis Wilson** and **Elizabeth Trent**. Maria died 6 Jan 1818 at "Bonbrook" and was buried there.[72] She married **John Park Wilson** 22 Sep 1814 in Cumberland Co.[73] He was born 26 Jun 1790 in Gerrardstown, Berkeley Co., Virginia (West Virginia), the son of **William Montgomery Wilson** and **Mary Park**. John died 2 May 1871 at "Bonbrook" and was buried there.[74]
ISSUE:[75]
   60. m   i.   **Willis Park Wilson**, born 31 Jul 1815 at "Bonbrook", died

---

[68] (...continued)
Historical Inventory, 4.

[69] "Cumberland County, Virginia, 1800 Tax List", *Virginia Genealogist* 17:197,252.

[70] *Cumb. Co. VA Hist. Bulletin*, 3(2):12, 15 and 13:31. Cumberland Co. VA Order Book 1788-1792:37. Hening, *Statutes*, 13:170-1.

[71] Cumberland Co. VA Will Book 7:105.

[72] WPA - Bonbrook Cemetery CUM86.

[73] Elliott, *Marriages, Cumberland Co. VA*, 139.

[74] Mitchell, "Trent Family". Brown, *Genealogy .... Wilson*.

[75] Brown, *Genealogy .... Wilson*.

28 Jun 1816, and was buried there.[76]

61. m   ii.   **William Willis Wilson**, born 31 Jul 1815 at "Bonbrook". He is mentioned often in letters written by his grandfather from 1815-1818.[77] In his grandfather's will, he and his younger brother Willis were to inherit "Bonbrook". In 1847, his brother deeded to William, his moiety in return for William's assumption of debts due the estate.[78] William is listed with his father in the 1850 and 1860 Cumberland Co. censuses as a lawyer. In his brother's 1862 will, Willis asked that William be appointed guardian of his children and that he build a house for them in Texas.[79] Notes on an application to the United Daughters of the Confederacy say William was Captain of a Cumberland Co. company commanded by Col. **Dick Booker**, that he was paroled on 7 Apr 1865 at Farmville, Virginia. After the Civil War, he carried out his brother's wishes. The children had fond memories of their uncle; they recalled hearing his body servant Dick tell of the officers that came to his tent and of how William "read Latin & Greek with as much ease as English".[80] In 1868 William wrote his will, which was proved in 1876.[81] He appears in the 1870 census of Rusk Co., Texas, with the children and other kin. He died 1 Oct 1875 at "Walnut Grove", Gregg Co., Texas, and was buried there.[82]

+ 62. m   iii.   **Willis Wilson**, born 15 Sep 1817, died 1 Dec 1865 <See pg. 15>.

John Park Wilson married (2) **Elizabeth Woodson Trent** 17 Oct 1832 at "Auburn", Cumberland Co., Virginia.[83] See Appendix for issue of this marriage.

---

[76] WPA - Bonbrook Cemetery CUM86.

[77] McCrary, *Wilson Families ... Correspondence .... 1785-1849*, 172-8, 187-190.

[78] Cumberland Co. VA Will Book 7:105, Deed Book 26:438

[79] Cumberland Co. VA Will Book 13:401, Order Book 1858-1869:522.

[80] Finley, Maria, Family history memories.   Letter 21 Aug 1934 by Mary Anna (Wilson) Mitchell to W. W. Finley in Finley, John M., Family history research. Transcription are in the appendix.

[81] Cumberland Co. VA Will Book 13:647. Gregg Co. TX Probate Docket A # 21.

[82] Gregg Co. Gen. Soc., *Cemeteries*, Walnut Grove, 3:189. Gregg Co. was created from Rusk Co. in 1873.

[83] Elliott, *Marriages, Cumberland Co. VA*, 139.

Maria's father mentioned her often in his letters from 1795; a letter written in 1807 told of her attending school in Richmond. Maria may also have attended Ann Smith Academy in Lexington, Virginia, meeting her future husband who attended Washington Academy (now Washington & Lee University).[84]

Maria's health was apparently rather fragile as shown in letters written in 1816 and 1817.[85]

- - - - - - - - - -

62. Willis⁴ Wilson <See pg. 14> (59.Maria³, 58.Willis², 1.Benjamin, Sr.¹) was born 15 Sep 1817 at "Bonbrook", Cumberland Co., Virginia,[86] the son of **John Park Wilson** and **Maria Willis Wilson**. Willis died 1 Dec 1865 at "Bonbrook".[87] He married **Mary Anna Wilson (See number 1704 - pg. 174)** 26 May 1847 at "Barter Hill", Cumberland Co., Virginia.[88] She was born 28 Jun 1822 at "Barter Hill", the daughter of **Matthew Wilson** and **Elizabeth "Betsy" Trent**.[89] Mary Anna died 11 Jul 1864 at "Bonbrook".[90]
ISSUE:[91]
+ 63. f   i.   **Elizabeth Trent Wilson**, born 10 Nov 1848, died 4 Jan 1875 <See pg. 17>.
  65. m   ii.   **Willis Wilson, Jr.**, born 25 Oct 1850 at "Bonbrook", Cumberland Co., Virginia, and died there 22 Jul 1869. After the death of his parents, he remained in Virginia to finish his education at Hampden-Sydney. The second wife of his grandfather wrote from "Bonbrook" to the kin in Texas of his death.[92]
  66. f   iii.   **Maria Louisa Wilson**, born 15 Mar 1853 at "Walnut

---

[84] Washington and Lee University, *Catalogue*, 63. Letter 21 Aug 1934, Finley, John M., Family history research.
[85] McCrary, *Wilson Families ... Correspondence .... 1785-1849*, 62-4, 127-8, 174-178, 182.
[86] Family Bible of Willis and Mary Anna Wilson.
[87] Cumberland Co. VA Register of Deaths 1853-1870, page 47.
[88] Cumberland Co. VA Marriage Bonds 1841-1854.
[89] McCrary, *Wilson Families ... Correspondence .... 1785-1849*, 212.
[90] Family Bible of Willis and Mary Anna Wilson. Letter 29 Jul 1864, Finley, John M., Family history research.
[91] Family Bible of Willis and Mary Anna Wilson. A transcription of the Bible is in the Appendix.
[92] Letters 22 Jul 1869, 21 Aug 1934, Finley, John M., Family history research.

Grove", Rusk Co., Texas, died 25 Aug 1853 and was buried in Walnut Grove Cemetery.[93]

+ 67. f   iv.   **Mary Anna Wilson**, born 7 May 1855, died 12 Oct 1940 <See pg. 18>.

85. f   v.   **Mary Isabella Wilson**, born 18 Sep 1857 at "Walnut Grove", died 19 Sep 1858, and was buried there..

+ 86. f   vi.   **Maria Willis Wilson**, born 9 Aug 1859, died 11 Jun 1947 <See pg. 21>.

169. f   vii.   **Laura Marye Wilson**, born 4 Feb 1862 at "Bonbrook", Cumberland Co., Virginia, died 15 Jun 1868 in Rusk Co., Texas.[94]

+ 170. f   viii.   **Caroline Louisa "Carrie" Wilson**, born 29 Jan 1864, died 2 Dec 1899 <See pg. 31>.

Willis is written of fondly by his grandfather while a child at "Bonbrook".[95] His mother died when he was a few months old, so he was reared primarily by his grandparents. In 1839 he delivered an address, "The Responsibilities of American Youth", at his commencement at Hampden-Sydney College in Prince Edward Co.[96] In 1847 he deeded his moiety of the estate he inherited from his grandfather to his brother.[97]

In the 1850 Marshall Co., Mississippi, census he is listed with his wife and daughter. By 1851 Willis and his wife were in the process of moving south and west. Letters in 1851 from his wife, who was probably in Virginia for the birth of their second child, addressed to him at Waterford, Marshall County, Mississippi, mentioned the move to Texas.[98] He wrote to his cousin in Missouri in 1859 about the birth of "another daughter ... mighty pretty for a Wilson".[99] In the 1860 census of Rusk Co., Texas, he is listed with his wife and four children.

His daughter, Maria, later wrote of what she was told of their trip in the spring of 1860 when the family traveled to Virginia for medical treatment for Willis. The "steamer on the Mississippi River ... caught fire and a kind .... Irishman held a rope between his teeth and swam ashore ... enabling men

---

[93]   Gregg Co. Gen. Soc., *Cemeteries*, Walnut Grove, 3:189.

[94]   Letter 16 Jun 1868, Finley, John M., Family history research.

[95]   McCrary, *Wilson Families ... Correspondence .... 1785-1849*, 187-9.

[96]   Bradshaw, *History of Hampden-Sydney College*, 237-8.

[97]   Cumberland Co. VA Deed Book 26:438.

[98]   Letters 9 Aug , 12 Aug 1851, Finley, John M., Family history research.

[99]   Letter 15 Aug 1859, Finley, John M., Family history research.

on the shore to draw the boat to the bank just in time that all escaped with their lives but no baggage. At this time, I was a babe in arms."[100]

Leaving his family at "Bonbrook", Willis went to New York for medical treatment. The three older children are listed with their grandfather at "Bonbrook" in the 1860 Cumberland Co. census. Before "the election", his wife, Mary Anna, wrote to her brother who was evidently tending the farm back in Texas for them. "Matt was gone to the University and Mr. Wilson in New York & and anxious to hear all he can from Texas".[101]

Willis died Dec 1, 1865. In his will, written 26 Nov 1862, he named his brother William executor, asking that if his wife died before the children were the age of 21, that William be appointed guardian; in a codicil written 28 Nov 1863, he asked that William build a comfortable house on his estate in Texas.[102]

His wife died in 1864. The eldest daughter, Elizabeth Trent Wilson, "Trent", wrote to her mother's sister, **Elizabeth Trent Wilson**, "Bettie", 29 Jul 1864, begging her to come live with them. "We've lost our dear mother and Father is in such bad health that I fear that we shall soon have no parent. Mother died the eleventh of July."[103] The aunt was living with her brother in Missouri at the time and received a pass dated Oct 7, 1864 written by President Lincoln to travel through the lines to Virginia. After the war was over, the bachelor uncle and maiden aunt took the children back to Rusk (now Gregg) County, Texas.

- - - - - - - - - - -

63. Elizabeth Trent[5] "Trent" Wilson <See pg. 15, 174> (62.Willis[4], 59.Maria[3], 58.Willis[2], 1.Benjamin, Sr.[1]) was born 10 Nov 1848 in Marshall Co., Mississippi, the daughter of **Willis Wilson** and **Mary Anna Wilson**. Trent died 4 Jan 1875 in Prairieville, Kaufman Co., Texas,[104] and was buried in Walnut Grove Cemetery, Gregg Co., Texas.[105] She married

---

[100] Finley, Maria, Family history memories.

[101] Letter 6 Nov 1860. Matt is cousin **Matthew John Wilson**, a student at the University of Virginia. Finley, John M., Family history research. Wilson, Papers of Eloise Wilson.

[102] Cumberland Co VA Will book 13:401. Texas State-wide Records Program, *Index ... Probate ... Rusk County*, 86-7, cases 917, 918.

[103] Letter 29 Jul 1864, Finley, John M., Family history research.

[104] Family Bible of Willis and Mary Anna Wilson.

[105] Gregg Co. Gen. Soc., *Cemeteries*, Walnut Grove, 3:189.

Joseph H. Trent (See number 1474 - pg. 144) 29 Jan 1874 in Rusk Co.,
Texas.[106] He was born 1839 at "Auburn", Cumberland Co., Virginia, the
son of **Carter Harrison Trent** and **Maria Alexandria Wilson**.[107] Joseph
died 5 Aug 1876 and was buried in Walnut Grove Cemetery.[108]

ISSUE:

64. m   i. **William Henry Trent**, born 21 Dec 1874 in Prairieville,
Kaufman Co., Texas, and died there 9 Jul 1875. He was
buried in Walnut Grove Cemetery.

Elizabeth T. Wilson, ("Trent"), is listed in the 1870 census for Rusk Co.,
Texas, with her uncle William and aunt Bettie. Her letter to her sisters from
Prairieville in 1874 tells of their horse "poking his head" into the windows
of the house. Joseph's 1875 letter to their aunt in Longview describes his
mother helping with the sick baby.[109]

- - - - - - - - - - -

67. Mary Anna⁵ Wilson <See pg. 16, 174> (62.Willis⁴, 59.Maria³, 58.Willis²,
1.Benjamin, Sr.¹) was born 7 May 1855 at "Walnut Grove", Rusk Co.,
Texas, the daughter of **Willis Wilson** and **Mary Anna Wilson**.[110] Anna
died 12 Oct 1940 in Gregg Co., Texas, and was buried in Elderville
Cemetery at the Centre Presbyterian Church, Gregg Co., Texas.[111] She
married **Pleasant J. Mitchell** 30 Oct 1879 in Gregg Co.[112] He was born
25 Sep 1851 in Warrenton, Alabama, the son of **P. J. Mitchell** and **Ann J.
_____**.[113] Pleasant died 27 Sep 1885 in Longview, Texas, and was buried in
Walnut Grove Cemetery, Gregg Co.[114]

ISSUE:

68. f   i. **Mary Preston Mitchell**, born 6 Mar 1881 at "Walnut
Grove", Gregg Co., Texas.[115] She married (1) **George
Teague** about 1901. He was born about 1873 in Texas.

[106] Ingmire, *Marriage .. Rusk* Co., 69.

[107] Trent Family Bible Record, Accession 25300, LVA.

[108] Gregg Co. Gen. Soc., *Cemeteries*, Walnut Grove, 3:189.

[109] Letter 20 Jul 1874, Finley, John M., Family history research. Letter written 1
Feb 1875, published in *Longview Daily News*, 23 Apr 1970.

[110] Family Bible of Willis and Mary Anna Wilson.

[111] Inscription on grave marker.

[112] Ruff, *Gregg Co. TX Marriage Licenses*, B:277.

[113] Family Bible of Willis and Mary Anna Wilson.

[114] Gregg Co. Gen. Soc., *Cemeteries*, Walnut Grove, 3:189.

[115] Family Bible of Willis and Mary Anna Wilson

Mary married (2) _____ **Flemister**. Mary died 13 Nov 1960 in Encino, California, and was buried in Walnut Grove Cemetery.[116]

+ 69. m   ii.   **William Gardiner Mitchell**, born 23 Mar 1885, died 3 Jun 1963.

Mary Anna is listed in the 1870 census for Rusk Co., Texas, with her uncle and aunt. In a letter written in 1929, she recalls being at "Bonbrook" from 1871 to 1874.[117] When "Bonbrook" was to be sold, there was family concern about the disposition of the books and furniture. She is said to have been the recipient of some items.

She usually went by the name Anna, was the eldest surviving child, and in 1879 was appointed guardian of the estate of her two younger sisters. Their aunt had deeded land to them in 1876.[118] Her husband died young leaving her with children to raise and a home and land to maintain. She had the first glass windows and first cotton gin in Gregg County.[119] Anna's letters and recorded recollections have added greatly to information on the Wilson family. She preferred to be buried in the Elderville Cemetery because the cattle roamed freely over the graves at "Walnut Grove".[120]

- - - - - - - - - - - -

69. William Gardiner[6] **Mitchell** (67.Mary[5], 62.Willis[4], 59.Maria[3], 58.Willis[2], 1.Benjamin, Sr.[1]) was born 23 Mar 1885 at "Walnut Grove", Gregg Co., Texas, the son of **Pleasant J. Mitchell** and **Mary Anna Wilson**.[121] William died 3 Jun 1963 in Longview, Texas, and was buried in Walnut Grove Cemetery.[122] He married **Ethel Mae Fall** 1 Mar 1909 in Gregg Co. She was born 25 Jan 1885 in Hot Springs, Arkansas, the daughter of **W. S. Fall** and **Mollie Harrell**. Ethel died 19 Feb 1963 in Longview, Texas, and was buried in Walnut Grove Cemetery.[123]

ISSUE:

70. m   i.   **William Gardiner "Red" Mitchell, Jr.**, born 2 Mar 1910 at "Walnut Grove". In 1995, he was in possession of the

---

[116] Wilkins, *Gregg Co. TX, South of the Sabine*, 16.

[117] Finley, John M., Family history research.

[118] Gregg Co. TX Probate Minutes "B", 164-5 file 50, Deed Book D:419.

[119] Obituary. Waxahachie TX newspaper 13 Oct 1940.

[120] Visits with descendants by John and Bonnie Finley of Austin TX.

[121] Family Bible of Willis and Mary Anna Wilson.

[122] Gregg Co. Gen. Soc., *Cemeteries*, Walnut Grove, 3:189.

[123] Wilkins, *Gregg Co. TX, South of the Sabine*, 15-16.

Family Bible of his grandparents. He married **Grace Martin** 25 Dec 1934 in Longview, Gregg Co., Texas.[124] She was born 27 Aug 1911. Grace died 4 May 1968, and was buried in Elderville Cemetery at Centre Presbyterian Church, Gregg Co., Texas.[125] Red died 29 Jan 2006 in Longview and was buried in Elderville Cemetery.[126]

+ 71. m   ii.   **Willis Wilson "Dick" Mitchell**, born 1 Feb 1912, died 29 Jul 2001.

+ 78. f   iii.   **Mary Ethel Mitchell**, born 20 Jul 1919, died 26 Sep 1982 <See pg. 21>.

+ 82. m   iv.   **Zack Fall Mitchell**, born 22 May 1921 <See pg. 21>.

In William Sr.'s obituary it is stated that he was an active church and civic leader, that he operated a cotton gin, installing the first electric gin in the county. He sold some of his land to the county for the local airport.

- - - - - - - - - - -

71. Willis Wilson "Dick"[7] **Mitchell** (69.William[6], 67.Mary[5], 62.Willis[4], 59.Maria[3], 58.Willis[2], 1.Benjamin, Sr.[1]) was born 1 Feb 1912 at "Walnut Grove", Gregg Co., Texas, the son of **William Gardiner Mitchell** and **Ethel Mae Fall**.[127] He died 29 Jul 2001 in Longview, Gregg Co., and was buried in Walnut Grove Cemetery. He married **Nell F. Mitcham** 1938.[128]

ISSUE:[129]

+ 72. m   i.   **Willis Wilson Mitchell, II**, born 3 Jan 1940.

   77. f   ii.   **Suzanne Mitchell**, born 7 Jul 1944.

- - - - - - - - - - -

72. Willis Wilson[8] **Mitchell, II** (71.Willis[7], 69.William[6], 67.Mary[5], 62.Willis[4], 59.Maria[3], 58.Willis[2], 1.Benjamin, Sr.[1]) was born 3 Jan 1940, the son of **Willis Wilson "Dick" Mitchell** and **Nell F. Mitcham**. He married (1) **JoAnne Johnson**; they divorced.

ISSUE:

   73. m   i.   **Todd Gardiner Mitchell**, born 29 Sep 1969.

   74. f   ii.   **Katherine Anne Mitchell**, born 1 Jul 1972.

---

[124] Finley, John M., Family history research.

[125] 1995 visit to cemetery with Eloise Wilson.

[126] Obituary.

[127] Finley, John M., Family history research.

[128] Obituary, Longview TX *News-Journal* 31 Jul 2001.

[129] Additional information from Willis Wilson Mitchell II of Dallas TX.

Willis, II married (2) **Beverly Ann Lebowitz** 1982.

ISSUE:

75. m   iii.   **Adam Fall Mitchell**, born 21 Mar 1983.
76. m   iv.   **Jake Lyons Mitchell**, born 8 Aug 1986.

- - - - - - - - - - -

78. Mary Ethel[7] Mitchell <See pg. 20> (69.William[6], 67.Mary[5], 62.Willis[4], 59.Maria[3], 58.Willis[2], 1.Benjamin, Sr.[1]) was born 20 Jul 1919 in Longview, Texas, the daughter of **William Gardiner Mitchell** and **Ethel Mae Fall**. Mary died 26 Sep 1982 in Longview. She married **Ralph Wesley Kutzer** 2 Jun 1942. He was born 4 Oct 1916 in Comfort, Texas. Ralph died 13 Oct 1970.[130]

ISSUE:

79. f   i.   **Carol Kutzer**, born 28 Jul 1943 in Tyler, Texas. She married **James Lawrence McBride** 31 May 1963. He was born 31 Jan 1943.
80. f   ii.   **Pamela Kutzer**.
81. m   iii.   **David Kutzer**.

- - - - - - - - - - -

82. Zack Fall[7] Mitchell <See pg. 20> (69.William[6], 67.Mary[5], 62.Willis[4], 59.Maria[3], 58.Willis[2], 1.Benjamin, Sr.[1]) was born 22 May 1921 at "Walnut Grove", Gregg Co., Texas, the son of **William Gardiner Mitchell** and **Ethel Mae Fall**. He married **Mary Evelyn Martin** 3 Oct 1947 in Longview, Gregg Co. She was born 28 May 1928 in Texas.[131]

ISSUE:

83. m   i.   **David Gardiner Mitchell**, born 6 Dec 1948.
84. m   ii.   **Ronald Hall "Ronnie" Mitchell**, born 8 May 1950.

- - - - - - - - - - -

86. Maria Willis[5] Wilson <See pg. 16, 175> (62.Willis[4], 59.Maria[3], 58.Willis[2], 1.Benjamin, Sr.[1]) was born 9 Aug 1859 at "Walnut Grove", Rusk Co., Texas,[132] the daughter of **Willis Wilson** and **Mary Anna Wilson**. Maria died 11 Jun 1947 in Ellis Co., Texas, and was buried in the old city cemetery in Waxahachie, Ellis Co., Texas. Maria married (1) **Walter B.**

---

[130]   DAR application of Carol (Kutzer) McBride, not submitted.

[131]   Finley, John M., Family history research.

[132]   Letter written by her father 15 Aug 1859, Finley, John M., Family history research. Family Bible of Willis and Mary Anna Wilson.

Mitchell 19 Jul 1887 in Longview, Gregg Co., Texas.[133] He was born 30 Oct 1858 in Warrenton, Alabama, the son of **P. J. Mitchell** and **Ann J. _____**. Walter died 30 Sep 1887 at "Walnut Grove" and was buried in the cemetery there.[134]

Maria married (2) **Olin Anthony Finley** 7 Aug 1894 in Longview, Gregg Co., Texas. He was born 16 Mar 1843 in Oxford, Newton Co., Georgia. He was the son of **John Jefferson Finley** and **Eliza Capers Lane**. Olin died 28 Mar 1922 in Ellis Co., Texas, and was buried in the old city cemetery in Waxahachie, Ellis Co., Texas.[135]

ISSUE:

+ 87. m   ii.   **Willis Wilson Finley**, born 17 May 1895, died 23 Oct 1971 <See pg. 23>.

166. m   iii.   **John Finley**, born 28 Sep 1897 in Ellis Co., Texas, died 13 Oct 1897 in Waxahachie, Ellis Co.

167. m   iv.   **Lane Finley**, born 28 Sep 1897 in Ellis Co. He married **Sara Margret Jarvis**. Sara died 20 Sep 1951, and was buried in Memorial Cemetery in Waxahachie,. Lane died before 1952 in Grand Prairie, Texas, and was buried in Memorial Cemetery.

168. m   i.   **Olin Wilber Finley, Sr.**, born 1883. He was the son of **Olin Anthony Finley** by a prior marriage.

Maria recorded valuable information about her ancestors and family. She wrote of the story told to her of the family trip from Texas to Virginia in 1860 when she was a baby and of her life in Virginia and Texas after the Civil War.[136] She kept many letters that were written by family, kin and friends between 1815 and 1943, adding so much to our knowledge of the family. She is listed in the 1870 census for Rusk Co., Texas, with her uncle and aunt. As a young woman, she spent a great deal of time from 1876 with her aunt **Maria Willis (Wilson) Marye** who was married and teaching in Tennessee. Maria was with them later when they moved to Virginia.

---

[133] Ruff, *Gregg Co. TX Marriage Licenses*, C:283.

[134] Family Bible of Willis and Mary Anna Wilson. Gregg Co. Gen. Soc., *Cemeteries*, Walnut Grove, 3:189.

[135] The material on the Finley descendants and ancestors was provided by John M. Finley of Austin TX, which includes information gathered by his father and papers and letters saved by his grandmother Maria Willis Wilson.

[136] Finley, Maria, Family history memories. A transcription of this is in the appendix.

When Maria returned to Texas in 1886 to help her sister, whose husband had died and who was ill herself, she met her first husband-to-be and alarmed the Virginia aunt and uncle. When Maria stated plans to marry him, the aunt wrote, "I was reproached once, when a girl, for weeping at the wedding of a dear friend. 'One w'd think she was dying', said my censor. To a reflecting mind the marriage of a Christian woman is a more appropriate time for solicitude than her death; for in the latter case, she enters upon certain happenings and even among sincerely good and upright people; marriage is a lottery."

A letter written to Maria from **Mary Coe (Wilson) Fuqua** Dec 20, 1894 mentions a book sent to Wilber, Maria's step-son from her second marriage.

- - - - - - - - - - -

87. Willis Wilson⁶ Finley <See pg. 22> (86.Maria⁵, 62.Willis⁴, 59.Maria³, 58.Willis², 1.Benjamin, Sr.¹) was born 17 May 1895 in Ellis Co., Texas, the son of **Olin Anthony Finley** and **Maria Willis Wilson**. Willis died 23 Oct 1971 in Ft. Worth, Texas, and was buried in Memorial Cemetery in Waxahachie, Ellis Co., Texas. He married **Georgia Page Sclater** 9 Nov 1918 in Hampton, Elizabeth City Co., Virginia. She was born 2 Oct 1896 in Hampton. Georgia died 30 Jul 1981 in Friendswood, Texas, and was buried in Memorial Cemetery in Waxahachie.

ISSUE:

+ 88. m	i.	**Willis Wilson Finley, Jr.**, born 30 Dec 1919.	
+ 108. f	ii.	**Ann Page Finley**, born 19 May 1921	<See pg. 25>.
+ 115. f	iii.	**Elizabeth Lane Finley**, born 8 Dec 1922	<See pg. 26>.
+ 121. f	iv.	**Virginia Louise Finley**, born 10 Sep 1924	<See pg. 27>.
+ 148. m	v.	**John Mallory Finley**, born 21 Nov 1929	<See pg. 29>.

- - - - - - - - - - -

88. Willis Wilson⁷ Finley, Jr. (87.Willis⁶, 86.Maria⁵, 62.Willis⁴, 59.Maria³, 58.Willis², 1.Benjamin, Sr.¹) was born 30 Dec 1919 in Hillsboro, Texas, the son of **Willis Wilson Finley** and **Georgia Page Sclater**. He married **Helen Ann "Jan" Miller** 3 Oct 1946 in Ft. Worth, Texas. She was born 8 Jun 1924 in New Haven, Connecticut.

ISSUE:

89. m	i.	**James Wilson Finley**, born 11 Nov 1946, died 17 Nov 1946.	
+ 90. m	ii.	**Robert Travis Finley**, born 21 May 1949.	
+ 98. f	iii.	**Lizabeth Lane Finley**, born 16 Feb 1952	<See pg. 24>.
+ 102. m	iv.	**Reed Anthony Finley**, born 25 Oct 1954	<See pg. 25>.

+ 105. f   v.   **Catherine Ann Finley**, born 30 Sep 1960 <See pg. 25>.

- - - - - - - - - -

90. Robert Travis[8] Finley (88.Willis, Jr.[7], 87.Willis[6], 86.Maria[5], 62.Willis[4], 59.Maria[3], 58.Willis[2], 1.Benjamin, Sr.[1]) was born 21 May 1949, the son of **Willis Wilson Finley, Jr.** and **Helen Ann "Jan" Miller**.
ISSUE:
+ 91. f   i.   **Misti Nada Wilson**, born 16 Jan 1972.

Robert married (2) **Janis Selby** 24 Mar 1973. She was born 1952.
ISSUE:
+ 94. m   ii. **Travis Wilson Finley**, born 22 Feb 1975.
  97. m iii. **John Charles Finley**, born 1978.

- - - - - - - - - -

91. Misti Nada[9] Wilson (90.Robert[8], 88.Willis, Jr.[7], 87.Willis[6], 86.Maria[5], 62.Willis[4], 59.Maria[3], 58.Willis[2], 1.Benjamin, Sr.[1]) was born 16 Jan 1972 in Salem, Oregon, the daughter of **Robert Travis Finley**. She married (1) **Naron Gabriel Wachten** 14 Nov 1990 in Salem; they divorced.
Misti married (2) **Kenneth Lee Rudloff** in 1999 in Houston, Texas. He was born 2 Aug 1968.
ISSUE:
  92. f   i.   **Madeline Diane Rudloff**, born 28 Oct 1999 in Houston, Texas.
  93. m ii. **Jacob Scott Rudloff**, born 22 Aug 2001 in Houston.

- - - - - - - - - -

94. Travis Wilson[9] Finley (90.Robert[8], 88.Willis, Jr.[7], 87.Willis[6], 86.Maria[5], 62.Willis[4], 59.Maria[3], 58.Willis[2], 1.Benjamin, Sr.[1]) was born 22 Feb 1975 in Houston, Texas, the son of **Robert Travis Finley and Janis Selby**. He married **Lori Ann Ward**. She was born 28 Nov 1974 in Webster, Texas.
ISSUE:
  95. f   i.   **Reagan Elizabeth Finley**, born 29 Jan 1999 in Houston, Texas.
  96. m ii. **Colin Wilson Finley**, born 23 Sep 2003 in Houston, Texas.

- - - - - - - - - -

98. Lizabeth Lane[8] Finley <See pg. 23> (88.Willis, Jr.[7], 87.Willis[6], 86.Maria[5], 62.Willis[4], 59.Maria[3], 58.Willis[2], 1.Benjamin, Sr.[1]) was born 16 Feb 1952, the daughter of **Willis Wilson Finley, Jr.** and **Helen Ann "Jan" Miller**. She married (1) **Mark Eugene Sabina** 27 Dec 1969. He was born 1951.

ISSUE:
99. u   i.   **David Mark Sabina**, born 4 Aug 1970.
100. m ii. **Michael John Sabina**, born 2 Jun 1974.
101. f iii. **Caryn Elizabeth Sabina**, born 5 Sep 1978.

Lizabeth married (2) **Richard Whitley Davis**. He was born 3 Feb 1947.

- - - - - - - - - - -

102. Reed Anthony^8 Finley <See pg. 23> (88.Willis, Jr.^{7}, 87.Willis^6, 86.Maria^5, 62.Willis^4, 59.Maria^3, 58.Willis^2, 1.Benjamin, Sr.^{1}) was born 25 Oct 1954 in Port Arthur, Texas, the son of **Willis Wilson Finley, Jr.** and **Helen Ann "Jan" Miller**. He married (1) **Sandra Gay Fox** 16 Feb 1974. She was born 4 Oct 1954.

ISSUE:
103. f i.   **Sharon Grace Finley**, born 21 Feb 1975.

Reed married (2) **Scarlett Reneé French** 20 Jun 1980. She was born 25 Jan 1958.

ISSUE:
104. f ii. **Tanya Nicole Finley**, born 19 May 1981.

- - - - - - - - - - -

105. Catherine Ann^8 Finley <See pg. 24> (88.Willis, Jr.^{7}, 87.Willis^6, 86.Maria^5, 62.Willis^4, 59.Maria^3, 58.Willis^2, 1.Benjamin, Sr.^{1}) was born 30 Sep 1960 in Port Arthur, Texas, the daughter of **Willis Wilson Finley, Jr.** and **Helen Ann "Jan" Miller**. She married **John Phillip Dixon** 23 Jun 1984 in La Jolla, California. He was born 1959.

ISSUE:
106. f i.   **Erin Elizabeth Dixon**, born 22 Dec 1990.
107. f ii. **Rebecca Paige Dixon**, born 17 Apr 1995.

- - - - - - - - - - -

108. Ann Page^7 Finley <See pg. 23> (87.Willis^6, 86.Maria^5, 62.Willis^4, 59.Maria^3, 58.Willis^2, 1.Benjamin, Sr.^{1}) was born 19 May 1921 in Hillsboro, Hill Co., Texas, the daughter of **Willis Wilson Finley** and **Georgia Page Sclater**. She married **William B. Lewis** 11 Jan 1941. He was born 27 Oct 1919 in Ft. Worth, Texas.

ISSUE:
109. m i.   **William Douglas Lewis**, born 22 Jul 1943. He married (1) **Patricia Anne Eaton** 28 Jan 1966. William married (2) **Lucinda White** about 1985. She was born 1945.

+ 110. f   ii.   **Suzanne Page Lewis,** born 13 Jan 1948 .
+ 112. f   iii. **Cynthia Kay "Cindy" Lewis,** born 20 Sep 1953.

- - - - - - - - - - -

110. Suzanne Page[8] Lewis (108.Ann[7], 87.Willis[6], 86.Maria[5], 62.Willis[4], 59.Maria[3], 58.Willis[2], 1.Benjamin, Sr.[1]) was born 13 Jan 1948, the daughter of **William B. Lewis** and **Ann Page Finley**. She married **James Bruce Harrell** 5 Sep 1969. He was born 14 Jun 1949.

ISSUE:

111. f   i.   **Carrie Anne Kathleen Harrell,** born 10 Apr 1980.

- - - - - - - - - - -

112. Cynthia Kay "Cindy"[8] Lewis (108.Ann[7], 87.Willis[6], 86.Maria[5], 62.Willis[4], 59.Maria[3], 58.Willis[2], 1.Benjamin, Sr.[1]) was born 20 Sep 1953, the daughter of **William B. Lewis** and **Ann Page Finley**. She married **Michael I. Thomas** 3 Jan 1976. He was born 14 Aug 1951 in Newark, New Jersey.

ISSUE:

113. f   i.   **Rachel Jan Thomas,** born 29 Mar 1979.
114. f   ii. **Amy Jessica Thomas,** born 21 Oct 1982.

- - - - - - - - - - -

115. Elizabeth Lane[7] Finley <See pg. 23> (87.Willis[6], 86.Maria[5], 62.Willis[4], 59.Maria[3], 58.Willis[2], 1.Benjamin, Sr.[1]) was born 8 Dec 1922 in Waxahachie, Ellis Co., Texas, the daughter of **Willis Wilson Finley** and **Georgia Page Sclater**. She married **William Larry "Dick" Richards** 13 Jun 1944 in Austin, Texas. He was born 17 Aug 1925. William died 29 Aug 1968.

ISSUE:

+ 116. f   i.   **Louise Page Richards,** born 21 Dec 1957 .
+ 118. f   ii. **Michelle Lane Wilson Richards,** born 17 Jul 1960 .

- - - - - - - - - - -

116. Louise Page[8] Richards (115.Elizabeth[7], 87.Willis[6], 86.Maria[5], 62.Willis[4], 59.Maria[3], 58.Willis[2], 1.Benjamin, Sr.[1]) was born 21 Dec 1957, the daughter of **William Larry "Dick" Richards** and **Elizabeth Lane Finley**. She married **Owen Ward Wilson** 3 Jun 1978. He was born 17 Oct 1956.

ISSUE:

117. m   i.   **Richard David Wilson,** born 26 Feb 1987.

- - - - - - - - - - -

118. Michelle Lane Wilson[8] Richards (115.Elizabeth[7], 87.Willis[6], 86.Maria[5], 62.Willis[4], 59.Maria[3], 58.Willis[2], 1.Benjamin, Sr.[1]) was born 17 Jul 1960, the daughter of **William Larry "Dick" Richards** and **Elizabeth Lane Finley**. She married (1) **Larry Paulk** 12 Jan 1980. He was born 1957. Larry died 10 May 1980.

ISSUE:

119. m   i.   **Phillip Jason Paulk**, born 12 Feb 1980, died 12 May 1980.

Michelle married (2) **James Riley Huckabee**.
Michelle married (3) **Stephen Jeffery Spears** 9 Sep 1995. He was born 1967.
Michelle married (4) **B. J. Fogle** 2001.

ISSUE:

120. f   ii.   **Magdalene Page Fogle**, born 4 Feb 2005 in Dallas, Texas. She is called Maggy.

- - - - - - - - - - -

121. Virginia Louise[7] Finley <See pg. 23> (87.Willis[6], 86.Maria[5], 62.Willis[4], 59.Maria[3], 58.Willis[2], 1.Benjamin, Sr.[1]) was born 10 Sep 1924 in Waxahachie, Ellis Co., Texas, the daughter of **Willis Wilson Finley** and **Georgia Page Sclater**. She married **Louis Edgar Holder** 10 Jan 1941. He was born 21 May 1920.

ISSUE:

+ 122. m   i.   **David Gordon Holder**, born 7 Aug 1942.
+ 139. f   ii.   **Elizabeth Page Holder**, born 31 Mar 1945 <See pg. 29>.
+ 145. f   iii.   **Deborah Louise Holder**, born 11 Oct 1948 <See pg. 29>.

- - - - - - - - - - -

122. David Gordon[8] Holder (121.Virginia[7], 87.Willis[6], 86.Maria[5], 62.Willis[4], 59.Maria[3], 58.Willis[2], 1.Benjamin, Sr.[1]) was born 7 Aug 1942, the son of **Louis Edgar Holder** and **Virginia Louise Finley**. He married **Blanch Ilene Cooper** 6 Aug 1960. She was born 31 Mar 1943.

ISSUE:

+ 123. f   i.   **Patricia Louise Holder**, born 2 Apr 1961.
+ 127. f   ii.   **Catherine Page Holder**, born 1964 <See pg. 28>.
+ 134. f   iii.   **Deborah Sue Holder**, born 22 Jan 1968.
  138. f   iv.   **Amy Elizabeth Holder**, born 1972. She married **John Frank Hark, Jr.** He was born 1967.

- - - - - - - - - - -

123. Patricia Louise[9] Holder (122.David[8], 121.Virginia[7], 87.Willis[6], 86.Maria[5], 62.Willis[4], 59.Maria[3], 58.Willis[2], 1.Benjamin, Sr.[1]) was born

2 Apr 1961, the daughter of **David Gordon Holder** and **Blanch Ilene Cooper**. She married (1) **Danny Andrew Wall** about 1985. He was born 2 May 1958.

ISSUE:

124. m   i.   **Daniel Andrew Wall**, born 25 Jul 1987.

Patricia married (2) **Jeffery Scott Wyman** after 2001. He was born 27 Apr 1960.

ISSUE:

125. m   iii.   **Samuel Scott Wyman**, born 26 Sep 2003.

Patricia had 1 stepchild:

126. f   ii.   **Allysa Ann Wyman**, born 5 Jul 2001. She is the daughter of Jeffery Scott Wyman.

- - - - - - - - - -

127. Catherine Page[9] Holder <See pg. 27> (122.David[8], 121.Virginia[7], 87.Willis[6], 86.Maria[5], 62.Willis[4], 59.Maria[3], 58.Willis[2], 1.Benjamin, Sr.[1]) was born 1964, the daughter of **David Gordon Holder** and **Blanch Ilene Cooper**. She married **Gerald Timothy Powell** 9 Sep 1982. He was born 3 Sep 1958.

ISSUE:

128. f   i.   **Tiffany Louise Powell**, born 14 Jul 1983.
129. f   ii.   **Virginia Page Powell**, born 20 May 1986.
130. f   iii.   **Amy Sue Powell**, born 1 Dec 1989.
131. m   iv.   **David Timothy Powell**, born 15 May 1992.
132. f   v.   **Courtney Blanch Powell**, born 23 Aug 1995.
133. m   vi.   **Hunter Louis Powell**, born 17 Jun 1997.

- - - - - - - - - -

134. Deborah Sue[9] Holder (122.David[8], 121.Virginia[7], 87.Willis[6], 86.Maria[5], 62.Willis[4], 59.Maria[3], 58.Willis[2], 1.Benjamin, Sr.[1]) was born 22 Jan 1968 in Houston, Texas, the daughter of **David Gordon Holder** and **Blanch Ilene Cooper**. She married (1) **Michael Alan Kent** 14 Feb 1987. He was born 10 Mar 1967 in Houston, Texas, the son of **Alan Kent** and **Janet _____**.

ISSUE:

135. f   i.   **Shelby Taylor Kent**, born 10 Jun 1990 in Houston.
136. f   ii.   **Jordan Michelle Kent**, born 29 Oct 1991 in Bay City, Texas.
137. m   iii.   **Cameron Michael Kent**, born 28 Aug 1996.

Deborah married (2) **Robert Mitchell Thompson**. He was born 13 Jul 1966.

- - - - - - - - - - -

139. Elizabeth Page[8] Holder <See pg. 27> (121.Virginia[7], 87.Willis[6], 86.Maria[5], 62.Willis[4], 59.Maria[3], 58.Willis[2], 1.Benjamin, Sr.[1]) was born 31 Mar 1945, the daughter of **Louis Edgar Holder** and **Virginia Louise Finley**. She married **Kenneth George Cunningham** 12 Sep 1964. He was born 1943.

ISSUE:

+ 140. m   i.   **Kenneth David Cunningham**, born 12 Sep 1965.
  143. m   ii.   **Kevin Louis Cunningham**, born 19 Dec 1968. He married **Juliette Louise Cummings**, born 29 Dec 1968.
  144. f   iii.   **Carolyn Page Cunningham**, born 10 Dec 1973. She married **Steven Ryan Shillcutt**.

- - - - - - - - - - -

140. Kenneth David[9] Cunningham (139.Elizabeth[8], 121.Virginia[7], 87.Willis[6], 86.Maria[5], 62.Willis[4], 59.Maria[3], 58.Willis[2], 1.Benjamin, Sr.[1]) was born 12 Sep 1965 in Lubbock, Texas, the son of **Kenneth George Cunningham** and **Elizabeth Page Holder**. He married **Rosemary Julia Petty**. She was born 31 May 1965.

ISSUE:

  141. f   i.   **Emily Grace Cunningham**, born 6 Apr 1994.
  142. m   ii.   **Kenneth Alan Cunningham**, born 11 Apr 1997.

- - - - - - - - - - -

145. Deborah Louise[8] Holder <See pg. 27> (121.Virginia[7], 87.Willis[6], 86.Maria[5], 62.Willis[4], 59.Maria[3], 58.Willis[2], 1.Benjamin, Sr.[1]) was born 11 Oct 1948, the daughter of **Louis Edgar Holder** and **Virginia Louise Finley**. She married **Kenneth R. Payne** 8 Jun 1968. He was born 1947.

ISSUE:

  146. f   i.   **Margaret Elizabeth Payne**, born 5 Oct 1970.
  147. f   ii.   **Diana Michelle Payne**, born 21 Dec 1973. She married **Kirk Richard Light**.

- - - - - - - - - - -

148. John Mallory[7] Finley <See pg. 23> (87.Willis[6], 86.Maria[5], 62.Willis[4], 59.Maria[3], 58.Willis[2], 1.Benjamin, Sr.[1]) was born 21 Nov 1929 in Ft. Worth, Texas, the son of **Willis Wilson Finley** and **Georgia Page Sclater**. He married **Bonnie Rae Graham** 3 May 1951 in Ft. Worth. She was born 2 May 1931 in Otumwa, Wapalo Co., Iowa, the daughter of **Ray Ott Graham** and **Mildred Bertina Moore**.

ISSUE:
+ 149. f   i.   **Nancy Page Finley,** born 12 Feb 1952 <See pg. 30>.
+ 154. f   ii. **Teresa Louise Finley,** born 27 Aug 1955 <See pg. 30>.
+ 158. m   iii. **William Neil Finley,** born 25 Sep 1957 <See pg. 31>.
+ 163. f   iv. **Laura Roxanne Finley,** born 18 Aug 1964 <See pg. 31>.

John shares very generously with copies of letters and other papers from his
family history research. He is a retired civil engineer in Austin, Texas.

- - - - - - - - - -

149. Nancy Page⁸ Finley <See pg. 30> (148.John⁷, 87.Willis⁶, 86.Maria⁵,
62.Willis⁴, 59.Maria³, 58.Willis², 1.Benjamin, Sr.¹) was born 12 Feb 1952,
the daughter of **John Mallory Finley** and **Bonnie Rae Graham**. She
married **Olen Ogden Wardlaw** 10 Jul 1971. He was born 27 Oct 1949 in El
Paso, Texas.
ISSUE:
+ 150. m   i.   **Christopher Olen Wardlaw,** born 29 Jun 1972.
  152. m   ii.   **Jeffrey Fredrick Wardlaw,** born 4 Nov 1973 in Austin,
                 Texas. He married **Zofya Alexandrovna Khorseeva** on
                 Mount Hood, Oregon. She was born 18 May 1979 in St.
                 Petersburg, Russia.
  153. f   iii. **Rebecca Rae Wardlaw,** born 20 Jul 1981 in Austin, Texas.
                 She married **Matthew Thomas Morales** 5 Jun 2004 in
                 Driftwood, Texas. He was born 4 Jun 1980.

- - - - - - - - - -

150. Christopher Olen⁹ Wardlaw (149.Nancy⁸, 148.John⁷, 87.Willis⁶,
86.Maria⁵, 62.Willis⁴, 59.Maria³, 58.Willis², 1.Benjamin, Sr.¹) was born
29 Jun 1972 in Austin, Texas, the son of **Olen Ogden Wardlaw** and **Nancy
Page Finley.** He married **Rynda Gayle Grauke.** She was born 26 Jun 1969
in Gonzales, Texas.
ISSUE:
  151. m   i.   **Tanner Scott Wardlaw,** born 17 Sep 2003 in Austin,
                 Texas.

- - - - - - - - - -

154. Teresa Louise⁸ Finley <See pg. 30> (148.John⁷, 87.Willis⁶, 86.Maria⁵,
62.Willis⁴, 59.Maria³, 58.Willis², 1.Benjamin, Sr.¹) was born 27 Aug 1955,
the daughter of **John Mallory Finley** and **Bonnie Rae Graham**. She
married **John Timothy Cloud** 1 May 1976. He was born 24 Jul 1949. John
died 21 Dec 1995.

ISSUE:

155. m i.   **John Thomas Cloud**, born 14 Nov 1978.
156. m ii. **David Nathan Cloud**, born 10 Jul 1980 in Austin, Texas. He married **Lauren Fay Pryor** 20 Jul 2002 in Austin. She was born 19 Aug 1983.
157. f iii. **Jamie Nicole "Nikki" Cloud**, born 20 May 1984.

Teresa married (2) **Gary Paul Whiteley** in 2002 in Austin, Texas.

- - - - - - - - - -

158. William Neil[8] Finley <See pg. 30> (148.John[7], 87.Willis[6], 86.Maria[5], 62.Willis[4], 59.Maria[3], 58.Willis[2], 1.Benjamin, Sr.[1]) was born 25 Sep 1957, the son of **John Mallory Finley** and **Bonnie Rae Graham**. He married **Tanna Lee Newberry**. She was born 14 Jul 1962.

ISSUE:

159. f i.   **Kathryn Elaine Finley**, born 27 Jul 1983. She married **Michael Holscher** 25 Jun 2005 in San Antonio, Texas.
160. f ii. **Lauren Anne Finley**, born 15 Mar 1988.
161. f iii. **Mallory Renee Finley**, born 6 Mar 1992.
162. m iv. **Nathaniel Scott Finley**, born 2 Aug 1993.

- - - - - - - - - -

163. Laura Roxanne[8] Finley <See pg. 30> (148.John[7], 87.Willis[6], 86.Maria[5], 62.Willis[4], 59.Maria[3], 58.Willis[2], 1.Benjamin, Sr.[1]) was born 18 Aug 1964, the daughter of **John Mallory Finley** and **Bonnie Rae Graham**. She married **Davey Keith Helton** 29 Sep 1984 in Hillsboro, Texas. He was born 15 Oct 1960.

ISSUE:

164. f i.   **Megan Michelle Helton**, born 3 Apr 1985.
165. f ii. **Heather Elizabeth Helton**, born 5 Jan 1988.

- - - - - - - - - -

170. Caroline Louisa "Carrie"[5] Wilson <See pg. 16, 175> (62.Willis[4], 59.Maria[3], 58.Willis[2], 1.Benjamin, Sr.[1]) was born 29 Jan 1864 at "Bonbrook", Cumberland Co., Virginia, the daughter of **Willis Wilson** and **Mary Anna Wilson**.[137] Caroline died 2 Dec 1899, and was buried in Walnut Grove Cemetery, Gregg Co., Texas.[138] She married **Frank Anderson Glenn** 17 Oct 1883 in Longview, Gregg Co., Texas.[139]

---

[137] Family Bible of Willis and Mary Anna Wilson.
[138] Gregg Co. Gen. Soc., *Cemeteries*, Walnut Grove, 3:189.
[139] Ruff, *Gregg Co. TX Marriage Licenses*, C:68.

ISSUE:[140]

171. f   i.   **Laura Orr Glenn**, born 15 Nov 1884 in Longview, Texas, and died there in 1885. She was buried in Walnut Grove Cemetery, Gregg Co., Texas.

172. f   ii.   **Mary Anna Glenn**, born 8 Feb 1888 in Henrietta, Texas. She married **John Thomas Wakefield**.

173. f   iii. **Elizabeth Wilson "Bettie" Glenn**, born 17 Feb 1891 in Huntsville, Texas.

+ 174. m iv. **John Wesley Glenn**, born 4 Sep 1894 <See pg. 32>.

181. f   v.   **Margaret Louise Glenn**, born 4 Sep 1894 at "Walnut Grove", Gregg Co., Texas.

+ 182. f vi. **Caroline Frarie Glenn**, born 6 Oct 1897.

184. m vii.   **Frank Anderson Glenn, Jr.**, born 6 Oct 1897 in San Angelo, Texas.

Carrie was recorded in the family Bible as being baptized on the day of her mother's burial.[141] She is listed in the 1870 census for Rusk Co., Texas, with her uncle and aunt. She was deeded land from her aunt in 1876, and her eldest sister became her guardian in 1879. Her aunt also named her in her 1886 will - "Mrs. Elizabeth T. Alston, (widow of Philip Alston deceased, died on 27th day of May A. D. 1886 at her residence in the city of Longview ... age 71 years ... to beloved niece Mrs. Caroline L. Glenn (formerly Caroline L. Wilson of Gregg Co. Tx) lots 13, 14, 15, 16 in Block No. 7 in Longview ..... household furniture, piano."[142]

- - - - - - - - - -

174. John Wesley[6] Glenn <See pg. 32> (170.Caroline[5], 62.Willis[4], 59.Maria[3], 58.Willis[2], 1.Benjamin, Sr.[1]) was born 4 Sep 1894 at "Walnut Grove", Gregg Co., Texas, the son of **Frank Anderson Glenn** and **Caroline Louisa "Carrie" Wilson**. He married **Laura Leigh Andrews**. She was the daughter of **W. F. Andrews**.

ISSUE:

175. f   i.   **Leigh Wilson Glenn**.

176. f   ii.   **Elizabeth Glenn**. She married **Robert E. "Bob" Walters**.

177. m iii.   **John Wesley Glenn, Jr.**, born about 1894.

178. f   iv.   **Laura Louise Glenn**. She married **E. L. Arnold**.

179. m   v.   **Frank Seay Glenn**. He married **Nila Sue Griffin**.

---

[140] Family Bible of Willis and Mary Anna Wilson. Unless documented otherwise, the Glenn information is from Finley, John M., Family history research.

[141] Family Bible of Willis and Mary Anna Wilson.

[142] Gregg Co. TX Probate Minutes "B", 164-5 file 50, Deed Book D:419, Probate Minutes "C",278-9, file 163.

180. m   vi.   **William Anderson "Bill" Glenn**. He married **Margaret Hitchcock**.

- - - - - - - - - -

182. Caroline Frarie[6] Glenn (170.Caroline[5], 62.Willis[4], 59.Maria[3], 58.Willis[2], 1.Benjamin, Sr.[1]) was born 6 Oct 1897 in San Angelo, Texas, the daughter of **Frank Anderson Glenn** and **Caroline Louisa "Carrie" Wilson**. She married **Thomas Bacon Cuny**.

ISSUE:[143]

183. m   i.   **Thomas Bacon Cuny, Jr.**, born 4 Aug 1919 in Hempstead, Texas.

---

[143] Family Bible of Willis and Mary Anna Wilson.

CHAPTER 4

Descendants of Benjamin Wilson, Jr. (1759-1839)

232. Benjamin[2] Wilson, Jr. <See pg. 1> (1.Benjamin, Sr.[1]) was born 24 Oct 1759 at "Somerset", Cumberland Co., Virginia, the son of **Benjamin Wilson, Sr.** and **Anne Seay**.[144] Benjamin, Jr. died 8 Sep 1839 in Woodford Co., Kentucky.[145] He married **Barbara Bullock** 5 Dec 1789. She was born 1 Sep 1768 in Hanover Co., Virginia, the daughter of **James Bullock** and **Rebecca Wingfield**. Barbara died 4 Feb 1837 in Woodford Co., Kentucky.[146]

ISSUE:[147]

+ 233. f   i.   **Ann Wilson**, born 26 Jan 1791, died Apr 1838 <See pg. 36>.

   321. m   ii.   **James P. Wilson**, born 2 Feb 1793 in Woodford Co. The family wrote affectionately of him from Cumberland Co., Virginia when he traveled back and forth for his education. He was encouraged in 1810 to attend a "Course of Medical Lectures in Philadelphia", which prompted his father to reply, "I wish you to Caution James against the disipation & in some Instances it might bear a harder name, that Come of the young men that attend the lectures Indulge themselves in." In his 1815 letter to his father, James described the mishaps of the trip by horseback, the man accompanying him falling in the Holston River in Tennessee.[148] He received his M. D. degree from the University of Pennsylvania in 1816.[149] His father wrote of "Dr. James in the neighborhood busy in the duties of his profession."[150] James died 2 Apr 1824 in Woodford Co., Kentucky.[151]

   322. m   iii.   **Willis Wilson**, born 27 May 1795 in Woodford Co.,

---

[144] Woodson Family, *Papers, 1740-1945*, Accession 29437-41, LVA.

[145] His will was dated 3 Sep 1839. McCrary, *Wilson Families ... Correspondence .... 1785-1849*, 270-1.

[146] Aker, *Bullocks of VA and KY*, 3, 15.

[147] Family Bible of Benjamin Wilson Jr. Wilson, Virginia, Family group sheets.

[148] McCrary, *Wilson Families ... Correspondence .... 1785-1849*, 94-134,151, 152, 169.

[149] University of Pennsylvania, (accessed 7 Mar 2006).

[150] McCrary, *Wilson Families ... Correspondence .... 1785-1849*, 205-6, 221-2.

[151] Clift, *KY Obituaries*, 34.

Kentucky. Willis also went to Cumberland Co. for his education. In 1811 his teacher/uncle, **James Meredith**, wrote to his father, "If he will hereafter apply himself in the proportion as nature has furnished him with intellectual faculties there is no doubt of his making an useful and respectable figure in any profession to which he shall apply himself."[152] Willis took oath as an attorney in 1817.[153] He was in Kentucky and married **Eliza Cosby** 20 Aug 1819 in Fayette Co., but he evidently returned to try to take care of his father's legal affairs in Virginia. Eliza was born probably in Louisa Co., Virginia, the daughter of **Garland Cosbie** and **Molly Poindexter**.[154] Willis died after 1840, serving with his brothers as executors of their father's will.

323. f   iv.   **Rebecca Wilson**, born 3 Dec 1797 in Woodford Co., Kentucky. She married **Stith Edgar Burton** 31 Mar 1841.[155] Rebecca died before 19 Aug 1870 in Versailles, Woodford Co., Kentucky.[156]

+ 324. m v.   **Samuel Wilson**, born 2 Jan 1800, died 31 Aug 1840 <See pg. 48>.

+ 328. m vi. **Benjamin Wilson, III**, born 3 Apr 1802, died 19 Jan 1853 <See pg. 49>.

346. f   vii. **Elizabeth Wilson**, born 26 Jan 1805 in Woodford Co., Kentucky. She married **Beverly H. Miller** 11 Nov 1846.[157] Elizabeth died after 2 Nov 1872 in Versailles, Woodford Co., Kentucky.[158]

+ 347. f viii. **Maria Wilson**, born 2 Jun 1807, died 4 Jul 1874 <See pg. 52>.

+ 375. f ix.   **Barbara Alexander Wilson**, born 24 Jun 1810, died 21 Jan 1899 <See pg. 55>.

+ 426. f x.   **Unita Mason Wilson**, born 24 Dec 1812, died 19 Nov 1847 <See pg. 60>.

Benjamin Wilson, Jr., wrote to his brother around 1830 that he had been in "Dan Country" near the North Carolina border 50 years earlier. He

---

[152] McCrary, *Wilson Families ... Correspondence .... 1785-1849*, 156, 213, 220.

[153] Cumberland Co. VA Order Book 1815-1818:248-9.

[154] Herndon, *VA Mag. Hist.*, 60:315.

[155] Railey, *History of Woodford Co. KY*, 126.

[156] Will probated 19 Aug 1870, Woodford Co. KY Will Book U:75.

[157] Railey, *History of Woodford Co. KY*, 126.

[158] 1872 appraisal of S. E. Burton's estate.

apparently owned land in Buckingham Co., Virginia from 1782 and was shown on the 1787 Buckingham Co. tax rolls.[159] His brothers wrote letters, 1793 and 1795, telling of their sister, Mason, and brother-in-law, **James Meredith**, being "at your old place".[160] He sold 300 acres on Randolph Creek to James Meredith in 1807.[161]

It appears from the papers and letters that Benjamin went to Kentucky by 1788, probably with General **Charles Scott**. His letters show him to be a carpenter, boat builder, horse trader, hemp grower and land speculator. He built a stone house in Woodford Co. around 1809.[162]

- - - - - - - - - - -

233. Ann[3] Wilson <See pg. 34> (232.Benjamin, Jr.[2], 1.Benjamin, Sr.[1]) was born 26 Jan 1791 in Woodford Co., Kentucky, the daughter of **Benjamin Wilson, Jr.** and **Barbara Bullock**. Ann died Apr 1838 in Lexington, Kentucky. She married **Benjamin Moore** 9 Aug 1825 in Woodford Co., Kentucky. He was born Jun 1788 in Lancaster Co., Pennsylvania, the son of **James Moore** and **Jane Canby**. Benjamin died 15 Sep 1871 in Petersburgh, Illinois.[163]

ISSUE:

+ 234. f   i.   **Jane Wilson Moore**, born 2 Dec 1826, died 9 Dec 1897
                 <See pg. 37>.

  319. f   ii. **Barbara Bullock Moore**, born 30 Mar 1828. She married
                 Benjamin F. Stephenson who was the founder of the
                 GAR.[164] Barbara died 7 Jan 1911 in Petersburgh IL. They
                 had three children.

  320. m   iii. **Benjamin Moore**, born 16 Nov 1829, died 16 Feb 1832.

Benjamin Moore was a teacher to his wife's brothers and neighbors

---

[159] Schreiner-Yantis, *1787 census of Virginia*, 2:685.

[160] Benjamin Wilson Papers 1785-1916. Transcriptions in McCrary, *Wilson Families ... Correspondence .... 1785-1849*, 51, 63.

[161] The tax records of Buckingham Co. list "Colo. Benjamin Wilson" with 300 acres in 1782, but entries from 1787 through 1805 say "Benjamin Wilson". James Meredith is listed with 300 acres from 1807-1813 (his residence on Randolph Creek). Buckingham Co. VA Land Tax 1782-1794, 1795-1813. Ward, *Buck. Co. Land Tax ....Deeds 1782-1814*, 203, 323.

[162] Railey, *History of Woodford Co. KY*, 126. The house which is located between Versailles and Midway is on the National Register. Information is available at the Woodford County Historical Society in Versailles KY.

[163] Passmore, *Andrew Moore*, 1:89-90.

[164] Knight, "Brief History ... Grand Army .... Republic", (accessed 5 Dec 2005).

evidently in Woodford Co. and in Lexington as shown by an 1825 tuition record and letters written later. He was a witness to his father-in-law's will, and he and his daughters are mentioned often in the estate settlement. [165]

- - - - - - - - - - -

234. Jane Wilson[4] Moore <See pg. 36> (233.Ann[3], 232.Benjamin, Jr.[2], 1.Benjamin, Sr.[1]) was born 2 Dec 1826, the daughter of **Benjamin Moore** and **Ann Wilson**. Jane died 9 Dec 1897. She married **James Ely Cowan** 18 Apr 1848 in Mercer Co., Kentucky. He was born 19 Aug 1828 in Mercer Co., Kentucky, the son of **Henry Jefferson Cowan** and **Chloe Ely**. James died 2 Apr 1888 in Danville, Kentucky.[166]

ISSUE:

235. f	i.	**Anna Wilson Cowan**, born 11 Mar 1849. She married **William Suffield** 18 Aug 1869. Anna died 28 Nov 1828.
236. f	ii.	**Chloe Cowan**, born 19 Mar 1851, died 6 Nov 1894.
237. m	iii.	**Harry J. Cowan**, born 26 Aug 1853, died 6 Aug 1854.
238. f	iv.	**Rebecca Jane Cowan**, born 19 Jun 1855, died 2 May 1927.
239. m	v.	**George B. Cowan**, born 2 Jun 1858. He married (1) **Lena Otterson**. George married (2) **Alida Bradley**. George married (3) **Marie Enriqueta Rodal**. George died 13 May 1939.
240. m	vi.	**John Cowan**, born 6 Feb 1862.
+ 241. f	vii.	**Letitia Caroline Craig "Lettie" Cowan**, born 9 Aug 1864, died 17 Jun 1955.
318. f	viii.	**Sarah Rice Cowan**, born 5 Jul 1868, died 23 Jun 1898.

Jane and her sister were named in their grandfather's 1839 will, their mother having died the year before. They spent some time with their aunt and uncle in the family stone house in Midway, Kentucky in 1840.[167]

- - - - - - - - - - -

241. Letitia Caroline Craig "Lettie"[5] Cowan (234.Jane[4], 233.Ann[3], 232.Benjamin, Jr.[2], 1.Benjamin, Sr.[1]) was born 9 Aug 1864 in Mason Co., Illinois, the daughter of **James Ely Cowan** and **Jane Wilson Moore**. Letitia died 17 Jun 1955 in Lexington, Kentucky, and was buried in Bellevue Cemetery in Danville, Kentucky. She married **Maurice MacKenzie Leach** 5 Oct 1892 in Danville. He was born 15 Sep 1865 in

---

[165] McCrary, *Wilson Families ... Correspondence .... 1785-1849*, 224, 233, 236, 271, 277-9, 281.

[166] Additional information from Maurice D. Leach Jr. of Lexington VA.

[167] McCrary, *Wilson Families ... Correspondence .... 1785-1849*, 270-1,273-4, 280-2, 292.

East Winch, Norfolk, England, the son of **John Henry Leach** and **Mary Henrietta Derby**. Maurice died 25 Jul 1922 in New York, New York, and was buried in Bellevue Cemetery in Danville, Kentucky.

ISSUE:

242. m   i.   **John Maurice Leach**, born 24 Jun 1893 in Danville, Kentucky, died there 10 Sep 1896, and was buried in Bellevue Cemetery.

+ 243. f   ii.   **Mary Moore Leach**, born 22 Jul 1895, died 14 May 1952.

+ 272. m   iii.   **Maurice Derby Leach**, born 21 Feb 1898, died 12 Mar 1963 <See pg. 41>.

+ 295. m   iv.   **James Robinson Leach**, born 2 Jul 1900, died 10 Jun 1976 <See pg. 45>.

+ 309. m   v.   **George Brown Leach**, born 21 Mar 1904, died 17 Oct 1980 <See pg. 47>.

- - - - - - - - - -

243. Mary Moore[6] Leach (241.Letitia[5], 234.Jane[4], 233.Ann[3], 232.Benjamin, Jr.[2], 1.Benjamin, Sr.[1]) was born 22 Jul 1895 in Danville, Kentucky, the daughter of **Maurice MacKenzie Leach** and **Letitia Caroline Craig "Lettie" Cowan**. Mary died 14 May 1952 in Detroit, Michigan, and was buried in Ferndale Cemetery in Detroit, Michigan. She married **Clarence Raymond Lynn** 19 Sep 1917. He was born 21 Feb 1897 in Madisonville, Kentucky. Clarence died 21 Aug 1967.

ISSUE:

+ 244. f   i.   **Mary Carolyn Lynn**, born 11 Jan 1922, died 26 Apr 2005.

+ 251. f   ii.   **Edith Glover Lynn**, born 10 Oct 1923, died 2001 <See pg. 39>.

+ 255. f   iii.   **Raymere Martha Lynn**, born 29 Nov 1925, died 6 Mar 1993 <See pg. 39>.

+ 260. f   iv.   **Margaret Ann Lynn**, born 1 Jul 1930 <See pg. 40>.

+ 264. f   v.   **Frances Scott Lynn**, born 1 Jan 1933 <See pg. 40>.

+ 270. f   vi.   **Nancy Dimple Lynn**, born 4 Mar 1934, died 13 Jul 1997 <See pg. 40>.

- - - - - - - - - -

244. Mary Carolyn[7] Lynn (243.Mary[6], 241.Letitia[5], 234.Jane[4], 233.Ann[3], 232.Benjamin, Jr.[2], 1.Benjamin, Sr.[1]) was born 11 Jan 1922 in Earlington, Kentucky, the daughter of **Clarence Raymond Lynn** and **Mary Moore Leach**. She died 26 Apr 2005. She married **Jack Burton Mann** 19 Sep 1941. He was born 11 Jun 1922 in Fort Wayne, Indiana. Jack died about 2001 probably in Wyandotte, Michigan.

ISSUE:

245. f   i.   **Martha Jill Mann**, born 25 Sep 1942 in Wyandotte, Michigan.

246. f   ii. **Judith Carol Mann**, born 7 Sep 1946, died 27 Sep 1946 in Trenton.

247. f   iii. **Cheryl Gail Mann**, born 27 Dec 1947 in Trenton, died about 2002.

248. f   iv. **Louann Mann**, born 16 Aug 1949 in Trenton.

249. m   v.   **Louis Lee Mann**, born 25 Aug 1951 in Trenton.

250. f   vi. **Debra Karen Mann**, born 26 Mar 1955 in Trenton.

- - - - - - - - - - -

251. Edith Glover[7] Lynn <See pg. 38> (243.Mary[6], 241.Letitia[5], 234.Jane[4], 233.Ann[3], 232.Benjamin, Jr.[2], 1.Benjamin, Sr.[1]) was born 10 Oct 1923 in Earlington, Kentucky, the daughter of **Clarence Raymond Lynn** and **Mary Moore Leach**. Edith died 2001 in Wyandotte, Michigan. She married **Omer Callaway** 22 Aug 1942 in Wyandotte, Michigan. He was born 20 May 1919 in West Liberty, Kentucky.

ISSUE:

252. m   i.   **Lynn Edward Callaway**, born 8 Sep 1943 in Wyandotte, Michigan.

253. m   ii. **Timothy Omer Callaway**, born 9 Jan 1947 in Wyandotte.

254. m   iii. **Richard Alan Callaway**, born 29 Dec 1947 in Wyandotte

- - - - - - - - - - -

255. Raymere Martha[7] Lynn <See pg. 38> (243.Mary[6], 241.Letitia[5], 234.Jane[4], 233.Ann[3], 232.Benjamin, Jr.[2], 1.Benjamin, Sr.[1]) was born 29 Nov 1925 in Detroit, Michigan, the daughter of **Clarence Raymond Lynn** and **Mary Moore Leach**. Raymere died 6 Mar 1993 in Southgate, Michigan. She married (1) **Milo Rodney Mann**. He was born 8 Apr 1923 in Fort Wayne, Indiana. Milo died 28 Sep 1945.

Raymere married (2) **Fred Howard**. He was born 25 Jan 1917 in Pineville, Kentucky. Fred died 19 Jun 1997 in Lincoln Park, Michigan.

ISSUE:

256. m   i.   **Raymond John Howard**, born 13 Oct 1947 in Lexington, Kentucky.

257. m   ii. **Fred Allen Howard**, born 29 Jan 1949 in Wyandotte, Michigan.

258. f   iii. **Mary Susan Howard**, born 31 Dec 1950 in Wyandotte.

259. m   iv. **James Frank Howard**, born 29 May 1954 in Wyandotte.

- - - - - - - - - - -

260. Margaret Ann[7] Lynn <See pg. 38> (243.Mary[6], 241.Letitia[5], 234.Jane[4], 233.Ann[3], 232.Benjamin, Jr.[2], 1.Benjamin, Sr.[1]) was born 1 Jul 1930 in Lincoln Park, Michigan, the daughter of **Clarence Raymond Lynn** and **Mary Moore Leach**. She married (1) **James Lee Wheatley** 22 Sep 1950 in Belleville, Michigan; they divorced. He was born 23 Sep 1931 in Big Sandy, Tennessee.

ISSUE:

261. m   i.   **Clarence Lee Wheatley**, born 23 May 1952 in Trenton, Michigan.

262. m   ii.   **Dennis James Wheatley**, born 24 Apr 1955 in Trenton.

263. m iii.   **James Bryan Wheatley**, born 30 Mar 1958 in Wyandotte, Michigan.

Margaret married (2) **Guy Stovall** 2 Aug 1974 in Riverview, Michigan. He was born 3 Apr 1918 in Cunningham, Kentucky.

- - - - - - - - - -

264. Frances Scott[7] Lynn <See pg. 38> (243.Mary[6], 241.Letitia[5], 234.Jane[4], 233.Ann[3], 232.Benjamin, Jr.[2], 1.Benjamin, Sr.[1]) was born 1 Jan 1933 in Lincoln Park, Michigan, the daughter of **Clarence Raymond Lynn** and **Mary Moore Leach**. She married **John Wilmer Hutchinson** 29 Sep 1950 in Wyandotte, Michigan. He was born 28 Sep 1931 in Dayton, Ohio. John died 1 May 2001 probably in Lancaster, Pennsylvania.

ISSUE:

265. f   i.   **Mary Frances Hutchinson**, born 5 Aug 1951 in Wyandotte.

266. f   ii.   **Judith Ann Hutchinson**, born 30 Apr 1953 in Wyandotte.

267. m iii.   **Donald Paul Hutchinson**, born 7 Sep 1955 in Wyandotte.

268. m iv.   **John Wayne Hutchinson**, born 29 Apr 1957 in Wyandotte, died 21 Nov 1977.

269. f   v.   **Nancy Emma Hutchinson**, born 29 Jan 1963 in Dearborn, Michigan.

- - - - - - - - - -

270. Nancy Dimple[7] Lynn <See pg. 38> (243.Mary[6], 241.Letitia[5], 234.Jane[4], 233.Ann[3], 232.Benjamin, Jr.[2], 1.Benjamin, Sr.[1]) was born 4 Mar 1934 in Lincoln Park, Michigan, the daughter of **Clarence Raymond Lynn** and **Mary Moore Leach**. Nancy died 13 Jul 1997 in South Lyon, Michigan. She married (1) **Harry Arthur Munion** 26 Feb 1953 in Lincoln Park, Michigan; they divorced. He was born 22 Feb 1924 in Lebanon, Pennsylvania.

ISSUE:

271. f   i.   **Pamela Sue Munion**, born 26 Jan 1954 in Trenton, Michigan.

Nancy married (2) **Norman Wilson Malone** 13 Jan 1967; they divorced. He was born 31 Aug 1939 in Brighton, England.
Nancy married (3) **Barry Don Oberg** 16 Apr 1975; they divorced. He was born 23 Dec 1931 in Detroit, Michigan.

- - - - - - - - - - -

272. Maurice Derby[6] Leach <See pg. 38> (241.Letitia[5], 234.Jane[4], 233.Ann[3], 232.Benjamin, Jr.[2], 1.Benjamin, Sr.[1]) was born 21 Feb 1898 in Danville, Kentucky, the son of **Maurice MacKenzie Leach** and **Letitia Caroline Craig "Lettie" Cowan**. Maurice died 12 Mar 1963 in Lexington, Kentucky, and was buried there. He married **Sarah Eleanor "Sallie" Woods** 7 Dec 1922 in Nicholasville, Kentucky. She was born 2 Mar 1892 in Keene, Kentucky, the daughter of **Lewis Richard Woods** and **Elizabeth Jane "Bettie" Collins**. Sarah died 28 May 1993 in Lexington, Kentucky, and was buried there.

ISSUE:

+ 273. m   i.   **Maurice Derby Leach, Jr.**, born 23 Jun 1923.
  277. m   ii.   **Kenneth Woods Leach**, born 18 Jul 1924 in Keene, Kentucky. He married **Chrystal Maxine Metcalf** 26 Jun 1948 in Rosebud, Illinois. She was born 22 Jul 1927 in Rosebud, the daughter of **Barney Samuel Metcalf** and **Elsie Little Obermark**. Kenneth died 11 Aug 1996 in Lexington, Kentucky, and was buried there.
+ 278. m iii.   **Lewis Cowan Leach**, born 30 May 1926 <See pg. 42>.
  287. m   iv.   **John Basil Leach**, born 21 Sep 1928 in Lexington, Kentucky. He married **Naomi Riggs** 10 Sep 1961 in Lexington. She was born 17 Sep 1927 in Myna, Clark Co., Kentucky, the daughter of **Henry Radford Riggs** and **Della Ashcraft**.
+ 288. f   v.   **Bettie Eleanor Leach**, born 27 Aug 1933 <See pg. 43>.

- - - - - - - - - - -

273. Maurice Derby[7] Leach, Jr. (272.Maurice[6], 241.Letitia[5], 234.Jane[4], 233.Ann[3], 232.Benjamin, Jr.[2], 1.Benjamin, Sr.[1]) was born 23 Jun 1923 in Lexington, Kentucky, the son of **Maurice Derby Leach** and **Sarah Eleanor "Sallie" Woods**. He married **Virginia Stuart Baskett** 16 Mar 1953 in Lexington, Kentucky. She was born 25 Aug 1924 in Shoshoni, Wyoming, the daughter of **Martin Tyra Baskett** and **Helen Lois Sanford**.

ISSUE:
+ 274. f   i.   **Sarah Stuart Leach**, born 10 Dec 1956.

Maurice, a retired librarian, now lives in Lexington, Virginia. He led a
group of Wilson descendants in a "Round Robin" which added greatly to
our research. [168]

- - - - - - - - - - -

274. Sarah Stuart[8] Leach (273.Maurice, Jr.[7], 272.Maurice[6], 241.Letitia[5],
234.Jane[4], 233.Ann[3], 232.Benjamin, Jr.[2], 1.Benjamin, Sr.[1]) was born 10 Dec
1956 in Naples, Italy, the daughter of **Maurice Derby Leach, Jr.** and
Virginia Stuart Baskett. She married **James Peter Davis** 14 Jun 1986 in
Lexington, Virginia. He was born 12 Jan 1957 in Lebanon, Pennsylvania,
the son of **James Kenneth Davis** and **Elizabeth Mary Sattazahn**.
ISSUE:
275. f   i.   **Margaret Stuart "Mollie" Davis**, born 21 Dec 1990 in
Fairfax, Virginia.
276. m   ii.   **Matthew Cowan "Matt" Davis**, born 23 Aug 1993 in
Fairfax.

- - - - - - - - - - -

278. Lewis Cowan[7] Leach <See pg. 41> (272.Maurice[6], 241.Letitia[5],
234.Jane[4], 233.Ann[3], 232.Benjamin, Jr.[2], 1.Benjamin, Sr.[1]) was born
30 May 1926 in Keene, Kentucky, the son of **Maurice Derby Leach** and
Sarah Eleanor "Sallie" Woods. He married (1) **Juanita Fox** 9 Jun 1947 in
Lexington, Kentucky. She was born 12 Jul 1925 in Mercer Co., Kentucky,
the daughter of **Oscar Fox** and **Susan Bill Baker**. Juanita died 27 Oct 1989
in Lexington, and was buried in Blue Grass Memorial Garden, Fayette Co.,
Kentucky.

ISSUE:
+ 279. m   i.   **Maurice Fox Leach**, born 9 May 1954 <See pg. 43>.
282. m   ii.   **Kenneth Lewis Leach**, born 2 Mar 1958 in Lexington,
Kentucky. He married **Karen Ann Johnson** 25 Aug 1979
in Hattiesburg, Mississippi; they divorced. She was born
28 Feb 1956 in Hinsdale, Illinois, the daughter of **Elliott H.
Johnson** and **Ellen Palmer**.
+ 283. m   iii. **Daniel Cowan Leach**, born 13 Mar 1961 <See pg. 43>.

Lewis married (2) **Barbara Ann Eaves** 9 Aug 1991 in Lexington,
Kentucky. She was born 15 Mar 1941 in Versailles, Kentucky, the daughter
of **Walter Lee Eaves** and **Marie Thomas**.

---

[168] Supplement to Who's Who in America, 45th ed., 695.

Barbara also married (1) **Fred Oliver**.
Barbara also married (2) **Byron Mullen**.

- - - - - - - - - -

279. Maurice Fox[8] Leach <See pg. 42> (278.Lewis[7], 272.Maurice[6],
241.Letitia[5], 234.Jane[4], 233.Ann[3], 232.Benjamin, Jr.[2], 1.Benjamin, Sr.[1]) was
born 9 May 1954 in Lexington, Kentucky, the son of **Lewis Cowan Leach**
and **Juanita Fox**. He married (1) **Terri Gayle Chowning** 1 Sep 1976 in
Lexington; they divorced. She was born 9 Nov 1958, the daughter of
Donald S. Chowning and **Nettie R. Corman**.

Maurice married (2) **Carla Lee Smith** 1 Sep 1984 in Lexington, Kentucky;
they divorced. She was born 19 Nov 1954 in Ironton, Ohio, the daughter of
Carl Martin Smith and **June Lee Smith**.
ISSUE:
  280. m   i. **Aaron Fox Leach**, born 30 Dec 1987 in Lexington.
  281. f   ii. **Meredith Ann Leach**, born 1 Mar 1990 in Lexington.

- - - - - - - - - -

283. Daniel Cowan[8] Leach <See pg. 42> (278.Lewis[7], 272.Maurice[6],
241.Letitia[5], 234.Jane[4], 233.Ann[3], 232.Benjamin, Jr.[2], 1.Benjamin, Sr.[1]) was
born 13 Mar 1961 in Lexington, Kentucky, the son of **Lewis Cowan Leach**
and **Juanita Fox**. He married **Sharon Gay Flynn** 15 Feb 1986 in Midway,
Kentucky. She was born 29 Mar 1964 in Lexington, Kentucky, the daughter
of **Roy Earl Flynn, Jr.** and **Edder Marie Whalen**.
ISSUE:
+ 284. f   i. **Tiffany Nicole Leach**, born 17 Feb 1987.
  286. f   ii. **Tara Daniella Leach**, born 13 Jan 1989 in Lexington,
           Kentucky.

- - - - - - - - - -

284. Tiffany Nicole[9] Leach (283.Daniel[8], 278.Lewis[7], 272.Maurice[6],
241.Letitia[5], 234.Jane[4], 233.Ann[3], 232.Benjamin, Jr.[2], 1.Benjamin, Sr.[1]) was
born 17 Feb 1987 in Lexington, Kentucky, the daughter of **Daniel Cowan
Leach** and **Sharon Gay Flynn**. She married **Christopher "Chris" Frazier**
13 Aug 2005 in Lexington, Kentucky.
ISSUE:
  285. f   i. **Skye Alexa Frazier**, born 22 Oct 2004 in Georgetown,
           Kentucky.

- - - - - - - - - -

288. Bettie Eleanor[7] Leach <See pg. 41> (272.Maurice[6], 241.Letitia[5],
234.Jane[4], 233.Ann[3], 232.Benjamin, Jr.[2], 1.Benjamin, Sr.[1]) was born 27 Aug

1933 in Lexington, Kentucky, the daughter of **Maurice Derby Leach** and **Sarah Eleanor "Sallie" Woods**. She married (1) **Albert Porter McCubbins** 14 Jul 1951. He was born 24 Jan 1933 in Lexington, Kentucky, the son of **John Thomas McCubbins** and **Jewel Cundiff**. Albert died 12 Feb 2001 in Homosassa Springs, Florida.

ISSUE:

+ 289. f   i.   **Sandra Eleanor McCubbins**, born 4 Feb 1953.
+ 291. f   ii.   **Gina Carol McCubbins**, born 24 Jan 1956.

Bettie married (2) **Emil C. Anderson** 29 Mar 2002 in Rainbow Springs State Park, Florida. He was born about 1920, the son of **August Ferdein Anderson** and **Kristen Samvold**. He died 3 Nov 2005.

- - - - - - - - - -

289. Sandra Eleanor[8] McCubbins (288.Bettie[7], 272.Maurice[6], 241.Letitia[5], 234.Jane[4], 233.Ann[3], 232.Benjamin, Jr.[2], 1.Benjamin, Sr.[1]) was born 4 Feb 1953 in Lexington, Kentucky, the daughter of **Albert Porter McCubbins** and **Bettie Eleanor Leach**. She married **David Dale Kellenberger** 19 Jun 1976 in Lexington; they divorced. He was born 15 Dec 1950, the son of **Leo Kellenberger** and **Betty Phillips**.

ISSUE:

290. m   i.   **Kevin Dale Kellenberger**, born 17 Feb 1983 in Sherman, Texas.

- - - - - - - - - -

291. Gina Carol[8] McCubbins (288.Bettie[7], 272.Maurice[6], 241.Letitia[5], 234.Jane[4], 233.Ann[3], 232.Benjamin, Jr.[2], 1.Benjamin, Sr.[1]) was born 24 Jan 1956 in Lexington, Kentucky, the daughter of **Albert Porter McCubbins** and **Bettie Eleanor Leach**. She married (1) **Gregory Kent Fightmaster** 5 Jul 1974 in Lexington; they divorced. He was born 27 Mar 1954 in Lexington, the son of **Wilbert Fightmaster** and **Sue Lowe**.

ISSUE:

292. f   i.   **Cari Beth Fightmaster**, born 28 Oct 1977. She married **Terry Lee Deifendeifer** 12 Dec 1998 in Yankeetown, Florida, the son of **Ronald Deifendeifer** and **Lavon Hunter**; they divorced.

Gina married (2) **Joseph Daniel Hill** 16 Jul 1981 in Homosassa Springs, Florida. He was born 29 Oct 1943 in Flushing, New York, the son of **Joseph Hill** and **Clara Sammis**.

ISSUE:

293. m   ii.   **Daniel Porter Hill**, born 2 Aug 1982 in Inverness, Florida.

294. m iii. **Joseph Patrick Hill**, born 12 Feb 1987 in Inverness.

- - - - - - - - - - -

295. James Robinson⁶ Leach <See pg. 38> (241.Letitia⁵, 234.Jane⁴, 233.Ann³, 232.Benjamin, Jr.², 1.Benjamin, Sr.¹) was born 2 Jul 1900 in Danville, Kentucky, the son of **Maurice MacKenzie Leach** and **Letitia Caroline Craig "Lettie" Cowan**. James died 10 Jun 1976 in Lexington, Kentucky, was cremated, and the ashes were scattered over the Kentucky River at Brooklyn Bridge. He married **Mary Elizabeth James** 7 Jul 1923 in Louisville, Kentucky. She was born 25 Dec 1899 in Louisville, the daughter of **Samuel James** and **Margaret Fulton**. Mary died 28 Jan 1984 in New Port Richey, Florida.

ISSUE:

+ 296. f   i. **Margaret Fulton Leach**, born 18 Mar 1924, died 16 Dec 1992.

- - - - - - - - - - -

296. Margaret Fulton⁷ Leach (295.James⁶, 241.Letitia⁵, 234.Jane⁴, 233.Ann³, 232.Benjamin, Jr.², 1.Benjamin, Sr.¹) was born 18 Mar 1924 in Lexington, Kentucky, the daughter of **James Robinson Leach** and **Mary Elizabeth James**. Margaret died 16 Dec 1992 in New Port Richey, Florida. She married (1) **Charles Orland Bradford** 15 Sep 1945 in Louisville, Kentucky; they divorced. He was born 11 Jul 1921 in Columbus, Ohio, the son of **Charles Henry Bradford** and **Rosa Pauline Norman**. Charles died 18 Feb 1996 in Louisville, Kentucky.

ISSUE:

+ 297. f   i. **Elizabeth Rose "Beth" Bradford**, born 22 Dec 1946 <See pg. 45>.

+ 303. m   ii. **Charles James Bradford**, born 7 Sep 1949, died 1 Feb 2000 <See pg. 46>.

+ 305. m iii. **John Fulton Bradford**, born 8 Dec 1951 <See pg. 47>.

  308. m iv. **Bruce MacKenzie Bradford**, born 20 Nov 1953 in Columbus, Ohio. He married **Janis Marie Damiano** 16 Jul 1983 in New Port Richey, Florida. She was born 6 May 1952 in Pittsburgh, Pennsylvania.

Margaret married (2) **Robert Ellis Higgson** 11 Dec 1976 in Lexington, Kentucky. Robert died 16 Dec 1991 in New Port Richey, Florida.

- - - - - - - - - - -

297. Elizabeth Rose "Beth"⁸ Bradford <See pg. 45> (296.Margaret⁷, 295.James⁶, 241.Letitia⁵, 234.Jane⁴, 233.Ann³, 232.Benjamin, Jr.², 1.Benjamin, Sr.¹) was born 22 Dec 1946 in Columbus, Ohio, the daughter of

Charles Orland Bradford and **Margaret Fulton Leach**. She married **Michael Carl West** 5 Oct 1968 in Jacksboro, Tennessee. He was born 27 May 1949 in Lexington, Kentucky, the son of **Carl J. West** and **Mildred Faye Holleran**.

ISSUE:

+ 298. m   i.   **Michael Carl West, Jr.**, born 19 Apr 1969.
+ 301. m   ii.   **James Russell West**, born 12 Feb 1973.

- - - - - - - - - -

298. Michael Carl[9] West, Jr. (297.Elizabeth[8], 296.Margaret[7], 295.James[6], 241.Letitia[5], 234.Jane[4], 233.Ann[3], 232.Benjamin, Jr.[2], 1.Benjamin, Sr.[1]) was born 19 Apr 1969 in Lexington, Kentucky, the son of **Michael Carl West** and **Elizabeth Rose "Beth" Bradford**. He married **Lori Jean Soule** 17 Nov 1991 in Fremont, Ohio. She was born 23 Feb 1970 in Fremont, the daughter of **James William Soule** and **Irene Mae Rufty**.

ISSUE:

299. f   i.   **Mariah Ellen West**, born 23 Oct 1993 in Fremont.
300. m   ii.   **Josiah Michael West**, born 7 Oct 1998 in Fremont.

- - - - - - - - - -

301. James Russell[9] West (297.Elizabeth[8], 296.Margaret[7], 295.James[6], 241.Letitia[5], 234.Jane[4], 233.Ann[3], 232.Benjamin, Jr.[2], 1.Benjamin, Sr.[1]) was born 12 Feb 1973 in Lexington, Kentucky, the son of **Michael Carl West** and **Elizabeth Rose "Beth" Bradford**. He married **Shawna Louise Rock** 28 Jan 2002 in Findlay, Ohio. She was born 22 Apr 1974 in Bellvue, Ohio.

ISSUE:

302. m   i.   **James Russell West, Jr.**, born 23 Sep 2002 in Fremont, Ohio.

- - - - - - - - - -

303. Charles James[8] Bradford <See pg. 45> (296.Margaret[7], 295.James[6], 241.Letitia[5], 234.Jane[4], 233.Ann[3], 232.Benjamin, Jr.[2], 1.Benjamin, Sr.[1]) was born 7 Sep 1949 in Columbus, Ohio, the son of **Charles Orland Bradford** and **Margaret Fulton Leach**. Charles died 1 Feb 2000 in Lexington, Kentucky. He married **Charlotte Ann Grose** 16 Aug 1969 in Lexington. She is the daughter of **Charles H. Grose**.

ISSUE:

304. m   i.   **Charles James Bradford, Jr.**, born 13 Jul 1971 in Lexington, Kentucky.

- - - - - - - - - -

305. John Fulton[8] Bradford <See pg. 45> (296.Margaret[7], 295.James[6], 241.Letitia[5], 234.Jane[4], 233.Ann[3], 232.Benjamin, Jr.[2], 1.Benjamin, Sr.[1]) was born 8 Dec 1951 in Columbus, Ohio, the son of **Charles Orland Bradford** and **Margaret Fulton Leach**. He married **Billie Jo Barker** 3 Jun 1972. She was born 11 Nov 1952 in Mansfield, Ohio.

ISSUE:

306. f   i.   **Jennifer Tracey Bradford**, born 19 Sep 1975 in Greenville, South Carolina. She married **Chad Schell** 17 Oct 1998. They have a son **Landon**, born 17 Apr 2005 in Atlanta. Georgia.

307. f   ii.   **Jamie Michele Bradford**, born 21 Sep 1979 in Greenville.

- - - - - - - - - -

309. George Brown[6] Leach <See pg. 38> (241.Letitia[5], 234.Jane[4], 233.Ann[3], 232.Benjamin, Jr.[2], 1.Benjamin, Sr.[1]) was born 21 Mar 1904 in Lexington, Kentucky, the son of **Maurice MacKenzie Leach** and **Letitia Caroline Craig "Lettie" Cowan**. George died 17 Oct 1980 in Louisville, Kentucky, and was buried in Lexington. He married **Frances Reynolds Scott** 20 Nov 1928 in Lexington. She was born 12 Jun 1906 in Lexington, the daughter of **Dan Scott** and **Maude Reynolds**. Frances died 21 Jan 1998 in Louisville, Kentucky, and was buried in Lexington.

ISSUE:

+ 310. m   i.   **Rice Cowan Leach**, born 10 Apr 1940.
+ 316. m   ii.   **George Brown Leach, Jr.**, born 1 Sep 1944 <See pg. 48>.

- - - - - - - - - -

310. Rice Cowan[7] Leach (309.George[6], 241.Letitia[5], 234.Jane[4], 233.Ann[3], 232.Benjamin, Jr.[2], 1.Benjamin, Sr.[1]) was born 10 Apr 1940 in Lexington, Kentucky, the son of **George Brown Leach** and **Frances Reynolds Scott**. He married **Isabel Mireille Labbe-Contreras** 26 Dec 1965 in Guatemala City, Guatemala. She was born 23 Jan 1942 in Guatemala City, the daughter of **Frederico Labbe** and **Stella Contreras**.

ISSUE:

311. m   i.   **George Frederick Leach**, born 12 Oct 1966 in New Orleans, Louisiana. He married **Lisa Nolan Lawson** 13 Sep 1996 in Louisville, Kentucky.

+ 312. f   ii.   **Mary Elizabeth Leach**, born 6 Mar 1970 <See pg. 47>.

315. m   iii.   **John Rice Cowan Leach**, born 19 Nov 1972 in Sells, Arizona. He married **Tiana Chidester** 1 Aug 2005.

- - - - - - - - - -

312. Mary Elizabeth[8] Leach <See pg. 47> (310.Rice[7], 309.George[6], 241.Letitia[5], 234.Jane[4], 233.Ann[3], 232.Benjamin, Jr.[2], 1.Benjamin, Sr.[1]) was born 6 Mar 1970 in New Orleans, Louisiana, the daughter of **Rice Cowan Leach** and **Isabel Mireille Labbe-Contreras**. She married **Bradford Paul Whitcomb** 12 Jun 1993 in Frankfort, Kentucky.

ISSUE:
- 313. m i. **Nicholas Cowan Whitcomb**, born 22 Apr 1995 in Bethesda, Maryland.
- 314. f ii. **Alyse Marie Whitcomb**, born 18 Dec 1996 in San Antonio, Texas.

- - - - - - - - - -

316. George Brown[7] Leach, Jr. <See pg. 47> (309.George[6], 241.Letitia[5], 234.Jane[4], 233.Ann[3], 232.Benjamin, Jr.[2], 1.Benjamin, Sr.[1]) was born 1 Sep 1944 in Lexington, Kentucky, the son of **George Brown Leach** and **Frances Reynolds Scott**. He married (1) **Prudence Owen White** 11 Jun 1966 in Scituate, Massachusetts; they divorced. She is the daughter of **Edward Pierce White**.

ISSUE:
- 317. m i. **Edward Owen Leach**, born 20 Jul 1969 in Bloomington, Indiana. His name was legally changed to **Edward Owen Miller** in 1973.

George, Jr. married (2) **Swallow Liu** 18 Jul 1983 in Hong Kong. She was born in China, the daughter of **Zhensheng Liu** and **Dehua Li.**

- - - - - - - - - -

324. Samuel[3] Wilson <See pg. 35> (232.Benjamin, Jr.[2], 1.Benjamin, Sr.[1]) was born 2 Jan 1800 in Woodford Co., Kentucky, the son of **Benjamin Wilson, Jr.** and **Barbara Bullock**. Samuel died 31 Aug 1840 in Woodford Co. He married **Jane Steele** 21 Jan 1829. She was born 1807, the daughter of **William Steele** and **Sarah Bullock.**[169]

ISSUE:.
- 325. f i. **Anna Mary Wilson**. She married **Charles Craig**. Charles also married (2) Barbara Wilson **(See number 326)**
- 326. f ii. **Barbara Wilson**. She married **Charles Craig**. Charles also married (1) Anna Mary Wilson **(See number 325).**
- 327. f iii. **Sally Wilson**. She married **William Wooldridge.**

Samuel is named in several of the family letters. In one written in 1831 he secretly asks his father for money owed to him by his brother, but very politely says, "I would not have him mortified about it." His uncle

---

[169] Family Bible of Benjamin Wilson Jr. Railey, *History of Woodford Co. KY*, 120-1, 126. Aker, *Bullocks of VA and KY*, 8, 15.

addressed a letter to him in 1836 as "Saml Wilson esqr". He and his brothers were executors of his father's 1839 will.[170]

- - - - - - - - - -

328. Benjamin[3] Wilson, III <See pg. 35> (232.Benjamin, Jr.[2], 1.Benjamin, Sr.[1]) was born 3 Apr 1802 in Woodford Co., Kentucky, the son of **Benjamin Wilson, Jr.** and **Barbara Bullock**. Benjamin, III died 19 Jan 1853 in Woodford Co. He married **Virginia Shouse** 17 Oct 1843. She was born 25 Feb 1825, the daughter of **William Shouse** and **Lucretia Smith**. Virginia died 23 Jul 1892 in Versailles, Woodford Co., Kentucky.[171]

ISSUE:[172]

   329. f   i.   **Lucretia Wilson**, born 13 Mar 1845, died 13 Apr 1919.

+ 330. f   ii.   **Inez Wilson**, born 22 Jun 1846, died 12 Feb 1915 <See pg. 50>.

   334. f iii.   **Anna Wilson**, born 27 Apr 1848, died 22 Dec 1925.

   335. f iv.   **Belle Wilson**, born 25 Dec 1849 in Woodford Co., Kentucky, died 18 Jul 1865. There are several letters written to Belle from a friend, one dated 11 Jul 1865 reporting "home is home again since my brother's return ... happy thought ... this cruel war is over".[173]

+ 336. m v.   **Benjamin Albert Wilson**, born 24 Jul 1851, died 24 Apr 1905 <See pg. 50>.

   344. f vi.   **Benella Wilson**, born 13 Feb 1853, died 13 Apr 1853.

   345. f vii.   **Virginia Wilson**, born 13 Feb 1853, died 11 Apr 1853.

Benjamin apparently made a trip south in 1827, shown in correspondence from Mississippi and Louisiana. His future brother-in-law, **Robert J. Thompson**, wrote from Mississippi in 1833 and in 1835 remembering their "school-boy intimacy" and. requesting that he send "any fine" horses to Natchez. Benjamin was named an executor of his father's will, in which he was given "the whole of the farm and tract of land on which I live". This included the stone house that his father built in 1809-1810.

His plan to be married is expressed in an 1840 letter, "I intend to get married this winter haveing sold all stock. I have nothing else to do though I have not commenced courting yet", but he was still single in 1841 when he and his sister made a trip to Virginia (probably Kanawha Co., now West

---

[170] McCrary, *Wilson Families ... Correspondence .... 1785-1849*, 241, 267, 270-1.

[171] Family Bible of Benjamin Wilson Jr. Railey, *History of Woodford Co. KY*, 126, 225. Aker, *Bullocks of VA and KY*, 15.

[172] Wilson, Virginia, Family group sheets.

[173] Benjamin Wilson Papers 1785-1916.

Virginia) by stage and steamboat. He evidently took his bride on a
honeymoon trip in 1843 to Mississippi, his brother-in-law, **William Dickey**,
taking care of things in Kentucky.[174]

In 1865 Virginia received a letter from her brother lamenting his loss of a
family watch, due to the "depredation of the guerillas in our little village"
who threatened him with a pistol. The funeral notice of their father shows
his burial in Versailles. In 1866 her account with Taylor & Railey, dealers
in Staple & Fancy Dry Goods showed among other things her purchase of
crape collars, whale bones, and hoop skirts. Later that year a letter from the
Frankfort "Office of the Commissioner's for the Compensation of Enlisted
Slaves" acknowledged her application for compensation for enlisted slave,
Frank Wilson. In early July 1892 her account with E. D. Scrogin & Co.,
Dealers in Pure Drugs, Patent Medicines, Paints, Oils, Varnishes, Etc.
Booksellers and Stationers showed her purchase of Port wine, Brandy,
Pepsin, Rx100039, Antikamnia, and charcoal tablets. [175]

Benjamin and Virginia are shown with their family in the 1850 Woodford
Co., Kentucky, census.

- - - - - - - - - - -

330. Inez[4] Wilson <See pg. 49> (328.Benjamin, III[3], 232.Benjamin, Jr.[2],
1.Benjamin, Sr.[1]) was born 22 Jun 1846, the daughter of **Benjamin Wilson,
III** and **Virginia Shouse**. Inez died 12 Feb 1915. She married **Albert W.
Thomson** 8 Jun 1870 in Woodford Co., Kentucky. He was born 1835.
Albert died 8 Jun 1876 in Woodford Co.[176]
ISSUE:
331. f   i.   **Virginia Wilson Thomson**, born 21 Feb 1876. She married
Joseph Thompson in 1897. Virginia died 28 Mar 1899,
shown printed in the 30 Mar 1899 issue of the *Woodford
Sun.*[177]
332. m   ii. **Harrison Thomson**, born 11 Jul 1878.
333. m   iii. **Roy B. Thomson**, born 17 Nov 1881.

- - - - - - - - - - -

336. Benjamin Albert[4] Wilson <See pg. 49> (328.Benjamin, III[3],
232.Benjamin, Jr.[2], 1.Benjamin, Sr.[1]) was born 24 Jul 1851 in Woodford

[174] McCrary, *Wilson Families ... Correspondence 1785-1849*, 227-8, 235, 246,
261-2, 270-1,280-2, 286, 293-4.
[175] Benjamin Wilson Papers 1785-1916.
[176] Wilson, Virginia, Family group sheets.
[177] Benjamin Wilson Papers 1785-1916.

Co., Kentucky, the son of **Benjamin Wilson, III** and **Virginia Shouse**. Benjamin died 24 Apr 1905 in Peru, Kansas. He married **Fannie Hawkins** 23 Mar 1886 in Harrisonville, Missouri. She was born 17 Sep 1863 in Woodford Co., the daughter of **Benjamin Luke Hawkins** and **Elizabeth Ann Sims**. Fannie died 9 Aug 1937 in Lexington, Kentucky.[178]

ISSUE:

337. f	i.	**Margaret Wilson**, born 6 Sep 1887, died 24 Jul 1889.
338. f	ii.	**Virginia Wilson**, born 21 Sep 1889 in Woodford Co., Kentucky, died Mar 1972 in Lexington, Kentucky. Virginia made transcriptions of many of the letters written by her ancestors and kin from 1788-1824. She recorded later family history which she left to her niece in Lexington.[179]
+ 339. m	iii.	**Benjamin Albert Wilson, Jr.**, born 26 Aug 1891, died 10 Sep 1943.
342. m	iv.	**John Sims Wilson**, born 21 Jan 1894 in Woodford Co., Kentucky. He married **Mary Tomlinson Fallis** 18 Jun 1919 in Lexington, Kentucky. She was born 24 May 1900 in Mercer Co., Kentucky, the daughter of **Samuel Kirkham Fallis** and **Rose Ella Buntin**. John died 20 Oct 1982 in Lexington, Kentucky.
343. f	v.	**Anna Wilson**, born 12 Oct 1896.

Benjamin went to Kansas in 1902 and died there in 1905, after which, according to the article in the *Peru Weekly Derrick*, he was taken by the undertaker to the Peru cemetery in "his beautiful funeral car." Fannie and the children returned to Kentucky.[180]

- - - - - - - - - -

339. Benjamin Albert[5] Wilson, Jr. (336.Benjamin[4], 328.Benjamin, III[3], 232.Benjamin, Jr.[2], 1.Benjamin, Sr.[1]) was born 26 Aug 1891 in Middlesboro, Kentucky,[181] the son of **Benjamin Albert Wilson** and **Fannie Hawkins**. Benjamin, Jr. died 10 Sep 1943 in Versailles, Woodford Co., Kentucky, and was buried in the Versailles Cemetery. He married **Blanche Burrus Butts** 15 Jun 1920 in Tyrone, Kentucky. She was born 26 Nov 1898 in Woodford Co. Blanche died in 1989 and was buried in the Versailles Cemetery.[182]

---

[178] Wilson, Virginia, Family group sheets.

[179] Benjamin Wilson Papers 1785-1916. Wilson, Virginia, Family group sheets.

[180] Benjamin Wilson Papers 1785-1916.

[181] His birth announcement. Benjamin Wilson Papers 1785-1916.

[182] Wilson, Virginia, Family group sheets. Hurst, *Versailles Cemetery*, 41.

ISSUE:

340. f   i.   **Mary Frances Wilson**, born 13 Mar 1921 in Woodford Co., Kentucky. She married **Clyde J. Gibson** 26 Aug 1950. Mary died after 1994.

341. f   ii.   **Anna Vernon Wilson**, born 21 Jan 1923 in Woodford Co.

- - - - - - - - - -

347. Maria³ Wilson <See pg. 35> (232.Benjamin, Jr.², 1.Benjamin, Sr.¹) was born 2 Jun 1807 in Woodford Co., Kentucky, the daughter of **Benjamin Wilson, Jr.** and **Barbara Bullock**. Maria died 4 Jul 1874 in Jefferson Co., Mississippi, and was buried in Greenwood Plantation Cemetery. She married **Louis Bonaparte Chamberlain** 30 Jan 1827 in Woodford Co., Kentucky. He was born 7 Mar 1802 in Jefferson Co., Mississippi, the son of **James Chamberlain** and **Paulina Burch**. Louis died 26 Jan 1844 in Jefferson Co. and was buried at "Mount Locust", Jefferson Co., Mississippi.

ISSUE:[183]

348. m   i.   **Paulinus Wilson Chamberlain**, born 5 May 1828 in Jefferson Co., Mississippi, died 11 Jul 1831.

349. f   ii.   **Louisa Barbara Chamberlain**, born 29 Apr 1831 in Jefferson Co., died 21 Jul 1860.

350. m   iii. **Samuel Benjamin Chamberlain**, born 5 Nov 1833 in Providence, Carroll Parish., Louisiana. He was left at his grandparents in Kentucky in 1835, "not being in good health", apparently stayed and went to school there,[184] was listed with his uncle in the 1850 Woodford Co., Kentucky, census. He married **Mary Darden**. They had four children. Samuel died 31 Oct 1867 in Mississippi.[185]

351. m   iv.   **Louis Willis Chamberlain**, born 15 Mar 1836 in Providence, Carroll Parish, Louisiana. He married **Lizzie Dickey**. They had one child. Louis died 19 Nov 1865.

352. m   v.   **Ferdinand Jefferson Chamberlain**, born 18 Jun 1839 in Union Town, Jefferson Co., Mississippi. He married **Sarah Coleman**. They had one child. Sarah died and was buried at "Mount Locust", Jefferson Co., Mississippi. Ferdinand died 9 Dec 1907, and was buried at "Mount Locust".

+ 353. m   vi.   **John Darden Chamberlain**, born 16 Sep 1841, died 17 Apr 1918 <See pg. 53>.

---

[183] Family Bible of Louis B. Chamberlain. Chamberlain, Eric S., Family history records.

[184] McCrary, *Wilson Families ... Correspondence .... 1785-1849*, 273, 282, 284, 287, 291.

[185] Wiltshire, *Mississippi .. ..Obituaries*, 115, 120.

Louis was educated in Kentucky with his future brothers-in-law as shown by the 1825 receipt and 1827 note regarding his Transylvania University law class. He was certified to practice law in Woodford Co., Kentucky, in 1830, and he later practiced in Carroll Parish, Louisiana.

The marriage bond of Louis and Maria was dated 30 Jan 1827 in Woodford Co., Kentucky.

His journal of his steamboat travels, 1826-1842, describes the fares, trips, etc.: "hurricane deck being twice on fire", "Ice has almost blocked up the river ...... next morning ... we go ashore ... on a firmer element", "May 1, 1827 ... my newly acquired family ... arrived at ..... Mother's ("Mount Locust") in the evening", "At the mouth of the Ohio .... we could proceed no further on account of low water", "S. B. Scotland ... an extremely filthy, foul and disagreeable old boat", "Dec 1835. . .returning home ... Mrs. C. ... daughter ... myself ... servant ... fare $45.00", "Providence Bayou ... Waters and that of the river to unite into one ...some said ... that the river (Mississippi) was to return to its old bed".[186]

In his journal and correspondence he wrote of his residences - with his mother at "Mount Locust",[187] his homes in Natchez, Mississippi and (Lake) Providence, Louisiana, inviting his father-in-law to visit with "bear meat & fish ... on our table at every meal .... a man ... killed twenty-five bears .. Another ... caught two in his trap at once", and then in Fayette, Mississippi, "desirous that our daughter sh^d go up to Ky & stay at school".[188]

Maria and 4 children appear in the 1850 Jefferson Co., Mississippi, census.[189]

- - - - - - - - - - -

353. John Darden[4] Chamberlain <See pg. 52> (347.Maria[3], 232.Benjamin, Jr.[2], 1.Benjamin, Sr.[1]) was born 16 Sep 1841 in Evergreen, Jefferson Co., Mississippi, the son of **Louis Bonaparte Chamberlain** and **Maria Wilson**. John died 17 Apr 1918, and was buried in Greenwood Plantation Cemetery. He married **Ellen Spence**. Ellen died 20 Mar 1882.

---

[186] Chamberlain, Eric S., Family history records.

[187] *Mount Locust*, 1, 8-21. Obernuefemann, *Travel, Old Natchez Trace*, 7-8, 15-17, 42-3, 54-5, 61.

[188] McCrary , *Wilson Families ... Correspondence .... 1785-1849*, 238, 241, 243, 257, 290.

[189] Additional information from Eric S. Chamberlain of Natchez MS. Chamberlain, Eric S., Family history records.

ISSUE:

354. f   i.   **Florence Chamberlain**, born 24 Feb 1866. She married **Isaac Ross**. Florence died 2 Jan 1889.

355. f   ii.   **Lizzie Chamberlain**, born 13 Jun 1867, died 13 Apr 1870.

+ 356. f iii. **Johnnie Chamberlain**, born 27 Dec 1868, died 17 Feb 1951.

370. f   iv. **Ellen Chamberlain**, born 3 Apr 1871, died 28 May 1941.

371. m   v. **Louis Jefferson Chamberlain**, born 6 Oct 1872, died 23 Jul 1967.

372. m vi. **William Spence Chamberlain**, born 11 Mar 1874, died 25 Apr 1947.

373. f vii. **Mary Effie Chamberlain**, born 18 Sep 1877. She married **Louis Campbell Stowers**. They had two children. Mary died 20 May 1951.

374. f viii. **Irene Wilson Chamberlain**, born 1881. She married **Clyde Stewart Cogan**. They had one child. Irene died 8 May 1956.

- - - - - - - - - - -

356. Johnnie[5] **Chamberlain** (353.John[4], 347.Maria[3], 232.Benjamin, Jr.[2], 1.Benjamin, Sr.[1]) was born 27 Dec 1868, the daughter of **John Darden Chamberlain** and **Ellen Spence**. Johnnie died 17 Feb 1951, and was buried at "Mount Locust", Jefferson Co., Mississippi. She married **Thomas Jefferson Chamberlain, II** 1890. He was born 11 Oct 1852, the son of **Thomas Jefferson Chamberlain** and **Mabelle Jane Duncan**. Thomas, II died 17 Aug 1929, and was buried at "Mount Locust".

ISSUE:

357. f   i.   **Sallie Pauline Chamberlain**, born 12 Dec 1890. She married **Floyd Kroh**. Sallie died 25 Aug 1990.

358. m   ii.   **Sidney Lee Chamberlain**, born 14 Sep 1892. He married **Cleora Fulton**. They had four children. Cleora died and was buried in Port Gibson, Mississippi. Sidney died 2 May 1964 and was buried in Port Gibson.

359. m iii. **Thomas Jefferson Chamberlain**, born 29 Oct 1895, died 25 Mar 1985 and was buried in Natchez Cemetery, Mississippi.

360. f   iv. **Elsie Barbara Chamberlain**, born 13 Sep 1898, died 3 Oct 1938 and was buried at "Mount Locust", Jefferson Co., Mississippi.

361. f   v. **Florence Mabelle Chamberlain**, born 31 Oct 1901. She married **Jack Echols**. Florence died 5 Mar 1996 and was buried at "Mount Locust".

362. f   vi.   **Johnnie Irene Chamberlain**, born 22 Jan 1904, died 4 Sep 1989.

+ 363. f   vii.   **Mary Louise Chamberlain**, born 4 Jul 1907, died 1 Mar 1977.

+ 365. m viii.   **Louis William Chamberlain**, born 15 Aug 1911, died 24 Dec 1989.

- - - - - - - - - -

363. Mary Louise⁶ Chamberlain (356.Johnnie⁵, 353.John⁴, 347.Maria³, 232.Benjamin, Jr.², 1.Benjamin, Sr.¹) was born 4 Jul 1907, the daughter of **Thomas Jefferson Chamberlain, II** and **Johnnie Chamberlain**. Mary died 1 Mar 1977, and was buried in Forest Lawn Cemetery in Houston, Texas. She married **Carey Wade**.

ISSUE:

364. m   i.   **Carey Wade, Jr.**

- - - - - - - - - -

365. Louis William⁶ Chamberlain (356.Johnnie⁵, 353.John⁴, 347.Maria³, 232.Benjamin, Jr.², 1.Benjamin, Sr.¹) was born 15 Aug 1911, the son of **Thomas Jefferson Chamberlain, II** and **Johnnie Chamberlain**. Louis died 24 Dec 1989 and was buried in Cayuga Cemetery in Utica, Mississippi. He married **Helen Smith** 25 Dec 1937. Helen died 2 Jan 1988 and was buried in Cayuga Cemetery.

ISSUE:

366. m   i.   **Louis William Chamberlain, Jr.**, born 1939.
367. m   ii.   **Eric "Rick" Spence Chamberlain**, born 19 Feb 1940. Rick, retired from a career with an oil company, became an interpreter/ranger with the National Park Service on the Natchez Trace at "Mount Locust", his ancestral home.[190]
368. m   iii.   **Bruce Chamberlain**, born 1941.
369. f   iv.   **Anita Chamberlain**, born 1951.

- - - - - - - - - -

375. Barbara Alexander³ Wilson <See pg. 35> (232.Benjamin, Jr.², 1.Benjamin, Sr.¹) was born 24 Jun 1810 in Woodford Co., Kentucky, the daughter of **Benjamin Wilson, Jr.** and **Barbara Bullock**. Barbara died 21 Jan 1899 in Versailles, Kentucky, and was buried in Versailles Cemetery. She married **Robert Joseph Thompson** 20 Mar 1835. He was born 23 Apr 1803 in Pennsylvania, the son of **William Robert Thompson**.

[190] "A Beautiful Day on the Trace", (accessed 7 Dec 2005). Solomon, "Off the Beaten Trace", (accessed 7 Dec 2005).

Robert died 3 Feb 1889, and was buried in Versailles Cemetery.[191]

ISSUE:

+ 376. m   i.   **William Thompson,** born 1836 <See pg. 57>.

387. m   ii.   **Benjamin Wilson Thompson,** born 24 Feb 1838 in Kentucky. He married **Fannie Goodwin.** She was born 25 Jan 1842. Fannie died 3 Oct 1914, and was buried in Versailles Cemetery, Woodford Co., Kentucky. Benjamin died 14 Apr 1889 and was buried in Versailles Cemetery.

388. f   iii.   **Harriet Rebecca Thompson,** born 1842 in Kentucky, died 26 Sep 1927, and was buried in Versailles Cemetery.

389. f   iv.   **Enna Thompson,** born 13 Dec 1845 in Kentucky, died 25 Aug 1937, and was buried in Versailles Cemetery.

390. m   v.   **Robert J. Thompson, Jr.,** born 1846 in Kentucky. He married **Maxey Ayres.** She was the daughter of **Walter Ayres.** Robert, Jr. died 21 Jun 1920 and was buried in Versailles Cemetery.

+ 391. f   vi.   **Katherine ODonahue Thompson,** born 11 Dec 1849, died 11 Dec 1929 <See pg. 57>.

416. f   vii.   **Anna Thompson.**

+ 417. m viii.   **Oakley Thompson** <See pg. 60>.

Robert wrote to his future brother-in-law in 1829 from Philadelphia where he was studying medicine.[192] As bachelors, he said, "Marry not untill thou findest one rich ....". In 1833 he wrote from Pine Ridge, Mississippi, that "... the treatment of the slaves is harsh in the extreme ..." and that he is the only physician in the area. Later he wrote, "There was an attempt made at insurrection in the county above ...". By 1834 he wrote, " ... present my most affectionate regards to Miss Barbara" enclosing "a small volume" for her.[193]

They must have been in Woodford Co. by 1841, her brother writing "Barbara and her two boys (are here) as often as she is able to come". Robert is listed with his family in the 1850 Woodford Co., Kentucky, census.

- - - - - - - - - -

---

[191] Aker, *Bullocks of VA and KY,* 15-16. Railey, *History of Woodford Co. KY,* 121. Hurst, *Versailles Cemetery,* 41. Additional information from Mary Jean (Brown) Reece of Versailles KY.

[192] University of Pennsylvania, (accessed 1 Apr 2006).

[193] McCrary, *Wilson Families ... Correspondence .... 1785-1849,* 231, 246, 253, 259.

376. William[4] Thompson <See pg. 56> (375.Barbara[3], 232.Benjamin, Jr.[2], 1.Benjamin, Sr.[1]) was born 1836 in Kentucky, the son of **Robert Joseph Thompson** and **Barbara Alexander Wilson**. He married **Virginia Campbell**. She was the daughter of **Alexander Campbell**.

ISSUE:

+ 377. m   i.   **Alexander Campbell Thompson**.
  384. m   ii.   **William Thompson**.
  385. f   iii.   **Virginia Campbell Thompson**.
  386. m   iv.   **Robert Joseph Thompson**. He married **Mary Nall**.

- - - - - - - - - -

377. Alexander Campbell[5] Thompson (376.William[4], 375.Barbara[3], 232.Benjamin, Jr.[2], 1.Benjamin, Sr.[1]). He was the son of **William Thompson** and **Virginia Campbell**. He married (1) **Mary Neal**.

ISSUE:

  378. m   i.   **Howard Neal Thompson**.

Alexander married (2) **Mary Barnard**.

ISSUE:

  379. m   ii.   **Alexander Campbell Thompson, Jr.**, born 1897.
  380. f   iii.   **Virginia Thompson**, born 1898.
  381. m   iv.   **Barnard Thompson**, born 1899.
  382. f   v.   **Matilda Thompson**, born 1901.
  383. f   vi.   **Margaret Thompson**, born 1907.

- - - - - - - - - -

391. Katherine ODonahue[4] Thompson <See pg. 56> (375.Barbara[3], 232.Benjamin, Jr.[2], 1.Benjamin, Sr.[1]) was born 11 Dec 1849, the daughter of **Robert Joseph Thompson** and **Barbara Alexander Wilson**. Katherine died 11 Dec 1929, and was buried in Versailles Cemetery, Woodford Co., Kentucky. She married **John Tilford Brown** 16 Nov 1882 in London, Kentucky. He was the son of **John Craig Brown**.

ISSUE:

+ 392. m   i.   **Oakley Thompson Brown**, born 6 May 1884.
+ 396. f   ii.   **Barbara Brown**, born 19 Dec 1885.
+ 400. m   iii.   **Frank Forrester Brown**, born 19 Sep 1888 <See pg. 58>.
+ 409. m   iv.   **Wesley Hale Brown**, born 8 Jun 1890 <See pg. 59>.

- - - - - - - - - -

392. Oakley Thompson[5] Brown (391.Katherine[4], 375.Barbara[3], 232.Benjamin, Jr.[2], 1.Benjamin, Sr.[1]) was born 6 May 1884, the son of **John Tilford Brown** and **Katherine ODonahue Thompson**. He married (1)

Mrs. Jean Notham.
ISSUE:

+ 393. f   i.   **Katherine Wildbridge Brown**, born 18 Dec 1914.
  395. m   ii.   **Oakley Francis Brown**, born 2 Nov 1916, died 27 Mar
                   1917.

Oakley married (2) **Barbara Ware Thompson (See number 419 - pg. 60)**
1939. She was the daughter of **Oakley Thompson** and **Jennie Fogg**.

- - - - - - - - - - -

393. Katherine Wildbridge[6] Brown (392.Oakley[5], 391.Katherine[4],
375.Barbara[3], 232.Benjamin, Jr.[2], 1.Benjamin, Sr.[1]) was born 18 Dec 1914,
the daughter of **Oakley Thompson Brown** and Mrs. **Jean Notham**. She
married **William McNee**.
ISSUE:

  394. f   i.   **Adelaide McNee**, born 1936.

- - - - - - - - - - -

396. Barbara[5] Brown (391.Katherine[4], 375.Barbara[3], 232.Benjamin, Jr.[2],
1.Benjamin, Sr.[1]) was born 19 Dec 1885, the daughter of **John Tilford
Brown** and **Katherine ODonahue Thompson**. She married **Logan Ewell**.
He was the son of **Richard L. Ewell** and **Julia Ann** ____.
ISSUE:

+ 397. m   i.   **Richard Tillford Ewell**, born 10 Dec 1911.
  399. f   ii.   **Katherine Logan Ewell**, born 1 Feb 1914, died 14 Dec
                   1943.

- - - - - - - - - - -

397. Richard Tillford[6] Ewell (396.Barbara[5], 391.Katherine[4], 375.Barbara[3],
232.Benjamin, Jr.[2], 1.Benjamin, Sr.[1]) was born 10 Dec 1911, the son of
Logan Ewell and **Barbara Brown**. He married **Freda Hack** 15 Jan 1942.
ISSUE:

  398. f   i.   **Carolyn Ewell**, born 18 Nov 1946.

- - - - - - - - - - -

400. Frank Forrester[5] Brown <See pg. 57> (391.Katherine[4], 375.Barbara[3],
232.Benjamin, Jr.[2], 1.Benjamin, Sr.[1]) was born 19 Sep 1888, the son of
John Tilford Brown and **Katherine ODonahue Thompson**. He married
Isabel Field. She was the daughter of **Willis Field** and **Elizabeth Shryock**.
ISSUE:

  401. f   i.   **Isabel Field Brown**, born 20 Oct 1914. She married
                   Bennett D. Taylor 1938.

402. m   ii.   **John Tilford Brown**, born 31 Jan 1920, died 17 Mar 1931.
+ 403. f   iii.   **Mary Jean Brown**, born 14 Mar 1927.

- - - - - - - - - -

403. Mary Jean[6] Brown (400.Frank[5], 391.Katherine[4], 375.Barbara[3], 232.Benjamin, Jr.[2], 1.Benjamin, Sr.[1]) was born 14 Mar 1927 in South Carolina, the daughter of **Frank Forrester Brown** and **Isabel Field**. She married **Fred E. Reece** Jun 1947.
ISSUE:
404. f   i.   **Susan Higbee Reece**, born 15 Jun 1950.
405. f   ii.   **Isabel Reece**.
406. m   iii.   **Fred E. Reece**.
407. f   iv.   **Margaret Reece**.
408. m   v.   **Bennett Reece**.

Mary Jean of Versailles, Kentucky, located the owner of the Wilson old family letters, papers and family Bible at a cousin's home in Lexington. The papers are now in the University of Kentucky library archives.[194] She shared copies with a group of Wilson cousins, adding greatly to the Wilson family history.

- - - - - - - - - -

409. Wesley Hale[5] Brown <See pg. 57> (391.Katherine[4], 375.Barbara[3], 232.Benjamin, Jr.[2], 1.Benjamin, Sr.[1]) was born 8 Jun 1890, the son of **John Tilford Brown** and **Katherine ODonahue Thompson**. He married **Cora F. Green**. She was the daughter of **Norvin Green** and **Ida** _____.
ISSUE:
410. f   i.   **Elizabeth Warren Brown**, born 17 Jan 1917.
+ 411. f   ii.   **Barbara Thompson Brown**, born 15 Jun 1918 <See pg. 59>.
415. m   iii.   **Joseph Wesley Brown**. He married **Barbara Fox**.

- - - - - - - - - -

411. Barbara Thompson[6] Brown <See pg. 59> (409.Wesley[5], 391.Katherine[4], 375.Barbara[3], 232.Benjamin, Jr.[2], 1.Benjamin, Sr.[1]) was born 15 Jun 1918, the daughter of **Wesley Hale Brown** and **Cora F. Green**. She married **J. C. Lindsey** 1 Nov 1937.
ISSUE:
412. m   i.   **Richard Wesley Lindsey**, born 25 Jun 1938.
413. m   ii.   **Joseph Bruce Lindsey**, born 30 Jul 1941.
414. m   iii.   **Donald Whatt Lindsey**, born Sep 1948.

[194] Benjamin Wilson Papers 1785-1916. Papers from 1785-1849 are published: McCrary, *Wilson Families ... Correspondence .... 1785-1849.*

- - - - - - - - - - -

417. Oakley⁴ Thompson <See pg. 56> (375.Barbara³, 232.Benjamin, Jr.²,
1.Benjamin, Sr.¹). He was the son of **Robert Joseph Thompson** and
Barbara Alexander Wilson. He married **Jennie Fogg**. She was the
daughter of **Elijah Fogg** and **Anne Richardson Ware**.
ISSUE:
  418. m   i.   **Edwin H. Thompson**.
+ 419. f   ii. **Barbara Ware Thompson**.
+ 420. f   iii. **Virginia Fogg Thompson**.
  425. m   iv. **Oakley Thompson**. He married **Ruby Smiley**.

- - - - - - - - - - -

419. Barbara Ware⁵ Thompson (417.Oakley⁴, 375.Barbara³,
232.Benjamin, Jr.², 1.Benjamin, Sr.¹). She was the daughter of **Oakley
Thompson** and **Jennie Fogg**. She married **Oakley Thompson Brown (See
number 392 - pg. 57)** 1939. He was born 6 May 1884, the son of **John
Tilford Brown** and **Katherine ODonahue Thompson**.

- - - - - - - - - - -

420. Virginia Fogg⁵ Thompson (417.Oakley⁴, 375.Barbara³,
232.Benjamin, Jr.², 1.Benjamin, Sr.¹). She was the daughter of **Oakley
Thompson** and **Jennie Fogg**. She married **James Clelland Johnson**.
ISSUE:
  421. f   i.   **Barbara Ware Johnson**. She married **Orin Green**.
  422. f   ii. **Mary Willis Johnson**.
  423. m   iii. **James Clelland Johnson, Jr.**
  424. f   iv. **Virginia Fogg Johnson**. She married **Robert T. Chase**.

- - - - - - - - - - -

426. Unita Mason³ Wilson <See pg. 35> (232.Benjamin, Jr.², 1.Benjamin,
Sr.¹) was born 24 Dec 1812 in Woodford Co., Kentucky, the daughter of
Benjamin Wilson, Jr. and **Barbara Bullock**. Unita died 19 Nov 1847.
She married **William M. Dickey** 25 Sep 1834. He was born 1814 in
Kentucky.
ISSUE:
  427. f   i.   **Barbara Dickey**, born 1838 in Woodford Co., Kentucky.
  428. f   ii. **Elizabeth Dickey**, born 1841 in Woodford Co.¹⁹⁵
  429. f   iii. **Margaret Dickey**, born 1844 in Woodford Co.

When his brother-in-law, **Benjamin Wilson**, was in Mississippi in 1843,

---
¹⁹⁵ She may be the Lizzie Dickey that married **Louis Willis Chamberlain**.

William apparently was taking care of the old home place, writing from Midway, "I shall finish sowing your wheat this week.. ... I shall remain at your place until you return."[196]

William also married (2) **Bettie** _____. She was born 1825 in Kentucky. He is listed with his children and second wife in the 1850 Woodford Co. Kentucky census.

---

[196] McCrary, *Wilson Families ... Correspondence .... 1785-1849*, 293.

CHAPTER 5

Descendants of James Wilson (1765-1847)

431. James[2] Wilson <See pg. 1> (1.Benjamin, Sr.[1]) was born 6 Feb 1765 at "Somerset", Cumberland Co., Virginia, the son of **Benjamin Wilson, Sr.** and **Anne Seay**.[197] James died 5 Jun 1847 in Kanawha Co., Virginia (West Virginia).[198] He married **Sarah Cox** 12 Apr 1789 in Buckingham Co., Virginia.[199] She was born about 1767 in Buckingham Co., the daughter of **John Cox** and **Mary Watkins**.[200] Sarah died after 20 Sep 1793 in Buckingham Co.[201]

ISSUE:

+ 432. f   i.   **Mary Wilson**, born before Jun 1790, died 27 Mar 1835 <See pg. 64>.

+ 704. f   ii.   **Ann Seay Wilson**, born 7 Mar 1791, died 17 Sep 1856 <See pg. 97>.

+ 1208. f   iii.   **Sarah "Sallie" Wilson**, born before 20 Mar 1793, died 5 Sep 1859 <See pg. 104>.

James, in his 1837 application for a Revolutionary War pension, stated that he volunteered in Cumberland Co. in 1780-1, was at Little York at the surrender of Cornwallis, and was one of the Sergeants in the guard that conducted the British prisoners of war to their barracks near Winchester. The application was rejected because he did not serve six months in any regularly organized corps.[202]

In the Cumberland County court 24 Apr 1786, "James Wilson Gentleman produced ... a license to practice as an attorney" taking the "oath of fidelity

---

[197] Woodson Family, *Papers, 1740-1945*, Accession 29437-41, LVA.

[198] DAR - Meredith Family Bible.

[199] Letter written by neighbor 12 Apr 1789, McCrary, *Wilson Families ... Correspondence .... 1785-1849*, 36-39.

[200] Stutesman, *Watkins Families*, 172-184. Pages 481-495 give documentation also on Mary Watkins' Hancock, Ligon and Harris ancestors in Virginia, **Thomas Ligon's** line going back to William the Conqueror. Richardson, *Plantagenet Ancestry*, 448-450.

[201] McCrary, *Wilson Families ... Correspondence .... 1785-1849*, 52-3.

[202] Wilson, James S., Pension Application, Revolutionary War, File R11659, Washington: National Archives. United States, *Rejected .... Applications*, 251/37. Other experiences are given in McLean, *Wilson Family*, 34, and DAR Application, National # 249591, Rosa (Moseley) Clarke.

and the oath of an attorney".[203]

After his marriage, James evidently lived in Buckingham County possibly on the property that was left to his wife in her father's will which was written in 1786.[204] Her father died in 1789. Sarah died by 1793 as shown when James wrote from Coxheath in 1796 of being a "widower of 3 years standing". He also mentioned buying "Clay Bank" plantation which was located in both Buckingham and Cumberland counties. In 1823 he exchanged "Clay Bank" for the portion of "Barter Hill" in Cumberland Co. that his son-in-law, **Alexander Trent**, inherited.[205]

James is listed as paying land tax in Buckingham Co. from 1791 through 1823. After that he is listed as a non-resident.[206] In Cumberland Co. his land records are shown from 1799 through 1823, portions showing his acquisition of "Clay Bank". He appears in the Buckingham Co. census in 1810 and 1820, in Cumberland Co. in 1830, and in Kanawha Co. in 1840.

James apparently took care of a great deal of his Kentucky brother's Cumberland and Buckingham, Virginia business. In 1795 James wrote to him, "The possession of a good & well gated horse & the company of a pleasing companion at an agreeable season of the year would tempt me to make a visit to your family," His brother named his first son **James**, whom James the elder enjoyed while the boy was at school in the Cumberland area. An 1801 letter states that the son urged his traveling companion "to ride fifty miles this day to reach my house". James made at least one trip to visit the Kentucky kin. He wrote a letter in 1808, in which he says, "You shall have another visit from me as soon as the new house is built".

James never remarried, one rejection ".... mortifying story of my having been yesterday rejected by my sweet heart Miss Venable", and later, "I feel not want of vigour or inclination of body or mind to engage a second time in matrimony; tho have not been luckily prepossessed in favour of a Suitable subject". A brother wrote in 1820 of an unsuccessful trip, "the only knight

---

[203] Cumberland Co. VA Order Book 1786-1788:2.

[204] "Buckingham County Will of John Cox", *The Southside Virginian*, 5:124-5.

[205] McCrary, *Wilson Families ... Correspondence .... 1785-1849*, 36-9, 68, 216-7. McCrary, *Cumberland County ... Historical Inventory*, 2-3, 11. Cumberland Co. VA Deed Books 8:235, 17:175. The 1796 purchase may have been recorded in Buckingham Co.

[206] Buckingham Co. VA Land Tax Books 1791-1833.

to a full stage of Ladies ... but he is still unconsorted".[207]

By 1831 James bought land in Kanawha County in what is now West
Virginia. More of the family joined him there, and in 1842 he deeded
property to his daughter and son-in-law, **John Meredith**, in exchange for
their caring for him and providing for him the rest of his life.[208]

James did not use the middle initial "S." until late in life.[209] His documents
in Kanawha are signed James S. Wilson, evidently to distinguish himself
from another James Wilson in the area.[210]

- - - - - - - - - - -

432. Mary³ Wilson <See pg. 62> (431.James², 1.Benjamin, Sr.¹) was born
before Jun 1790 in Buckingham Co., Virginia, the daughter of **James
Wilson** and **Sarah Cox**.[211] Mary died 27 Mar 1835 in Virginia. She
married **Alexander Trent, V** 17 Sep 1807 in Buckingham Co.[212] He was
born 18 Nov 1786 probably at "Barter Hill" in Cumberland Co., Virginia,
the son of **Alexander Trent, IV** and **Ann "Nancy" Anderson**.[213]
Alexander, V died 6 Mar 1873 at "Clay Bank", Buckingham Co.

ISSUE:[214]

+ 433. f   i.   **Ann Anderson Trent**, born 5 Aug 1808, died 17 Dec 1891
                 <See pg. 65>.
   658. m   ii. **Alexander Trent, VI**, born 1808 probably in Buckingham
                 Co., Virginia, died Nov 1872 in Buckingham Co.[215]
   659. f   iii. **Sally Trent**, born after 1810. She married **James A.**

---

[207] McCrary, *Wilson Families ... Correspondence 1785-1849*, 32-6, 44-5. 59-61,
68, 89, 94, 130, 202.

[208] Kanawha Co. VA (WV) Deed Book M:374-6.

[209] McCrary, *Wilson Families ... Correspondence .... 1785-1849*, 267. No record
has been found of his having the middle name Stuart as shown in McLean, *Wilson
Family*, 34.

[210] The other James Wilson, Dayton, *Pioneers ... Upper Kanawha*, 143. His will
written and proven 1835, Kanawha Co. WV Will Book A:15.

[211] Letter written 13 Sep 1790 names daughter Mary. McCrary, *Wilson Families ...
Correspondence .... 1785-1849*, 44-5.

[212] Kidd, *Marriages Buckingham Co. VA*, 90.

[213] Avant, *Southern Colonial Families*, 4:750.

[214] *Notes on Peter Field Trent*, 15/28. Brown, *Genealogy .... Wilson*. Additional
information from Mary Carolyn (Steger) Mitton of Salem IN.

[215] Buckingham Co. VA Register of Deaths, 11.

Armistead 26 Dec 1831 in Cumberland Co., Virginia.[216]

660. f iv. **Mary Elizabeth Trent**, born 1810 in Buckingham Co., Virginia, died after Sep 1840.

+ 661. m v. **James Wilson Trent**, born about 1817, died 1863 <See pg. 94>.

+ 691. f vi. **Emeline Frances Trent**, born 6 Aug 1819, died 15 Dec 1892 <See pg. 96>.

Alexander, V also married (2) **Elizabeth Meade Randolph** 18 Oct 1837 in Henrico Co., Virginia.[217] She was born 8 May 1803 at "Ampthill", Virginia, the daughter of **Isham Randolph** of Dungeness and **Ann Randolph "Nancy" Coupland**. Elizabeth died 1 Apr 1882 at "Claybank", Buckingham Co., Virginia.

Issue:[218]

699. f vii. **Mary Trent**. She died before 1876.

700. m viii. **James Trent**. He died before 1876.

701. f ix. **Julia Randolph Trent**, born 10 Nov 1841 at "Clay Bank", died after 1884. She married **John Taylor Gray** 1 May 1867. He was born 13 Feb 1829. John died 24 Aug 1876.[219]

703. m x. **Edward Trent**, born 1846, died before 1876.

The marriage record shown in the *Richmond Argus* 26 Sep 1807 issue stated that Alexander Trent and Mary Wilson were married 17 Sep 1807 by **Christopher McRae**, that the groom was born in Cumberland Co. and the bride in Buckingham Co., daughter of James Wilson.[220]

Alexander inherited a portion of "Barter Hill" at his father's death in 1804. He exchanged this property with his father-in-law in 1823. In his will, dated 4 May 1871, he left his home "Clay Bank" to his wife [221]

- - - - - - - - - - -

433. Ann Anderson⁴ Trent <See pg. 64> (432.Mary³, 431.James², 1.Benjamin, Sr.¹) was born 5 Aug 1808 at "Clay Bank", Buckingham Co., Virginia, the daughter of **Alexander Trent, V** and **Mary Wilson**. Ann died

---

[216] Mitchell, "Trent Family".

[217] Valentine, *Papers*, 3:1463.

[218] *Notes on Peter Field Trent*, 15/28.

[219] Valentine, *Papers*, 4:2262, 2266.

[220] Kidd, *Marriages Buckingham Co. VA*, 90.

[221] Cumberland Co. VA Deed Book 17:175. Buckingham Co. VA Will Book 1:195.

17 Dec 1891 in Corsicana, Navarro Co., Texas, and was buried in Mexia City Cemetery, Limestone Co., Texas. She married **William Perkins Moseley** 14 Dec 1826 in Cumberland Co., Virginia. He was born 31 May 1794 in Buckingham Co., Virginia, the son of **Arthur Richard Moseley** and **Sarah Perkins**. William died 2 Apr 1863 in Buckingham Co. and was buried at "Wheatland", Buckingham Co. [222]

ISSUE:

+ 434. m   i.   **Arthur Perkins Moseley**, born 16 Oct 1827, died 20 May 1883.

+ 440. f   ii.   **Maria Louisa Moseley**, born 15 Jul 1829, died 20 Mar 1893 <See pg. 67>.

+ 447. m iii.   **Alexander Trent Moseley**, born 16 Sep 1831, died 7 May 1891 <See pg. 68>.

+ 544. m iv.   **Samuel Perkins Moseley**, born 28 Jul 1833, died 14 Mar 1912 <See pg. 81>.

  558. m   v.   **Henry Lee Moseley**, born 23 Dec 1834 in Buckingham Co., Virginia, died 6 Apr 1862 at "Wheatland", Buckingham Co.

  559. m vi.   **Edgar Fearn Moseley**, born 16 Feb 1836 in Buckingham Co., died 16 Dec 1864 in Petersburg, Virginia, and was buried at "Wheatland".

+ 560. f vii.   **Mary Wilson Moseley**, born 30 Mar 1838, died Oct 1915 <See pg. 83>.

+ 563. m viii.   **William Perkins Moseley**, born 8 Aug 1841, died 16 Jun 1885 <See pg. 83>.

+ 567. f ix.   **Emeline Elizabeth Moseley**, born 11 Jan 1844, died 22 Aug 1881 <See pg. 83>.

  573. f   x.   **Ann Trent "Nannie" Moseley**, born 27 May 1846 in Buckingham Co., died 26 May 1950 in Miami, Dade Co., Florida.

+ 574. m xi.   **Stanley Page Moseley**, born 24 Jun 1849, died 17 Feb 1933 <See pg. 84>.

+ 610. m xii.   **Franklin Pierce Moseley**, born 1 Sep 1852, died 17 Apr 1906 <See pg. 88>.

+ 644. m xiii.   **Richard Thornton Moseley**, born 10 Aug 1855, died 14 Dec 1925 <See pg. 93>.

- - - - - - - - - -

434. Arthur Perkins[5] Moseley (433.Ann[4], 432.Mary[3], 431.James[2], 1.Benjamin, Sr.[1]) was born 16 Oct 1827 in Buckingham Co., Virginia, the son of **William Perkins Moseley** and **Ann Anderson Trent**. Arthur died

---

[222] D'Aiutolo .... Mitton, *Moseley*, 314-7.

20 May 1883 in Buckingham Co. and was buried at "Wheatland",
Buckingham Co. He married **Lavinia Blanchard Williams** 13 May 1856
in Philadelphia, Pennsylvania. She was born 20 Dec 1832 in Philadelphia,
the daughter of **Thomas Williams** and **Anna Maria Friend**. Lavinia died
27 Aug 1888 in Buckingham Co. and was buried at "Wheatland". [223]

ISSUE:

435. f   i.   **Anna Friend Moseley**, born 1858. She married _____
                   Smith. Anna died 15 Dec 1939, and was buried at
                   "Wheatland".

+ 436. m   ii.   **Arthur Guyon Moseley**, born 23 Feb 1859, died after
                   1917.

439. f   iii.   **Emma Morton Moseley**, born 25 Apr 1861 at
                   "Wheatland". She married **William Moseley Eldridge**
                   22 Jan 1891. He was born 18 Oct 1863 in Buckingham Co.
                   William died 18 May 1919 in Paint Lick, Garrard Co.,
                   Kentucky. Emma died 12 Sep 1931, and was buried in
                   Paint Lick.[224]

- - - - - - - - - - -

436. Arthur Guyon[6] Moseley (434.Arthur[5], 433.Ann[4], 432.Mary[3],
431.James[2], 1.Benjamin, Sr.[1]) was born 23 Feb 1859, the son of **Arthur
Perkins Moseley** and **Lavinia Blanchard Williams**. Arthur died after
1917. He married (1) **Antonette Jackson** in Mexia, Texas. She was born
1865 in Mexia. Antonette died about 1889.

ISSUE:

437. f   i.   **Ellen Douglas Moseley**, born about 1889.

Arthur married (2) **Lucy K. Gadberry** 1890; they divorced. She was born
1870 in Yazoo City, Mississippi. Lucy died after 1940.

ISSUE:

438. m   ii.   **Arthur Guyon Moseley, Jr.**, born 13 Dec 1891 in
                   Denison, Grayson Co., Texas.

- - - - - - - - - - -

440. Maria Louisa[5] Moseley <See pg. 66> (433.Ann[4], 432.Mary[3],
431.James[2], 1.Benjamin, Sr.[1]) was born 15 Jul 1829 in Buckingham Co.,
Virginia, the daughter of **William Perkins Moseley** and **Ann Anderson
Trent**. Maria died 20 Mar 1893. She married **Richard Clough Thornton**
16 Nov 1848 in Virginia. He was born 1826 at "Oak Hill", Cumberland Co.,
Virginia. Richard died Aug 1861.

---

[223] D'Aiutolo ... Mitton, *Moseley*, 430-1.

[224] D'Aiutolo ... Mitton, *Moseley*, 514-5.

ISSUE:
441. m   i. **William Nynn Thornton**, born 1859.
+ 442. f   ii. **Ann Trent Thornton**, born 1861.

- - - - - - - - - - -

442. Ann Trent [6] Thornton (440.Maria[5], 433.Ann[4], 432.Mary[3],
431.James[2], 1.Benjamin, Sr.[1]) was born 1861, the daughter of **Richard
Clough Thornton** and **Maria Louisa Moseley**. She married **Charles
Johnston**. He was born about 1861 in Salem, Roanoke Co., Virginia.[225]
ISSUE:
443. f   i. **Maria Louisa Johnston**, born about 1891. She married **P.
S. Polster**. He was born about 1891. P. S. died probably in
California.
444. m ii. **Frederick Johnston**, born about 1893, died probably in
California.
445. f iii. **Kate Courtnay Johnston**, born about 1895, died in New
York, New York.
446. m iv. **John Thornton Johnston**, born about 1897. He married
Grace Carlton.

- - - - - - - - - - -

447. Alexander Trent[5] Moseley <See pg. 66> (433.Ann[4], 432.Mary[3],
431.James[2], 1.Benjamin, Sr.[1]) was born 16 Sep 1831 at "Rose Cottage",
Buckingham Co., Virginia, the son of **William Perkins Moseley** and **Ann
Anderson Trent**. Alexander died 7 May 1891 at "Trenton", Buckingham
Co., and was buried at Maysville Presbyterian Church, Buckingham Co.[226]
He married **Maria Louise Housewright** 23 Dec 1852 in Buckingham Co.
She was born 28 Nov 1832 in Lovingston, Nelson Co., Virginia, the
daughter of **John Montgomery Housewright** and **Elizabeth Cobbs
Bradshaw**. Maria died 8 Jul 1908 at "Trenton", Buckingham Co., and was
buried at Maysville Presbyterian Church.[227]
ISSUE:
448. m i. **Nicholas Bocock Moseley**, born 25 Aug 1853 in
Buckingham Co., Virginia. He married **Pattie Moss** 8 Jun
1893 in Buckingham Court House, Buckingham Co. Pattie
died 6 Oct 1894. Nicholas died 1 May 1902, and was
buried at Maysville Presbyterian Church.
+ 449. f ii. **Florence LaSalle Moseley**, born 31 Mar 1855, died 5 Jun
1951.

---

[225] D'Aiutolo ... Mitton, *Moseley*, 515.

[226] Rosen, *History of Maysville Presbyterian Church*, 204.

[227] D'Aiutolo ... Mitton, *Moseley*, 431-5

524. m iii. **Perkins Moseley**, born 30 Aug 1857 in Buckingham Co.,
Virginia. He married **Isadora Minette Cruse** Aug 1901 in
Washington, District of Columbia. She was the daughter of
Elias T. Cruse. Isadora died after 1907. Perkins died
24 May 1907 in Baltimore, Maryland, and was buried at
Maysville Presbyterian Church, Buckingham Co., Virginia.

525. f iv. **Katherine May "Kate" Moseley**, born 15 Aug 1859 in
Buckingham Co., Virginia and died there 29 Apr 1861.

+ 526. f v. **Carrie Trent Moseley**, born 11 Apr 1861, died 1907 <See
pg. 80>.

+ 532. f vi. **Lucy Page Moseley**, born 10 Sep 1863, died 9 Jan 1943
<See pg. 80>.

536. f vii. **Elizabeth Montgomery "Betty" Moseley**, born 14 Aug
1866 in Buckingham Co., died 6 Feb 1944 at "Wheatland",
Buckingham Co., and was buried at Maysville Presbyterian
Church, Buckingham Co.

537. f viii. **Ann Meredith "Nannie" Moseley**, born 23 Nov 1868 in
Buckingham Co., died May 1918 at "Dixie", Buckingham
Co., and was buried at Maysville Presbyterian Church.

538. m ix. **Alexander Trent Moseley**, born 10 Jan 1871 in
Buckingham Co. and died there 12 Jan 1871.

539. m x. **Arthur Moseley**, born 10 Jan 1871 in Buckingham Co. and
died there 12 Jan 1871.

+ 540. f xi. **Hattie Heath Hawes Moseley**, born 22 May 1872, died
8 Jun 1902 <See pg. 81>.

- - - - - - - - - -

449. Florence LaSalle[6] Moseley (447.Alexander[5], 433.Ann[4], 432.Mary[3],
431.James[2], 1.Benjamin, Sr.[1]) was born 31 Mar 1855 in Hardwicksville,
Nelson Co., Virginia, the daughter of **Alexander Trent Moseley** and
Maria Louise Housewright. Florence died 5 Jun 1951 in Danville,
Virginia, and was buried at Maysville Presbyterian Church, Buckingham
Co., Virginia. She married **Whitcomb Eliphalet Pratt (See number 692 -
pg. 97)** 6 Apr 1887 in Buckingham Co. He was born 28 Feb 1849 at "Clay
Bank", Buckingham Co., the son of **Bryce McClelland Pratt** and **Emeline
Frances Trent**. Whitcomb died 16 May 1901 in Richmond, Virginia, and
was buried at Maysville Presbyterian Church. [228]

ISSUE:

450. f i. **Mariah Emeline Pratt**, born 30 Nov 1888 in Buckingham
Co., Virginia, died there 19 Oct 1974, and was buried at
Maysville Presbyterian Church, Buckingham Co.

---

[228] D'Aiutolo ... Mitton, *Moseley*, 515.

+ 451. f   ii.   **Mary Wilson Pratt**, born 25 Jul 1890, died 21 Oct 1978.
+ 497. f   iii.   **Trent Moseley Pratt**, born 16 Mar 1892, died 11 Feb 1953
            <See pg. 76>.
   523. m   iv.   **Whitcomb Bryce Pratt**, born 29 Nov 1895 in Buckingham
                   Co., Virginia, died about 1917.

- - - - - - - - - - -

451. Mary Wilson[7] Pratt (449.Florence[6], 447.Alexander[5], 433.Ann[4],
432.Mary[3], 431.James[2], 1.Benjamin, Sr.[1]) was born 25 Jul 1890 in
Buckingham Co., Virginia, the daughter of **Whitcomb Eliphalet Pratt** and
Florence LaSalle Moseley. Mary died 21 Oct 1978 in Petersburg, Virginia,
and was buried at "Dixie", Buckingham Co. She married **James Gray
Spencer** 16 Oct 1911 in Buckingham Co. He was born 27 Dec 1877 in
Buckingham Co., the son of **Samuel Franklin Spencer** and **Eubelia
Buchner Richardson**. James died 24 May 1964 in Buckingham Co. and
was buried at "Dixie".[229]

ISSUE:

+ 452. m   i.   **James Gray Spencer, Jr.**, born 5 Jan 1913, died 27 Aug
                  1988.
+ 464. f   ii.   **Mary Wilson Pratt Spencer**, born 28 Mar 1915 <See pg.
                  72>.
   480. m iii.   **Whitcomb Pratt Spencer**, born 23 Aug 1916 in
                  Buckingham Co., Virginia. He married **Joyce Baird** 11 Oct
                  1954. She was born 27 Jun 1933 in Virginia. Whitcomb
                  died 2 Mar 2002 and was buried in Buckingham Co.
   481. m iv.   **Samuel Franklin Spencer**, born 28 Jul 1921 at "Dixie",
                  Buckingham Co., Virginia, died there 16 Nov 1923, and
                  was buried there.
+ 482. m   v.   **Franklin Moseley Spencer**, born 25 Dec 1924 <See pg. 75>.
+ 489. f   vi.   **Florence Diller "Polly" Spencer**, born 14 Sep 1926 <See
                  pg. 75>.
+ 492. f   vii.   **Meredith Page Spencer**, born 28 Jun 1932 <See pg. 76>.

- - - - - - - - - - -

452. James Gray[8] Spencer, Jr. (451.Mary[7], 449.Florence[6],
447.Alexander[5], 433.Ann[4], 432.Mary[3], 431.James[2], 1.Benjamin, Sr.[1]) was
born 5 Jan 1913 in Buckingham Co., Virginia, the son of **James Gray
Spencer** and **Mary Wilson Pratt**. James, Jr. died 27 Aug 1988 in
Richmond, Virginia, and was buried in Buckingham Cemetery, Virginia.
He married (1) **Nellie Marie Gray** before 1940; they divorced. She was

---

[229] D'Aiutolo ... Mitton, *Moseley*, 572-3.

born about 1913.[230]

ISSUE:

+ 453. f   i.   **Doris Marie Spencer**, born 14 Jun 1940.
+ 457. m   ii.   **James Gray Spencer, III**, born 21 May 1943.
  461. m iii.   **Charles Bryce Spencer**, born 22 May 1944.
+ 462. f   iv.   **Betty May Spencer**, born 18 Jul 1945 <See pg. 72>.

James, Jr. married (2) **Ruth Elizabeth Snoddy** 19 Jan 1957 in Buckingham Co., Virginia. She was born 6 Jun 1915.

- - - - - - - - - - -

453. Doris Marie[9] Spencer (452.James, Jr.[8], 451.Mary[7], 449.Florence[6], 447.Alexander[5], 433.Ann[4], 432.Mary[3], 431.James[2], 1.Benjamin, Sr.[1]) was born 14 Jun 1940 in Stanley, Page Co., Virginia, the daughter of **James Gray Spencer, Jr.** and **Nellie Marie Gray**. She married **Robert Whorley** 19 Oct 1963 in Maysville Presbyterian Church, Buckingham Co., Virginia. He was born 31 May 1941 in Buckingham Co.[231]

ISSUE:

  454. m   i.   **Robert Whorley**, born 25 Jul 1966 in Farmville, Prince Edward Co., Virginia, died 14 May 1989 in Buckingham Co., Virginia, and was buried in Buckingham Cemetery.
  455. f   ii.   **Elizabeth Ann Whorley**, born 1 Mar 1971 in Farmville.
  456. f   iii.   **Crystal Gail Whorley**, born 6 Jan 1977 in Farmville.

- - - - - - - - - - -

457. James Gray[9] Spencer, III (452.James, Jr.[8], 451.Mary[7], 449.Florence[6], 447.Alexander[5], 433.Ann[4], 432.Mary[3], 431.James[2], 1.Benjamin, Sr.[1]) was born 21 May 1943 in Buckingham Co., Virginia, the son of **James Gray Spencer, Jr.** and **Nellie Marie Gray**. He married **Sarah Elizabeth Newton**. She was born about 1945.

ISSUE:

+ 458. m   i.   **James Gray Spencer, IV**, born about 1969.

- - - - - - - - - - -

458. James Gray[10] Spencer, IV (457.James, III[9], 452.James, Jr.[8], 451.Mary[7], 449.Florence[6], 447.Alexander[5], 433.Ann[4], 432.Mary[3], 431.James[2], 1.Benjamin, Sr.[1]) was born about 1969, the son of **James Gray Spencer, III** and **Sarah Elizabeth Newton**. He married **Sandy**

---

[230] D'Aiutolo ... Mitton, *Moseley*, 628.
[231] D'Aiutolo ... Mitton, *Moseley*, 683.

_____. She was born about 1970. [232]

ISSUE:
459. f   i.   **Brittany Spencer**, born 1989.
460. m   ii.   **Hayden Spencer**, born 1993.

- - - - - - - - - - -

462. Betty May[9] Spencer <See pg. 71> (452.James, Jr.[8], 451.Mary[7],
449.Florence[6], 447.Alexander[5], 433.Ann[4], 432.Mary[3], 431.James[2],
1.Benjamin, Sr.[1]) was born 18 Jul 1945, the daughter of **James Gray
Spencer, Jr.** and **Nellie Marie Gray**. She married **Leonard A. Mauck**;
they divorced. He was born about 1944. [233]

ISSUE:
463. f   i.   **Kimberly Lynn Mauck**, born Nov 1977.

- - - - - - - - - - -

464. Mary Wilson Pratt[8] Spencer <See pg. 70> (451.Mary[7], 449.Florence[6],
447.Alexander[5], 433.Ann[4], 432.Mary[3], 431.James[2], 1.Benjamin, Sr.[1]) was
born 28 Mar 1915 at "Dixie", Buckingham Co., Virginia, the daughter of
James Gray Spencer and **Mary Wilson Pratt**. She married **Herbert
Dancy Steger** 26 Mar 1937 in Lovingston, Nelson Co., Virginia. He was
born 20 Dec 1913 in Buckingham Co., the son of **Herbert Dancy Steger**
and **Lelia Virginia Smith**. Herbert died 18 Nov 1984 in Petersburg,
Virginia.[234]

ISSUE:
+ 465. f   i.   **Mary Carolyn Steger**, born 18 May 1939.
+ 472. m   ii.   **Herbert Dancy Steger**, born 27 Jun 1942 <See pg. 74>.

- - - - - - - - - - -

465. Mary Carolyn[9] Steger (464.Mary[8], 451.Mary[7], 449.Florence[6],
447.Alexander[5], 433.Ann[4], 432.Mary[3], 431.James[2], 1.Benjamin, Sr.[1]) was
born 18 May 1939 in Farmville, Prince Edward Co., Virginia, the daughter
of **Herbert Dancy Steger** and **Mary Wilson Pratt Spencer**. She married
(1) **James George Jenkins** 9 Jun 1962 in Midland, Midland Co., Michigan;
they divorced. He was born 15 May 1938 in Midland, the son of **James
George Jenkins** and **Lois Love McKeith**. James died after 1997. [235]

ISSUE:
+ 466. f   i.   **Mary Sue Jenkins**, born 15 Nov 1962.

_____

[232] D'Aiutolo ... Mitton, *Moseley*, 709.

[233] D'Aiutolo ... Mitton, *Moseley*, 683.

[234] D'Aiutolo ... Mitton, *Moseley*, 628.

[235] D'Aiutolo ... Mitton, *Moseley*, 683-5

+ 469. m   ii.   **James George Jenkins, Jr.**, born 17 Sep 1965.

Mary Carolyn married (2) **Carl Greger "Greg" Mitton** 22 Jul 1979 in Beaverton, Gladwin Co., Michigan. He was born 3 Feb 1941 in Terre Haute, Vigo Co., Indiana, the son of **Henry Vandeveer Mitton** and **Katherine Elma Greger**.

Mary Carolyn became an airline pilot in 1980 and was the first female captain with Comair. She has shared an abundance of family history records.

- - - - - - - - - -

466. Mary Sue[10] Jenkins (465.Mary[9], 464.Mary[8], 451.Mary[7], 449.Florence[6], 447.Alexander[5], 433.Ann[4], 432.Mary[3], 431.James[2], 1.Benjamin, Sr.[1]) was born 15 Nov 1962 in Midland, Midland Co., Michigan, the daughter of **James George Jenkins** and **Mary Carolyn Steger**. She married **Theodore Bruno Sylwestrzak** 18 Aug 1981 in Midland. He was born 20 Nov 1961 in Mount Clemens, Macomb Co., Michigan, the son of **Theodore Bruno Sylwestrzak** and **Geraldine M. French**. [236]
ISSUE:
467. f   i.   **Kristen Marie Sylwestrzak**, born 2 Jun 1988 in Detroit, Michigan.
468. f   ii.   **Rachael Ann Sylwestrzak**, born 13 Feb 1990 in Detroit.

- - - - - - - - - -

469. James George[10] Jenkins, Jr. (465.Mary[9], 464.Mary[8], 451.Mary[7], 449.Florence[6], 447.Alexander[5], 433.Ann[4], 432.Mary[3], 431.James[2], 1.Benjamin, Sr.[1]) was born 17 Sep 1965 in Midland, Midland Co., Michigan, the son of **James George Jenkins** and **Mary Carolyn Steger**. He married (1) **Shannon Barringer** 19 Aug 1989 in Sanford, Midland Co., Michigan; they divorced. She is the daughter of **Richard Barringer** and **Barbara** _____.
ISSUE:
470. f   i.   **Allisha Marie Jenkins**, born 16 Oct 1987 in Midland.

James, Jr. married (2) **Donna Jean Sinke** 24 Jul 1992 in Midland. She was born 22 Sep 1961 in Midland, the daughter of **Gerard Clarence Sinke** and **Dolores Kay Stark**.
ISSUE:
471. m   ii.   **Michael Gerard Jenkins**, born 24 Oct 1991 in Midland,

---

[236] D'Aiutolo ... Mitton, *Moseley*, 709.

Midland Co., Michigan.

- - - - - - - - - - -

472. Herbert Dancy⁹ Steger <See pg. 72> (464.Mary⁸, 451.Mary⁷,
449.Florence⁶, 447.Alexander⁵, 433.Ann⁴, 432.Mary³, 431.James²,
1.Benjamin, Sr.¹) was born 27 Jun 1942 in Petersburg, Virginia, the son of
Herbert Dancy Steger and **Mary Wilson Pratt Spencer**. He married
Linda Lou Redford 27 Jun 1964 in Ettrick, Chesterfield Co., Virginia. She
was born 6 Jan 1947 in Portsmouth, Virginia, the daughter of **Wallace
Alfred Redford** and **Vermadel Berkeley Burke**. [237]

ISSUE:

+ 473. f   i.   **Catherine Burke Steger**, born 17 Jul 1966.
+ 476. f   ii. **Claire Whitney Steger**, born 17 Jul 1966.

- - - - - - - - - - -

473. Catherine Burke¹⁰ Steger (472.Herbert⁹, 464.Mary⁸, 451.Mary⁷,
449.Florence⁶, 447.Alexander⁵, 433.Ann⁴, 432.Mary³, 431.James²,
1.Benjamin, Sr.¹) was born 17 Jul 1966 in Petersburg, Virginia, the daughter
of **Herbert Dancy Steger** and **Linda Lou Redford**. She married **Steven
Thomas Childers** 7 Apr 1990 in Huntsville, Madison Co., Alabama. He
was born 16 Dec 1966 in Arab, Marshall Co., Alabama, the son of **William
Thomas Childers** and **Helen Fay Oden**. [238]

ISSUE:

474. f   i.   **Taylor Catherine Noel Childers**, born 14 Dec 1990 in
Jackson, Hinds Co., Mississippi.

475. m   ii. **Jacob Thomas Childers**, born 8 Feb 1995 in Huntsville,
Madison Co., Alabama.

- - - - - - - - - - -

476. Claire Whitney¹⁰ Steger (472.Herbert⁹, 464.Mary⁸, 451.Mary⁷,
449.Florence⁶, 447.Alexander⁵, 433.Ann⁴, 432.Mary³, 431.James²,
1.Benjamin, Sr.¹) was born 17 Jul 1966 in Petersburg, Virginia, the daughter
of **Herbert Dancy Steger** and **Linda Lou Redford**. She married (1) **Edwin
Scott Hicklen** 8 Mar 1986 in Huntsville, Madison Co., Alabama; they
divorced.

ISSUE:

477. m   i.   **Dustin Burke Hicklen**, born 29 Jun 1987 in Huntsville,
Madison Co., Alabama.

478. m   ii. **Michael Spencer Hicklen**, born 9 Sep 1989 in Huntsville.

---

[237] D'Aiutolo ... Mitton, *Moseley*, 685.

[238] D'Aiutolo ... Mitton, *Moseley*, 710.

Claire married (2) **Daniel Todd Renner** 4 Oct 1993 in Huntsville. He is the son of **Cecil Loring Renner**.

ISSUE:

479. f   iii.   **Zoe Danielle Renner**, born 26 Nov 1995 in Huntsville.

- - - - - - - - - - -

482. Franklin Moseley[8] Spencer <See pg. 70> (451.Mary[7], 449.Florence[6], 447.Alexander[5], 433.Ann[4], 432.Mary[3], 431.James[2], 1.Benjamin, Sr.[1]) was born 25 Dec 1924 in Buckingham Co., Virginia, the son of **James Gray Spencer** and **Mary Wilson Pratt**. He married (1) **Minnie Dunkum**; they divorced.[239]

ISSUE:

483. m   i.   **Franklin Moseley Spencer**, born about 1958.
484. m   ii.   **Michael Wayne Spencer**, born about 1960.

Franklin married (2) **Margarette McAllester**.

ISSUE:

485. m   iii.   **Joseph Spencer Spencer**, christened 23 Sep 1973 in Mulberry Grove, Buckingham Co., Virginia.
+ 486. f   iv.   **Mary Frances Spencer**, born 26 Feb 1967.

- - - - - - - - - - -

486. Mary Frances[9] Spencer (482.Franklin[8], 451.Mary[7], 449.Florence[6], 447.Alexander[5], 433.Ann[4], 432.Mary[3], 431.James[2], 1.Benjamin, Sr.[1]) was born 26 Feb 1967 in Virginia, the daughter of **Franklin Moseley Spencer** and **Margarette McAllester**. She married **Randy Scott Hickman** 29 Sep 1990 at Maysville Baptist Church, Buckingham Co., Virginia.

ISSUE:

487. m   i.   **Jesse Scott Hickman**, born 1995.
488. m   ii.   **Kevin Shawn Hickman**, born 1997.

- - - - - - - - - - -

489. Florence Diller "Polly"[8] Spencer <See pg. 70> (451.Mary[7], 449.Florence[6], 447.Alexander[5], 433.Ann[4], 432.Mary[3], 431.James[2], 1.Benjamin, Sr.[1]) was born 14 Sep 1926 in Buckingham Co., Virginia, the daughter of **James Gray Spencer** and **Mary Wilson Pratt**. She married **Noyes Watters Willett** 24 May 1952 in Valley Mills, Texas. He was born 23 Aug 1924 in Wichita Falls, Texas.

ISSUE:

490. m   i.   **Noyes Watters Willett**, born 31 Aug 1955 in Austin, Texas.

---

[239] D'Aiutolo ... Mitton, *Moseley*, 629-630.

491. m   ii.   **James Spencer Willett**, born 19 Dec 1956 in Austin.

- - - - - - - - - -

492. Meredith Page[8] Spencer <See pg. 70> (451.Mary[7], 449.Florence[6], 447.Alexander[5], 433.Ann[4], 432.Mary[3], 431.James[2], 1.Benjamin, Sr.[1]) was born 28 Jun 1932 in Buckingham Co., Virginia, the daughter of **James Gray Spencer** and **Mary Wilson Pratt**. She married **John Emmett Staton** 16 Aug 1953 in Farmville, Prince Edward Co., Virginia. He was born 17 Aug 1922 in Dillwyn, Buckingham Co., the son of **Charles Staton** and **Mary Catherine Fitzgerald**. John died 10 Oct 1980 in Richmond, Virginia, and was buried in Staton Family Cemetery in Dillwyn.

ISSUE:
+ 493. m   i.   **John Emmett Staton**, born 9 Aug 1954.
   496. f   ii.   **Mary Catherine Staton**, born 19 Aug 1958 in Richmond, Virginia.

- - - - - - - - - -

493. John Emmett[9] Staton (492.Meredith[8], 451.Mary[7], 449.Florence[6], 447.Alexander[5], 433.Ann[4], 432.Mary[3], 431.James[2], 1.Benjamin, Sr.[1]) was born 9 Aug 1954 in Richmond, Virginia, the son of **John Emmett Staton** and **Meredith Page Spencer**. He married **Dianne Lynn Perutelli** in Charleston, South Carolina.[240]

ISSUE:
   494. m   i.   **John Emmett Staton**, born 27 Feb 1976 in Charlottesville, Albemarle Co., Virginia.
   495. f   ii.   **Jennifer Lynn Staton**, born 30 Aug 1978 in Charlottesville.

- - - - - - - - - -

497. Trent Moseley[7] Pratt <See pg. 70> (449.Florence[6], 447.Alexander[5], 433.Ann[4], 432.Mary[3], 431.James[2], 1.Benjamin, Sr.[1]) was born 16 Mar 1892 in Buckingham Co., Virginia, the daughter of **Whitcomb Eliphalet Pratt** and **Florence LaSalle Moseley**. Trent died 11 Feb 1953 in Danville, Virginia, and was buried in Mount View Cemetery, Danville Co., Virginia. She married **William Gannaway Crute** 19 Jan 1918 in Maysville Presbyterian Church, Buckingham Co., Virginia. He was born 1 Apr 1885 in Buckingham Co., the son of **John Nicholas Crute** and **Hattie America Gannaway**. William died 18 May 1963 in Staunton, Augusta Co., Virginia.[241]

---
[240] D'Aiutolo ... Mitton, *Moseley*, 685.
[241] D'Aiutolo ... Mitton, *Moseley*, 573-4.

ISSUE:

+ 498. f   i.   **Lorna Hubard Crute**, born 14 Oct 1918, died 24 Oct 1994 <See pg. 77>.

+ 502. f   ii.   **Frances Carroll Crute**, born 5 Feb 1920 <See pg. 77>.

+ 509. f   iii.   **Hattie Gannaway Crute**, born 14 Jul 1922, died 28 Feb 1963 <See pg. 78>.

+ 517. f   iv.   **Florence Moseley Crute**, born 29 Mar 1927 <See pg. 79>.

- - - - - - - - - - -

498. Lorna Hubard[8] Crute <See pg. 77> (497.Trent[7], 449.Florence[6], 447.Alexander[5], 433.Ann[4], 432.Mary[3], 431.James[2], 1.Benjamin, Sr.[1]) was born 14 Oct 1918 in Buckingham Co., Virginia, the daughter of **William Gannaway Crute** and **Trent Moseley Pratt**. Lorna died 24 Oct 1994. She married **Lovick Harden Kernodle** 1 Sep 1947 in Cheraw, South Carolina. He was born 17 Jan 1899 in Graham, North Carolina, the son of **John David Kernodle** and **Cora Harden**. Lovick died 27 Dec 1985 in Durham, North Carolina, and was buried in Mt. View Cemetery, Danville Co., Virginia.[242]

ISSUE:

+ 499. m   i.   **Trent Moseley Kernodle**, born 9 Mar 1951.

- - - - - - - - - - -

499. Trent Moseley[9] Kernodle (498.Lorna[8], 497.Trent[7], 449.Florence[6], 447.Alexander[5], 433.Ann[4], 432.Mary[3], 431.James[2], 1.Benjamin, Sr.[1]) was born 9 Mar 1951 in Danville, Virginia, the son of **Lovick Harden Kernodle** and **Lorna Hubard Crute**. He married **Carol Anne Costen** 16 Oct 1976 in Richmond, Virginia. She was born 24 Mar 1952 in Richmond.[243]

ISSUE:

500. f   i.   **Anne Crute Kernodle**, born 25 Oct 1983 in Danville, Virginia.

501. m   ii.   **William Harden Kernodle**, born 7 May 1989 in Danville.

- - - - - - - - - - -

502. Frances Carroll[8] Crute <See pg. 77> (497.Trent[7], 449.Florence[6], 447.Alexander[5], 433.Ann[4], 432.Mary[3], 431.James[2], 1.Benjamin, Sr.[1]) was born 5 Feb 1920 at "Dixie", Buckingham Co., Virginia, the daughter of **William Gannaway Crute** and **Trent Moseley Pratt**. She married **Oscar Peebles Estes** 4 Jan 1947 in Chatam, Virginia. He was born 18 Jul 1913 in Danville, Virginia, the son of **Oscar Peebles Estes** and **Mary Norma**

---

[242] D'Aiutolo ... Mitton, *Moseley*, 630.

[243] D'Aiutolo ... Mitton, *Moseley*, 685-6.

Sneed. Oscar died 14 Dec 1981 in Staunton, Augusta Co., Virginia.[244]

ISSUE:

+ 503. m   i.   **John Swanson Estes**, born 21 Sep 1947.

+ 506. m   ii.   **William Gannaway Estes**, born 4 Jan 1949.

- - - - - - - - - - -

503. John Swanson[9] **Estes** (502.Frances[8], 497.Trent[7], 449.Florence[6], 447.Alexander[5], 433.Ann[4], 432.Mary[3], 431.James[2], 1.Benjamin, Sr.[1]) was born 21 Sep 1947 in Danville, Virginia, the son of **Oscar Peebles Estes** and **Frances Carroll Crute**. He married **Rose Marie Hayter** 6 Nov 1976 in Intervale, Virginia, the daughter of **William Howard Hayter** and **Virginia Sarah Gilmer**. [245]

ISSUE:

504. m   i.   **William Howard Estes**, born 14 Jul 1977 in Richmond, Virginia.

505. f   ii.   **Christine Crute Estes**, born 5 Sep 1980 in Richmond.

- - - - - - - - - - -

506. William Gannaway[9] **Estes** (502.Frances[8], 497.Trent[7], 449.Florence[6], 447.Alexander[5], 433.Ann[4], 432.Mary[3], 431.James[2], 1.Benjamin, Sr.[1]) was born 4 Jan 1949 in Danville, Virginia, the son of **Oscar Peebles Estes** and **Frances Carroll Crute**. He married **Claudia Jean Conley** 25 Mar 1972 in Seekonk, Massachusetts; they divorced. She is the daughter of **George Vincent Conley** and **Eleanor Isabelle Fernandes**.

ISSUE:

507. f   i.   **Laureen Maureen Estes**, born 3 Mar 1979 in Richmond, Virginia.

508. f   ii.   **Jillian Conley Estes**, born 5 Dec 1981 in Richmond.

- - - - - - - - - - -

509. Hattie Gannaway[8] **Crute** <See pg. 77> (497.Trent[7], 449.Florence[6], 447.Alexander[5], 433.Ann[4], 432.Mary[3], 431.James[2], 1.Benjamin, Sr.[1]) was born 14 Jul 1922 in Buckingham Co., Virginia, the daughter of **William Gannaway Crute** and **Trent Moseley Pratt**. Hattie died 28 Feb 1963 in Berwyn, Pennsylvania. She married **Charles Francis McManus** 3 Sep 1949 in Danville, Virginia. He was born 27 Jun 1919 in Omaha, Nebraska, the son of **Edward James McManus** and **Lenore Jeanette Giblin**.[246]

ISSUE:

510. m   i.   **Edward Moseley McManus**, born 16 Jan 1951 in Dothan,

---

[244] D'Aiutolo ... Mitton, *Moseley*, 630-1.

[245] D'Aiutolo ... Mitton, *Moseley*, 686.

[246] D'Aiutolo ... Mitton, *Moseley*, 631.

Alabama.

511. f ii. **Mary Gannaway McManus**, born 16 Sep 1952 in Mt. Lakes, New Jersey.

512. m iii. **William Crute McManus**, born 14 Dec 1954 in Mt. Lakes.

513. f iv. **Frances Carroll McManus**, born 27 Sep 1956 in Mt. Lakes.

+ 514. f v. **Trent Pratt McManus**, born 2 Sep 1959.

- - - - - - - - - -

514. Trent Pratt[9] McManus (509.Hattie[8], 497.Trent[7], 449.Florence[6], 447.Alexander[5], 433.Ann[4], 432.Mary[3], 431.James[2], 1.Benjamin, Sr.[1]) was born 2 Sep 1959 in Mt. Lakes, New Jersey, the daughter of **Charles Francis McManus** and **Hattie Gannaway Crute**. She married **Christos M. Liakris** 19 Oct 1985 in Corfu, Greece. He was born 3 Jun 1960 in Anthousa, Greece, the son of **Mikhail Liakris** and **Anna Hadsi**.[247]

ISSUE:

515. f i. **Samantha Anne Liakris**, born 14 Mar 1987 in Princeton, New Jersey.

516. m ii. **Michael Charles Liakris**, born 1 Jul 1989 in Princeton.

- - - - - - - - - -

517. Florence Moseley[8] Crute <See pg. 77> (497.Trent[7], 449.Florence[6], 447.Alexander[5], 433.Ann[4], 432.Mary[3], 431.James[2], 1.Benjamin, Sr.[1]) was born 29 Mar 1927 in Chatam, Virginia, the daughter of **William Gannaway Crute** and **Trent Moseley Pratt**. She married **Richard Anthony Batiuk** 30 Mar 1957 in Danville, Virginia. He was born 25 Jan 1928 in Scranton, Pennsylvania, the son of **Anthony Batiuk** and **Zinaida Stepanova Opolska**.[248]

ISSUE:

+ 518. f i. **Suzanne Trent Batiuk**, born 13 Jan 1958.

520. f ii. **Nancy Hubard Batiuk**, born 10 Feb 1960 in Abington, Pennsylvania. She married **Kenneth Doherty Morin** 30 Dec 1983 in Westborough, Massachusetts.

+ 521. m iii. **Richard Anthony Batiuk**, born 25 Jul 1962 <See pg. 80>.

- - - - - - - - - -

518. Suzanne Trent[9] Batiuk (517.Florence[8], 497.Trent[7], 449.Florence[6], 447.Alexander[5], 433.Ann[4], 432.Mary[3], 431.James[2], 1.Benjamin, Sr.[1]) was born 13 Jan 1958 in Abington, Pennsylvania, the daughter of **Richard Anthony Batiuk** and **Florence Moseley Crute**. She married **John Michael**

---

[247] D'Aiutolo ... Mitton, *Moseley*, 686-7.

[248] D'Aiutolo ... Mitton, *Moseley*, 631.

Chalmers 4 Aug 1984 in Belfast, Maine. [249]

ISSUE:

519. m   i.   **Owen Michael Chalmers**, born 10 Sep 1990.

- - - - - - - - - - -

521. Richard Anthony[9] Batiuk <See pg. 79> (517.Florence[8], 497.Trent[7],
449.Florence[6], 447.Alexander[5], 433.Ann[4], 432.Mary[3], 431.James[2],
1.Benjamin, Sr.[1]) was born 25 Jul 1962 in Abington, Pennsylvania, the son
of **Richard Anthony Batiuk** and **Florence Moseley Crute**. He married
Susan Marcia Panciera 13 Oct 1985 in Granby, Connecticut.

ISSUE:

522. f   i.   **Sarah Elizabeth Batiuk**, born 7 Nov 1990.

- - - - - - - - - - -

526. Carrie Trent[6] Moseley <See pg. 69> (447.Alexander[5], 433.Ann[4],
432.Mary[3], 431.James[2], 1.Benjamin, Sr.[1]) was born 11 Apr 1861 in
Buckingham Co., Virginia, the daughter of **Alexander Trent Moseley** and
Maria Louise Housewright. Carrie died 1907. She married **James
Franklin Morrow** 18 Apr 1883 in Buckingham Co. He was born 1865.[250]

ISSUE:

527. m   i.   **Frank Trent Morrow**, born 4 Jun 1884 in Buckingham
                Co., Virginia, died 26 Feb 1886 in Newville, Pennsylvania.
528. f   ii. **Rachel Talbot Morrow**, born 7 Jan 1887 in Cumberland
                Co., Virginia.
529. f   iii. **Meredith Morrow**, born about 1889.
530. f   iv. **Adelaide Morrow**, born Mar 1892.
531. f   v.   **Julia Morrow**, born about 1894.

- - - - - - - - - - -

532. Lucy Page[6] Moseley <See pg. 69> (447.Alexander[5], 433.Ann[4],
432.Mary[3], 431.James[2], 1.Benjamin, Sr.[1]) was born 10 Sep 1863 at
"Wheatland", Buckingham Co., Virginia, the daughter of **Alexander Trent
Moseley** and **Maria Louise Housewright**. Lucy died 9 Jan 1943 in
Farmville, Prince Edward Co., Virginia. She married (1) **John Eppes
Hubard** 15 Jun 1885 in Buckingham Co. He was born 27 Sep 1847 at
"Millbrook", Buckingham Co., the son of **Edmund Wilcox Hubard** and
Sarah Ann Eppes. John died 14 Feb 1892 at "Saratoga", Buckingham Co.,
and was buried in Hubard Cemetery at "Chellowe", Buckingham Co. [251]

---

[249] D'Aiutolo ... Mitton, *Moseley*, 687.

[250] D'Aiutolo ... Mitton, *Moseley*, 517.

[251] D'Aiutolo ... Mitton, *Moseley*, 517-9.

ISSUE:

533. m   i.   **John Eppes Hubard, Jr.**, born 21 Jul 1887 at "Saratoga" and died there 26 Sep 1889.

534. m   ii.   **Edmund Wilcox Hubard**, born 4 Nov 1888, died 1 Aug 1952.[252]

535. f   iii.   **Lorna Doone Hubard**, born 4 Aug 1890 at "Saratoga". She married **Bernard Brown Forbes** 29 Oct 1913 at "Saratoga". He was born 17 Jan 1893 in Andersonville, Buckingham Co., Virginia. Bernard died 3 Jul 1947, and was buried at Trinity Methodist Church, Buckingham Co. Lorna died 12 Mar 1915 at "Saratoga" and was buried in Hubard Cemetery at "Chellowe", Buckingham Co., Virginia.

Lucy married (2) **David Elwood Davidson** 14 Sep 1904 in Washington, District of Columbia. He was born 1858 in Buckingham Co., Virginia. David died 1 Jan 1952 in Farmville, Prince Edward Co., Virginia.

- - - - - - - - - -

540. Hattie Heath Hawes[6] Moseley <See pg. 69> (447.Alexander[5], 433.Ann[4], 432.Mary[3], 431.James[2], 1.Benjamin, Sr.[1]) was born 22 May 1872 in Buckingham Co., Virginia, the daughter of **Alexander Trent Moseley** and **Maria Louise Housewright**. Hattie died 8 Jun 1902, and was buried at Maysville Presbyterian Church, Buckingham Co. She married **Edward Estes Hunter** 8 Aug 1894 in Buckingham Co. He was born about 1872 in Washington, District of Columbia.[253]

ISSUE:

541. f   i.   **Annie Louise Hunter**, born 1895.

542. f   ii.   **Irene Hunter**, born 1898.

543. f   iii.   **Hattie Heath Hunter**, born 1900.

- - - - - - - - - -

544. Samuel Perkins[5] Moseley <See pg. 66> (433.Ann[4], 432.Mary[3], 431.James[2], 1.Benjamin, Sr.[1]) was born 28 Jul 1833 in Buckingham Co., Virginia, the son of **William Perkins Moseley** and **Ann Anderson Trent**. Samuel died 14 Mar 1912 in Virginia, and was buried at Maysville Presbyterian Church, Buckingham Co. He married **Pattie Lewis Hickok** 3 Sep 1871 in Buckingham Co. She was born 29 Sep 1850 in Buckingham Co., the daughter of **Patrick Henry Hickok**. Pattie died 21 Jul 1909, and

---

[252] D'Aiutolo ... Mitton, *Moseley*, 574-5, 631-5,687-691. I apologize to this family for failing to enter more of the family data.

[253] D'Aiutolo ... Mitton, *Moseley*, 519-520.

was buried at Maysville Presbyterian Church.[254]

ISSUE:

545. f   i. **Rosa Clinton Moseley**, born 1872, died 1935, and was buried at Maysville Presbyterian Church.

546. m ii. **John Hitchcock Moseley**, born 1874, died 1910, and was buried at Maysville Presbyterian Church.

547. m iii. **Charles Moseley**, born about 1876.

548. m iv. **William Washburn Moseley**, born 1880, died 1937, and was buried at Maysville Presbyterian Church.

+ 549. f   v. **Ann Pratt "Nannie" Moseley**, born 29 Jul 1883, died 1974.

- - - - - - - - - - -

549. Ann Pratt "Nannie"[6] Moseley (544.Samuel[5], 433.Ann[4], 432.Mary[3], 431.James[2], 1.Benjamin, Sr.[1]) was born 29 Jul 1883, the daughter of **Samuel Perkins Moseley** and **Pattie Lewis Hickok**. Ann died 1974, and was buried in Buckingham Co., Virginia. She married **Frank Hill Spencer** 7 Sep 1905 in Virginia. He was born 2 May 1880 in Virginia. Frank died 19 Feb 1948, and was buried in Buckingham Co.[255]

ISSUE:

550. m   i. _____ **Spencer**, born 30 Sep 1911 in Buckingham Co.

+ 551. m ii. **Frank Addison Spencer**, born 29 Jun 1913.

555. m iii. **Charles Moseley Spencer**, born Jul 1915. He married **Emma Lee**.

556. f iv. **Susie Virginia Spencer**, born Jul 1915 in Buckingham Co. She married **Herbert Adams**. Herbert died in Charlotte Co., Virginia.

557. m v. **Edward Clinton Spencer**, born 1917 in Buckingham Co. died in Lynchburg, Virginia.

- - - - - - - - - - -

551. Frank Addison[7] Spencer (549.Ann[6], 544.Samuel[5], 433.Ann[4], 432.Mary[3], 431.James[2], 1.Benjamin, Sr.[1]) was born 29 Jun 1913 in Buckingham Co., Virginia, the son of **Frank Hill Spencer** and **Ann Pratt "Nannie" Moseley**. He married **Mary L. Clark** 29 Nov 1941. She was born 20 Dec 1915. [256]

ISSUE:

552. m   i. **Frank Addison Spencer**, born 12 Jan 1944.

553. m ii. **Louis Clark Spencer**, born 9 Dec 1946.

---

[254] D'Aiutolo ... Mitton, *Moseley*, 435.

[255] D'Aiutolo ... Mitton, *Moseley*, 520.

[256] D'Aiutolo ... Mitton, *Moseley*, 575.

554. m   iii.   **Charles William Spencer**, born 27 Jun 1950.

- - - - - - - - - -

560. Mary Wilson⁵ Moseley <See pg. 66> (433.Ann⁴, 432.Mary³, 431.James², 1.Benjamin, Sr.¹) was born 30 Mar 1838 in Buckingham Co., Virginia, the daughter of **William Perkins Moseley** and **Ann Anderson Trent**. Mary died Oct 1915. She married **Seymour Wright Holman** 10 Dec 1872 in Virginia. He was born 21 Sep 1836 at "Linwood", Cumberland Co., Virginia, the son of **Benjamin Holman** and **Sarah Elizabeth Allen**. Seymour died 15 Mar 1880 in Limestone Co., Texas. [257]
ISSUE:
561. m   i.   **Henry Lee Holman**, born about 1876 in Texas. He married **Emma Gume**. She was born about 1880 in Beaumont, Texas.
562. f   ii.   **Mary Ruth Holman**, born about 1879 in Texas.

- - - - - - - - - -

563. William Perkins⁵ Moseley <See pg. 66> (433.Ann⁴, 432.Mary³, 431.James², 1.Benjamin, Sr.¹) was born 8 Aug 1841 in Buckingham Co., Virginia, the son of **William Perkins Moseley** and **Ann Anderson Trent**. William died 16 Jun 1885 in Mexia, Limestone Co., Texas, and was buried in the Mexia City Cemetery. He married (1) **Juvernia Rosa Lowe** 1870. She was born 10 Oct 1844 in Georgia. Juvernia died 4 Mar 1877 in Mexia and was buried in the Mexia City Cemetery.
ISSUE:
564. m   i.   **Edgar Fearn Moseley**, born 11 Jun 1873.
565. m   ii.   **Thomas Lowe Moseley**, born 25 Sep 1875 in Mexia, died 7 Mar 1906 in Whitesburg, Letcher Co., Kentucky, and was buried in Mexia.

William married (2) **Mary Murphy** after May 1877 in Texas. She was born about 1841. Mary died in Texas.
ISSUE:
566. m   iii.   **David Murphy Moseley**, born 25 Nov 1882 in Texas, died 28 Jun 1897 in Limestone Co., Texas.

- - - - - - - - - -

567. Emeline Elizabeth⁵ Moseley <See pg. 66> (433.Ann⁴, 432.Mary³, 431.James², 1.Benjamin, Sr.¹) was born 11 Jan 1844 in Buckingham Co., Virginia, the daughter of **William Perkins Moseley** and **Ann Anderson Trent**. Emeline died 22 Aug 1881, and was buried at "Wheatland",

---

[257] D'Aiutolo ... Mitton, *Moseley*, 435-6.

Buckingham Co. She married **Houston Hall** 23 Sep 1868 at "Wheatland". He was born 1836 in Augusta Co., Virginia, the son of **Alexander S. Hall** and **Jane S. _____**. Houston died Oct 1920 in Staunton, Virginia. [258]

ISSUE:

   568. f   i. **Nannie Hall**, born about 1874.

+ 569. f   ii. **Emmie Hall**, born about 1876.

   572. f   iii. **Elizabeth "Bessie" Hall**, born about 1880.

- - - - - - - - - - -

569. Emmie⁶ Hall (567.Emeline⁵, 433.Ann⁴, 432.Mary³, 431.James², 1.Benjamin, Sr.¹) was born about 1876, the daughter of **Houston Hall** and **Emeline Elizabeth Moseley**. She married **Clarence Beardslee**. He was born about 1876. [259]

ISSUE:

  570. f   i. **Caroline Beardslee**, born about 1906.

  571. m   ii. **Emmitt Houston Beardslee**, born about 1908.

- - - - - - - - - - -

574. Stanley Page⁵ Moseley <See pg. 66> (433.Ann⁴, 432.Mary³, 431.James², 1.Benjamin, Sr.¹) was born 24 Jun 1849 in Buckingham Co., Virginia, the son of **William Perkins Moseley** and **Ann Anderson Trent**. Stanley died 17 Feb 1933 in Texas, and was buried in Rose Hill Park in Arlington, Texas. He married (1) **Mary Jane Miller** 25 Nov 1872 in Virginia. She was born 6 Feb 1854 in Georgia. Mary died Nov 1885.[260]

ISSUE:

  575. m   i. **William Perkins Moseley**, born 1 Nov 1873 in Mexia, Limestone Co., Texas, died in California.

  576. m   ii. **Joseph Miller Moseley**, born 20 Sep 1875, died 9 Feb 1935.

+ 577. f   iii. **Katherine Page "Kate" Moseley**, born 7 Apr 1878, died 2 May 1971 <See pg. 85>.

  602. f   iv. **Eve Frances "Fannie" Moseley**.

  603. f   v. **Edna Pearle Moseley**, born 14 Jan 1883 in Mexia, Limestone Co., Texas and died there 22 Jun 1884.

  604. f   vi. **Mary Miller Moseley**, born about 1884 in Mexia and died there Nov 1885.

Stanley married (2) **Ella Clark Morrow**. She was born 15 Feb 1861 in Mexia. Ella died 28 Mar 1935 in Mexia, and was buried in Rose Hill Park

---

[258] D'Aiutolo ... Mitton, *Moseley*, 437.

[259] D'Aiutolo ... Mitton, *Moseley*, 520-1.

[260] D'Aiutolo ... Mitton, *Moseley*, 437-8.

in Arlington, Texas.

ISSUE:

605. f   vii.   **Ella Morrow Moseley.**
606. f   viii. **Esther Trent Moseley.**
607. f   ix.   **Grace Permela Moseley.**
608. f   x.   **Mildred Lee Moseley.**
609. m   xi.   **Stanley Page Moseley, Jr.**

- - - - - - - - - -

577. Katherine Page "Kate"[6] Moseley <See pg. 84> (574.Stanley[5], 433.Ann[4], 432.Mary[3], 431.James[2], 1.Benjamin, Sr.[1]) was born 7 Apr 1878 in Mexia, Limestone Co., Texas, the daughter of **Stanley Page Moseley** and **Mary Jane Miller**. Katherine died 2 May 1971 in Mexia, and was buried in Wortham, Freestone Co., Texas. She married **Thomas LeRoy Simmons** 1899 in Mexia. He was born May 1876 in Cotton Gin, Texas. Thomas died May 1941 in Ennis, Ellis Co., Texas, and was buried in Wortham.[261]

ISSUE:

+ 578. m   i.   **Ed Roy Simmons**, born 24 Dec 1901, died 25 Mar 1971.
+ 590. m   ii.   **Franklin Page Simmons**, born 2 Aug 1907, died 3 Apr 1982 <See pg. 86>.

- - - - - - - - - -

578. Ed Roy[7] Simmons (577.Katherine[6], 574.Stanley[5], 433.Ann[4], 432.Mary[3], 431.James[2], 1.Benjamin, Sr.[1]) was born 24 Dec 1901 in Wortham, Freestone Co., Texas, the son of **Thomas LeRoy Simmons** and **Katherine Page "Kate" Moseley**. Ed Roy died 25 Mar 1971 in Mexia, Limestone Co., Texas, and was buried in Wortham. He married **Sallejo Simmons**. She was born 11 Oct 1903 in Wortham. Sallejo died after 1996.[262]

ISSUE:

+ 579. m   i.   **Roy Dean Simmons**, born 8 Sep 1924, died 22 May 1992.
+ 584. f   ii.   **Sally Simmons**, born 3 Feb 1927 <See pg. 86>.

- - - - - - - - - -

579. Roy Dean[8] Simmons (578.Ed Roy[7], 577.Katherine[6], 574.Stanley[5], 433.Ann[4], 432.Mary[3], 431.James[2], 1.Benjamin, Sr.[1]) was born 8 Sep 1924 in Wortham, Freestone Co., Texas, the son of **Ed Roy Simmons** and **Sallejo Simmons**. Roy died 22 May 1992 in San Antonio, Bexar Co., Texas. He married **Virginia Grogan**. She was born 12 Aug 1924 in Boston, Suffolk

---

[261] D'Aiutolo ... Mitton, *Moseley*, 521.

[262] D'Aiutolo ... Mitton, *Moseley*, 575.

Co., Massachusetts. [263]

ISSUE:
580. m   i.   **Patrick H. Simmons**, born 11 Dec 1954 in Washington, District of Columbia.
581. f   ii. **Rebecca Simmons**, born 8 Nov 1956 in Washington.
582. m   iii. **Roy T. Simmons**, born 18 Sep 1958 in Washington.
583. m   iv. **Joseph B. Simmons**, born 14 Oct 1960 in Washington.

- - - - - - - - - - -

584. Sally^8 Simmons <See pg. 85> (578.Ed Roy^7, 577.Katherine^6, 574.Stanley^5, 433.Ann^4, 432.Mary^3, 431.James^2, 1.Benjamin, Sr.^{1}) was born 3 Feb 1927 in Teague, Freestone Co., Texas, the daughter of **Ed Roy Simmons** and **Sallejo Simmons**. She married **Edmund LeGros Smith** 11 Jun 1949 in Corsicana, Navarro Co., Texas. He was born 19 Sep 1920 in Houston, Harris Co., Texas.

ISSUE:
+ 585. f   i.   **Melissa Smith**, born about 1955.
  589. f   ii. **Sally LeGros Smith**, born 20 Sep 1956 in New York, New York.

- - - - - - - - - - -

585. Melissa^9 Smith (584.Sally^8, 578.Ed Roy^7, 577.Katherine^6, 574.Stanley^5, 433.Ann^4, 432.Mary^3, 431.James^2, 1.Benjamin, Sr.^{1}) was born about 1955 in New York, New York, the daughter of **Edmund LeGros Smith** and **Sally Simmons**. She married **Stanton Pyburn Champion** 3 Jan 1975 in Houston, Harris Co., Texas. He was born 23 Jul 1944 in Houston.[264]

ISSUE:
586. m   i.   **Stanton Pyburn Champion, Jr.**, born 23 Jul 1979 in Tyler, Smith Co., Texas.
587. m   ii. **Austin Smith Champion**, born 11 Nov 1982 in Tyler.
588. f   iii. **Lauren Kate Champion**, born 24 Feb 1986 in Tyler.

- - - - - - - - - - -

590. Franklin Page^7 Simmons <See pg. 85> (577.Katherine^6, 574.Stanley^5, 433.Ann^4, 432.Mary^3, 431.James^2, 1.Benjamin, Sr.^{1}) was born 2 Aug 1907 in Wortham, Freestone Co., Texas, the son of **Thomas LeRoy Simmons** and **Katherine Page "Kate" Moseley**. Franklin died 3 Apr 1982 in Wortham. He married (1) **Maurine Dearing**; they divorced. She was born

---

[263] D'Aiutolo ... Mitton, *Moseley*, 635.

[264] D'Aiutolo ... Mitton, *Moseley*, 693.

about 1907.[265]

ISSUE:
+ 591. m   i.   **Franklin Page Simmons**, born 17 Nov 1928.
+ 593. f   ii.   **Nancy Katherine Simmons**, born 17 Jan 1930.

Franklin married (2) **Mildred Marie Wolters** 6 Nov 1942 in Dallas, Texas.
She was born 21 Jul 1921 in Lewisville, Denton Co., Texas.
ISSUE:
+ 597. f   iii. **Karla Page Simmons**, born 14 Jul 1945.
+ 599. f   iv.   **Cynthia Marie Simmons**, born 31 Oct 1952 <See pg. 88>.

- - - - - - - - - -

591. Franklin Page[8] Simmons (590.Franklin[7], 577.Katherine[6],
574.Stanley[5], 433.Ann[4], 432.Mary[3], 431.James[2], 1.Benjamin, Sr.[1]) was born
17 Nov 1928 in Wortham, Freestone Co., Texas, the son of **Franklin Page
Simmons** and **Maurine Dearing**. He married **Jesse Jewel Nard** 11 Nov
1951 in Wortham. She was born 15 Oct 1930 in Wortham. [266]
ISSUE:
592. m   i.   **Thomas Randall Simmons**, born 27 Dec 1967 in Dallas,
Texas. Adopted.

- - - - - - - - - -

593. Nancy Katherine[8] Simmons (590.Franklin[7], 577.Katherine[6],
574.Stanley[5], 433.Ann[4], 432.Mary[3], 431.James[2], 1.Benjamin, Sr.[1]) was born
17 Jan 1930 in Mexia, Limestone Co., Texas, the daughter of **Franklin
Page Simmons** and **Maurine Dearing**. She married **William Lawrence
Benfer** Jun 1951 in Dallas, Texas. He was born 28 Feb 1928.
ISSUE:
594. f   i.   **Sherry Lynn Benfer**, born 8 May 1953 in Dallas, Texas.
She married **Robert Little** Aug 1974 in Dallas. He was
born about 1950.
595. f   ii.   **Patricia Leann Benfer**, born 15 Oct 1955 in Dallas.
596. m   iii. **Paul Dean Benfer**, born 25 Sep 1960 in Dallas.

- - - - - - - - - -

597. Karla Page[8] Simmons (590.Franklin[7], 577.Katherine[6], 574.Stanley[5],
433.Ann[4], 432.Mary[3], 431.James[2], 1.Benjamin, Sr.[1]) was born 14 Jul 1945
in Mexia, Limestone Co., Texas, the daughter of **Franklin Page Simmons**
and **Mildred Marie Wolters**. She married (1) **Terry Lee Hagle** 16 Oct
1965 in Nacogdoches, Texas. He was born about 1945.

---

[265] D'Aiutolo ... Mitton, *Moseley*, 575-6.
[266] D'Aiutolo ... Mitton, *Moseley*, 636-7.

Karla married (2) **Dale Alexander** 1 Feb 1970 in Texas; they divorced.
                            ISSUE:
   598. f   i.   **Alisha Lauren Alexander**, born Mar 1973 in Denver, Colorado.

Karla married (3) **Joseph Friedman** 12 Jul 1991 in Dallas, Texas. He was born about 1945.

- - - - - - - - - - -

599. Cynthia Marie[8] Simmons <See pg. 87> (590.Franklin[7], 577.Katherine[6], 574.Stanley[5], 433.Ann[4], 432.Mary[3], 431.James[2], 1.Benjamin, Sr.[1]) was born 31 Oct 1952 in Corsicana, Navarro Co., Texas, the daughter of **Franklin Page Simmons** and **Mildred Marie Wolters**. She married **Robert Wayne Gage** 2 Sep 1978 in Wortham, Freestone Co., Texas. He was born about 1950.
                            ISSUE:
   600. m   i.   **Brent Franklin Gage**, born 9 Mar 1983 in Waco, McLennan Co., Texas.
   601. f   ii. **Kathryn Marie Gage**, born 17 Jan 1986 in Waco.

- - - - - - - - - - -

610. Franklin Pierce[5] Moseley <See pg. 66> (433.Ann[4], 432.Mary[3], 431.James[2], 1.Benjamin, Sr.[1]) was born 1 Sep 1852 at "Wheatland", Buckingham Co., Virginia, the son of **William Perkins Moseley** and **Ann Anderson Trent**. Franklin died 17 Apr 1906 in Lexington, Oklahoma. He married (1) **Florence Dunson** 10 Nov 1872 in Virginia. She was born 1852 in Georgia. Florence died 4 Jul 1877 in Georgia.[267]
                            ISSUE:
 + 611. f   i.   **Minnie Otis Moseley**, born 26 Jan 1875, died 17 Jul 1934 <See pg. 89>.
   626. f   ii. **Elizabeth Goss "Bessie" Moseley**, born 1 Apr 1877. She married (1) _____ **Brown**. Elizabeth married (2) _____ **Finn**. Elizabeth married (3) **Con Brundensh**. Elizabeth died 1939 in Wisconsin.

Franklin married (2) **Nettie Beardslee** 25 Dec 1887. She was born 3 Feb 1860 in Honesdale, Florida. Nettie died 9 Feb 1897 in Lexington, Oklahoma.
                            ISSUE:
 + 627. m   iii. **Guyon Ernald Moseley**, born 15 Jul 1889 <See pg. 91>.
 + 633. f   iv. **Rowena Lee Moseley**, born 14 Jan 1891, died 1975 <See pg.

---

[267] D'Aiutolo ... Mitton, *Moseley*, 438-9.

92>.

+ 639. m   v.   **Minven Upton "Jack" Moseley**, born 8 Aug 1894, died 26 Jan 1940 <See pg. 93>.

   643. m   vi.   **Franklin Pierce Moseley, Jr.**, born 31 Oct 1896 in Sulphur, Murray Co., Oklahoma, and died there 30 Jun 1898.

Franklin married (3) **Sarah Elizabeth Trent (See number 687 - pg. 96)** 31 Jan 1901 in Gainesville, Texas. She was born 4 Jan 1852 in St. Louis, Missouri. She was the daughter of **James Wilson Trent** and **Ann Wilson "Nannie" Meredith.** Sarah died 3 Jan 1928 in Miami, Dade Co., Florida.

- - - - - - - - - - -

611. Minnie Otis[6] Moseley <See pg. 88> (610.Franklin[5], 433.Ann[4], 432.Mary[3], 431.James[2], 1.Benjamin, Sr.[1]) was born 26 Jan 1875 in Georgia, the daughter of **Franklin Pierce Moseley** and **Florence Dunson**. Minnie died 17 Jul 1934 in Colorado. She married **Fred W. James** 16 Jun 1896 in Lexington, Oklahoma. He was born about 1875 in Louisville, Kentucky. Fred died about 1921 in Boulder, Colorado.[268]
                                     ISSUE:
+ 612. m   i.   **Donnelly Trent James**, born Oct 1901, died 26 Nov 1967.
+ 617. f   ii.   **Frances Moseley James**, born 22 Aug 1906, died Mar 1990 <See pg. 90>.

- - - - - - - - - - -

612. Donnelly Trent[7] James (611.Minnie[6], 610.Franklin[5], 433.Ann[4], 432.Mary[3], 431.James[2], 1.Benjamin, Sr.[1]) was born Oct 1901 in Lexington, Oklahoma, the son of **Fred W. James** and **Minnie Otis Moseley**. Donnelly died 26 Nov 1967 in Arlington Co., Virginia, and was buried in Oakwood Cemetery, Arlington Co. He married **Cleo Simmons**. She was born 1905 in Dallas, Texas. Cleo died 20 May 1977 in Arlington Co., Virginia, and was buried in Oakwood Cemetery.[269]
                                     ISSUE:
+ 613. m   i.   **Frederick Lee James**, born 2 Jan 1938 <See pg. 89>.
   616. m   ii.   **Michael Howard James**, born 2 Jan 1938 in Denver, Colorado.

- - - - - - - - - - -

613. Frederick Lee[8] James <See pg. 89> (612.Donnelly[7], 611.Minnie[6], 610.Franklin[5], 433.Ann[4], 432.Mary[3], 431.James[2], 1.Benjamin, Sr.[1]) was

---

[268] D'Aiutolo ... Mitton, *Moseley*, 523.

[269] D'Aiutolo ... Mitton, *Moseley*, 580-1.

born 2 Jan 1938 in Denver, Colorado, the son of **Donnelly Trent James** and **Cleo Simmons**. He married **Laureen O'Neill** 3 Jul 1965. She was born 4 Jun 1942 in Glasgow, Scotland.[270]

ISSUE:

614. m   i.   **Frederick Donnelly Francis James**, born 27 Jun 1966 in Paisley, Scotland.

615. m ii.   **Robert David Michael James**, born 5 Jul 1968 in Bryn Mawr, Pennsylvania.

- - - - - - - - - - -

617. Frances Moseley[7] James <See pg. 89> (611.Minnie[6], 610.Franklin[5], 433.Ann[4], 432.Mary[3], 431.James[2], 1.Benjamin, Sr.[1]) was born 22 Aug 1906 in Lexington, Oklahoma, the daughter of **Fred W. James** and **Minnie Otis Moseley**. Frances died Mar 1990 in Hemet, Riverside Co., California. She married **Herbert Jefferson Fenn**. He was born 13 Dec 1903 in Pueblo, Colorado. Herbert died Jun 1988 in Hemet, Riverside Co., California.[271]

ISSUE:

+ 618. m   i.   **Donnelly Moseley Fenn**, born 15 Sep 1934.

+ 621. f   ii.   **Dorothy Ann Fenn**, born 15 Sep 1934, died after 1996 <See pg. 91>.

625. f iii.   **Margaret Frances "Peggy" Fenn**, born 17 Jul 1936 in Boulder, Colorado.

- - - - - - - - - - -

618. Donnelly Moseley[8] Fenn (617.Frances[7], 611.Minnie[6], 610.Franklin[5], 433.Ann[4], 432.Mary[3], 431.James[2], 1.Benjamin, Sr.[1]) was born 15 Sep 1934 in Boulder, Colorado, the son of **Herbert Jefferson Fenn** and **Frances Moseley James**. He married (1) **Louise Ann McCluskey** 16 Jun 1957 in Pasadena, Los Angeles Co., California. She was born 29 Nov 1934 in Long Beach, Los Angeles Co.[272]

ISSUE:

619. f   i.   **Laura Frances Fenn**, born 29 Jun 1962 in Long Beach, Los Angeles Co., California.

620. m ii.   **Donald Howard Fenn**, born 16 May 1966 in Torrance, Los Angeles Co., California.

Donnelly married (2) **Joanna Kubicka** 30 Dec 1990 in Topanga Canyon, California; they divorced. She was born 22 Dec 1936 in Cairo, Egypt.

---

[270] D'Aiutolo ... Mitton, *Moseley*, 643.

[271] D'Aiutolo ... Mitton, *Moseley*, 581.

[272] D'Aiutolo ... Mitton, *Moseley*, 644.

- - - - - - - - - -

621. Dorothy Ann[8] Fenn <See pg. 90> (617.Frances[7], 611.Minnie[6], 610.Franklin[5], 433.Ann[4], 432.Mary[3], 431.James[2], 1.Benjamin, Sr.[1]) was born 15 Sep 1934 in Boulder, Colorado, the daughter of **Herbert Jefferson Fenn** and **Frances Moseley James**. Dorothy died after 1996. She married **Andrew Rudolph Pearson, Jr.** in Long Beach, Los Angeles Co., California. He was born 24 Jul 1934 in New Orleans, Louisiana. Andrew, Jr. died Nov 1984 in California.

ISSUE:

+ 622. m   i.   **Andrew Rudolph Pearson, III**, born 9 Jun 1970.
   624. m   ii.   **Scott James Pearson**, born 25 Jul 1975 in Long Beach, Los Angeles Co., California.

- - - - - - - - - -

622. Andrew Rudolph[9] Pearson, III (621.Dorothy[8], 617.Frances[7], 611.Minnie[6], 610.Franklin[5], 433.Ann[4], 432.Mary[3], 431.James[2], 1.Benjamin, Sr.[1]) was born 9 Jun 1970 in Long Beach, Los Angeles Co., California, the son of **Andrew Rudolph Pearson, Jr.** and **Dorothy Ann Fenn**. He married **Robin Jackson** Feb 1995 in Hayward, Alameda Co., California. She was born 8 Apr 1969 in Fresno, California.[273]

ISSUE:

   623. m   i.   **Isaac Andrew Pearson**, born 3 Dec 1995 in San Lorenzo, Alameda Co., California.

- - - - - - - - - -

627. Guyon Ernald[6] Moseley <See pg. 88> (610.Franklin[5], 433.Ann[4], 432.Mary[3], 431.James[2], 1.Benjamin, Sr.[1]) was born 15 Jul 1889 in Lexington, Oklahoma, the son of **Franklin Pierce Moseley** and **Nettie Beardslee**. Guyon died in Florida. He married **Rosina Emmajean Heine** 18 Apr 1941 in Fort Lauderdale, Florida. She was born 17 Feb 1901 in Caseyville, Union Co., Kentucky. [274]

ISSUE:

+ 628. m   i.   **Donald Lee Moseley**, born 24 Feb 1942 <See pg. 91>.

- - - - - - - - - -

628. Donald Lee[7] Moseley <See pg. 91> (627.Guyon[6], 610.Franklin[5], 433.Ann[4], 432.Mary[3], 431.James[2], 1.Benjamin, Sr.[1]) was born 24 Feb 1942 in Miami, Dade Co., Florida, the son of **Guyon Ernald Moseley** and **Rosina Emmajean Heine**. He married **Susan Lee Gibson** 28 Sep 1968 in Orlando, Florida. She was born 14 Dec 1941 in Rio de Janeiro, Brazil, the

---

[273] D'Aiutolo ... Mitton, *Moseley*, 695.

[274] D'Aiutolo ... Mitton, *Moseley*, 523-4.

daughter of **Robert Gibson** and **Sophie Walto**. [275]

ISSUE:

629. m   i.   **Guyon Ernald Moseley, II**, born 12 Jul 1969 in Miami, Dade Co., Florida.

630. m   ii. **Donald Lee Moseley, Jr.**, born 17 Nov 1970 in Miami.

631. m   iii. **Walton G. Moseley**, born 23 May 1972 in Miami.

632. f   iv. **Katherine Lee Moseley**, born 23 Sep 1973 in Miami.

- - - - - - - - - - -

633. Rowena Lee[6] Moseley <See pg. 89> (610.Franklin[5], 433.Ann[4], 432.Mary[3], 431.James[2], 1.Benjamin, Sr.[1]) was born 14 Jan 1891 in Lexington, Oklahoma, the daughter of **Franklin Pierce Moseley** and **Nettie Beardslee**. Rowena died 1975 in Miami, Dade Co., Florida. She married **Monroe Osborn** 25 May 1912. He was born 15 Jul 1887. Monroe died 1947 in Oklahoma City, Oklahoma.[276]

ISSUE:

+ 634. f   i.   **Nancy Trent Osborn**, born 20 Jul 1913, died 14 Apr 1990.

- - - - - - - - - - -

634. Nancy Trent[7] Osborn (633.Rowena[6], 610.Franklin[5], 433.Ann[4], 432.Mary[3], 431.James[2], 1.Benjamin, Sr[1]) was born 20 Jul 1913 in Paula Valley, Garvin Co., Oklahoma, the daughter of **Monroe Osborn** and **Rowena Lee Moseley**. Nancy died 14 Apr 1990 in Carrollton, Carroll Co., Ohio. She married **Robert Marshall Beckley** 15 Jun 1946 in New Orleans, Louisiana. He was born 27 Mar 1913 in Carrollton. [277]

ISSUE:

+ 635. f   i.   **Lynda Rowena Beckley**, born 18 May 1953.

638. f   ii. **Nancy Trent Beckley**, born 9 Aug 1954 in Honolulu, Hawaii, died about May 1986 in Lake Tahoe, Nevada.

- - - - - - - - - - -

635. Lynda Rowena[8] Beckley (634.Nancy[7], 633.Rowena[6], 610.Franklin[5], 433.Ann[4], 432.Mary[3], 431.James[2], 1.Benjamin, Sr.[1]) was born 18 May 1953 in Honolulu, Hawaii, the daughter of **Robert Marshall Beckley** and **Nancy Trent Osborn**. She married **David Paul Williams** 1969 in Boulder, Colorado. He was born about 1950. [278]

ISSUE:

636. m   i.   **Elliott Williams**, born about 1985 in Arkansas.

[275] D'Aiutolo ... Mitton, *Moseley*, 581-2.

[276] D'Aiutolo ... Mitton, *Moseley*, 524.

[277] D'Aiutolo ... Mitton, *Moseley*, 582.

[278] D'Aiutolo ... Mitton, *Moseley*, 644.

637. f   ii.   **Kathryn Trent Williams**, born about 1987 in Arkansas.

- - - - - - - - - -

639. Minven Upton "Jack"[6] Moseley <See pg. 89> (610.Franklin[5],
433.Ann[4], 432.Mary[3], 431.James[2], 1.Benjamin, Sr.[1]) was born 8 Aug 1894
in Noble, Cleveland Co., Oklahoma, the son of **Franklin Pierce Moseley**
and **Nettie Beardslee**. Minven died 26 Jan 1940 in Miami, Dade Co.,
Florida. He married **Lillie Nichols** about 1922. She was born about 1894.
[279]

ISSUE:
640. m   i.   **Franklin Pierce Moseley**, born about 1924.
641. m   ii.   **Dale Upton Moseley**, born about 1920.
642. f   iii.   **Joy Moseley**, born about 1930.

- - - - - - - - - -

644. Richard Thornton[5] Moseley <See pg. 66> (433.Ann[4], 432.Mary[3],
431.James[2], 1.Benjamin, Sr.[1]) was born 10 Aug 1855 in Buckingham Co.,
Virginia, the son of **William Perkins Moseley** and **Ann Anderson Trent**.
Richard died 14 Dec 1925 in Oklahoma. He married (1) **May O. Tague**
4 Jan 1877 in Virginia. She was born 1855 in Mexia, Texas.[280]
ISSUE:
645. m   i.   **Robert Bruce Moseley**, born 4 Nov 1878 in Texas, died
                 22 Mar 1905 in Texas, and was buried in Mexia City
                 Cemetery, Texas.
646. f   ii.   **Hinda Moseley**, born about 1887. She married **L. T. Voltz**.
                 He was born about 1887 in Oklahoma City, Oklahoma.

Richard married (2) **Martha "Mattie" Long**. She was born about 1855.
Martha died Nov 1883 in Texas.
ISSUE:
647. m iii.   **Lamar Moseley**, born about 1874.
648. m   iv.   **Aubry Moseley**, born about 1876.
649. f   v.   **Adrian Moseley**, born about 1878.
650. f   vi.   **Erin Moseley**, born about 1880.
651. f vii.   **Edith Moseley**, born about 1880. She married **Vernon
                Moore**.
652. f viii.   **Maury Trent Moseley**, born about 1883.

Richard married (3) **Dorothy Means** 5 Nov 1902 in Lexington, Oklahoma.
She was born about 1865.

---

[279] D'Aiutolo ... Mitton, *Moseley*, 524.

[280] D'Aiutolo ... Mitton, *Moseley*, 439.

ISSUE:

653. m ix. **Lowell Moseley**, born about 1895.

+ 654. f x. **Dorothy Lee Moseley**, born 14 Feb 1909.

- - - - - - - - - - -

654. Dorothy Lee⁶ Moseley (644.Richard⁵, 433.Ann⁴, 432.Mary³,
431.James², 1.Benjamin, Sr.¹) was born 14 Feb 1909, the daughter of
Richard Thornton Moseley and **Dorothy Means**. She married **O. Alton
Watson** 22 Jun 1934 in Oklahoma City, Oklahoma. He was born about
1909. [281]

ISSUE:

655. f i. **Ann Sheridan Watson**, born about 1929.

656. f ii. **Marcia Moseley Watson**, born about 1931.

657. m iii. **O. Alton Watson, Jr.**, born about 1933.

- - - - - - - - - - -

661. James Wilson⁴ Trent <See pg. 65> (432.Mary³, 431.James², 1.Benjamin,
Sr.¹) was born about 1817 in Virginia, the son of **Alexander Trent, V** and
Mary Wilson.[282] James died 1863.[283] He married **Ann Wilson "Nannie"
Meredith (See number 1093 - pg. 100)** 1 Jun 1843.[284] She was born
16 Apr 1826 in Buckingham Co., Virginia, the daughter of **John Meredith**
and **Ann Seay Wilson**. Ann died after 1880 probably in St. Clair Co.,
Missouri.

ISSUE:[285]

662. f i. **Mary "Mollie" Willis Trent**, born 1844. She married (1)
            Goodridge Wilson (See number 765 - pg. 99, 228). He
            was born 24 Dec 1847 in Virginia, the son of **Samuel
            Venable Wilson** and **Sarah Cox Meredith**. Mollie married
            (2) **Joseph Bunberry**.

+ 663. f ii. **Anne M. Trent**, born 1845.

+ 678. m iii. **James Wilson Trent**, born 1847, died 1908 <See pg. 96>.

+ 687. f iv. **Sarah Elizabeth Trent**, born 4 Jan 1852, died 3 Jan 1928
              <See pg. 96>.

688. m v. **John Trent**, born 1855 in Missouri.

---

[281] D'Aiutolo ... Mitton, *Moseley*, 524.

[282] *Notes on Peter Field Trent*, 15/28.

[283] McLean, *Wilson Family*, 35.

[284] DAR - Meredith Family Bible.

[285] *Notes on Peter Field Trent*, 16/29. McLean, *Wilson Family*, 35-6. The
children of deceased son James W. Trent, though not named, received land from
their grandfather in his 1871 will. Buckingham Co. VA Will Book 1:195.

689. f   vi.   **Ellen C. Trent,** born 1859 in Missouri. She married
                Robert McMarth.
690. f   vii. **Martha Spencer Trent,** born 1862 in Missouri, died 1903.

In 1848, Nannie's mother deeded land to them as specified in a the 1842
deed of Nannie's grandfather.[286] The family is listed in the 1850 Putnam
Co., Virginia (West Virginia), census.

In James' father's 1871 will, land is left to the children of his deceased son
James W. Trent.[287] Nannie is listed with three children in the 1880 St.
Clair Co., Missouri, census.

- - - - - - - - - - -

663. Anne M.[5] Trent (661.James[4], 432.Mary[3], 431.James[2], 1.Benjamin,
Sr.[1]) was born 1845, the daughter of **James Wilson Trent** and **Ann Wilson
"Nannie" Meredith.** She married **James M. Becraft.**[288]
                                ISSUE:
  664. f   i.   **Mary Wilson Becraft,** born 1878, died 1904.
+ 665. f   ii.   **Nancy Becraft.**
+ 672. m iii. **Trent Becraft,** born 1882 <See pg. 95>.
  676. m iv.   **Cecil Becraft,** born 1884, died 1906.
  677. f   v.   **Nellie Trent Becraft,** died 1891.

- - - - - - - - - - -

665. Nancy[6] Becraft (663.Anne[5], 661.James[4], 432.Mary[3], 431.James[2],
1.Benjamin, Sr.[1]). She was the daughter of **James M. Becraft** and **Anne M.
Trent.** She married **John O. Wilson.**
                                ISSUE:
  666. f   i.   **Mary Becraft Wilson,** born 1900, died 1920.
  667. m ii.   **Paul Wilson.**
  668. f   iii. **Mildred Wilson.**
  669. f   iv.   **Nellie Wilson.**
  670. f   v.   **Lavinia Wilson.**
  671. f   vi.   **Christine Wilson.**

- - - - - - - - - - -

672. Trent[6] Becraft <See pg. 95> (663.Anne[5], 661.James[4], 432.Mary[3],
431.James[2], 1.Benjamin, Sr.[1]) was born 1882, the son of **James M. Becraft**
and **Anne M. Trent.** He married **Maria DeBuston.**

---
[286] Kanawha Co. VA (WV) Deed Books M:374, P:471.

[287] Buckingham Co. VA Will Book 1:195.

[288] McLean, *Wilson Family,* 35-6.

ISSUE:

673. m   i.   **George Becraft.**
674. f   ii.   **Nellie Becraft.**
675. f   iii.   **Florence Becraft.**

- - - - - - - - - - -

678. James Wilson⁵ Trent <See pg. 94, 100> (661.James⁴, 432.Mary³,
431.James², 1.Benjamin, Sr.¹) was born 1847, the son of **James Wilson
Trent** and **Ann Wilson "Nannie" Meredith**. James died 1908 in Arkansas.
He married **Iowa Fakes**. [289]

ISSUE:

679. f   i.   **Mary E. Trent.** She married **Sidney Burke.**
680. f   ii.   **Judith Trent.**
681. f   iii.   **Nannie Trent.** She married _____ **Steine.**
682. f   iv.   **Emeline Trent.**
683. f   v.   **Lillie B. Trent.**
684. m   vi.   **John M. Trent.**
685. m   vii.   **James Wilson Trent.**
686. m viii.   **Henry Trent.**

- - - - - - - - - - -

687. Sarah Elizabeth⁵ Trent <See pg. 94, 101> (661.James⁴, 432.Mary³,
431.James², 1.Benjamin, Sr.¹) was born 4 Jan 1852 in St. Louis, Missouri,
the daughter of **James Wilson Trent** and **Ann Wilson "Nannie"
Meredith**. Sarah died 3 Jan 1928 in Miami, Dade Co., Florida. She married
Franklin Pierce Moseley (See number 610 - pg. 88) 31 Jan 1901 in
Gainesville, Texas. He was born 1 Sep 1852 at "Wheatland", Buckingham
Co., Virginia, the son of **William Perkins Moseley** and **Ann Anderson
Trent**.[290]

- - - - - - - - - - -

691. Emeline Frances⁴ Trent <See pg. 65> (432.Mary³, 431.James²,
1.Benjamin, Sr.¹) was born 6 Aug 1819 in Buckingham Co., Virginia, the
daughter of **Alexander Trent, V** and **Mary Wilson**. Emeline died 15 Dec
1892 in Buckingham Co. She married **Bryce McClelland Pratt** 13 Apr
1848 at "Clay Bank", Buckingham Co. He was born 9 May 1817 in
Bloomfield, Somerset Co., Maine, the son of **Whitcomb Pratt** and **Abigail
Halsey Gardiner**. Bryce died 19 Jan 1886 in Rogers, Benton Co.,

---

[289]   *Notes on Peter Field Trent*, 16/29.

[290]   *Notes on Peter Field Trent*, 16/29. D'Aiutolo ... Mitton, *Moseley*, 438-9.

Arkansas. [291]

ISSUE:

+ 692. m   i.   **Whitcomb Eliphalet Pratt**, born 28 Feb 1849, died 16 May 1901.

  693. m   ii.   **Alexander Trent Pratt**, born 8 Jul 1850 in Buckingham Co., Virginia, died 4 Oct 1870 in Virginia.

+ 694. f   iii.   **Mary Wilson Pratt**, born 23 Feb 1852, died 18 Jun 1883.

- - - - - - - - - - -

692. Whitcomb Eliphalet[5] Pratt (691.Emeline[4], 432.Mary[3], 431.James[2], 1.Benjamin, Sr.[1]) was born 28 Feb 1849 at "Clay Bank", Buckingham Co., Virginia, the son of **Bryce McClelland Pratt** and **Emeline Frances Trent**. Whitcomb died 16 May 1901 in Richmond, Virginia, and was buried at Maysville Presbyterian Church, Buckingham Co. He married **Florence LaSalle Moseley (See number 449 - pg. 69)** 6 Apr 1887 in Buckingham Co. She was born 31 Mar 1855 in Hardwicksville, Nelson Co., Virginia, the daughter of **Alexander Trent Moseley** and **Maria Louise Housewright**.[292]

- - - - - - - - - - -

694. Mary Wilson[5] Pratt (691.Emeline[4], 432.Mary[3], 431.James[2], 1.Benjamin, Sr.[1]) was born 23 Feb 1852 in Buckingham Co., Virginia, the daughter of **Bryce McClelland Pratt** and **Emeline Frances Trent**. Mary died 18 Jun 1883 in Rogers, Benton Co., Arkansas. She married **Charles Lucas Gibbs** 12 Apr 1874 in Concordia, Cloud Co., Kansas. He was born in Massachusetts, the son of **Lucas Gibbs** and **Electta** _____. [293]

ISSUE:

  695. m   i.   **Bryce Pratt Gibbs**.

  696. f   ii.   **Virginia Whitcomb Gibbs**.

  697. u   iii.   **Alexander Trent Gibbs**.

  698. f   iv.   **Lettie Gibbs**.

- - - - - - - - - - -

704. Ann Seay[3] Wilson <See pg. 62> (431.James[2], 1.Benjamin, Sr.[1]) was born 7 Mar 1791 in Buckingham Co., Virginia, the daughter of **James Wilson** and **Sarah Cox**. Ann died 17 Sep 1856 at "Thornhill", St. Louis Co., Missouri. She married **John Meredith (See number 1236 - pg. 109)** 6 Oct 1815 probably in Buckingham Co. He was born 4 May 1793 in Virginia, the son of **James Meredith** and **Mason Wilson**. John died 26 May 1846 in

---

[291] *Notes on Peter Field Trent*, 15/28.

[292] D'Aiutolo ... Mitton, *Moseley*, 515-7.

[293] *Notes on Peter Field Trent*, 15/28.

Kanawha Co., Virginia (West Virginia). [294]
ISSUE:

705. m i. **James Wilson Meredith**, born 27 Jul 1816, died 2 Mar 1818.
706. m ii. **William Alexander Meredith**, born 16 Dec 1818, died 16 Mar 1820.
+ 707. f iii. **Sarah Cox Meredith**, born 21 Jan 1821, died 9 Dec 1867 <See pg. 99>.
1091. m iv. **Samuel Meredith**, born 23 Nov 1822, died 15 Dec 1823.
1092. m v. **Benjamin Meredith**, born 24 Nov 1824, died 4 Apr 1825.
+ 1093. f vi. **Ann Wilson "Nannie" Meredith**, born 16 Apr 1826, died after 1880 <See pg. 100>.
+ 1094. f vii. **Mary Hetty Meredith**, born 28 Feb 1828, died 17 Jul 1891 <See pg. 101>.
1198. f viii. **Margaret Virginia Meredith**, born 17 Feb 1830, died 25 Jun 1833.
1199. m ix. **John Meredith**, born 24 Sep 1832, died 7 Oct 1832.
+ 1200. f x. **Lavinia J. Meredith**, born 6 May 1834, died 1910 <See pg. 103>.
1207. f xi. **Elizabeth Meredith**, born 18 Mar 1837, died 10 May 1838.

Ann was named in the 1812 will of her grandfather.[295] In 1824 she is listed as a charter member of the Maysville Presbyterian Church in Buckingham Co., then "dismissed to Charlestown, Kanawha, November 1835". She rejoined in June 1836.[296]

Her father's 1842 deed gave Ann and her husband property in exchange for their taking care of his comfort and expenses the rest of his life.[297] According to her father's deed, at the death of either Ann or her husband, the survivor, after paying debts was to give portions of the land to their 4 daughters.[298] She is shown in the 1850 Putnam Co., Virginia (West Virginia), census with her daughter Lavinia, next to the household of her daughter Nannie.

In 1853 a letter from kin in St. Louis states that Lavinia is expected again next winter. Ann must have moved about that time to St. Louis Co.,

[294] DAR - Meredith Family Bible.
[295] Will of Benjamin Wilson, LVA.
[296] Rosen, *History of Maysville Presbyterian Church*, 15, 20.
[297] Kanawha Co. VA (WV) Deed Book M:374.
[298] Kanawha Co. VA (WV) Deed Book P:471.

Missouri, to be with her other two daughters. A note on the back of a
picture of Ann Seay, obviously later in life, says she died at "Thornhill" 17
Sep 1856. [299]

- - - - - - - - - -

707. Sarah Cox[4] Meredith <See pg. 98, 109> (704.Ann[3], 431.James[2],
1.Benjamin, Sr.[1]) was born 21 Jan 1821 probably in Buckingham Co.,
Virginia, the daughter of **John Meredith** and **Ann Seay Wilson**. Sarah died
9 Dec 1867 in Poplar Bluff, Butler Co., Missouri,[300] and was buried in
Wilson/Rose Hill Cemetery, Butler Co.[301]   She married **Samuel Venable
Wilson (See number 2130 - pg. 228)** 2 Dec 1843 in Kanawha Co., Virginia
(West Virginia).[302]   He was born 3 Mar 1821 in Prince Edward Co.,
Virginia, the son of **Goodridge Wilson** and **Elizabeth Woodson Venable**.
Samuel died 17 Apr 1870 in Poplar Bluff, and was buried in Wilson/Rose
Hill Cemetery.

ISSUE:

+ 708. m   i.   **James Meredith Wilson,** born 23 Sep 1845, died 14 Dec
                1933 <See pg. 229>.

 765. m   ii.   **Goodridge Wilson,** born 24 Dec 1847 in Virginia. He
                married **Mary "Mollie" Willis Trent (See number 662 -
                pg. 94, 100).** She was born 1843, the daughter of **James
                Wilson Trent** and **Ann Wilson "Nannie" Meredith.**
                Goodridge died 8 Nov 1870 in Butler Co. and was buried in
                Wilson/Rose Hill Cemetery.

+ 766. m   iii. **Samuel Venable Wilson,** born 4 Jun 1850, died 27 Feb
                1935 <See pg. 235>.

+ 795. m   iv. **Robert Faris Wilson,** born 3 Nov 1852, died 15 Feb 1937
                <See pg. 238>.

+ 838. f   v.   **Anne "Nancy" Meredith Wilson,** born 2 Jun 1855, died
                16 Sep 1901 <See pg. 240>.

+ 903. m   vi. **Benjamin Francis Wilson,** born Nov 1857, died after
                26 Mar 1919 <See pg. 247>.

 918. f   vii. **Hetty Meredith Wilson,** born 9 Nov 1860, died 26 Nov
                1870 in Butler Co., Missouri, and was buried in
                Wilson/Rose Hill Cemetery, Butler Co.

+ 919. f   viii. **Elizabeth Venable "Bessie" Wilson,** born 14 Mar 1864,
                 died 22 Mar 1927 <See pg. 249>.

---

[299] Copy of 1853 Aug 25 letter and picture with handwritten note from Watson
sisters of Kirkwood MO.

[300] DAR - Meredith Family Bible.

[301] Hanks, "Wilson/ Rose Hill" Cemetery (accessed 15 Dec 2005).

[302] DAR - Meredith Family Bible.

+ 1070. f   ix.   **Sarah Stonewall Wilson**, born 27 May 1865, died 11 Nov
                    1951 <See pg. 259>.

Sarah was admitted to membership in the Maysville Presbyterian Church in
Buckingham Court House in 1834, dismissed to Charleston , Kanawha Co.,
in 1835 but rejoined in 1836.[303]   She wrote a letter to a cousin 25 Aug 1836
saying they would not be in Kanawha in the fall, that she was happy at
home and school, evidently in Buckingham Co.[304]

After her marriage in Kanawha Co. and after her father's death in 1846, she
and her husband received land inherited from her grandfather;[305]   by 1850
they were listed in the St. Louis Co., Missouri, census. Sarah attached a
note to a letter her husband wrote from Missouri to Kanawha in 1850 saying
she was sending books to her mother and sisters. She is said to have
recorded family history from her grandfather, and perhaps at one time she
owned family furniture, the portrait of her great-grandfather, and the prayer
book in which her great-grandmother recorded the births of her children.[306]

- - - - - - - - - - -

1093. Ann Wilson "Nannie"[4] Meredith <See pg. 98, 109> (704.Ann[3],
431.James[2], 1.Benjamin, Sr.[1]) was born 16 Apr 1826 in Buckingham Co.,
Virginia, the daughter of **John Meredith** and **Ann Seay Wilson**. Ann died
after 1880 probably in St. Clair Co., Missouri. She married **James Wilson
Trent (See number 661 - pg. 94)** 1 Jun 1843. He was born about 1817 in
Virginia. He was the son of **Alexander Trent, V** and **Mary Wilson**.
                              ISSUE:[307]
    662. f   i.   **Mary "Mollie" Willis Trent**, born 1844. She married (1)
                    Goodridge Wilson (See number 765 - pg. 99, 228). He
                    was born 24 Dec 1847 in Virginia, the son of **Samuel
                    Venable Wilson** and **Sarah Cox Meredith**. Mollie married
                    (2) **Joseph Bunberry**.
+ 663. f   ii.   **Anne M. Trent**, born 1845 <See pg. 95>.
+ 678. m   iii.   **James Wilson Trent**, born 1847, died 1908 <See pg. 96>.
+ 687. f   iv.   **Sarah Elizabeth Trent**, born 4 Jan 1852, died 3 Jan 1928

---

[303]   Rosen, *History of Maysville Presbyterian Church*, 19, 20.

[304]   Wilson, Nath'l V. *Papers, 1834-1878.*

[305]   Kanawha Co. VA (WV) Deed Book P:471.

[306]   Copy of letter from Watson sisters of Kirkwood MO. Woodson Family,
Papers, 1740-1945, Accession 29437-41, LVA.

[307]   *Notes on Peter Field Trent*, 16/29. McLean, *Wilson Family*, 35-6. The
children of deceased son James W. Trent, though not named, received land from
their grandfather in his 1871 will. Buckingham Co. VA Will Book 1:195.

<See pg. 96>.

688. m   v.   **John Trent**, born 1855 in Missouri.

689. f   vi.   **Ellen C. Trent**, born 1859 in Missouri. She married
              Robert McMarth.

690. f   vii.   **Martha Spencer Trent**, born 1862 in Missouri, died 1903.

Nannie painted a picture of the Maysville Church at Buckingham Court
House in 1838 and removed to Kanawha Co. in 1840.[308] Deeds in Kanawha
Co. show that she and her husband had land in 1848 and 1850.[309] The
family is shown in the 1850 Putnam Co., Virginia (West Virginia), census.

Nannie is listed with three children in the 1880 St. Clair Co., Missouri,
census.

- - - - - - - - - - -

1094. Mary Hetty[4] Meredith <See pg. 98, 109> (704.Ann[3], 431.James[2],
1.Benjamin, Sr.[1]) was born 28 Feb 1828 in Buckingham Co., Virginia, the
daughter of **John Meredith** and **Ann Seay Wilson**. Mary died 17 Jul 1891
in Fisher Co., Texas, was buried in Sweetwater, Nolan Co., Texas. She
married **James Willis Wilson (See number 2131 - pg. 260)** 25 Feb 1847 in
Kanawha Co., Virginia (West Virginia).[310] He was born 3 Dec 1823 at
"Milnwood", Prince Edward Co., Virginia, the son of **Goodridge Wilson**
and **Elizabeth Woodson Venable**. James died 2 Sep 1899 in St. Charles,
Missouri, and was buried in Frayser Burying Ground, St. Charles Co.[311]

ISSUE:[312]

+ 1095. m   i.   **John Meredith Wilson**, born 22 Feb 1848, died before
              1926 <See pg. 263>.

   1102. f   ii.   **Julia Bates Wilson**, born 2 Dec 1850 in St. Louis,
              Missouri, died after 1870.

+ 1103. f   iii.   **Margaret Virginia Wilson**, born 6 Jul 1852, died 5 Jun
              1925 <See pg. 264>.

+ 1111. m   iv.   **Charles Woodson Wilson**, born 5 Aug 1854, died 16 Apr
              1926 <See pg. 265>.

   1144. f   v.   **Elizabeth Venable Wilson**, born 4 May 1856 in Franklin
              Co., Missouri, and died there 17 May 1857.

   1145. m   vi.   **Willis Wilson**, born 19 Feb 1858 in Franklin Co., died

---

[308] Rosen, *History of Maysville Presbyterian Church*, iii, 21.

[309] Kanawha Co. WV Deed Books Q:318, 395.

[310] Kanawha Co. WV Marriage Records, 147.

[311] DAR - Meredith Family Bible.

[312] Copy of "Old notebook" from Watson sisters of Kirkwood MO.

                12 May 1862.

+ 1146. m vii. **Nathaniel Venable Wilson**, born 5 Nov 1859, died 24 Jun 1911 <See pg. 269>.

  1147. m viii. **Goodridge Wilson**, born 12 Oct 1861 at "Thornhill", St. Louis Co., Missouri, died Dec 1928 in West Plains, Howell Co., Missouri, and was buried in Evergreen Cemetery, Howell Co.

+ 1148. f ix. **Nancy Meredith Wilson**, born 11 Jul 1864, died after 1928 <See pg. 276>.

  1149. f x. **Mary Hetty "Polly" Wilson**, born 26 Sep 1866 in Rapides Parish, Louisiana, died 19 Feb 1932 in Howell Co., Missouri, and was buried in Blue Mound Cemetery, Howell Co.

  1150. m xi. **James W. Wilson**, born 26 Sep 1866 in Rapides Parish. He married **Alice W. Clark** 7 Nov 1925 in Howell Co. James died 1939 in West Plains, Howell Co., and was buried in Blue Mound Cemetery.

+ 1151. m xii. **Samuel Venable Wilson**, born 27 Mar 1868, died 12 Aug 1951 <See pg. 276>.

Mary Hetty Meredith was baptized at Maysville Presbyterian Church in Buckingham Co., Virginia, 27 Dec 1828.[313] The family moved to Kanawha Co. about 1842. After her father's death, she and her husband received land left to her by her grandfather's will.[314]

"Het" wrote to her new sister-in-law Mar 7 about the "knock-off" on Feb 25 1847 and the surrounding celebrations. Her new husband wrote, "I ... have the greatest wife that ever come along." Her letters in 1870 and soon after are from South Point in Franklin Co., Missouri. She describes their home as close to the railroad depot "and the Mo. River not much farther off" and mentions "my little folks bustling around me". A letter written probably in 1872 with garden, chicken, and family news signs off with "If you could see the pile of work laying at my side you would say 'Hetty had better go to sewing' and so she had". [315]

It is said that she was trained in music and that she played and taught piano. It interesting to consider the many moves the family made from Missouri, to Texas, then to Louisiana, back to Missouri, and her last move, to West Texas. Her son remembered putting rocks on her grave in Fisher Co.,

---

[313] Rosen, *History of Maysville Presbyterian Church*, 43.

[314] Kanawha Co. VA (WV) Deed Books M:374-6, P:471.

[315] Copies of letters from Watson sisters of Kirkwood MO.

Texas. Her body was later moved to the Germany plot in the Sweetwater, Texas, cemetery.

- - - - - - - - - - -

1200. Lavinia J.[4] Meredith <See pg. 98, 109> (704.Ann[3], 431.James[2], 1.Benjamin, Sr.[1]) was born 6 May 1834 probably in Buckingham Co., Virginia, the daughter of **John Meredith** and **Ann Seay Wilson**.[316] Lavinia died 1910 probably in Escondido, California.[317] She married (1) **Frederick Bates, Jr.** 1861. He was born 1 Feb 1826, the son of **Frederick Bates** and **Nancy Opie Ball**. Frederick, Jr. died 18 Oct 1862 probably at "Thornhill", St. Louis Co., Missouri.[318]

ISSUE:
1201. m   i.   **Woodville Bates**, born 1862 in Missouri.

Lavinia married (2) **Samuel Conway** after 1868. He was born 1799 in Missouri. Samuel died after 1870.[319]

ISSUE:
+ 1202. m   ii.   **Meredith Conway**, born 1869 <See pg. 104>.

Lavinia married (3) **Benjamin Kenney** 1874.

ISSUE:[320]
1205. m   iii.   **Benjamin Kenney, Jr.**, born 1877 in Missouri.
1206. m   iv.   **William Kenney**, born 1879 in Missouri, died 1932

Lavinia was baptized in 1835 at the Maysville Presbyterian Church at Buckingham Court House, Virginia.[321] She is shown in the 1850 Putnam Co., Virginia (West Virginia), census with her mother and in the 1860 St. Louis Co., Missouri, census with her married sister Hetty and family in the household next to Frederick Bates, who was probably the heir to "Thornhill".

On 1 Dec 1859 and 8 Oct 1860, Lavinia Meredith is mentioned as visiting at the home of **Edward Bates**. From Dec 1865 to Jan 1866, Lavinia, later

---

[316] DAR - Meredith Family Bible.

[317] Boddie, *Historical Southern Families*, 3:65. McLean, *Wilson Family*, 36-7.

[318] Bates, *Bates, et al*, 75. Bryan, *Pioneer Families of Missouri*, 130-1.

[319] Samuel's age compared to Lavinia's makes one wonder if there was a Samuel Jr.

[320] The 1940 query, by Dr. **John Meredith Kenney** in *William and Mary Quarterly*, 20 (2)433, suggests that he is a descendant.

[321] Rosen, *History of Maysville Presbyterian Church*, 44.

as "Mrs. Dr. Fred: Bates" of Bonhomme, is named in the diary.[322]

An 1868 plat of the "Thornhill" Bonhomme area in St. Louis Co., Missouri, shows land owners Lavinia Bates and Samuel Conway.[323]

Lavinia is listed in the 1870 St. Louis Co., Missouri, census as Lavinia Conway with husband and sons Woodville Bates, age 8 and Meredith Conway age 8 months, and in the 1880 St. Louis Co., Missouri, census as Lavinia Kinney with two additional sons.

Sometime after 1881, Lavinia and her family moved to California, where her kin visited through the years and where according to family tradition, they had an avocado and orange ranch near Escondido.

- - - - - - - - - - -

1202. Meredith⁵ Conway <See pg. 103> (1200.Lavinia⁴, 704.Ann³, 431.James², 1.Benjamin, Sr.¹) was born 1869 in Missouri, the son of **Samuel Conway** and **Lavinia J. Meredith**. His spouse has not been identified.

ISSUE:
1203. f   i.   **Anne Meredith Conway**.
1204. m   ii.   _____ **Conway**.

- - - - - - - - - - -

1208. Sarah "Sallie"³ Wilson <See pg. 62> (431.James², 1.Benjamin, Sr.¹) was born before 20 Mar 1793 in Buckingham Co., Virginia, the daughter of **James Wilson** and **Sarah Cox**.[324] Sarah died 5 Sep 1859 in Buckingham Co.[325] She married (1) **Benajah Brown Jr.** about 1817 probably in Buckingham Co. He was the son of **Benajah Brown** and **Mary** _____. Benajah Jr. died Nov 1822.[326]

ISSUE:
1209. m   i.   **John James Brown**, born about 1818 probably in Buckingham Co., Virginia, died about 1894 probably in Kanawha Co., West Virginia. His grandfather and his

[322] Beale, *Diary of Edward Bates*, xvi, 71, 151, 525, 527, 533.

[323] http://www.usgennet.org/usa/mo/county/stlouis/1wslu50red.gif, (accessed 9 Jan 2006).

[324] McCrary, *Wilson Families ... Correspondence .... 1785-1849*, 49.

[325] Rosen, *History of Maysville Presbyterian Church*, 18.

[326] McCrary, *Wilson Families ... Correspondence .... 1785-1849*, 215. The will of his father, Benajah, is found in the Burned County Records Collection, Library of Virginia.

uncle deeded land to him in Kanawha Co. in 1839 and
1850.[327]

Sarah married (2) **William Francis Moseley** 21 Dec 1827. He was born
10 May 1774 in Chesterfield Co., Virginia, the son of **Robert Peter
Moseley** and **Mary Magdalen Guerrant**. William died 11 Jan 1852 in
Buckingham Co., Virginia.[328]

ISSUE:

+ 1210. m iii. **Daniel Willis Moseley**, born 21 Oct 1828, died 15 Jun
                  1904.
+ 1227. m iv. **Benjamin Wilson Moseley**, born 19 Apr 1836, died 1898
                  <See pg. 107>.

William also married (1) **Mary Saunders** 22 Mar 1792. She was born about
1774. Mary died 13 Jun 1822 in Buckingham Co., Virginia.

ISSUE:

+ 1233. m ii. **Grandison Moseley**, born 26 Jan 1799, died 29 Dec 1877
                  <See pg. 107>.

- - - - - - - - - - -

1210. Dr. Daniel Willis[4] Moseley (1208.Sarah[3], 431.James[2], 1.Benjamin,
Sr.[1]) was born 21 Oct 1828 in Buckingham Co., Virginia, the son of
William Francis Moseley and **Sarah "Sallie" Wilson**.[329] Daniel died
15 Jun 1904 in Richmond, Virginia. He married (1) **Mary Elizabeth
Stevenson** 21 Feb 1853 in Richmond, Virginia. She was born Sep 1834 in
Richmond, Virginia, the daughter of **Thomas Stevenson**. Mary died Jun
1872.[330]

ISSUE:

+ 1211. m i. **James Wilson Moseley**, born 12 Jan 1854 <See pg. 106>.
  1216. m ii. **Wyatt G. Moseley**, born about 1856, died about 1859.
+ 1217. m iii. **William Grandison Moseley**, born 24 Mar 1861, died
                  4 Mar 1932.
  1220. f iv. **Mary E. Moseley**, born in Richmond, Virginia. She
                  married **Albert C. Floyd**.
  1221. m v. **Stevenson Moseley**.

Daniel married (2) **Mollie Lyne** 1872. She was born 1841. Mollie died

---

[327] Kanawha Co. WV Deed Books K:604, Q:270.

[328] D'Aiutolo ... Mitton, *Moseley*, 114, 208-9.

[329] Rosen, *History of Maysville Presbyterian Church*, 43.

[330] D'Aiutolo ... Mitton, *Moseley*, 333. Additional information from Mary Carolyn
(Steger) Mitton of Salem IN.

1914.
ISSUE:

1222. f   vi.   **Mamie Moseley**, born about 1874. She married ___
               Brown.

1223. f   vii.   **Lyne Ella Moseley**, born about 1876 in Richmond, Henrico
               Co., Virginia.

1224. f   viii.   **Frances Moseley**.

1225. f   ix.   **Sue May Moseley**, born in Virginia.

1226. f   x.   **Sallie Moseley**. She married _____ **Brosnaham**.

- - - - - - - - - - -

1211. James Wilson[5] Moseley <See pg. 105> (1210.Daniel[4], 1208.Sarah[3],
431.James[2], 1.Benjamin, Sr.[1]) was born 12 Jan 1854, the son of **Daniel
Willis Moseley** and **Mary Elizabeth Stevenson**. He married **Mary
Valentine** 5 Jul 1875. She was born 31 Jul 1856. Mary died 15 Mar 1882.[331]
ISSUE:

1212. m   i.   **William Gray Moseley**, born 1877. He married **Clothilda
               Caroline Amelia Fishback**. She was born about 1880.

1213. f   ii.   **Maria Goodrich Moseley**, born 3 Apr 1878.

1214. f   iii.   **Helen Preston Moseley**, born 27 Feb 1880. She married
               (1) **Clay Drewry, Jr.** about 1900. He was born about 1880.
               Helen married (2) **Henry Reese**. He was born about 1879.

1215. m   iv.   **Alexander Moseley**, born 7 Mar 1881. He married
               Kathleen Elizabeth Reese 27 May 1910. She was born
               about 1885, the daughter of **Lycurgus Reese** and **Emily
               Espy**.

- - - - - - - - - - -

1217. William Grandison[5] Moseley <See pg. 106> (1210.Daniel[4],
1208.Sarah[3], 431.James[2], 1.Benjamin, Sr.[1]) was born 24 Mar 1861 in
Virginia, the son of **Daniel Willis Moseley** and **Mary Elizabeth
Stevenson**. William died 4 Mar 1932. He married **Rosa Adelaide Hewitt**
19 Jan 1886. She was born 1 Mar 1865. Rosa died after 27 Sep 1932. [332]
ISSUE:

1218. f   i.   **Rosa Moseley**, born in Richmond, Virginia. She married **G.
               Stanley Clarke**.[333]

1219. m   ii.   **William Grandison Moseley**, born 6 Jul 1888 in
               Richmond, Henrico Co., Virginia.

---

[331] D'Aiutolo ... Mitton, *Moseley*, 458.

[332] D'Aiutolo ... Mitton, *Moseley*, 459.

[333] DAR - Application # 249591, Rosa Moseley Clarke.

- - - - - - - - - -

1227. Benjamin Wilson[4] Moseley <See pg. 105> (1208.Sarah[3], 431.James[2], 1.Benjamin, Sr.[1]) was born 19 Apr 1836 in Buckingham Co., Virginia, the son of **William Francis Moseley** and **Sarah "Sallie" Wilson**. Benjamin died 1898 in Virginia. He married **Elizabeth W. Blair** 15 Nov 1859 in Richmond, Virginia. She was born about 1844 in Virginia. [334]

ISSUE:

1228. f   i.   **Anna Beverly Moseley**, born 24 Oct 1863 in Richmond, Virginia.

1229. m ii. **John Henry Blair Moseley**, born 30 Nov 1865 in Richmond.

1230. m iii. **Harris Grandison Moseley**, born 16 Mar 1869 in Richmond.

1231. f   iv. **Lula Moseley**, born about 1870.

1232. m v. **Wilson Moseley**, born about 1873.

- - - - - - - - - -

1233. Grandison[4] Moseley <See pg. 105> (stepchild of 1208.Sarah[3], 431.James[2], 1.Benjamin, Sr.[1]) was born 26 Jan 1799 in Buckingham Co., Virginia, the son of **William Francis Moseley** and **Mary Saunders**. Grandison died 29 Dec 1877 in Buckingham Co. and was buried in Willow Lake Cemetery, Buckingham Co. He married **Elizabeth Fearn Moseley** in Buckingham Co. She was born 4 May 1804 in Buckingham Co., the daughter of **Arthur Richard Moseley** and **Sarah Perkins**. Elizabeth died 15 Aug 1874 in Buckingham Co. and was buried in Willow Lake Cemetery. [335]

ISSUE:

1234. f   i. **Sarah Perkins Moseley**, born 11 Oct 1830 in Buckingham Co. She married **John Eldridge** 4 Jun 1856. He was born 9 Sep 1827 in Buckingham Co., the son of **Rolfe Eldridge, Jr.** and **Mary Moseley**. John died 11 Jun 1912 at "Rolfton", Buckingham Co., and was buried in Willow Lake Cemetery. Sarah died 28 Sep 1908.

---

[334] Rosen, *History of Maysville Presbyterian Church*, 45. D'Aiutolo ... Mitton, *Moseley*, 334-5.

[335] D'Aiutolo ... Mitton, *Moseley*, 319, 332. They were probably married 1 Nov 1825.

CHAPTER 6

Descendants of Mason Wilson (1768-1837)

1235. Mason² Wilson <See pg. 1> (1.Benjamin, Sr.¹) was born 21 Dec 1768 at "Somerset", Cumberland Co., Virginia, the daughter of **Benjamin Wilson, Sr.** and **Anne Seay**.³³⁶ Mason died 1837 in Buckingham Co., Virginia. She married **James Meredith** about 1792. He was born about 1770. James died after 1841.³³⁷

ISSUE:

+ 1236. m   i.   **John Meredith**, born 4 May 1793, died 26 May 1846 <See pg. 109>.

+ 1237. m   ii.   **James Meredith**, born 1795 <See pg. 110>.

+ 1243. f   iii.   **Anne Meredith**, born 1800, died after 1850 <See pg. 110>.

+ 1245. f   iv.   **Martha Meredith**, born 1805, died 1880 <See pg. 111>.

Mason is named in her father's will, and in family letters in 1793 and 1795, "Mason and Meredith" are spoken of in reference to her Kentucky brother's land.³³⁸ The members' register of the Maysville Presbyterian Church at Buckingham Court House, Virginia, notes that Mason was a charter member in 1824 and died in 1837.

James Meredith is named in many of the letters and is also shown in the 1810, 1820 and 1830 Buckingham Co., Virginia, censuses. He was a teacher, probably first at "Somerset" in 1790 where "the master & all most the whole School" boarded. Later his wife's brother sent his children from Kentucky to be educated.³³⁹ He appears in the land tax records of Buckingham Co. from 1807 through 1836 when it appears that he sold land to his sons-in-law. His last appearance as an elder of Maysville Presbyterian Church is dated 3 Jun 1841. He and Mason may have been buried at the church. There are several unmarked graves.³⁴⁰

There are no records found yet to show who James Meredith's parents were, but he may have been the son of the James Meredith named in Cumberland Co. who in 1753 was surveyor and appeared in court to file a lawsuit and was named in other lawsuits in 1757 and 1767. Also in 1767, James

---

³³⁶ Woodson Family, *Papers, 1740-1945*, Accession 29437-41, LVA.

³³⁷ Rosen, *History of Maysville Presbyterian Church*, 1, 7, 15, 58.

³³⁸ Will of Benjamin Wilson, LVA. McCrary, *Wilson Families ... Correspondence .... 1785-1849*, 51, 63, 81.

³³⁹ McCrary, *Wilson Families ... Correspondence .... 1785-1849*, 45, 99, 156.

³⁴⁰ WPA - Maysville Presbyterian Church and Cemetery BU70 and BU71.

Meredith of the county of Cumberland sold 300 acres of land.[341]   James
Meredith is shown with land in Buckingham Co. in 1764.[342]

- - - - - - - - - -

1236. John[3] Meredith <See pg. 108> (1235.Mason[2], 1.Benjamin, Sr.[1]) was
born 4 May 1793 in Virginia, the son of **James Meredith** and **Mason
Wilson**. John died 26 May 1846 in Kanawha Co., Virginia (West Virginia).
He married **Ann Seay Wilson (See number 704 - pg. 97)** 6 Oct 1815
probably in Buckingham Co., Virginia. She was born 7 Mar 1791 in
Buckingham Co., the daughter of **James Wilson** and **Sarah Cox**.

ISSUE:[343]

705. m   i.   **James Wilson Meredith**, born 27 Jul 1816, died 2 Mar
1818.

706. m   ii.   **William Alexander Meredith**, born 16 Dec 1818, died
16 Mar 1820.

+ 707. f   iii.   **Sarah Cox Meredith**, born 21 Jan 1821, died 9 Dec 1867
<See pg. 99>.

1091. m   iv.   **Samuel Meredith**, born 23 Nov 1822, died 15 Dec 1823.

1092. m   v.   **Benjamin Meredith**, born 24 Nov 1824, died 4 Apr 1825.

+ 1093. f   vi.   **Ann Wilson "Nannie" Meredith**, born 16 Apr 1826, died
after 1880 <See pg. 100>.

+ 1094. f   vii.   **Mary Hetty Meredith**, born 28 Feb 1828, died 17 Jul 1891
<See pg. 101>.

1198. f   viii.   **Margaret Virginia Meredith**, born 17 Feb 1830, died
25 Jun 1833.

1199. m   ix.   **John Meredith**, born 24 Sep 1832, died 7 Oct 1832.

+ 1200. f   x.   **Lavinia J. Meredith**, born 6 May 1834, died 1910 <See pg.
103>.

1207. f   xi.   **Elizabeth Meredith**, born 18 Mar 1837, died 10 May 1838.

In John's letters to his cousin **James** in Kentucky, one in 1809 complains,
"I am now studying chemistry ... the most difficult thing I ever undertook. I
expect to go to Philadelphia next fall, Deo Volente." Both studied to
become physicians, John receiving his M. D. degree in 1813. John may have
written his cousin's eulogy in 1824.[344]

---

[341] Hopkins, *Story of Cumberland* Co., 98. Cumberland Co. VA Order Books
1752-1758:67, 484 and 1767-1770:53, 76, 119. Deed Book 4:227-8.

[342] Grundset, *Buckingham Co Plat Book*, 3(9, 10).

[343] DAR - Meredith Family Bible.

[344] McCrary, *Wilson Families ... Correspondence 1785-1849*, 135-6, 143-4,
221-2. University of Pennsylvania, (accessed 22 Mar 2006).

John is shown at the Maysville Presbyterian Church in Buckingham Co., Virginia, from 1830 through 1838[345] and in the Buckingham Co. censuses 1820, 1830, and 1840. In 1841 he was named as an executor in his uncle's will as "my nephew Dr. John Meredith".[346] John appears in the Buckingham Co. land tax records from 1832 to1842.

After the family moved to Kanawha Co., his father-in-law, in 1842, left property to him and his wife in exchange for their caring for him. After John's death, his wife distributed her father's land as requested. A letter written in Sep 1846 from Charleston, Virginia (West Virginia), to Buckingham Co. mentions "the estate of the late Dr. Meredith".[347]

- - - - - - - - - - -

1237. James³ Meredith <See pg. 108> (1235.Mason², 1.Benjamin, Sr.¹) was born 1795 in Virginia, the son of **James Meredith** and **Mason Wilson**. He married **Mary** _____ about 1828 probably in Buckingham Co., Virginia. She was born 1793 in Virginia.

ISSUE:

1238. m	i.	**John W. Meredith**, born 1829 in Virginia.	
1239. f	ii.	**Susan A. Meredith**, born 1830 in Virginia.	
1240. m	iii.	**James L. Meredith**, born 1832 in Virginia.	
1241. m	iv.	**Robert J. Meredith**, born 1833 in Virginia.	
1242. f	v.	**Mary E. Meredith**, born 1838 in Virginia.	

James was named in an 1802 letter to his father, sending love to "little John & James".[348] He may be the James Meredith concerning the "sheriffality" in Buckingham Co. in 1842 and 1845.[349] He and his family are possibly the ones shown in the 1850 Franklin Co., Virginia, census.

- - - - - - - - - - -

1243. Anne³ Meredith <See pg. 108> (1235.Mason², 1.Benjamin, Sr.¹) was born 1800 probably in Buckingham Co., Virginia, the daughter of **James Meredith** and **Mason Wilson**. Anna died after 1850. She married **John Garrott**.

---

[345] Rosen, *History of Maysville Presbyterian Church*, 16, 43-4, 57.

[346] Cumb. Co. VA Will Book 10:319.

[347] Kanawha Co. VA (WV) Deed Books, M:374, P:471. Rosen, *Papers of Col. Richard H. Gilliam*, 63.

[348] McCrary, *Wilson Families ... Correspondence .... 1785-1849*, 99.

[349] Rosen, *Papers of Col. Richard H. Gilliam*, 62-3.

ISSUE:
1244. m   i. **John Garrott,** born 1824 in Buckingham Co.

Anne was a charter member of Maysville Presbyterian Church and apparently married by 1824. John was baptized as an adult in 1831, but was excommunicated in 1858.[350] Ann is shown in the household of her son in the 1850 Buckingham Co. census.

John is shown with Nathan Spencer on the 1836-1840 Buckingham land tax records for land which they received from their father-in-law James Meredith.

- - - - - - - - - -

1245. Martha[3] Meredith <See pg. 108> (1235.Mason[2], 1.Benjamin, Sr.[1]) was born 1805 in Buckingham Co., Virginia, the daughter of **James Meredith** and **Mason Wilson**. Martha died 1880 in Buckingham Co. She married **Nathan Spencer** 21 May 1828 in Buckingham Co.[351] He was born 1787. Nathan died 1854 in Buckingham Co.

ISSUE:
1246. f   i. **Elizabeth Mason Spencer,** christened 23 Oct 1830 in Maysville Presbyterian Church., Buckingham Co.
1247. f   ii. **Anna Spencer,** born 1833.
1248. f   iii. **Mildred Spencer,** born 1835.
1249. f   iv. **Martha Spencer,** born 1839.
1250. m   v. **John Spencer,** born 1842.
1251. f   vi. **Alice Spencer,** born 1847.

Nathan probably married (1) **Judith Daniel Fuqua** 14 Nov 1815. She was born 22 May 1798, the daughter of **William Fuqua** and **Jane Anderson.**[352]

Martha was an 1824 charter member of Maysville Presbyterian Church, and Nathan joined in 1831. He dismissed to Cumberland in 1844.[353] The family appears in the 1840 and 1850 Buckingham Co. censuses. Nathan is shown in the Buckingham Co. tax records from 1813 to 1841.[354]

---

[350] Rosen, *History of Maysville Presbyterian Church,* 7, 15, 16, 43, 62, 63.

[351] Kidd, *Marriages Buckingham Co. VA,* 152-3.

[352] *Cumb Co. VA and Its People,* 2nd Supplement, 89.

[353] Rosen, *History of Maysville Presbyterian Church,* 7, 15, 16, 43.

[354] Buckingham Co. VA Land Tax Records, Library of Virginia, Richmond.
Additional information from Mary Carolyn (Steger) Mitton of Salem IN.

CHAPTER 7

Descendants of Matthew Wilson (1772-1833)

1253. Matthew² Wilson <See pg. 2> (1.Benjamin, Sr.¹) was born 25 Mar 1772 at "Somerset", Cumberland Co., Virginia, the son of **Benjamin Wilson, Sr.** and **Anne Seay**.³⁵⁵ Matthew died before 18 Nov 1833 probably in Pittsylvania Co., Virginia.³⁵⁶ He married **Elizabeth "Betsy" Trent** 14 Jul 1808 in Cumberland Co.³⁵⁷ She was born 22 May 1785 in Cumberland Co., the daughter of **Alexander Trent, IV** and **Ann "Nancy" Anderson**.³⁵⁸ Betsy died 24 Oct 1851 in Cumberland Co. and was buried at "Barter Hill", Cumberland Co.³⁵⁹

ISSUE:³⁶⁰

+ 1254. f   i.   **Anne Elizabeth Wilson**, born 8 Jun 1809, died before 7 Nov 1878 <See pg. 114>.

+ 1261. m   ii.   **Samuel Wilson**, born 17 Jan 1811, died 26 Nov 1886 <See pg. 114>.

+ 1462. m   iii.   **Benjamin Wilson**, born 8 Jun 1812, died 14 Aug 1900 <See pg. 141>.

+ 1472. f   iv.   **Maria Alexandria Wilson**, born 17 Jan 1814, died 10 Jun 1879 <See pg. 143>.

+ 1484. f   v.   **Elizabeth Trent "Bettie" Wilson**, born 27 Feb 1815, died 27 May 1886 <See pg. 144>.

   1488. m   vi.   **Matthew Wilson**, born 3 Aug 1817 at "Barter Hill", died 1877 at the Western Lunatic Asylum in Staunton, Virginia. In 1852 Matthew, because of his epilepsy, was placed at the Asylum. His brother Edward, "Committee of Matthew Wilson" managed his finances.³⁶¹

+ 1489. m   vii.   **Goodrich Wilson**, born 24 Nov 1818, died 10 Jun 1890 <See pg. 146>.

---

³⁵⁵ Woodson Family, *Papers, 1740-1945*, Accession 29437-41, LVA.

³⁵⁶ Will of Matthew Wilson, Pittsylvania Co. VA Will Book 1:250-2. Proved 18 Nov 1833. Division of estate of Matthew Wilson, 4 Apr 1835, Cumberland Co. VA Will Book 9:240-1. Cumberland Co. VA Chancery Order Book 1831-1851:46.

³⁵⁷ Elliott, *Marriages, Cumberland Co. VA*, 140.

³⁵⁸ Avant, *Southern Colonial Families*, 4:750.

³⁵⁹ Picture of headstone at "Barter Hill" Cemetery taken by John C. Reid in 1993.

³⁶⁰ A list of birth dates for his children is given in his estate papers. Nash family, *Papers, 1734-1889*.

³⁶¹ Cumberland Co. VA "Ended Chancery Papers, January term 1909", Chancery Order Books 1852-1872, 1872-1882, Will Book 13:547-8, 682.

+ 1512. m viii. **Edward Wilson**, born 26 Aug 1820, died Aug 1893 <See pg. 149>.

+ 1704. f   ix. **Mary Anna Wilson**, born 28 Jun 1822, died 11 Jul 1864 <See pg. 174>.

   1705. m   x. **Willis Alexander Wilson**, born 25 Jan 1825 at "Barter Hill", Cumberland Co., Virginia. He was listed as a carpenter in the 1850 Shelby Co., Texas, census, with his brother Ben. He apparently took care of his brother-in-law's property when he and his wife, Mary Anna, were in Virginia from 1860-1865. Willis died 1 Oct 1866 at "Walnut Grove", Rusk/Gregg Co., Texas, and was buried there.[362]

As a young man, Matthew wrote to his brother in Kentucky in 1793, telling of his plans for beginning in "mercantile Business". After his marriage, he lived at "Barter Hill". In 1809 his nephew wrote, "Trents estate was redivided some time last winter and Uncle Matt's lot was Barter Hill", and his brother wrote, "Matt. Wilson has married & settled at Barter Hill a near & very acceptable neighbor".[363] He had land transactions in Buckingham Co. from 1798 through 1814.[364] In 1817 he was appointed by the Cumberland Co. court as one of the overseers of the poor, and in 1819 he gave bond as treasurer of the school and was named treasurer of the Literary Fund.[365] He and several of his brothers were subscribers to the Willis River Navigation Company.[366]

By 1826, Matthew and his older sons, eldest daughter and some slaves were in Pittsylvania Co., Virginia.[367] Betsy appears with some children in the 1830 Cumberland Co. census, while Matthew appears with others in the 1830 Pittsylvania Co. census.

---

[362] Family Bible of Willis and Mary Anna Wilson. Gregg Co. Gen. Soc., *Cemeteries*, Walnut Grove, 3:189. Texas State-wide Records Program, *Index ... Probate ... Rusk County*, 87, case 879.

[363] McCrary, *Wilson Families ... Correspondence .... 1785-1849*, 49, 143, 145-6. McCrary, *Cumberland County ... Historical Inventory*, 2-3 (an error in this entry refers to Will Book 6:556, which should be Deed Book 6:556).

[364] Grundset, *Buckingham Co. Plat Book*, 31, 35. Ward, *Buck. Co. Land Tax ....Deeds 1782-1814*, 323.

[365] Cumberland Co. VA Order Books 1815-1818:291, 1818-1821:107, 246.

[366] Trout, *Slate and Willis Rivers*, 38.

[367] Deposition by Daniel Talley, overseer of "Barter Hill", Cumberland Co. VA Chancery Records 1828-012, Archives, Library of Virginia, Richmond.

- - - - - - - - - -

1254. Anne Elizabeth³ Wilson <See pg. 112> (1253.Matthew², 1.Benjamin, Sr.¹) was born 8 Jun 1809 at "Barter Hill", Cumberland Co., Virginia, the daughter of **Matthew Wilson** and **Elizabeth "Betsy" Trent**.[368] Anne died before 7 Nov 1878 in Missouri. She married **William Howard** 18 Sep 1827 in Warren Co., North Carolina.[369] William died after 7 Nov 1878 probably in Missouri.

ISSUE:

1255. m   i.   **John Howard.**
1256. f   ii.   **Nannie Howard.** She married _____ **Dunn.**
1257. f   iii. **Mary P. Howard.**
1258. f   iv.   **Lizzie Howard.** She married _____ **Pearson.**
1259. m   v.   **Alexander Howard.**
1260. m   vi.   **Augustus Howard.**

Anne and family moved to Missouri by 1842 when her sister **Bettie** wrote from Pettys, Missouri, apparently on a visit with their brother **Matt**, to their brother **Ben** in Cumberland, Virginia, about "... Howards family", helping "Sister" with the children and about returning home to their mother. Their brother **Goodrich** wrote in 1874 that "Mr. Howard is in bad health."[370]

The sale of "Somerset", which was left to the children of Matthew by their uncle **Samuel**, was complicated by the status of the epileptic brother, and was still being settled in the 7 Nov 1878 term records of the Chancery Court, in which were named William Howard and his children, his wife Anne, deceased.[371]

- - - - - - - - - -

1261. Samuel³ Wilson <See pg. 112> (1253.Matthew², 1.Benjamin, Sr.¹) was born 17 Jan 1811 at "Barter Hill", Cumberland Co., Virginia, the son of **Matthew Wilson** and **Elizabeth "Betsy" Trent**.[372] Samuel died 26 Nov 1886 in San Augustine Co., Texas. He married (1) **Susan A. Jones** 7 Dec 1835 in Cumberland Co.[373] She was born 15 Jun 1813 in Virginia,[374] the

---

[368] Nash family, *Papers, 1734-1889.*

[369] Holcomb, *Marriages ....Warren ....*, 86.

[370] Martin and Johnson, *Brooks Manuscript, Descendants of John Edwards*, 182-188.

[371] Cumberland Co. VA Will Book 10:319, Chancery Order Book 1872-1882:357.

[372] Nash family, *Papers, 1734-1889.*

[373] Elliott, *Marriages, Cumberland Co VA*, 140. McLean was given incorrect

(continued...)

THE DESCENDANTS OF MATTHEW WILSON (1772-1833)   115

daughter of **John H. Jones** and **Mary Ann S. Jones**. Susan died 27 Apr 1843 probably in Cumberland Co.[375]

ISSUE:

+ 1262. f i. **Victoria Marie Wilson**, born 31 Jul 1837, died 6 Sep 1877 <See pg. 116>.
+ 1314. m ii. **Matthew John Wilson**, born 17 Jun 1840, died 8 Dec 1890 <See pg. 122>.
+ 1405. f iii. **Mary E. Wilson**, born 27 May 1842 <See pg. 135>.

Samuel married (2) **Cornelia Williamson McLaurine** 11 Jun 1849 in Cumberland Co.[376] She was born 5 Aug 1821 in Cumberland Co., the daughter of **James McLaurine** and **Jane St. Clair Williamson**.[377] Cornelia died 15 Feb 1891 in San Augustine Co., Texas.

ISSUE:

+ 1407. f iv. **Flora Willie Wilson**, born 29 Apr 1850, died Feb 1881 <See pg. 136>.
  1413. m v. **Samuel Esten Wilson**, born 13 Dec 1851 in Cumberland Co., Virginia. He married **Kate Wyatt** Oct 1880 in Washington, District of Columbia. She was born in Charlottesville, Virginia. Samuel died 3 Dec 1880 in Philadelphia, Pennsylvania, and was buried in Charlottesville.
+ 1414. f vi. **Lelia James Wilson**, born 11 Aug 1853, died 8 Feb 1936 <See pg. 136>.
+ 1429. f vii. **Rosa St. Clair Maria Wilson**, born 20 Apr 1855, died 1924 <See pg. 138>.
+ 1443. f viii. **Courtney Jennetta Wilson**, born 27 Feb 1857 <See pg. 139>.
  1448. f ix. **Alice Virginia Wilson**, born 11 Dec 1858 in San Augustine Co., Texas, died there 23 Jul 1867.
+ 1449. f x. **Eglantine Cornelia Wilson**, born 14 Feb 1861, died 28 Sep 1938 <See pg. 140>.

---

[373] (...continued)
information about the names of Samuel's wives and his brother's wives. McLean, *Wilson Family*, 11. Boddie, *Historical Southern Families*, 3: 63-4.

[374] Wilson, Cornelia, *Genealogical notes on McLaurine*. Wilson,Cornelia, "Family History", (accessed Jul 28, 2005).

[375] Cumberland Co. VA Chancery Records 1837-016 (John H. Jones will, etc.), 1849-015, Archives, Library of Virginia, Richmond.

[376] Cumberland Co VA Marriage Bonds 1841-1854.

[377] Wilson, Cornelia, *Genealogical notes on McLaurine*. Wilson, Cornelia, "Family History", (accessed Jul 28, 2005).

Samuel and Susan sold land in 1837, probably land she had inherited from her father.[378] Samuel was named an executor of his uncle's 1841 will in which he was given land they had bought together. The property was possibly, "View Mont" where Samuel was living when he married his second wife, Cornelia, "Monday Morn at 10 o clock by Henry Brown. Went to his plantation, View Mont to dinner. 12 miles." [379] Before their marriage, Cornelia wrote a letter from "Edgemont" calling him "one of the best men ...my sincere friend".[380] In 1851 he bought land in Powhatan Co. which they sold in 1853.[381]

Cornelia wrote of their move to San Augustine Co. Texas. "Samuel Wilson came to Texas Nov. 1853. Came by land through half of Virginia, part of Tenn., Alabama, Mississippi and La. The crowd was Mrs Jane McLaurine and her daughter, Maria. Samuel and Cornelia Wilson, her three children born in Va., Flora, Sam amd Lelia (2 months old) Vic. Matt and Mary, the three children by his 1st wife, an overseer named Goodman, 22 Servants, wagon, Carry all, barouch, about 5 horses. Stopped at 12 Saturday to wash. Rested Sunday - were about 2 months on the road."[382]

They appeared in the 1860, 1870, and 1880 censuses there. In 1957 a descendant took pictures of their graves which were located on private property in San Augustine Co., Texas.[383]

- - - - - - - - - - -

1262. Victoria Marie[4] Wilson <See pg. 115> (1261.Samuel[3], 1253.Matthew[2], 1.Benjamin, Sr.[1]) was born 31 Jul 1837 at "View Mont", Cumberland Co., Virginia, the daughter of **Samuel Wilson** and **Susan A. Jones**. Victoria died 6 Sep 1877 in Milford, Ellis Co., Texas, and was buried in the Milford Cemetery. She married **Thomas Coleman Edwards** 26 Aug 1858 in San Augustine Co., Texas. He was born 7 Oct 1827 in Big Spring, Tennessee, the son of **John E. Edwards** and **Julia Coleman**. Thomas died 18 Jun 1888 in Milford and was buried there. [384]

---

[378] Cumberland Co VA Deed Book 23:133.

[379] Cumberland Co. VA Will Book 10:319, 378, Deed Book 24:99. Wilson, Cornelia, "Family History", (accessed Jul 28, 2005).

[380] Wilson, Eloise. Papers of Eloise Wilson.

[381] Powhatan Co. VA Deed Books 18:402-3, 19:142.

[382] Wilson, Cornelia, "Family History", (accessed Jul 28, 2005).

[383] Wilson, Eloise. Papers of Eloise Wilson.

[384] 18 Apr 1950 affidavit signed by her son **Samuel Wilson Edwards**, quoting

(continued...)

ISSUE:

+ 1263. f   i.   **Launa Edwards**, born 11 Jun 1860, died 28 Oct 1893 <See pg. 118>.

1278. m ii. **Lilburn Ulysses Edwards**, born 3 Mar 1862, died 11 Jul 1866.

1279. m iii. **Thomas Crump Edwards**, born 4 Jul 1864, died 19 Jan 1893 and was buried in Milford Cemetery, Ellis Co., Texas.

+ 1280. m iv. **Samuel Wilson Edwards**, born 16 Feb 1868, died 25 Nov 1951 <See pg. 119>.

1308. m v. **Mathew Edwards**, born 25 Sep 1870, died 11 Feb 1885 and was buried in Milford Cemetery.

1309. m vi. **Randolph McFadden Edwards**, born 24 Nov 1872, died 23 Jul 1899 and was buried in Milford Cemetery.

1310. f vii. **Grace Lee Edwards**, born 23 Mar 1875. She married **George R. Mabry** 31 Jul 1895. Grace died 19 Jun 1899.

1311. m viii. **Victor Edwards**, born 6 Sep 1877 in Milford, Ellis Co., Texas, died 26 May 1878, and was buried in Milford Cemetery.

1312. m ix. **(twin) Edwards**, born 6 Sep 1877, died 6 Sep 1877 in Milford, Ellis Co., Texas, and was buried in Milford Cemetery.

Thomas married (2) **Nancy Eleanor Norford** 29 Apr 1879. She was born 3 Jun 1849 in Texas, the daughter of **G. A. Norford** and **Mildred Weatherred**. Nancy died 26 Sep 1928 and was buried in Milford Cemetery.

ISSUE:

1313. f x. **Wilna Edwards**, born 18 Sep 1886. She married **Godfrey Holmes** 12 May 1931 in Milford, Texas. He was born in Sheffield, England. Wilna died Dec 1973.

Victoria is shown in the 1850 Powhatan Co., Virginia, census. In 1860 she is listed with her husband and daughter in the San Augustine Co., Texas, census.

Thomas "entered the Confederate Army as Captain of Col. W. P. Lane's

---

[384] (...continued)

family Bible and his parents' statements. Original in possession of **Sydney Ann (Witten) Barr**. Martin and Johnson, *Brooks Manuscript, Descendants of John Edwards*, 53-6, 65-6, 69, 73, 76-7, 205, 264. Ingmire, *San Augustine Co .... Marriage Records*, 11. Bivona, *Ancestors of Brian & Melissa Bivona*, (accessed 24 Apr 2005).

Partisan Rangers."[385]

- - - - - - - - - - -

1263. Launa[5] Edwards <See pg. 117> (1262.Victoria[4], 1261.Samuel[3], 1253.Matthew[2], 1.Benjamin, Sr.[1]) was born 11 Jun 1860 in San Augustine Co., Texas, the daughter of **Thomas Coleman Edwards** and **Victoria Marie Wilson**. Launa died 28 Oct 1893. She married **John Reece "Jack" Morrel** 20 Mar 1878. He was born 5 Feb 1856 in Navarro Co., Texas, the son of **R. D. Morrel** and **S. Arnold**. John died 11 Apr 1930 in Milford, Texas. [386]

ISSUE:

+ 1264. m   i.   **Ralph Edwards Morrel**, born 23 Feb 1879, died 1 Oct 1949.
+ 1267. f   ii. **Helen Victoria Morrel**, born 30 Aug 1881, died Sep 1926.
  1270. m   iii. **John Greene "Jack" Morrel**, born 5 Feb 1883 in Ellis Co., Texas. He married **Annie Moore** 1913.
  1271. m   iv. **Matthew Morrel**, born 24 Apr 1886, died 22 Mar 1887.
  1272. m   v.   **William Lamar Morrel**, born 18 Feb 1888. He married **Alice Ruth Taylor** 25 Feb 1923.
  1273. f   vi. **Launa Grace Morrel**, born 2 Aug 1890.
+ 1274. f   vii. **Anna Gladys Morrel**, born 3 May 1893 <See pg. 119>.

- - - - - - - - - - -

1264. Ralph Edwards[6] Morrel (1263.Launa[5], 1262.Victoria[4], 1261.Samuel[3], 1253.Matthew[2], 1.Benjamin, Sr.[1]) was born 23 Feb 1879 in Milford, Texas, the son of **John Reece "Jack" Morrel** and **Launa Edwards**. Ralph died 1 Oct 1949. He married **Mary Olive Smylie** 30 Jan 1898. She was born about 1865 in Milford.

ISSUE:

+ 1265. m   i.   **Victor Munroe Morrel**.

- - - - - - - - - - -

1265. Victor Munroe[7] Morrel (1264.Ralph[6], 1263.Launa[5], 1262.Victoria[4], 1261.Samuel[3], 1253.Matthew[2], 1.Benjamin, Sr.[1]). He was the son of **Ralph Edwards Morrel** and **Mary Olive Smylie**. His spouse has not been identified.

ISSUE:

  1266. m   i.   **John Newton Morrel**.

[385] Martin and Johnson, *Brooks Manuscript, Descendants of John Edwards*, 57.
[386] Martin and Johnson, *Brooks Manuscript, Descendants of John Edwards*, 56, 71-2.

- - - - - - - - - -

1267. Helen Victoria[6] Morrel (1263.Launa[5], 1262.Victoria[4], 1261.Samuel[3], 1253.Matthew[2], 1.Benjamin, Sr.[1]) was born 30 Aug 1881 in Texas, the daughter of **John Reece "Jack" Morrel** and **Launa Edwards**. Helen died Sep 1926, and was buried in Milford Cemetery, Texas. She married **J. E. Pittman** 31 Jan 1898. [387]

ISSUE:

1268. m   i.   **J. D. Pittman.**
1269. f   ii. **Patricia Pittman.**

- - - - - - - - - -

1274. Anna Gladys[6] Morrel <See pg. 118> (1263.Launa[5], 1262.Victoria[4], 1261.Samuel[3], 1253.Matthew[2], 1.Benjamin, Sr.[1]) was born 3 May 1893, the daughter of **John Reece "Jack" Morrel** and **Launa Edwards**. She married **Fred J. Bryan** 13 Jun 1913.

ISSUE:

1275. f   i.   **Launa Charlsey Bryan**, born 1914, died 1933.
1276. f   ii.   **Helen Victoria Bryan**, born 1916. She married **Kirby Power Murphy** in Tyler, Texas.
1277. m   iii.   **Jack Robert Bryan**, born 1925. He married **Vera Sparks**.

- - - - - - - - - -

1280. Samuel Wilson[5] Edwards <See pg. 117> (1262.Victoria[4], 1261.Samuel[3], 1253.Matthew[2], 1.Benjamin, Sr.[1]) was born 16 Feb 1868 in Milford, Ellis Co., Texas, the son of **Thomas Coleman Edwards** and **Victoria Marie Wilson**. He went by the name Wilson. He died 25 Nov 1951 in Waxahachie, Ellis Co., and was buried in Milford Cemetery. He married (1) **Minnie Galbraith** 10 Dec 1890 in Milford. She was born 15 Jan 1872 in Ontario, Canada, the daughter of **Hurbert Galbraith** and **Mary Richardson**. Minnie died 2 Dec 1900 in Milford, and was buried in Milford Cemetery.[388]

ISSUE:

+ 1281. f   i.   **Lurline Edwards**, born 6 Aug 1891 <See pg. 120>.
+ 1287. m   ii.   **Hugh Thomas Edwards**, born 22 Jan 1893, died 17 Jul 1957 <See pg. 120>.
  1291. u   iii. **(infant) Edwards**, born 7 Oct 1894, died 10 Oct 1894, and was buried in Milford Cemetery, Ellis Co., Texas.
+ 1292. f   iv. **Alice Evelyn Edwards**, born 17 Oct 1896, died 23 Sep

---

[387] Obituary of Mrs. J. E. Pittman. Martin and Johnson, *Brooks Manuscript, Descendants of John Edwards*, 197.

[388] Martin and Johnson, *Brooks Manuscript, Descendants of John Edwards*, 70, 73-6. Additional information from Martha (Witten) Johnson of Benbrook TX.

1983 <See pg. 121>.

1304. f   v.   **Grace Ruth Edwards**, born 8 Apr 1899, died 23 Oct 1900, and was buried in Milford Cemetery.

Wilson married (2) **Elizabeth Marney** 31 Dec 1902. She was born 1868. Elizabeth died 1956.

ISSUE:

1305. m   vi.   **Marney Amos Edwards**, born 12 Mar 1905 in Milford, Ellis Co., Texas, died there 12 Jul 1907, and was buried in Milford Cemetery.

1306. m   vii. **Samuel Wilson Edwards, Jr.**, born 16 Apr 1906 in Milford, Ellis Co., Texas, died 1 Feb 1981, and was buried in Milford Cemetery.

1307. u   viii. **(infant) Edwards**, born 10 Oct 1907 in Milford.

- - - - - - - - - - -

1281. Lurline⁶ Edwards <See pg. 119> (1280.Samuel⁵, 1262.Victoria⁴, 1261.Samuel³, 1253.Matthew², 1.Benjamin, Sr.¹) was born 6 Aug 1891, the daughter of **Samuel Wilson Edwards** and **Minnie Galbraith**. She married **Walter Smith** 22 Jul 1913. Walter died 14 Aug 1948. [389]

ISSUE:

1282. f   i.   **Mary Beth Smith**.
1283. m   ii.   **Paul Edwards Smith**.
1284. f   iii. **Grace Smith**.
1285. f   iv.   **Dorothy Smith**.
1286. f   v.   **Mildred Smith**.

- - - - - - - - - - -

1287. Hugh Thomas⁶ Edwards <See pg. 119> (1280.Samuel⁵, 1262.Victoria⁴, 1261.Samuel³, 1253.Matthew², 1.Benjamin, Sr.¹) was born 22 Jan 1893 in Milford, Ellis Co., Texas, the son of **Samuel Wilson Edwards** and **Minnie Galbraith**. Hugh died 17 Jul 1957 in El Paso, Texas. He married **Alice Higgins** 4 Dec 1918. She was born 4 May 1894 in London, England. Alice died 6 Sep 1987.[390]

ISSUE:

1288. m   i.   **Hugh Thomas Edwards, Jr.**, born 25 Nov 1920 in Corregidor, Phillipine Islands. He married **Beatrice Denis**. Hugh, Jr. died 5 Aug 1994 in Whittier, California.

+ 1289. f ii.   **Sydney Alice Edwards**, born 12 Oct 1924, died 9 Mar 1999.

---

[389] Martin and Johnson, *Brooks Manuscript, Descendants of John Edwards*, 74.

[390] Martin and Johnson, *Brooks Manuscript, Descendants of John Edwards*, 74-5.

- - - - - - - - - -

1289. Sydney Alice⁷ Edwards (1287.Hugh⁶, 1280.Samuel⁵, 1262.Victoria⁴, 1261.Samuel³, 1253.Matthew², 1.Benjamin, Sr.¹) was born 12 Oct 1924 in Milford, Texas, the daughter of **Hugh Thomas Edwards** and **Alice Higgins**. Sydney died 9 Mar 1999. She married (1) **Marion Preston Martin** 7 Feb 1942. He was born 12 May 1920 in Lexington, Kentucky.

ISSUE:

1290. f   i. **Sydney Marion Martin**. She married **Ben Gillis**.

Sydney married (2) **Ralph Eugene Stoughton**.
Sydney married (3) **Everett Coleman** 1 Jul 1978.

- - - - - - - - - -

1292. Alice Evelyn⁶ Edwards <See pg. 120> (1280.Samuel⁵, 1262.Victoria⁴, 1261.Samuel³, 1253.Matthew², 1.Benjamin, Sr.¹) was born 17 Oct 1896 in Milford, Ellis Co., Texas, the daughter of **Samuel Wilson Edwards** and **Minnie Galbraith**. Alice died 23 Sep 1983 in Waxahachie, Ellis Co., Texas. She married **Sidney Gipson Witten** 21 Dec 1921 in Milford. He was born 26 Jun 1892, the son of **Patrick Witten** and **Lucy Clement**. Sidney died 10 Dec 1958 in Waxahachie.

ISSUE:

+ 1293. m   i. **Patrick Wilson Witten**, born 17 Oct 1922, died 15 Nov 1961.
+ 1300. f   ii. **Sydney Ann Witten**, born 28 Nov 1930 <See pg. 122>.

- - - - - - - - - -

1293. Patrick Wilson⁷ Witten (1292.Alice⁶, 1280.Samuel⁵, 1262.Victoria⁴, 1261.Samuel³, 1253.Matthew², 1.Benjamin, Sr.¹) was born 17 Oct 1922 in Waxahachie, Ellis Co., Texas, the son of **Sidney Gipson Witten** and **Alice Evelyn Edwards**. Patrick died 15 Nov 1961 in Waxahachie. He married **Ann Ruth Claunch** 8 Jul 1948. She was born 6 May 1925 in Maypearl, Ellis Co., Texas.[391]

ISSUE:

+ 1294. f   i. **Cynthia Ann Witten**, born 19 Jun 1949.
+ 1297. f   ii. **Martha Alice Witten**, born 26 Aug 1950 <See pg. 122>.

- - - - - - - - - -

1294. Cynthia Ann⁸ Witten (1293.Patrick⁷, 1292.Alice⁶, 1280.Samuel⁵, 1262.Victoria⁴, 1261.Samuel³, 1253.Matthew², 1.Benjamin, Sr.¹) was born 19 Jun 1949, the daughter of **Patrick Wilson Witten** and **Ann Ruth**

---

[391] Martin and Johnson, *Brooks Manuscript, Descendants of John Edwards*, 75.

Claunch. She married **Carl Alan Jacobson** 24 Apr 1981 in Midland, Texas. He was born 15 Sep 1948 in Medford, Oregon.

ISSUE:

1295. m   i.   **Scott Carlton Jacobson**, born 1 Mar 1984.

1296. f   ii.   **Rebecca Carling Jacobson**, born 20 Aug 1985.

- - - - - - - - - - -

1297. Martha Alice[8] Witten <See pg. 121> (1293.Patrick[7], 1292.Alice[6], 1280.Samuel[5], 1262.Victoria[4], 1261.Samuel[3], 1253.Matthew[2], 1.Benjamin, Sr.[1]) was born 26 Aug 1950 in Fort Worth, Tarrant Co., Texas, the daughter of **Patrick Wilson Witten** and **Ann Ruth Claunch**. She married **Edwin Wayne Johnson** 3 Aug 1972 in Lubbock, Texas. He was born 5 Sep 1949 in Lubbock, Texas.

ISSUE:

1298. f   i.   **Laura Marie Johnson**, born 27 Apr 1978 in Corpus Christi, Nueces Co., Texas.

1299. m   ii.   **Patrick Wayne Johnson**, born 16 Jun 1984 in Fort Worth.

- - - - - - - - - - -

1300. Sydney Ann[7] Witten <See pg. 121> (1292.Alice[6], 1280.Samuel[5], 1262.Victoria[4], 1261.Samuel[3], 1253.Matthew[2], 1.Benjamin, Sr.[1]) was born 28 Nov 1930 in Waxahachie, Ellis Co., Texas, the daughter of **Sidney Gipson Witten** and **Alice Evelyn Edwards**. She married **Earl Clifton Barr, Jr.** 8 Jun 1952 in Waxahachie; they divorced. He was born 26 Nov 1924 in Denton, Texas.[392]

ISSUE:

1301. m   i.   **Britten Barr**, born 1 Nov 1956. He married **Laurie McCall** 16 Aug 1980.

1302. f   ii.   **Bevelyn Barr**, born 23 Jan 1961. She married **Gregory Paul Jacobs** 3 Dec 1983; they divorced.

1303. m   iii.   **Burlin Barr**, born 22 May 1963. He married **Linda Clark Wentworth** 12 Jul 1992; they divorced.

- - - - - - - - - - -

1314. Matthew John[4] Wilson <See pg. 115> (1261.Samuel[3], 1253.Matthew[2], 1.Benjamin, Sr.[1]) was born 17 Jun 1840 at "View Mont", Cumberland Co., Virginia, the son of **Samuel Wilson** and **Susan A. Jones**. Matthew died 8 Dec 1890 in Danville, Gregg Co., Texas, and was buried in the cemetery there. He married **Johnnie Lamar Butts** 26 May 1869 in Danville, Rusk

---

[392] Martin and Johnson, *Brooks Manuscript, Descendants of John Edwards*, 75.

Co., Texas.[393] She was born 20 Apr 1851 in Hancock Co., Georgia, the daughter of **George Washington Butts** and **Charlotte Bivens**. Johnnie died 5 Feb 1905 in Longview, Gregg Co., Texas, and was buried in Danville Cemetery, Gregg Co.[394]

ISSUE:

+ 1315. m   i.   **Samuel Washington Wilson**, born 20 May 1871, died 8 Dec 1940 <See pg. 124>.

  1353. f   ii.   **Alice Bivens Wilson**, born 5 Mar 1874 in Danville, Gregg Co., Texas, died 11 Jun 1945 in Longview, Gregg Co., Texas, and was buried in Grace Hill Cemetery in Longview.[395]

  1354. f   iii.   **Mamie Charlott Wilson**, born 2 Nov 1876 in Danville, died 26 Feb 1968 in Longview and was buried in Grace Hill Cemetery.

  1355. f   iv.   **Lela Vic Wilson**, born 13 Aug 1879 in Danville. She married (1) **William Gregg Rosson** 21 Apr 1915 in Longview. He was born 3 Jul 1874. William died 25 Oct 1918 in Silverton, Colorado, and was buried in Danville Cemetery. Lela married (2) **A. B. Eddleman** in Longview; they divorced. Lela died 27 Jul 1955 in Longview and was buried in Grace Hill Cemetery.

+ 1356. m   v.   **John Butts Wilson**, born 17 Dec 1881, died 6 Nov 1939 <See pg. 128>.

+ 1361. m   vi.   **Emory Stuart Wilson**, born 27 Dec 1883, died 15 Jun 1971 <See pg. 129>.

+ 1379. f   vii.   **Emma Eloise Wilson**, born 4 Sep 1886, died 5 Sep 1922 <See pg. 132>.

  1404. f   viii.   **Mollie Ione Wilson**, born 13 Mar 1890 in Danville, died there 10 Feb 1891, and was buried in Danville Cemetery.

Matthew is shown in the 1860 Cumberland Co., Virginia, census with his uncle **Edward**. He enlisted in the Confederate Army while he was in school at the University of Virginia; he served in General J. E. B. Stuart's calvary and was a prisoner of war for 18 months.[396]

---

[393] Rusk Co. TX Marriage Records Vol. E:362. Gregg Co. was created from Rusk Co. in 1873.

[394] Boddie, *Historical Southern Families*, 3:63. Wilson, Eloise. Papers of Eloise Wilson. Gregg Co. TX Probate Records, #20, 1875 will of George W. Butts. Gregg County Cemeteries, (accessed 3 Mar 2006).

[395] Gregg County Cemeteries, (accessed 3 Mar 2006).

[396] Wilson, Eloise. Papers of Eloise Wilson.

His wife Johnnie was postmistress at Claybank in Gregg Co.[397]

- - - - - - - - - - -

1315. Samuel Washington[5] Wilson <See pg. 123> (1314.Matthew[4],
1261.Samuel[3], 1253.Matthew[2], 1.Benjamin, Sr.[1]) was born 20 May 1871 in
Danville, Rusk Co., Texas, the son of **Matthew John Wilson** and **Johnnie
Lamar Butts**. Samuel died 8 Dec 1940 in Longview, Gregg Co., Texas, and
was buried in Grace Hill Cemetery in Longview. He married (1) **Foy
Stroud** 8 Jan 1895 in Gregg Co. She was born Oct 1875. Foy died 1900.[398]
ISSUE:
+ 1316. f   i.   **Louise Ione "Irene" Wilson**, born 20 Mar 1896, died
           14 Oct 1976.
+ 1337. m   ii.   **Matthew Thomas Wilson**, born 4 Dec 1897, died 30 Jun
           1962 <See pg. 127>.

Samuel married (2) **May Dee Owens** 1911. She was born 1891, the
daughter of **John Owens**. May died 22 Jun 1978 in Longview and was
buried in Memory Park Cemetery, Gregg Co., Texas.
ISSUE:
+ 1340. f   iii.   **Edna Jeanette Wilson**, born 2 Jan 1913 <See pg. 127>.
   1351. m   iv.   **Samuel Wilson**.
   1352. m   v.   **John Dee Wilson**, born 1922, died 7 Oct 1981 in Baton
           Rouge, Louisiana, and was buried in Memory Park
           Cemetery.

- - - - - - - - - - -

1316. Louise Ione "Irene"[6] Wilson (1315.Samuel[5], 1314.Matthew[4],
1261.Samuel[3], 1253.Matthew[2], 1.Benjamin, Sr.[1]) was born 20 Mar 1896 in
Longview, Gregg Co., Texas, the daughter of **Samuel Washington Wilson**
and **Foy Stroud**. Louise died 14 Oct 1976 in Inglewood, California. She
married (1) **Dexter E. Inman** 22 Oct 1914 in Longview; they divorced.
ISSUE:
+ 1317. m   i.   **Dexter E. "Lester" Inman, Jr.**, born 19 Jan 1916, died
           21 Aug 1941 <See pg. 125>.
   1319. m   ii.   **Thomas Richard Inman**, born 19 Dec 1919 in Toledo,
           Ohio, died 1 Mar 1936 in Los Angeles Co., California.

Louise married (2) **James Chester Cagle** before 1923 in Toledo, Ohio. He
was born 24 Dec 1892 in Crawfordsville, Indiana. James died 28 Jun 1936

---

[397] Phillips, *Gregg Co. Postoffices*.

[398] Wilson, Eloise. Papers of Eloise Wilson. Gregg County Cemeteries, (accessed
3 Mar 2006).

in Southgate, California.

ISSUE:

+ 1320. m iii. **James Chester Cagle, Jr.**, born 3 Sep 1923, died 1999 <See pg. 125>.

+ 1323. m iv. **Marion Eugene "Gene" Cagle**, born 6 Jun 1925.

+ 1325. m v. **Robert Milburn Cagle**, born 20 Jul 1927, died 10 Feb 1999.

Louise married (3) **Albert Eck** about 1940; they divorced.

- - - - - - - - - - -

1317. Dexter E. "Lester"[7] Inman, Jr. <See pg. 124> (1316.Louise[6], 1315.Samuel[5], 1314.Matthew[4], 1261.Samuel[3], 1253.Matthew[2], 1.Benjamin, Sr.[1]) was born 19 Jan 1916 in Marshall, Texas, the son of **Dexter E. Inman** and **Louise Ione "Irene" Wilson**. Dexter, Jr. died 21 Aug 1941 in Los Angeles Co., California. He married **Vanelia M. Gee**. She was born about 1921.[399]

ISSUE:

1318. m i. **Thomas Richard Cagle**, born 6 Jul 1937.

- - - - - - - - - - -

1320. James Chester[7] Cagle, Jr. <See pg. 125> (1316.Louise[6], 1315.Samuel[5], 1314.Matthew[4], 1261.Samuel[3], 1253.Matthew[2], 1.Benjamin, Sr.[1]) was born 3 Sep 1923 in Maywood, California, the son of **James Chester Cagle** and **Louise Ione "Irene" Wilson**. James, Jr. died 1999 in Huntington Beach, Orange Co., California. He married **Hazel** _____ about 1946.

ISSUE:

1321. m i. **Jamie Cagle**.

1322. m ii. **Terry Cagle**, died about 1998 in Huntington Beach.

- - - - - - - - - - -

1323. Marion Eugene "Gene"[7] Cagle (1316.Louise[6], 1315.Samuel[5], 1314.Matthew[4], 1261.Samuel[3], 1253.Matthew[2], 1.Benjamin, Sr.[1]) was born 6 Jun 1925 in Maywood, California, the son of **James Chester Cagle** and **Louise Ione "Irene" Wilson**. He married **Louise** _____.

ISSUE:

1324. f i. **Mariana Cagle**, born 1955.

- - - - - - - - - - -

1325. Robert Milburn[7] Cagle (1316.Louise[6], 1315.Samuel[5], 1314.Matthew[4], 1261.Samuel[3], 1253.Matthew[2], 1.Benjamin, Sr.[1]) was born

---

[399] Wilson, Eloise. Papers of Eloise Wilson.

20 Jul 1927 in Maywood, California, the son of **James Chester Cagle** and
Louise Ione "Irene" Wilson. Robert died 10 Feb 1999 in Los Angeles Co.,
California. He married **Shirley Darlene Zabolio** 25 Jul 1952 in Los
Angeles Co. She was born 1 Jan 1936 in Los Angeles Co.[400]

ISSUE:

+ 1326. f   i.   **Donna Irene Cagle**, born 1 Aug 1953.
+ 1330. f   ii.   **Jody Lee Cagle**, born 20 Nov 1957.
+ 1332. m   iii.   **Lane Richard Cagle**, born 31 Jul 1962.
   1335. m   iv.   **Michael Loren Cagle**, born 20 Jun 1966.
   1336. f   v.   **Tracy Lou Cagle**, born 8 Jun 1968 in Los Angeles.

- - - - - - - - - - -

1326. Donna Irene[8] Cagle (1325.Robert[7], 1316.Louise[6], 1315.Samuel[5],
1314.Matthew[4], 1261.Samuel[3], 1253.Matthew[2], 1.Benjamin, Sr.[1]) was born
1 Aug 1953 in Los Angeles Co., California, the daughter of **Robert
Milburn Cagle** and **Shirley Darlene Zabolio**. She married **Michael
Patrick Gannon**. He was born about 1955.

ISSUE:

   1327. m   i.   **Michael Gannon**.
   1328. m   ii.   **Jonathan Gannon**.
   1329. f   iii.   **Katie Gannon**.

- - - - - - - - - - -

1330. Jody Lee[8] Cagle (1325.Robert[7], 1316.Louise[6], 1315.Samuel[5],
1314.Matthew[4], 1261.Samuel[3], 1253.Matthew[2], 1.Benjamin, Sr.[1]) was born
20 Nov 1957 in Downey, Los Angeles Co., California, the daughter of
Robert Milburn Cagle and **Shirley Darlene Zabolio**. She married **Gary
Lee Vermillion** 31 Oct 1998 in Las Vegas, Nevada. He was born 2 Jan
1962 in Los Angeles Co., California.

ISSUE:

   1331. m   i.   **Jonathan Michael Vermillion**, born 3 Mar 1998.

- - - - - - - - - - -

1332. Lane Richard[8] Cagle (1325.Robert[7], 1316.Louise[6], 1315.Samuel[5],
1314.Matthew[4], 1261.Samuel[3], 1253.Matthew[2], 1.Benjamin, Sr.[1]) was born
31 Jul 1962 in Downey, Los Angeles Co., California, the son of **Robert
Milburn Cagle** and **Shirley Darlene Zabolio**. He married (1) **Brenda
Marie Gunnari**.

ISSUE:

   1333. f   i.   **Amanda Marie Cagle**, born 31 Jul 1987.

---

[400] Wilson, Eloise. Papers of Eloise Wilson.

Lane married (2) **Donna Gay Patterson** 9 Dec 1988 in Las Vegas, Nevada. She was born 4 Dec 1961 in Inglewood, California.

ISSUE:

1334. m   ii.   **Bradley Kevin Cagle**, born 16 Dec 1993.

- - - - - - - - - - -

1337. Matthew Thomas⁶ Wilson <See pg. 124> (1315.Samuel⁵, 1314.Matthew⁴, 1261.Samuel³, 1253.Matthew², 1.Benjamin, Sr.¹) was born 4 Dec 1897 in Gregg Co., Texas, the son of **Samuel Washington Wilson** and **Foy Stroud**. Matthew died 30 Jun 1962 in Houston, Harris Co., Texas, and was buried in Grace Hill Cemetery in Longview, Gregg Co., Texas. He married **Edith _____** 8 Sep 1959 in Houston.[401]

Matthew had 2 stepchildren:

1338. m   i.   **Cary Coole**
1339.   ii.   **Edana Coole**.

Edith also married (1) _____ **Coole**.
Edith also married (3) _____ **Treadwell**.

- - - - - - - - - - -

1340. Edna Jeanette⁶ Wilson <See pg. 124> (1315.Samuel⁵, 1314.Matthew⁴, 1261.Samuel³, 1253.Matthew², 1.Benjamin, Sr.¹) was born 2 Jan 1913 in Humble, Houston Co., Texas, the daughter of **Samuel Washington Wilson** and **May Dee Owens**. She married (1) **Minter Robert Cooke**.[402]

ISSUE:

+ 1341. f   i.   **Mary Loye Cooke** <See pg. 128>.

Edna married (2) **Frank E. Patterson**. He was born 1914. Frank died 23 Jan 1978 in Longview, Gregg Co., Texas, and was buried in Memory Park Cemetery, Gregg Co.

ISSUE:

1345. m   ii.   **Don Evan Patterson**.
+ 1346. f   iii.   **Helen Patterson** <See pg. 128>.
1348. f   iv.   **Diane J. Patterson**.
+ 1349. f   v.   **Linda Patterson** <See pg. 128>.

- - - - - - - - - - -

---

[401] Wilson, Eloise. Papers of Eloise Wilson. Gregg County Cemeteries, (accessed 3 Mar 2006).

[402] Wilson, Eloise. Papers of Eloise Wilson.

1341. Mary Loye⁷ Cooke <See pg. 127> (1340.Edna⁶, 1315.Samuel⁵, 1314.Matthew⁴, 1261.Samuel³, 1253.Matthew², 1.Benjamin, Sr.¹). She is the daughter of **Minter Robert Cooke** and **Edna Jeanette Wilson**. She married **Ed McAlister**.

ISSUE:

   1342. f   i.   **Gail McAlister**.
   1343. f   ii.   **Kay McAlister**.
   1344. f iii.   **Dee McAlister**.

- - - - - - - - - -

1346. Helen⁷ Patterson <See pg. 127> (1340.Edna⁶, 1315.Samuel⁵, 1314.Matthew⁴, 1261.Samuel³, 1253.Matthew², 1.Benjamin, Sr.¹). She is the daughter of **Frank E. Patterson** and **Edna Jeanette Wilson**. She married **J. R. Bivin**.

ISSUE:

   1347. m   i.   **Bill Bivin**.

- - - - - - - - - -

1349. Linda⁷ Patterson <See pg. 127> (1340.Edna⁶, 1315.Samuel⁵, 1314.Matthew⁴, 1261.Samuel³, 1253.Matthew², 1.Benjamin, Sr.¹). She is the daughter of **Frank E. Patterson** and **Edna Jeanette Wilson**. She married _____ **Stanley**.

ISSUE:

   1350. m   i.   **Anthony Stanley**.

- - - - - - - - - -

1356. John Butts⁵ Wilson <See pg. 123> (1314.Matthew⁴, 1261.Samuel³, 1253.Matthew², 1.Benjamin, Sr.¹) was born 17 Dec 1881 in Danville, Gregg Co., Texas, the son of **Matthew John Wilson** and **Johnnie Lamar Butts**. John died 6 Nov 1939 in Vivian, Louisiana, and was buried in Grace Hill Cemetery in Longview, Gregg Co. He married **Myrtle White** 23 Dec 1911 in San Antonio, Texas. Myrtle died 17 Mar 1977.[403]

ISSUE:

+ 1357. m   i.   **Cyrus Wilson**, born 12 Dec 1912, died 28 Dec 1954.

- - - - - - - - - -

1357. Cyrus⁶ Wilson (1356.John⁵, 1314.Matthew⁴, 1261.Samuel³, 1253.Matthew², 1.Benjamin, Sr.¹) was born 12 Dec 1912 in Humble, Texas, the son of **John Butts Wilson** and **Myrtle White**. Cyrus died 28 Dec 1954 in Panola Co., Mississippi, and was buried in Fayette Co., Texas. He

---

[403] Wilson, Eloise. Papers of Eloise Wilson. Gregg County Cemeteries, (accessed 3 Mar 2006).

married **Charleen Thornton** 30 Jun 1938. Charleen died after 2004.[404]
ISSUE:

1358. m   i.   **John Thornton Wilson**, born 7 Sep 1939. He married
"Pinky" _____. John died, assistant presiding
officer of the Texas Senate ,19 Sep 1982 in Fayette Co.,
Texas.[405]

+ 1359. f   ii. **Judith Carter Wilson**, born 13 Nov 1940.

Col. Cy served as a pilot in Word War II. His plane was hit on a mission, so he flew to the North Sea and bailed out. He was declared missing in action 27 Aug 1944. In October, his wife wrote to her aunt that she had received letters from men using short wave radios in New York telling her that a message had been sent October 7 from Cy Wilson to Mrs. Cy Wilson "Everything is under control. I am having a short vacation in Germany. I get plenty to eat so don't you worry. I have given up cigars though. Remember, we still have a date. All my love to all. Cy."[406]

- - - - - - - - - - -

1359. Judith Carter[7] Wilson (1357.Cyrus[6], 1356.John[5], 1314.Matthew[4], 1261.Samuel[3], 1253.Matthew[2], 1.Benjamin, Sr.[1]) was born 13 Nov 1940, the daughter of **Cyrus Wilson** and **Charleen Thornton**. She married **Mark Walsh**.
ISSUE:

1360. m   i.   **John Walsh**.

- - - - - - - - - - -

1361. Emory Stuart[5] Wilson <See pg. 123> (1314.Matthew[4], 1261.Samuel[3], 1253.Matthew[2], 1.Benjamin, Sr.[1]) was born 27 Dec 1883 in Danville, Gregg Co., Texas, the son of **Matthew John Wilson** and **Johnnie Lamar Butts**. Emory died 15 Jun 1971 in Longview, Gregg Co., and was buried in Grace Hill Cemetery in Longview. He married **Alice Middleton Ross** 20 Dec 1911 in Longview. She was born 19 Feb 1887 in Longview, the daughter of **George Taylor Ross** and **Emma Jane Dodson**. Alice died 27 Sep 1975 in Longview, and was buried in Grace Hill Cemetery.[407]

---

[404] Wilson, Eloise. Papers of Eloise Wilson.

[405] Obituary, *Longview Daily News*, 20 Sep 1982.

[406] "Col. Cy Wilson Remembered", (accessed 3 Mar 2006). Whitehouse, "The Loco Boys Go Wild", 6-7, 92-5. Fayette Co. TX Cemeteries, (accessed 3 Mar 2006).

[407] Wilson, Eloise. Papers of Eloise Wilson. Gregg County Cemeteries, (accessed 3 Mar 2006). Gregg Co. Gen. Soc., *Cemeteries*. Grace Hill 4:53.

ISSUE:

1362. f   i.   **Emma Eloise Wilson**, born 15 Sep 1912 in Longview, Gregg Co., Texas, died 20 Jun 2003 in Longview, Gregg Co., Texas.[408]

+ 1363. m   ii.   **Emory Stuart Wilson, Jr.**, born 9 Sep 1915.

+ 1371. f   iii.   **Glenna Vic Wilson**, born 16 Apr 1925, died 7 Feb 1999 <See pg. 131>.

- - - - - - - - - - -

1363. Emory Stuart[6] Wilson, Jr. (1361.Emory[5], 1314.Matthew[4], 1261.Samuel[3], 1253.Matthew[2], 1.Benjamin, Sr.[1]) was born 9 Sep 1915 in Longview, Gregg Co., Texas, the son of **Emory Stuart Wilson** and **Alice Middleton Ross**. He married **Marian Miller Moyer** 12 Jun 1947 in Longview. She was born 10 Nov 1922 in Kaufman, Kaufman Co., Texas, the daughter of **Shirley Russell Moyer** and **Willie Irene Miller**. Marian died 4 Dec 2000 in Longview.

ISSUE:

1364. m   i.   **Emory Stuart Wilson, III**, born 28 May 1948 in Longview. He married (1) **Sherry Ann Davis**; they divorced. Emory, III married (2) **Carolyn Hoppel** 6 Aug 1988 in Desoto, Missouri. She is the daughter of **Raymond Hoppel** and **Lillian** _____. Carolyn also married (1) _____ **Whitman**. Emory, III died 2 Aug 2001.

+ 1365. m   ii.   **Russell Moyer Wilson**, born 10 May 1952.

1370. f   iii.   **Miriam Annette Wilson**, born 8 Aug 1960 in Longview.

- - - - - - - - - - -

1365. Russell Moyer[7] Wilson (1363.Emory, Jr.[6], 1361.Emory[5], 1314.Matthew[4], 1261.Samuel[3], 1253.Matthew[2], 1.Benjamin, Sr.[1]) was born 10 May 1952 in Longview, Gregg Co., Texas, the son of **Emory Stuart Wilson, Jr.** and **Marian Miller Moyer**. He married (1) **Rita Burns** 16 Jun 1978 in Tatum, Rusk Co., Texas; they divorced. She was the daughter of **James Burns** and **Pat** _____. Rita died 30 Jan 1983 in Longview and was buried in Granbury, Texas.

ISSUE:

1366. m   i.   **Christopher Wade Wilson**, born 8 May 1979 in Longview.

Russell married (2) **Eva Marie Ryan** 23 Jun 1989 in Longview. She was born 9 Dec 1960 in Naples, Florida, the daughter of **Dan Ryan** and **Martha**

---

[408] Eloise's papers in the Longview TX library, which contain many primary documents on her ancestors, provided most of the information on this family.

_____. Eva died 30 Oct 1997 in Gilmer, Gregg Co., Texas.

ISSUE:

1367. f   iv.   **Amy Lynn Wilson**, born 11 Apr 1990 in Longview.

Eva also married (1) _____ **Wood**.

ISSUE:

1368. m   ii.   **Christopher Wood**.
1369. f   iii. **Kimberly Elizabeth Wood**..

- - - - - - - - - -

1371. Glenna Vic[6] Wilson <See pg. 130> (1361.Emory[5], 1314.Matthew[4], 1261.Samuel[3], 1253.Matthew[2], 1.Benjamin, Sr.[1]) was born 16 Apr 1925 in Longview, Gregg Co., Texas, the daughter of **Emory Stuart Wilson** and **Alice Middleton Ross**. Glenna died 7 Feb 1999 in Runaway, Wise Co., Texas. She married **Ashley Baird Moore** 1 Mar 1946 in Kilgore, Gregg Co., Texas. He was born 27 Mar 1916 in Dallas, Texas, the son of **Ashley Baird Moore** and **Estelle Rutledge**. Ashley died 27 Jul 1996 in Bridgeport, Wise Co., Texas.[409]

ISSUE:

+ 1372. m   i.   **David Allen Moore**, born 22 Jun 1948.
+ 1376. f   ii. **Janis Gayle Moore**, born 12 May 1952 <See pg. 131>.

- - - - - - - - - -

1372. David Allen[7] Moore (1371.Glenna[6], 1361.Emory[5], 1314.Matthew[4], 1261.Samuel[3], 1253.Matthew[2], 1.Benjamin, Sr.[1]) was born 22 Jun 1948 in Kilgore, Gregg Co., Texas, the son of **Ashley Baird Moore** and **Glenna Vic Wilson**. He married **Lynn Gail Wassel** 17 Mar 1973 in Atlanta, Georgia. She was born 5 Jul 1948 in Chicago, Illinois, the daughter of **Eugene S. Wassel** and **Olga Margantini**.

ISSUE:

1373. m   i.   **Brian David Moore**, born 30 Dec 1976 in Palatine, Illinois.
1374. m   ii.   **Collin Wassel Moore**, born 29 Dec 1978 in Chicago, Illinois.
1375. m   iii. **Daniel Wilson Moore**, born 28 Oct 1983 in Rolling Meadows, Illinois.

- - - - - - - - - -

1376. Janis Gayle[7] Moore <See pg. 131> (1371.Glenna[6], 1361.Emory[5], 1314.Matthew[4], 1261.Samuel[3], 1253.Matthew[2], 1.Benjamin, Sr.[1]) was born 12 May 1952 in Glen Ridge, New Jersey, the daughter of **Ashley Baird**

---

[409] Wilson, Eloise. Papers of Eloise Wilson.

Moore and **Glenna Vic Wilson**. She married **James Howe Meyers** 31 Aug 1974 in Bridgeport, Wise Co., Texas. He was born 13 Jun 1963 in Dallas, Texas, the son of **Howard F. Meyers, Jr.** and **Martha Mott**.

ISSUE:

1377. f   i.   **Kristy Lynn Meyers**, born 3 Jul 1980 in Denton, Texas.
1378. m   ii.   **Luke James Meyers**, born 3 Oct 1982 in Denton.

- - - - - - - - - -

1379. Emma Eloise[5] Wilson <See pg. 123> (1314.Matthew[4], 1261.Samuel[3], 1253.Matthew[2], 1.Benjamin, Sr.[1]) was born 4 Sep 1886 in Danville, Gregg Co., Texas, the daughter of **Matthew John Wilson** and **Johnnie Lamar Butts**. Emma died 5 Sep 1922 in Dallas, Texas, and was buried in Grace Hill Cemetery in Longview, Gregg Co., Texas. She married **William Fleming Brown** 20 Nov 1912 in Longview. He was born 31 Aug 1888, the son of **Ervin F. Brown** and **Icy P. Burns**. William died 17 Mar 1953 in Brenham, Texas.[410]

ISSUE:

+ 1380. m   i.   **Ervin Wilson Brown**, born 22 Nov 1914, died 5 Dec 1986.
+ 1383. m   ii.   **William Matthew Brown**, born 15 Oct 1916, died 4 Dec 1985 <See pg. 133>.
+ 1394. m   iii. **Marion Hartfield Brown**, born 21 Nov 1918, died 13 Jan 1999 <See pg. 134>.

- - - - - - - - - -

1380. Ervin Wilson[6] Brown (1379.Emma[5], 1314.Matthew[4], 1261.Samuel[3], 1253.Matthew[2], 1.Benjamin, Sr.[1]) was born 22 Nov 1914 in Manor, Travis Co., Texas, the son of **William Fleming Brown** and **Emma Eloise Wilson**. Ervin died 5 Dec 1986 in Amarillo, Potter Co., Texas. He married **Carolyn Culwell McMahan** 21 Mar 1943 in Longview, Gregg Co., Texas. She was born 10 Oct 1921 in Bay City, Texas, the daughter of **John Wesley McMahan** and **Mary Aileen Culwell**. [411]

ISSUE:

1381. m   i.   **Richard Fleming Brown**, born 17 Jan 1946 in Texarkana, Arkansas. He married **Kay Carter** 17 Aug 1968 in Amarillo, Potter Co., Texas.
1382. f   ii.   **Catherine Eloise Brown**, born 28 Nov 1948 in Gladewater, Gregg Co., Texas. She married (1) **Karl Orrin**

---

[410] Wilson, Eloise. Papers of Eloise Wilson. The family Bible of Ervin F. Brown, which gives births, deaths, and marriages from 1847-1986 is in the possession of Richard Brown.

[411] Wilson, Eloise. Papers of Eloise Wilson. Additional information from Carolyn (McMahan) Brown Askew of Amarillo TX.

Bayer, Jr. 28 Jun 1972 in Texas. Catherine married (2) **Jack Dodson**.

Carolyn also married (2) _____ **Askew**.

- - - - - - - - - - -

1383. William Matthew⁶ Brown <See pg. 132> (1379.Emma⁵, 1314.Matthew⁴, 1261.Samuel³, 1253.Matthew², 1.Benjamin, Sr.¹) was born 15 Oct 1916, the son of **William Fleming Brown** and **Emma Eloise Wilson**. William died 4 Dec 1985 in Cincinnatti, Ohio, and was buried in Somerset, Kentucky. He married **Lavelle Sparks** 5 Oct 1940 in Longview, Texas. She was born 24 Nov 1921, the daughter of **Roy Sparks**.⁴¹²
ISSUE:
+ 1384. m   i.   **William Lamont Brown**, born 29 Apr 1944.
+ 1387. m   ii.   **Ted Ridgley Brown**, born 30 Aug 1946.

- - - - - - - - - - -

1384. William Lamont⁷ Brown <See pg. 133> (1383.William⁶, 1379.Emma⁵, 1314.Matthew⁴, 1261.Samuel³, 1253.Matthew², 1.Benjamin, Sr.¹) was born 29 Apr 1944, the son of **William Matthew Brown** and **Lavelle Sparks**. He married **Anne Bonham Taylor** 29 Jun 1973. She was born 4 Aug 1943.
ISSUE:
1385. f   i.   **Lori Suzanne Brown**, born 22 Oct 1975.

Anne also married (1) **A. O. Evans**.
ISSUE:
1386. m   ii.   **Lance Barkley Evans**, born 19 Mar 1970, the son of **A. O. Evans** and **Anne Bonham Taylor**.

- - - - - - - - - - -

1387. Ted Ridgley⁷ Brown (1383.William⁶, 1379.Emma⁵, 1314.Matthew⁴, 1261.Samuel³, 1253.Matthew², 1.Benjamin, Sr.¹) was born 30 Aug 1946, the son of **William Matthew Brown** and **Lavelle Sparks**. He married **Cynthia Lynn Scoffield** 3 Apr 1971. She was born 24 Sep 1949.
ISSUE:
+ 1388. f   i.   **Brook Nicole Brown**, born 19 Jul 1974 <See pg. 134>.
1393. f   ii.   **Lee Aren Brown**, born 22 Feb 1977.

- - - - - - - - - - -

---

⁴¹² Wilson, Eloise. Papers of Eloise Wilson. Additional information from Lavelle (Sparks) Brown of Somerset KY.

1388. Brook Nicole[8] Brown <See pg. 133> (1387.Ted[7], 1383.William[6], 1379.Emma[5], 1314.Matthew[4], 1261.Samuel[3], 1253.Matthew[2], 1.Benjamin, Sr.[1]) was born 19 Jul 1974, the daughter of **Ted Ridgley Brown** and **Cynthia Lynn Scoffield**.

Born to Brook Nicole Brown and **Christopher Bosch**.
  1389. f   i.   **Abigail Elise Bosch**, born 27 Apr 1994.
  1390. f   ii. **Katelyn Rose Bosch**, born 26 Jun 1995.

Born to Brook Nicole Brown and **Thomas Edward Carroll**.
  1391. m   iii. **Jacob Thomas McCracken Carroll**, born 16 Dec 1998.
  1392. m   iv. **Joshua Sloan Carroll**, born 6 May 2000.

- - - - - - - - - - -

1394. Marion Hartfield[6] Brown <See pg. 132> (1379.Emma[5], 1314.Matthew[4], 1261.Samuel[3], 1253.Matthew[2], 1.Benjamin, Sr.[1]) was born 21 Nov 1918 in Chapel Hill, Washington Co., Texas, the son of **William Fleming Brown** and **Emma Eloise Wilson**. Marion died 13 Jan 1999 in Kirkland, Washington. He married **Betty Ruth Murray McCormick** 4 Sep 1943 in Oklahoma City, Oklahoma. She was born 27 Dec 1923 in Shawnee, Potowatame Co., Oklahoma, the daughter of **Alfred Garver Murray** and **Lois Opal Ownbey**. [413]
ISSUE:
  1395. f   i.   **Carol Jeane Brown**, born 23 Jun 1944 in Oklahoma City, Oklahoma.
+ 1396. m   ii.   **James Randolph Brown**, born 10 Mar 1946.
+ 1400. f   iii. **Marilyn Leigh Brown**, born 21 Jun 1952 <See pg. 135>.

- - - - - - - - - - -

1396. James Randolph[7] Brown (1394.Marion[6], 1379.Emma[5], 1314.Matthew[4], 1261.Samuel[3], 1253.Matthew[2], 1.Benjamin, Sr.[1]) was born 10 Mar 1946 in Oklahoma City, Oklahoma, the son of **Marion Hartfield Brown** and **Betty Ruth Murray McCormick**. He married **Phyllis Joan Pitts** 14 Dec 1968 in Anaheim, California. She was born 4 Oct 1942 in Dardanelle, Arkansas.
ISSUE:
  1397. f   i.   **Susan Alissa Brown**, born 6 Jan 1972 in Anaheim, California.
  1398. m   ii. **Gregory Ryan Brown**, born 28 Feb 1974 in Yreka, California.

---

[413] Wilson, Eloise. Papers of Eloise Wilson. Additional information from Betty (McCormick) Brown of Kirkland WA.

Phyllis also married (1) _____ **Peters.**
ISSUE:
1399. f   iii.   **Karol Jenae Peters**, born 4 Aug 1962 in Downey,
California. She is the daughter of _____ **Peters** and
Phyllis Joan Pitts.

- - - - - - - - - - -

1400. Marilyn Leigh[7] Brown <See pg. 134> (1394.Marion[6], 1379.Emma[5],
1314.Matthew[4], 1261.Samuel[3], 1253.Matthew[2], 1.Benjamin, Sr.[1]) was born
21 Jun 1952 in Longview, Gregg Co., Texas, the daughter of **Marion
Hartfield Brown** and **Betty Ruth Murray McCormick**. She married
Anthony Bartuch 3 Aug 1974.
ISSUE:
1401. f   i.   **Marcy Allison Bartuch**, born 29 Mar 1975 in Arlington
Heights, Illinois.
+ 1402. m   ii.   **Anthony Matthew Bartuch**, born 12 Jan 1978.

- - - - - - - - - - -

1402. Anthony Matthew[8] Bartuch (1400.Marilyn[7], 1394.Marion[6],
1379.Emma[5], 1314.Matthew[4], 1261.Samuel[3], 1253.Matthew[2], 1.Benjamin,
Sr.[1]) was born 12 Jan 1978 in Arlington Heights, Illinois, the son of
Anthony Bartuch and **Marilyn Leigh Brown**. He married **Geralyn
Balatbat** 9 May 1999.
ISSUE:
1403. m   i.   **Anthony Francis Bartuch**, born 15 Nov 1999 in Arlington
Heights, Illinois.

- - - - - - - - - - -

1405. Mary E.[4] Wilson <See pg. 115> (1261.Samuel[3], 1253.Matthew[2],
1.Benjamin, Sr.[1]) was born 27 May 1842 at "View Mont", Cumberland Co.,
Virginia, the daughter of **Samuel Wilson** and **Susan A. Jones**. Mary died
probably in Itasca, Hill Co., Texas. She married **A. W. Weatherred**
11 Nov 1880. He was born 25 Jul 1844, the son of **William Carroll
Weatherred** and **Mary Ann Lawhon**. A. W. died 28 Mar 1895.[414]
ISSUE:
1406. m   i.   **Samuel Homer Weatherred**, born 18 Jan 1883.

Mary is listed in the 1850 Cumberland Co., Virginia, census and in the 1870
Rusk Co., Texas, census.

---

[414] Martin and Johnson, *Brooks Manuscript, Descendants of John Edwards*, 65,
231, 238. Wilson, Eloise. Papers of Eloise Wilson.

- - - - - - - - - - -

1407. Flora Willie⁴ Wilson <See pg. 115> (1261.Samuel³, 1253.Matthew²,
1.Benjamin, Sr.¹) was born 29 Apr 1850 in Powhatan Co., Virginia, the
daughter of **Samuel Wilson** and **Cornelia Williamson McLaurine**. Flora
died Feb 1881 in Cass Co., Texas. She married **Charley Heard** 11 Feb
1869. Charley died Apr 1890.[415]

ISSUE:

1408. f   i.   **Lola McLaurine Heard**, born 27 Oct 1872.
1409. f   ii. **Starr St. Clair Heard**, born May 1878 in Cass Co.

Flora had 3 stepchildren:

1410. f   iii. **May Heard**, born 1884.
1411. m   iv. **Cleaveland Heard**, born 1886.
1412. m   v.   _____ **Heard**, born 1888.

- - - - - - - - - - -

1414. Lelia James⁴ Wilson <See pg. 115> (1261.Samuel³, 1253.Matthew²,
1.Benjamin, Sr.¹) was born 11 Aug 1853 in Cumberland Co., Virginia, the
daughter of **Samuel Wilson** and **Cornelia Williamson McLaurine**. Lelia
died 8 Feb 1936 in Dallas, Texas. She married (1) **William Stanley
McFadden** 25 Dec 1875 in San Augustine Co., Texas.[416] He was born
26 Apr 1850 in Chester Co., South Carolina, the son of **Isaac McFadden**
and **Jane Susan** _____. William died 28 Mar 1890 in Hillsboro,
Texas.

ISSUE:

1415. f   i.   **Clara Gray McFadden**, born 29 Dec 1876 in Milford,
                Ellis Co., Texas, died 3 Sep 1897 in Dallas, Texas.
1416. f   ii. **Lelia Alyne McFadden**, born 11 Jan 1880 in San
                Augustine Co., Texas, died 22 Sep 1946 in Tulsa,
                Oklahoma.
1417. f   iii. **Maude Randolph McFadden**, born 18 Sep 1882 in
                Milford, Ellis Co., Texas. She married **Philip Cass** 2 Apr
                1902 in Dallas, Texas. He was born Aug 1875 in Illinois.
                Philip died before 7 Dec 1956 in Wynnewood,
                Pennsylvania. Maude died 15 Sep 1973 in Wynnewood.
+ 1418. f iv. **Mabel McFadden**, born 29 Aug 1885, died 3 Aug 1968
                <See pg. 137>.

Lelia married (2) **Reade Macon Washington, II** 12 Jun 1892 in Dallas,

---

[415] Wilson, Cornelia, "Family History", (accessed Jul 28, 2005). Wilson, Cornelia,
Genealogical notes on McLaurine.

[416] Ingmire, *San Augustine Co .... Marriage Records*, 26.

Texas. He was born 1 Jan 1848 in Pittsburgh, Pennsylvania, the son of **E. C. Washington.** Reade, II died before 1936 in Dallas.

- - - - - - - - - - -

1418. Mabel⁵ McFadden <See pg. 136> (1414.Lelia⁴, 1261.Samuel³, 1253.Matthew², 1.Benjamin, Sr.¹) was born 29 Aug 1885 in Hillsboro, Texas, the daughter of **William Stanley McFadden** and **Lelia James Wilson.** Mabel died 3 Aug 1968 in Tulsa, Oklahoma. She married **Walter Hamilton Peck** 8 Jan 1909 in Dallas, Texas. He was born 3 Dec 1877 in Toledo, Ohio. Walter died 24 Mar 1952 in Tulsa.*⁴¹⁷*

ISSUE:

+ 1419. f   i. **Alyne Maude Peck,** born 18 Sep 1914, died 2 Jan 1989.
  1425. f   ii. **Waltyne Sweet Peck,** born 11 Apr 1917 in Dallas, Texas, and died there.
+ 1426. f   iii. **Philippa Wilson Peck,** born 11 Apr 1917, died 20 Jan 1997 <See pg. 138>.

- - - - - - - - - - -

1419. Alyne Maude⁶ Peck (1418.Mabel⁵, 1414.Lelia⁴, 1261.Samuel³, 1253.Matthew², 1.Benjamin, Sr.¹) was born 18 Sep 1914 in Dallas, Texas, the daughter of **Walter Hamilton Peck** and **Mabel McFadden.** Alyne died 2 Jan 1989 in Tulsa, Oklahoma. She married **William E. Miller, Jr.** 15 Oct 1938 in Tulsa. He was born 26 Feb 1913.*⁴¹⁸*

ISSUE:

+ 1420. m   i. **Cass Hamilton Miller,** born 7 Mar 1946.
+ 1423. f   ii. **Cathy Claire Miller,** born 26 Sep 1954 <See pg. 138>.

- - - - - - - - - - -

1420. Cass Hamilton⁷ Miller (1419.Alyne⁶, 1418.Mabel⁵, 1414.Lelia⁴, 1261.Samuel³, 1253.Matthew², 1.Benjamin, Sr.¹) was born 7 Mar 1946 in Tulsa, Oklahoma, the son of **William E. Miller, Jr.** and **Alyne Maude Peck.** His spouse has not been identified.

ISSUE:

  1421. f   i. **Pamela Jaye Miller.**
  1422. m   ii. **David Hamilton Miller,** born Dec 1987.

- - - - - - - - - - -

---

⁴¹⁷ Boddie, *Historical Southern Families,* 3:63. Wilson, Eloise. Papers of Eloise Wilson. Additional information from Philip Lawless of Durham NC.

⁴¹⁸ Alyne did a great deal of family history research which corrected some errors of McLean's book. Boddie, *Historical Southern Families,* 3: 59-. Wilson, Eloise. Papers of Eloise Wilson.

1423. Cathy Claire[7] Miller <See pg. 137> (1419.Alyne[6], 1418.Mabel[5], 1414.Lelia[4], 1261.Samuel[3], 1253.Matthew[2], 1.Benjamin, Sr.[1]) was born 26 Sep 1954, the daughter of **William E. Miller, Jr.** and **Alyne Maude Peck**. She married (1) **Richard Eugene McKim** before 17 Jun 1978.

ISSUE:

1424. m   i.   **Matthew Scott McKim**, born 21 Sep 1979.

Cathy married (2) _____ **McNamar**.

- - - - - - - - - -

1426. Philippa Wilson[6] Peck <See pg. 137> (1418.Mabel[5], 1414.Lelia[4], 1261.Samuel[3], 1253.Matthew[2], 1.Benjamin, Sr.[1]) was born 11 Apr 1917 in Dallas, Texas, the daughter of **Walter Hamilton Peck** and **Mabel McFadden**. Philippa died 20 Jan 1997 in Asheville, North Carolina. She married **John Austin Lawless** 26 Oct 1940. He was born 23 Mar 1914 in Columbia, South Dakota. John died 10 May 1997 in Asheville, North Carolina.

ISSUE:

1427. m   i.   **Philip Austin Lawless**, born 7 Jun 1943 in Tulsa, Oklahoma.

1428. m   ii.   **Walter James Lawless**, born 8 Apr 1947 in Tulsa.

- - - - - - - - - -

1429. Rosa St. Clair Maria[4] Wilson <See pg. 115> (1261.Samuel[3], 1253.Matthew[2], 1.Benjamin, Sr.[1]) was born 20 Apr 1855 in San Augustine Co., Texas, the daughter of **Samuel Wilson** and **Cornelia Williamson McLaurine**. Rosa died 1924 in Dallas, Texas. She married **William Clarkston "Clark" Nash** 4 Nov 1874 in San Augustine Co. William died 1907 in Beaumont, Texas.[419]

ISSUE:

+ 1430. m   i.   **Elzie A. Nash**, born 25 Aug 1875 <See pg. 139>.

1433. m   ii.   **Samuel Esten Wilson Nash**, born 4 Jan 1878.

1434. f   iii. **Alice Nash**, born 4 Jul 1879. She married **Earnest Silsbee**. Earnest died 1918.

1435. f   iv.   **Sarah Nash**, born 1882.

+ 1436. m   v.   **William Clark Nash, II**, born 9 Feb 1884, died 1951 <See pg. 139>.

1442. f   vi.   **Kate Nash**, born 12 Dec 1886.

- - - - - - - - - -

---

[419] Wilson, Cornelia, "Family History", (accessed Jul 28, 2005). Ingmire, *San Augustine Co ..... Marriage Records*, 21.

1430. Elzie A.⁵ Nash <See pg. 138> (1429.Rosa⁴, 1261.Samuel³, 1253.Matthew², 1.Benjamin, Sr.¹) was born 25 Aug 1875 in San Augustine Co., Texas, the son of **William Clarkston "Clark" Nash** and **Rosa St. Clair Maria Wilson**. He married **Jennie** _____. She was born 1882 in Mississippi.

ISSUE:
1431. m   i.   **Albert Nash**, born 1902 in Texas, died 1933.
1432. m   ii.   **George Nash**, born 1908 in Texas, died before 1969.

- - - - - - - - - - -

1436. William Clark⁵ Nash, II <See pg. 138> (1429.Rosa⁴, 1261.Samuel³, 1253.Matthew², 1.Benjamin, Sr.¹) was born 9 Feb 1884 in Nacogdoches, Texas, the son of **William Clarkston "Clark" Nash** and **Rosa St. Clair Maria Wilson**. William, II died 1951. He married **Nora Bell Neal**. She was born 1895. Nora died 1974.

ISSUE:
+ 1437. f   i.   **Mary Estes Nash**.

- - - - - - - - - - -

1437. Mary Estes⁶ Nash (1436.William, II⁵, 1429.Rosa⁴, 1261.Samuel³, 1253.Matthew², 1.Benjamin, Sr.¹). She was the daughter of **William Clark Nash, II** and **Nora Bell Neal**. She married _____ **Edwards** 12 Jan 1904 in Nashville, Tennessee.

ISSUE:
1438. m   i.   **William Richard Edwards**.
1439. m   ii.   **Steven Alan Edwards**.
1440. f   iii.   **Nora Isabelle Edwards**.
1441. m   iv.   **Clark Nash Edwards**.

- - - - - - - - - - -

1443. Courtney Jennetta⁴ Wilson <See pg. 115> (1261.Samuel³, 1253.Matthew², 1.Benjamin, Sr.¹) was born 27 Feb 1857 in San Augustine Co., Texas, the daughter of **Samuel Wilson** and **Cornelia Williamson McLaurine**. She married (1) **Bonneau Brodnax** Nov 1873 in San Augustine Co. Bonneau died Apr 1883 in San Augustine Co. [420]

ISSUE:
1444. f   i.   **Pearl Brodnax**, born 1874, died 1876.
1445. f   ii.   **Edna Cordelia Brodnax**, born 27 Jan 1877.
1446. f   iii.   **Mary Olive Brodnax**, born 17 Feb 1879.
1447. m   iv.   **Leslie Brodnax**, born 18 Mar 1882.

---

[420] Wilson, Cornelia, "Family History", (accessed Jul 28, 2005). Ingmire, *San Augustine Co ... Marriage Records*, 20.

Courtney married (2) **James B. Johnson** 13 Jun 1888.

- - - - - - - - - - -

1449. Eglantine Cornelia[4] **Wilson** <See pg. 115> (1261.Samuel[3],
1253.Matthew[2], 1.Benjamin, Sr.[1]) was born 14 Feb 1861 in San Augustine
Co., Texas, the daughter of **Samuel Wilson** and **Cornelia Williamson
McLaurine**. Eglantine died 28 Sep 1938 in Dallas, Texas. She married (1)
Samuel B. Beckham 20 Dec 1877 in San Augustine Co. He was born Jan
1853 in Alabama.[421]

ISSUE:
- 1450. m   i.   **Edwin Leon Beckham**, born 26 Jan 1879.
- + 1451. m   ii.   **Samuel Esten Beckham**, born 29 Jan 1881.
- 1455. m iii.   **Addison Earnest Beckham**, born 18 Jan 1884 in
Nacogdoches, Texas.
- + 1456. f   iv.   **May Forest Beckham**, born 1 Aug 1888, died after 6 Aug
1978.
- 1461. m   v.   **Frank Waggoner Beckham**, born 1 Aug 1888 in
Colmesneil, Tyler Co., Texas. He married **Estella**
_____. She was born 1891.

Eglantine married (2) **Thomas P. Vinson** about 1896 in Texas. He was born
1877 in Georgia.

- - - - - - - - - - -

1451. Samuel Esten[5] **Beckham** (1449.Eglantine[4], 1261.Samuel[3],
1253.Matthew[2], 1.Benjamin, Sr.[1]) was born 29 Jan 1881 in Texas, the son
of **Samuel B. Beckham** and **Eglantine Cornelia Wilson**. He married
Frances Pearl Boon. She was born 1 Nov 1882 in Queen City, Cass Co.,
Texas. Frances died 11 May 1975.

ISSUE:
- 1452. f   i.   **Winnifred Beckham**, born in Lufkin, Angelina Co., Texas,
died 1939.
- 1453. f   ii.   **Lottie W. Beckham**, born 1907 in Lufkin. She married
_____ **Hook**.
- 1454. f iii.   **Emma M. Beckham**, born 1909 in Lufkin.

- - - - - - - - - - -

1456. May Forest[5] **Beckham** (1449.Eglantine[4], 1261.Samuel[3],
1253.Matthew[2], 1.Benjamin, Sr.[1]) was born 1 Aug 1888 in Colmesneil,
Tyler Co., Texas, the daughter of **Samuel B. Beckham** and **Eglantine**

---

[421] Wilson, Cornelia, "Family History", (accessed Jul 28, 2005). Ingmire, *San
Augustine Co ... Marriage Records*, 23.

Cornelia Wilson. May died after 6 Aug 1978 in Lexington, Kentucky. She married **Grover C. Bridger**. He was born 1884.
ISSUE:
+ 1457. m   i.   **Grover Leon Bridger**, born 11 Jul 1911, died Nov 1978.

- - - - - - - - - - -

1457. Grover Leon⁶ Bridger (1456.May⁵, 1449.Eglantine⁴, 1261.Samuel³, 1253.Matthew², 1.Benjamin, Sr.¹) was born 11 Jul 1911 in Tennessee, the son of **Grover C. Bridger** and **May Forest Beckham**. Grover died Nov 1978 in Atlanta, Georgia. He married **Elizabeth Lou Everett**. She was born 12 Sep 1914. Elizabeth died Apr 1984 in Lexington, Kentucky.
ISSUE:
1458. f   i.   **Carolyn Bridger**.
1459. f   ii.   **Susan Bridger**.
1460. f   iii. **Elizabeth Bridger**.

- - - - - - - - - - -

1462. Benjamin³ Wilson <See pg. 112> (1253.Matthew², 1.Benjamin, Sr.¹) was born 8 Jun 1812 at "Barter Hill", Cumberland Co., Virginia, the son of **Matthew Wilson** and **Elizabeth "Betsy" Trent**.[422] Benjamin died 14 Aug 1900 in Texas.[423] He married (1) **Mary Brown** before 1840 possibly in Missouri. Mary died before 25 Sep 1840 probably in Grand Pass, Missouri. Benjamin married (2) **Elizabeth James K. Polk "Lizzie" Edwards** 5 Feb 1856 probably in Shelby Co., Texas. She was born 9 Jan 1841 in Shelby Co., the daughter of **John E. Edwards** and **Julia Coleman**. Elizabeth died 21 Jul 1875 in Shelby Co.[424]
ISSUE:
1463. f   i.   **Julia Elizabeth Wilson**, born 16 Dec 1856, died 29 Sep 1857.
1464. m   ii.   **Benjamin Wilson**, born 19 Aug 1860, died 14 Aug 1869, and was buried in East Hamilton, Shelby Co., Texas. [425]
1465. f   iii. **Leonora Wilson**, born 19 Jul 1863. She married _____ **Lawrence**.

---

[422] Nash family, *Papers, 1734-1889.*

[423] A letter written by his son 13 Feb 1899 says "Papa's health is good". Wilson, Eloise. Papers of Eloise Wilson. Bivona, *Ancestors of Brian & Melissa Bivona*, (accessed 24 Apr 2005).

[424] McLean, *Wilson Family*, 11. McLean was given incorrect information about Benjamin's wives. Martin and Johnson, *Brooks Manuscript, Descendants of John Edwards*, 175-195, 248-251. Wilson, Cornelia, "Family History", (accessed Jul 28, 2005).

[425] Sanders, *Our Dead,* 300.

1466. f   iv.   **Sarah Inez "Queen" Wilson**, born 15 Jan 1866. She married **W. Vessie Carraway** 16 Apr 1884.[426]

1467. f   v.   **Rowena Wilson**, born 11 Apr 1868. She married **Jefferson Hicks** Nov 1888. He was born 30 Jun 1858. Jefferson died 20 Feb 1933. Rowena died after 1932.[427]

1468. m vi.   **Willis Alexander Wilson**, born 25 May 1870. He married (1) **Addie Florie Nethery** 18 Sep 1897 in Shelby Co., Texas.[428] She was born 29 Dec 1874, the daughter of **Alexander Matthew Nethery** and **Mary Cornelia Swindall**. Addie died 30 Apr 1900 probably in Shelby Co., Texas.[429] Willis married (2) **Lydia** _____ 7 Jan 1918. Lydia also married (1) **Ed Hicks**. Lydia died after 1932. Willis lost his right arm in an accident in his father's gin. In a letter to kin in 1898 he wrote, "do not miss my arm so much as I thought I would." Willis died 11 Mar 1932 in Harlingen, Texas.[430]

+ 1469. f vii.   **Elizabeth Edwards "Lizzie" Wilson**, born 9 Dec 1872, died 14 Apr 1963.

Benjamin's brother **Samuel** wrote him a letter 25 Sep 1840 from Cumberland Co., Virginia to Grand Pass, Missouri giving sympathy for his loss, evidently the death of his wife Mary. **Bettie**, a sister visiting in Missouri wrote to him in Cumberland Co. in July 1842.[431]

In the 1850 census of Shelby Co., Texas, he is listed with his youngest brother. He is shown with his family in that county's 1870 and 1880 censuses.

- - - - - - - - - -

1469. Elizabeth Edwards "Lizzie"⁴ Wilson (1462.Benjamin³, 1253.Matthew², 1.Benjamin, Sr.¹) was born 9 Dec 1872, the daughter of **Benjamin Wilson** and **Elizabeth James K. Polk "Lizzie" Edwards**. Elizabeth died 14 Apr 1963 in Shreveport, Caddo Parish, Louisiana. She

---

[426] Sanders, *Marriage Records ... Shelby Co* TX, 220.

[427] DRT Daughters of the Republic of Texas, 268.

[428] Sanders, *Marriage Records ... Shelby Co* TX, 230.

[429] Nethery, (accessed 4 Mar 2006). Sanders, *Our Dead,* 300.

[430] Notes from Martha (Witten) Johnson. 14 Dec 1898 letter in Wilson, Eloise. Papers of Eloise Wilson. Obituary. *Center TX Daily News,* Mar 16, 1932.

[431] Martin and Johnson, *Brooks Manuscript, Descendants of John Edwards,* 177-180, 182-185.

married (1) **Herd McDonald Reeves** 2 Dec 1892 in Shelby Co., Texas;[432] they divorced.

ISSUE:

1470. f   i.   **Sybil Reeves**. She married **R. F. Williams**.[433]
1471. m   ii.   **Powell Reeves**.

Elizabeth married (2) **Henry W. Hedgecock** 1923 in San Augustine, Texas.

- - - - - - - - - - -

1472. Maria Alexandria[3] Wilson <See pg. 112> (1253.Matthew[2], 1.Benjamin, Sr.[1]) was born 17 Jan 1814 at "Barter Hill", Cumberland Co., Virginia, the daughter of **Matthew Wilson** and **Elizabeth "Betsy" Trent**.[434] Maria died 10 Jun 1879 in Prairieville, Kaufman Co., Texas. She married **Carter Harrison Trent** 7 May 1834 at "Barter Hill". He was born 13 Dec 1804 at "Auburn", Cumberland Co., Virginia, the son of **Stephen Woodson Trent** and **Elizabeth Bassett Coupland**. Carter died 26 Mar 1885 in Athens, Texas.[435]

ISSUE:

1473. m   i.   **Willis W. Trent**, born 1835 at "Auburn", Cumberland Co., Virginia.
+ 1474. m ii.   **Joseph H. Trent**, born 1839, died 5 Aug 1876 <See pg. 144>.
1475. m   iii.   **Stephen W. Trent**, born 1841 at "Auburn".
1476. f   iv.   **Ann E. Trent**, born 1843 at "Auburn". She married **George Jones**, probably in Missouri.
+ 1477. f   v.   **Elizabeth C. Trent**, born 1845 <See pg. 144>.
1479. m   vi.   **Carter H. Trent**, born 1847 at "Auburn".
1480. m   vii.   **Goodridge A. Trent**, born Jan 1850 at "Auburn".
1481. m viii.   **Carter Trent**.
1482. m   ix.   **Edward Alexander Trent**, born after 1851.
1483. f   x.   **Virginia Carol Trent**.

The family, showing seven children, is shown in the 1850 Cumberland Co., Virginia, census. The Virginia home was sold in 1851 and the family may have moved to Missouri. By 1875 they were living in Prairieville, Texas, helping their son and grandson; their daughter-in-law died soon after the

---

[432] Sanders, *Marriage Records ... Shelby Co TX*, 220.

[433] Wilson, Eloise. Papers of Eloise Wilson. Martin and Johnson, *Brooks Manuscript, Descendants of John Edwards*, 176, 248.

[434] Nash family, *Papers, 1734-1889*.

[435] Trent Family Bible Record, Accession 25300, LVA. Elliott, *Marriages, Cumberland Co. VA*, 130. McLean, *Wilson Family*, 11.

birth of her baby. The baby died soon after.

In a letter written in 1876 by Maria to her sister in Longview, Texas, she spoke of a daughter Nannie in Missouri wanting her help with a baby expected soon. Maria's sister wrote in 1880 of being "all that is left of 4 daughters". Maria and Carter's daughter Betty Bond wrote in 1885 of her father's death.[436]

- - - - - - - - - - -

1474. Joseph H.[4] Trent <See pg. 143> (1472.Maria[3], 1253.Matthew[2], 1.Benjamin, Sr.[1]) was born 1839 at "Auburn", Cumberland Co., Virginia, the son of **Carter Harrison Trent** and **Maria Alexandria Wilson**. Joseph died 5 Aug 1876 in Texas, and was buried in Walnut Grove Cemetery, Gregg Co., Texas.[437] He married **Elizabeth Trent Wilson (See number 63 - pg. 17)** 29 Jan 1874 in Rusk Co., Texas. She was born 10 Nov 1848 in Marshall Co., Mississippi, the daughter of **Willis Wilson** and **Mary Anna Wilson**.

ISSUE:

64. m   i. **William Henry Trent**, born 21 Dec 1874 in Prairieville, Kaufman Co., Texas, died there 9 Jul 1875, and was buried in Walnut Grove Cemetery.

- - - - - - - - - - -

1477. Elizabeth C.[4] Trent <See pg. 143> (1472.Maria[3], 1253.Matthew[2], 1.Benjamin, Sr.[1]) was born 1845 at "Auburn", Cumberland Co., Virginia, the daughter of **Carter Harrison Trent** and **Maria Alexandria Wilson**. She married **Dr. John L. Bond** before 19 Jan 1876 probably in Kaufman Co., Texas.[438]

ISSUE:

1478. m   i. **Judge John L. Bond**.

- - - - - - - - - - -

1484. Elizabeth Trent "Bettie"[3] Wilson <See pg. 112> (1253.Matthew[2], 1.Benjamin, Sr.[1]) was born 27 Feb 1815 at "Barter Hill", Cumberland Co., Virginia, the daughter of **Matthew Wilson** and **Elizabeth "Betsy" Trent**.[439] Elizabeth died 27 May 1886 in Longview, Gregg Co., Texas, and

---

[436] Wilson, Eloise. Papers of Eloise Wilson. Finley, John M., Family history research.

[437] Gregg Co. Gen. Soc., *Cemeteries*, Walnut Grove, 3:189.

[438] Carlton, "Trent Family", 4.

[439] Nash family, *Papers, 1734-1889*.

was buried in Walnut Grove Cemetery, Gregg Co., Texas.[440]   She married **Phillips Alston** 26 Mar 1878 in Gregg Co.[441] Phillips died before 3 Jun 1879.

Elizabeth had 1 stepchild:

+ 1485. m   i.   _____ **Alston** <See pg. 146>.

Bettie wrote a letter from Pettys, Missouri, in 1842 after a visit with her sister Anne and others planning her return home to Virginia soon "if the watter is not very low".[442] In 1864 her namesake niece, **Elizabeth Trent "Trent" Wilson**, wrote from "Bonbrook", her grandparents home in Cumberland Co., Virginia, to her aunt Bettie in Boonville, Missouri, saying her mother had died and that her father was in poor health. "I write to beg you to come back to live with us."[443]

Bettie contacted **Edward Bates**, the Attorney General in the cabinet of **Abraham Lincoln**. In his diary he wrote, "Oct 6 .... Miss Eliz 'th. T. Wilson (called Betty) of Boonville Mo. called to get my aid to procure a pass to go into Va. Her Sister, (wife of Willis Wilson of Cumberland Cy Va.) is lately dead, leaving several Orphan children, and she is urged by the family to go and take care of them - passes are refused just now, but I hope to make out hers to be an exceptional case. She is staying with us till it can be known whether or no she can go. Sunday the 9th. I got her pass, from the Prest. direct, as a special favor, and she started in the mail boat, at 3. p. m. better accomodated than I had hoped."[444]

> "Allow the bearer, Miss Elizabeth T. Wilson, to pass to our lines with transportation thereto, and ordinary baggage through the lines Southward, A. Lincoln, Oct. 7, 1864"[445]

The children's father, Willis Wilson, died 1 Dec 1865 at "Bonbrook". (**See pg. 15**). In his will, he asked that his brother be appointed guardian of his children and that he erect "a comfortable dwelling place ..... on my estate in Texas" (Walnut Grove in Rusk/Gregg Co., Texas). After the war, Bettie, the aunt on their mother's side, and **William**, the uncle on their father's side, took the children back to Texas. Bettie wrote to William from Walnut

---

[440] Gregg Co. Gen. Soc., *Cemeteries*, Walnut Grove, 3:189.

[441] Ruff, *Gregg Co. TX Marriage Licenses*, B:130.

[442] Martin and Johnson, *Brooks Manuscript, Descendants of John Edwards*, 182.

[443] Letter 29 Jul 1864, Finley, John M., Family history research.

[444] Beale, *Diary of Edward Bates*, 416-7.

[445] Robert A. Siegel Auction Galleries, Inc. (accessed 10 Jan 2006).

Grove in 1868 giving him the status of things in his absence. He was evidently back in, Virginia to tend to some business. The uncle, aunt, and children are shown in the 1870 Rusk Co., Texas, census.

In a letter dated 3 Jun 1879, Bettie spoke of "my sainted husband in Heaven".[446] She is shown in the 1880 Gregg Co., Texas, census with her step-grandson. In 1878 she deeded land to her nieces and in her will named the youngest niece and her step-grandsons.[447]

- - - - - - - - - -

1485. _____ Alston <See pg. 145> (stepchild of 1484.Elizabeth[3], 1253.Matthew[2], 1.Benjamin, Sr.[1]). He was the son of Phillips Alston.
ISSUE:
1486. m   i.   **Robert Alston**.
1487. m   ii.   **Angus Alston**, born 1862.

- - - - - - - - - -

1489. Goodrich[3] Wilson <See pg. 112> (1253.Matthew[2], 1.Benjamin, Sr.[1]) was born 24 Nov 1818 at "Barter Hill", Cumberland Co., Virginia, the son of **Matthew Wilson** and **Elizabeth "Betsy" Trent**.[448] Goodrich died 10 Jun 1890 in Blackburn, Missouri, and was buried in the cemetery there.[449] He married **Ellen West Drane** in 1869 probably in Missouri. She was born in Frederick Co., Maryland. Ellen died 1 Jun 1917 in Phoenix, Arizona at her daughter's home. [450]
ISSUE:
1490. f   i.   **Mary Goodrich Wilson**, born 18 Oct 1870, died 31 Aug 1891, and was buried in Blackburn Cemetery, Missouri.
+ 1491. m   ii.   **Richard Drane Wilson**, born about 1872, died 1912 <See pg. 147>.
+ 1500. f   iii. **Eleanora Wilson**, born 8 Feb 1875 <See pg. 148>.

Goodrich is shown in the 1850 Cumberland Co., Virginia, census with his mother and sister. He is shown having interest in "Somerset" in 1842 and

---

[446] Letters 16 Jun 1868, 3 Jun 1879, Finley, John M., Family history research.

[447] Gregg Co. TX Deed Book D:419, Probate Minutes C:278-9 (File #163).

[448] Nash family, *Papers, 1734-1889*.

[449] 1997 letter to John Finley from Joe Auer gave the inscription for Goodrich and his daughter.

[450] McLean, *Wilson Family*, 11-13.

1847, and he sold "Barter Hill" in 1859.[451]

By 15 Aug 1859 a letter from kin shows Goodrich and his sister living in Boonville, Missouri, and in 1874 he wrote a letter from Blackburn to a brother in Texas about crops and financial affairs.[452]

- - - - - - - - - -

1491. Dr. Richard Drane[4] Wilson <See pg. 146> (1489.Goodrich[3], 1253.Matthew[2], 1.Benjamin, Sr.[1]) was born about 1872, the son of **Goodrich Wilson** and **Ellen West Drane**. He died 1912 in Phoenix, Arizona. He married **Rachel DePoorter** 8 Sep 1898 in New Orleans, Louisiana, where Rachel died.
                    ISSUE:
+ 1492. f   i.   **Rose Marie Wilson,** born 4 Nov 1899.
+ 1498. m   ii.   **Joseph Goodrich Wilson,** born 20 Jun 1903 <See pg. 148>.

- - - - - - - - - -

1492. Rose Marie[5] Wilson (1491.Richard[4], 1489.Goodrich[3], 1253.Matthew[2], 1.Benjamin, Sr.[1]) was born 4 Nov 1899 in New Orleans, Louisiana, the daughter of **Richard Drane Wilson** and **Rachel DePoorter**. She married **Francis A. Comerford** 10 Sep 1918 in New Orleans.
                    ISSUE:
+ 1493. f   i.   **Rosemarie Jack Comerford,** born 4 Aug 1920.
+ 1495. f   ii.   **Frances Ellen Comerford,** born 27 Sep 1921.

- - - - - - - - - -

1493. Rosemarie Jack[6] Comerford (1492.Rose[5], 1491.Richard[4], 1489.Goodrich[3], 1253.Matthew[2], 1.Benjamin, Sr.[1]) was born 4 Aug 1920 probably in New Orleans, Louisiana, the daughter of **Francis A. Comerford** and **Rose Marie Wilson**. She married **Arthur De Pra Guy** an attorney at law in Los Angeles CA.
                    ISSUE:
  1494. f   i.   **Malissa De Pra Guy,** born 28 Jan 1948 probably in Los Angeles, California.

- - - - - - - - - -

1495. Frances Ellen[6] Comerford (1492.Rose[5], 1491.Richard[4], 1489.Goodrich[3], 1253.Matthew[2], 1.Benjamin, Sr.[1]) was born 27 Sep 1921, the daughter of **Francis A. Comerford** and **Rose Marie Wilson**. She

---

[451] Cumberland Co. VA Will Book 10:319, Deed Books 26:510-1, 28:667-8.

[452] Letter 15 Aug 1859, Finley, John M., Family history research. Letter 7 Oct 1874, Martin and Johnson, *Brooks Manuscript, Descendants of John Edwards*, 186.

married **John Synon Roche** 10 May 1941 in Los Angeles, California.
ISSUE:
1496. f   i.   **Eldridge Ellen Roche**, born 19 Apr 1942 probably in Los Angeles Co., California.
1497. m   ii.   **John Francis Roche**, born 21 Oct 1944 probably in Los Angeles Co.

- - - - - - - - - - -

1498. Joseph Goodrich[5] Wilson <See pg. 147> (1491.Richard[4], 1489.Goodrich[3], 1253.Matthew[2], 1.Benjamin, Sr.[1]) was born 20 Jun 1903 probably in New Orleans, Louisiana, the son of **Richard Drane Wilson** and **Rachel DePoorter**. He married **Lillian Wright** 1923.
ISSUE:
1499. f   i.   **Rose Marie Wilson**, born 1925.

- - - - - - - - - - -

1500. Eleanora[4] Wilson <See pg. 146> (1489.Goodrich[3], 1253.Matthew[2], 1.Benjamin, Sr.[1]) was born 8 Feb 1875, the daughter of **Goodrich Wilson** and **Ellen West Drane**. Eleanora died probably in Tucson, Arizona. She married **Chalmers Barbour Wood** of Washington DC 24 Nov 1896. He died in 1915 probably in Phoenix AZ.[453]
ISSUE:
+ 1501. m   i.   **Wilson Barbour Wood**, born 30 Jan 1898.
1507. f   ii.   **Mary Adele Wood**, born 3 Jan 1901.
+ 1508. f   iii.   **Helen West Wood**, born 21 Oct 1902 <See pg. 149>.

- - - - - - - - - - -

1501. Col. Wilson Barbour[5] Wood (1500.Eleanora[4], 1489.Goodrich[3], 1253.Matthew[2], 1.Benjamin, Sr.[1]) was born 30 Jan 1898, the son of **Chalmers Barbour Wood** and **Eleanora Wilson**. He married **Effie Davey** 15 Jun 1921 in Tucson, Arizona.
ISSUE:
+ 1502. m   i.   **Edward Chalmers Wood**, born 30 Apr 1923.
1505. m   ii.   **Thomas Davey Wood**, born 18 Jan 1826. He married **Shulamith Appel** 1 Jun 1947.
1506. f   iii.   **Kathleen Marie Wood**, born 27 Apr 1930.

- - - - - - - - - - -

1502. Edward Chalmers[6] Wood (1501.Wilson[5], 1500.Eleanora[4], 1489.Goodrich[3], 1253.Matthew[2], 1.Benjamin, Sr.[1]) was born 30 Apr 1923, the son of **Wilson Barbour Wood** and **Effie Davey**. He married **Victoria**

---

[453] McLean, *Wilson Family*, 12-13.

Doan 7 Nov 1943.
ISSUE:
1503. m   i.   **Edward Chalmers Wood, Jr.**, born 7 Nov 1944.
1504. f   ii. **Leslie Teresa Wood**, born 7 Nov 1948.

- - - - - - - - - -

1508. Helen West[5] Wood <See pg. 148> (1500.Eleanora[4], 1489.Goodrich[3], 1253.Matthew[2], 1.Benjamin, Sr.[1]) was born 21 Oct 1902, the daughter of **Chalmers Barbour Wood** and **Eleanora Wilson**. She married **Walter C. Roediger** 3 Sep 1924.[454]
ISSUE:
1509. m   i.   **Walter C. Roediger, Jr.**, born 7 Mar 1926.
1510. m   ii. **Robert Gordon Roediger**, born 14 Feb 1931.
1511. f   iii. **Margaret Jean Roediger**, born 4 Jul 1938.

- - - - - - - - - -

1512. Edward[3] Wilson <See pg. 113> (1253.Matthew[2], 1.Benjamin, Sr.[1]) was born 26 Aug 1820 at "Barter Hill", Cumberland Co., Virginia, the son of **Matthew Wilson** and **Elizabeth "Betsy" Trent**.[455] Edward died Aug 1893 at "Mill View", Cumberland Co., Virginia, and was buried at "Barter Hill". He married (1) **Sarah Linton Powell** 1852. She was born about 1830 in Virginia. Sarah died after Aug 1870.[456]
ISSUE:
1513. f   i.   **Mary Wilson**, born 1853 at "Somerset", Cumberland Co., Virginia, died 1855.
+ 1514. m ii. **Goodrich Wilson**, born 6 Mar 1855, died 3 May 1941 <See pg. 150>.
+ 1521. f iii. **Anna Maria "Annie" Wilson**, born 28 Jul 1857, died 11 Mar 1929 <See pg. 151>.
+ 1558. m iv. **William Henry Wilson**, born 28 Aug 1859, died 3 Sep 1904 <See pg. 156>.
+ 1608. f v.   **Elizabeth Trent "Lizzie" Wilson**, born 1 Dec 1862, died 24 Jun 1946 <See pg. 162>.
+ 1669. m vi. **Edward C. Wilson**, born 1 Jan 1865, died 18 Sep 1940 <See pg. 171>.
+ 1682. m vii. **Gallatin Trent Wilson**, born 10 Feb 1867, died 6 Oct 1926 <See pg. 172>.
1702. f   viii.**Affiah Catherine "Affie" Wilson**, born 19 Apr 1870 at

---
[454] McLean, *Wilson Family*, 13.
[455] Nash family, *Papers, 1734-1889*.
[456] McLean, *Wilson Family*, 14-31. Picture of Edward's grave marker at "Barter Hill" Cemetery taken by John C. Reid in 1993.

"Somerset". She married (1) **J. George Schupp** 19 Sep 1914. George died 19 Jun 1917. Affiah married (2) **M. W. Candless** 1 Oct 1919. M. W. died 4 Dec 1932. Affiah died 10 Mar 1948 in Blair, Washington Co., Nebraska.

Edward married (2) **Virginia Scott** 1872.

ISSUE:

1703. f   ix.   **Virginia "Jennie" Edmonia Wilson**, born 1873 at "Somerset", Cumberland Co., Virginia, died Aug 1898 at "Mill View", Cumberland Co., Virginia.

Edward's family is shown in the 1860, 1870, and 1880 censuses of Cumberland Co., Virginia.

He, being the only of his siblings to remain in Virginia, was appointed "Committee of Matthew Wilson" for his epileptic brother who had to be put in a hospital, the Western Lunatic Asylum in Staunton, Virginia. Evidently the income from "Somerset" was used to pay for Matthew's expenses there from 1852-1877. Edward and his siblings inherited both "Somerset" and "Barter Hill". Because of Matthew's condition, there were many legal documents involved in the ownership and sale of "Somerset". In 1890, "Somerset" was sold.[457]

A deed dated 19 Jan 1899 between Virginia Scott Wilson, widow of Edward Wilson and mother of Jennie E. Wilson deceased, and **W. H. Wilson** of Braxton Co., West Virginia, **Edward Wilson, G. T. Wilson** of Oklahoma Territory, **Annie W. Donnohue, Lizzie Pheasants** and **Affie C. Wilson** of St. Clair Co., Missouri described "Millview Farm ... owned and occupied by ... Edward Wilson, deceased".[458]

- - - - - - - - - - -

1514. Goodrich[4] Wilson <See pg. 149> (1512.Edward[3], 1253.Matthew[2], 1.Benjamin, Sr.[1]) was born 6 Mar 1855 at "Somerset", Cumberland Co., Virginia, the son of **Edward Wilson** and **Sarah Linton Powell**. Goodrich died 3 May 1941 in Carpenter, Oklahoma. He married **Flora May Wells** 24 Oct 1888 probably in St. Clair Co., Missouri. Flora died 13 May 1945.[459]

ISSUE:

1515. m   i.   **Donnohue Elvin Wilson**, born 24 Sep 1890, died 12 Mar

---

[457] Cumberland Co. VA "Ended Chancery Papers, January term 1909", Chancery Order Books 1852-1872, 1872-1882, Will Book 13:547-8,682, Deed Book 36:218.

[458] Cumberland Co. VA Deed Book 38:381.

[459] McLean, *Wilson Family*, 15-16.

1898.

1516. f   ii.   **Mary Louise Wilson,** born 10 Nov 1892.
1517. f   iii. **Henry Edward Wilson,** born 8 Feb 1895, died 20 Mar 1937.
1518. m iv. **Daniel Milton Wilson,** born 4 Nov 1901.
1519. m v.   **William Homer Wilson,** born 23 Jun 1904, died 25 Aug 1904.
1520. m vi. **George Leslie Wilson,** born 20 Mar 1908.

Goodrich homesteaded near Elk City, Chester Co., Oklahoma, in 1893.

- - - - - - - - - -

1521. Anna Maria "Annie"[4] Wilson <See pg. 149> (1512.Edward[3], 1253.Matthew[2], 1.Benjamin, Sr.[1]) was born 28 Jul 1857 at "Somerset", Cumberland Co., Virginia, the daughter of **Edward Wilson** and **Sarah Linton Powell.** Anna died 11 Mar 1929 in Appleton City, St. Clair Co., Missouri. She married **Daniel Donnohue** 26 Dec 1877 in St. Clair Co. He was born 26 Feb 1844 in Missouri. Daniel died 8 May 1910.[460]

ISSUE:

+ 1522. m   i.   **Henry Edward "Harry" Donnohue,** born 18 Jan 1879, died 3 Jun 1948 <See pg. 152>.
  1534. f   ii.   **Sarah Linton Donnohue,** born 24 Jan 1881, died 24 Jan 1881.
  1535. m iii. **Herbert Spencer Donnohue,** born 2 Dec 1883. He married **Ida Clarkson** 24 Mar 1921.
+ 1536. m iv. **Jerome Trent Donnohue,** born 26 Dec 1887, died 7 Dec 1968 <See pg. 153>.
  1554. m v.   **Lawrence Dillard Donnohue,** born 21 Oct 1889. He married **Verda F. Samples** 5 Aug 1928 in Los Angeles, California.
  1555. m vi. **John Jay Donnohue,** born 20 Feb 1892, died 26 Jun 1918 in Paris, France.
  1556. f   vii. **Mary Affie Donnohue,** born 25 Nov 1894 in Hudson, Bates Co., Missouri. She married **Leroy Edgar "Jack" Bailey** 18 Feb 1936 in Butler, Bates Co., Missouri. He was born 12 Aug 1885. Leroy died 26 Aug 1972. Mary died 11 Dec 1961 in Appleton City, St. Clair Co., Missouri.
  1557. f   viii. **Lizzie Elnora Donnohue,** born 12 Dec 1897. She married **Arthur F. Arnold** 21 Feb 1915 in La Tour, Missouri. Arthur died in Los Angeles, California. Lizzie died in Los

---

[460] McLean, *Wilson Family*, 16-18. Additional information from Don and Barbara (Nelson) Donnohue of Appleton City MO.

Angeles.

- - - - - - - - - - -

1522. Henry Edward "Harry"⁵ Donnohue <See pg. 151> (1521.Anna⁴,
1512.Edward³, 1253.Matthew², 1.Benjamin, Sr.¹) was born 18 Jan 1879, the
son of **Daniel Donnohue** and **Anna Maria "Annie" Wilson**. Henry died
3 Jun 1948 in Denver, Colorado, and was buried in Appleton City, St.
Claire Co., Missouri. He married **Etta Mable Deyo** 6 Oct 1902.
ISSUE:
  1523. f   i. **Grace Vivian Donnohue**, born 8 Nov 1903, died 24 Jan
          1904.
+ 1524. f ii. **Myrtle Florence Donnohue**, born 12 Mar 1905, died
          5 Dec 1988.
+ 1527. f iii. **Henrietta May Donnohue**, born 22 May 1910.
  1529. m iv. **Jerome Daniel Donnohue**, born 18 Sep 1911, died 23 Oct
          1928.
+ 1530. f v. **Mabel Florence Donnohue**, born 12 Oct 1914 <See pg. 153>.
  1532. f vi. **Olive Marie Donnohue**, born 23 Aug 1913, died 30 Nov
          1913.
  1533. f vii. **Martha Donnohue**, born 6 Oct 1915, died 27 Oct 1915.

- - - - - - - - - - -

1524. Myrtle Florence⁶ Donnohue (1522.Henry⁵, 1521.Anna⁴,
1512.Edward³, 1253.Matthew², 1.Benjamin, Sr.¹) was born 12 Mar 1905,
the daughter of **Henry Edward "Harry" Donnohue** and **Etta Mable
Deyo**. Myrtle died 5 Dec 1988, and was buried in Mason, Michigan. She
married **Clifford B. Douglas** 2 Jun 1927 in Mason.
ISSUE:
  1525. m i. **Burnet Donnohue Douglas**, born 9 Sep 1928 in South
          Bend, Indiana.
  1526. m ii. **Daniel Frank Douglas**, born 30 Jul 1930 in South Bend.

- - - - - - - - - - -

1527. Henrietta May⁶ Donnohue (1522.Henry⁵, 1521.Anna⁴,
1512.Edward³, 1253.Matthew², 1.Benjamin, Sr.¹) was born 22 May 1910 in
Appleton City, St. Clair Co., Missouri, the daughter of **Henry Edward
"Harry" Donnohue** and **Etta Mable Deyo**. She married **Robert Angelo
Cito** 11 Jul 1941.
ISSUE:
  1528. m i. **Robert Angelo Cito, Jr.**, born 30 Aug 1942 in Denver,
          Colorado.

- - - - - - - - - - -

1530. Mabel Florence⁶ Donnohue <See pg. 152> (1522.Henry⁵, 1521.Anna⁴, 1512.Edward³, 1253.Matthew², 1.Benjamin, Sr.¹) was born 12 Oct 1914 in Appleton City, St. Clair Co., Missouri, the daughter of **Henry Edward "Harry" Donnohue** and **Etta Mable Deyo**. She married **Rex Asquith** 27 Jun 1940 in Mason, Michigan. He was born in Stockbridge, Michigan.

ISSUE:

1531. m   i.   **Don Gaylord Asquith**, born 23 May 1947 in Stockbridge.

- - - - - - - - - - -

1536. Jerome Trent⁵ Donnohue <See pg. 151> (1521.Anna⁴, 1512.Edward³, 1253.Matthew², 1.Benjamin, Sr.¹) was born 26 Dec 1887 in Hudson, Bates Co., Missouri, the son of **Daniel Donnohue** and **Anna Maria "Annie" Wilson**. Jerome died 7 Dec 1968 in El Dorado Springs, Missouri, and was buried in Appleton City, St. Clair Co., Missouri. He married **Minnie Helen Deller** 25 Mar 1912 in Rich Hill, Bates Co., Missouri. She was born 17 Jul 1890 in Rich Hill, the daughter of **Henry Deller** and **Agnes Ramage**. Minnie died 2 Oct 1973 in Appleton City and was buried there.⁴⁶¹

ISSUE:

+ 1537. m   i.   **Vern Guy Donnohue**, born 27 Jan 1913, died 21 Feb 1991.
+ 1540. m   ii.   **Harry Owen Donnohue**, born 21 Feb 1914 <See pg. 154>.
+ 1546. m   iii.   **Albert Jerome Donnohue**, born 22 Oct 1915, died 3 Mar 1996 <See pg. 154>.

- - - - - - - - - - -

1537. Vern Guy⁶ Donnohue (1536.Jerome⁵, 1521.Anna⁴, 1512.Edward³, 1253.Matthew², 1.Benjamin, Sr.¹) was born 27 Jan 1913 in Bates Co., Missouri, the son of **Jerome Trent Donnohue** and **Minnie Helen Deller**. Vern died 21 Feb 1991 in Appleton City, St. Clair Co., Missouri, and was buried there. He married (1) **Hazel Marie Hines** 17 Apr 1938 in Kansas City, Jackson Co., Missouri. She was born 1914. Hazel died 1979 in McAlister, Oklahoma, and was buried in Appleton City.

ISSUE:

+ 1538. f   i.   **Janice K. Donnohue.**

Vern married (2) **Ruby Della Piepmeier** 1980. She was born 1911.

- - - - - - - - - - -

1538. Janice K.⁷ Donnohue (1537.Vern⁶, 1536.Jerome⁵, 1521.Anna⁴, 1512.Edward³, 1253.Matthew², 1.Benjamin, Sr.¹). She was the daughter of **Vern Guy Donnohue** and **Hazel Marie Hines**. She married **Terry Wright**.

---

⁴⁶¹ McLean, *Wilson Family*, 17-18.

ISSUE:
1539. f   i.   **Jamie Wright**, born 10 Jun 1976.

- - - - - - - - - - -

1540. Harry Owen⁶ Donnohue <See pg. 153> (1536.Jerome⁵, 1521.Anna⁴, 1512.Edward³, 1253.Matthew², 1.Benjamin, Sr.¹) was born 21 Feb 1914 in Bates Co., Missouri, the son of **Jerome Trent Donnohue** and **Minnie Helen Deller**. He married **Julia Miller** 23 Jul 1937 in Centralia, Missouri. She was born 6 Mar 1911 in Sturgeon, Missouri, the daughter of **George Miller** and **Edna Chedester**. Julia died 17 Feb 2002.
ISSUE:
+ 1541. f   i.   **Carol Ann Donnohue**, born 2 Apr 1941.

- - - - - - - - - - -

1541. Carol Ann⁷ Donnohue (1540.Harry⁶, 1536.Jerome⁵, 1521.Anna⁴, 1512.Edward³, 1253.Matthew², 1.Benjamin, Sr.¹) was born 2 Apr 1941 in Columbia, Boone Co., Missouri, the daughter of **Harry Owen Donnohue** and **Julia Miller**. She married **Webb L. Wallace** 29 Jun 1963 in Dallas, Texas. He was born 18 Dec 1940 in Dallas, the son of **James E. Wallace** and **Rosland Lindsley**.
ISSUE:
+ 1542. f   i.   **Susan Lindsley Wallace**, born 27 Apr 1968.
  1545. m   ii.   **Mike Wallace**, born 1 Dec 1965 in Dallas. He married **Kathran Elizabeth Whitsit** 9 Aug 2004. She was born 9 Feb 1974 in Denver, Colorado.

- - - - - - - - - - -

1542. Susan Lindsley⁸ Wallace (1541.Carol⁷, 1540.Harry⁶, 1536.Jerome⁵, 1521.Anna⁴, 1512.Edward³, 1253.Matthew², 1.Benjamin, Sr.¹) was born 27 Apr 1968 in Dallas, Texas, the daughter of **Webb L. Wallace** and **Carol Ann Donnohue**. She married **Robert E. Lee** 25 Jun 1994 in Santa Fe, New Mexico.
ISSUE:
  1543. m   i.   **Webb Ryan Lee**, born 23 Sep 1997.
  1544. f   ii.   **Meaghan Alexander Lee**, born 13 May 2000.

- - - - - - - - - - -

1546. Albert Jerome⁶ Donnohue <See pg. 153> (1536.Jerome⁵, 1521.Anna⁴, 1512.Edward³, 1253.Matthew², 1.Benjamin, Sr.¹) was born 22 Oct 1915 in Bates Co., Missouri, the son of **Jerome Trent Donnohue** and **Minnie Helen Deller**. Albert died 3 Mar 1996 in Kansas City, Missouri, and was buried in Appleton City, St. Clair Co., Missouri. He married **Lucille**

Schlichtman 1 Oct 1937 in Centralia, Missouri. She was born 13 Nov 1918 in Appleton City, the daughter of **Harry C. Schlichtman** and **Viola Spencer**. Lucille died 28 Oct 2000 in Kansas City, Missouri, and was buried in Appleton City.[462]

ISSUE:

+ 1547. m   i.   **Don Trent Donnohue**, born 29 Sep 1940 <See pg. 155>.

- - - - - - - - - - -

1547. Don Trent[7] Donnohue <See pg. 155> (1546.Albert[6], 1536.Jerome[5], 1521.Anna[4], 1512.Edward[3], 1253.Matthew[2], 1.Benjamin, Sr.[1]) was born 29 Sep 1940 in Appleton City, St. Clair Co., Missouri, the son of **Albert Jerome Donnohue** and **Lucille Schlichtman**. He married **Barbara E. Nelson** 23 Dec 1965 in Raytown, Missouri. She was born 19 Mar 1942 in Hays, Ellis Co., Kansas, the daughter of **Ray E. Nelson** and **Helen Campbell**.

ISSUE:

+ 1548. m   i.   **Don Trent Donnohue, Jr.**, born 18 Mar 1969.
+ 1551. m   ii. **Matt Jerome Donnohue**, born 10 Apr 1973.

- - - - - - - - - - -

1548. Don Trent[8] Donnohue, Jr. (1547.Don[7], 1546.Albert[6], 1536.Jerome[5], 1521.Anna[4], 1512.Edward[3], 1253.Matthew[2], 1.Benjamin, Sr.[1]) was born 18 Mar 1969 in Denver, Colorado, the son of **Don Trent Donnohue** and **Barbara E. Nelson**. He married **Stephanie Read** 2 Nov 1996 in El Dorado Springs, Missouri. She was born 1 Feb 1972 in Glendale, Arizona, the daughter of **John Read** and **Carol Reeves**.

ISSUE:

1549. f   i.   **Morgan Rae Donnohue**, born 12 Jun 1999 in Clinton, Missouri.
1550. m   ii. **Lane William Donnohue**, born 27 May 2002 in Clinton.

- - - - - - - - - - -

1551. Matt Jerome[8] Donnohue (1547.Don[7], 1546.Albert[6], 1536.Jerome[5], 1521.Anna[4], 1512.Edward[3], 1253.Matthew[2], 1.Benjamin, Sr.[1]) was born 10 Apr 1973 in Englewood, Colorado, the son of **Don Trent Donnohue** and **Barbara E. Nelson**. He married **Ann Parks** 11 Oct 1997 in Eureka Springs, Arkansas. She was born 25 Feb 1975 in El Dorado Springs, Cedar Co., Missouri, the daughter of **Ronnie Parks** and **Kristine Kreissler**.

ISSUE:

1552. f   i.   **Paige Jannette Donnohue**, born 10 Mar 2000 in El Dorado Springs, Missouri.

---

[462] McLean, *Wilson Family*, 18.

1553. f   ii.   **Matti Don Charlese Donnohue**, born 6 Jul 2004 in Kansas City, Missouri.

- - - - - - - - - - -

1558. William Henry⁴ Wilson <See pg. 149> (1512.Edward³, 1253.Matthew², 1.Benjamin, Sr.¹) was born 28 Aug 1859 at "Somerset", Cumberland Co., Virginia, the son of **Edward Wilson** and **Sarah Linton Powell**. William died 3 Sep 1904 in Stanley Creek, North Carolina. He married **Sallie Ashlin** 28 Oct 1891 in Wilmington, Virginia. Sallie died 2 Apr 1947 in Fredericksburg, Virginia, and was buried in Oak Hill Cemetery, Fredericksburg Co., Virginia.[463]

ISSUE:[464]

+ 1559. f   i.   **Sarah Henderson Wilson**, born 26 Sep 1892, died 29 Jun 1984 <See pg. 157>.

  1566. f   ii.   **Mary Powell Wilson**, born 11 Apr 1894 at "Riverside", Buckingham Co., Virginia. She married **William Samuel Scott** 30 Jul 1924. William died 1947. Mary died 12 Mar 1983.

+ 1567. m   iii.   **William Stoddart Wilson**, born 20 Sep 1895, died 26 Sep 1978 <See pg. 157>.

+ 1569. m   iv.   **Edward Ashlin Wilson**, born 19 May 1898, died 12 Mar 1983 <See pg. 158>.

  1583. m   v.   **Robert Ashlin Wilson**, born 26 Jun 1900 in Stanley Creek, Gaston Co., North Carolina. He married **Mary Lewis Bailey** 4 Nov 1939. Mary died 14 May 1972. Robert died 23 Aug 1970.

+ 1584. m   vi.   **Willis Trent Wilson**, born 28 Aug 1902, died 13 Sep 1980 <See pg. 160>.

+ 1589. m   vii.   **Fielding Lewis Wilson**, born 14 Oct 1904, died 21 Jun 1965 <See pg. 160>.

Sallie also married (2) **Harry H. McLean**.

ISSUE:

1607. m   **Harry Herndon McLean**.[465]

---

[463] McLean, *Wilson Family*, 19-24. William is the person who originally gathered the data which was used as the basis of the McLean book. .

[464] Additional information from Anne (Wilson) Rowe of Fredericksburg VA, Frances (Bleight) Elliott of Williamsburg VA, and Jean (Wilson) Micklem of Hopewell VA.

[465] The author of *The Wilson Family - Somerset and Barter Hill Branch.* Charlotte NC: Observer Printing House, 1950.

- - - - - - - - - -

1559. Sarah Henderson[5] **Wilson** <See pg. 156> (1558.William[4], 1512.Edward[3], 1253.Matthew[2], 1.Benjamin, Sr.[1]) was born 26 Sep 1892 at "Riverside", Buckingham Co., Virginia, the daughter of **William Henry Wilson** and **Sallie Ashlin**. Sarah died 29 Jun 1984, and was buried at St. Paul's Church in Haymarket, Virginia. She married **Winston Carter Bleight** 16 Jun 1920. Winston died 3 May 1963 and was buried at St. Paul's Church.[466]

ISSUE:

1560. f   i.   **Sarah Ashlin Bleight**, born 19 Aug 1921. She married **Paul Scheffler** 4 Dec 1950. Paul died 1985, and was buried in Haymarket, Virginia. Sarah died 21 Feb 1984, and was buried in Haymarket.

+ 1561. f   ii.   **Frances Carter Bleight**, born 21 Nov 1925.

- - - - - - - - - -

1561. Frances Carter[6] **Bleight** (1559.Sarah[5], 1558.William[4], 1512.Edward[3], 1253.Matthew[2], 1.Benjamin, Sr.[1]) was born 21 Nov 1925, the daughter of **Winston Carter Bleight** and **Sarah Henderson Wilson**. She married **Richard Sealy Elliott** 14 Feb 1948. Richard died Jun 2004.

ISSUE:

1562. f   i.   **Sarah Carter Elliott**, born 8 Jul 1949.

+ 1563. f   ii.   **Nancy Wright Elliott**, born 2 Nov 1952.

- - - - - - - - - -

1563. Nancy Wright[7] **Elliott** (1561.Frances[6], 1559.Sarah[5], 1558.William[4], 1512.Edward[3], 1253.Matthew[2], 1.Benjamin, Sr.[1]) was born 2 Nov 1952, the daughter of **Richard Sealy Elliott** and **Frances Carter Bleight**. She married **John Webb Lesesne** 5 Jul 1980.

ISSUE:

1564. m   i.   **Brian Elliott Lesesne**, born 12 Apr 1983.

1565. f   ii.   **Sarah Bancroft Lesesne**, born 14 Sep 1985.

- - - - - - - - - -

1567. Dr. William Stoddart[5] **Wilson** <See pg. 156> (1558.William[4], 1512.Edward[3], 1253.Matthew[2], 1.Benjamin, Sr.[1]) was born 20 Sep 1895 at "Riverside", Buckingham Co., Virginia, the son of **William Henry Wilson** and **Sallie Ashlin**. William died 26 Sep 1978. He married **Virginia Wallace** 14 Oct 1922. Virginia died about 2002.

---

[466] McLean, *Wilson Family*, 22. Additional information from Frances (Bleight) Elliot of Williamsburg VA.

ISSUE:

1568. m   i.   **Warren Scott Wilson**, born 8 Aug 1936, died 25 Nov 1986, and was buried in Fredericksburg, Virginia.

- - - - - - - - - - -

1569. Edward Ashlin[5] Wilson <See pg. 156> (1558.William[4], 1512.Edward[3], 1253.Matthew[2], 1.Benjamin, Sr.[1]) was born 19 May 1898 in Sutton, West Virginia, the son of **William Henry Wilson** and **Sallie Ashlin**. Edward died 12 Mar 1983, and was buried at St. John's Church in Warsaw, Virginia. He married **Ruth Ellen Garland** 24 May 1924 in Alexandria, Virginia. Ruth died 23 May 1980, and was buried at St. John's Church.[467]

ISSUE:

+ 1570. f   i.   **Jean Garland Wilson**, born 3 Nov 1926.
+ 1577. f   ii.   **Elizabeth Warner Wilson**, born 30 Aug 1930, died 26 Apr 2005 <See pg. 159>.
+ 1580. f   iii.   **Sarah McLean Wilson**, born 26 Apr 1933, died 22 Aug 1999 <See pg. 159>.
  1582. f   iv.   **Lucy Jeffries Wilson**, born 23 Aug 1939. She married **Roger Paul Schultz** 20 Jun 1964.

- - - - - - - - - - -

1570. Jean Garland[6] Wilson (1569.Edward[5], 1558.William[4], 1512.Edward[3], 1253.Matthew[2], 1.Benjamin, Sr.[1]) was born 3 Nov 1926, the daughter of **Edward Ashlin Wilson** and **Ruth Ellen Garland**. She married **James T. Micklem**, the son of **Austen Clifton Micklem** and **Alice Trahern Cook**.

ISSUE:

  1571. m   i.   **James T. Micklem, Jr.**, born 29 Jul 1953.
+ 1572. f   ii.   **Ruth Garland Micklem**, born 1 Feb 1958.

- - - - - - - - - - -

1572. Ruth Garland[7] Micklem (1570.Jean[6], 1569.Edward[5], 1558.William[4], 1512.Edward[3], 1253.Matthew[2], 1.Benjamin, Sr.[1]) was born 1 Feb 1958, the daughter of **James T. Micklem** and **Jean Garland Wilson**. She married **Marshall Eugene Shepherd**.

ISSUE:

+ 1573. f   i.   **Suzanne Ashlin Shepherd**, born 8 Sep 1978.
+ 1575. f   ii.   **Elizabeth Garland Shepherd**, born 17 Apr 1980.

- - - - - - - - - - -

---

[467] McLean, *Wilson Family*, 23-24.

1573. Suzanne Ashlin[8] Shepherd (1572.Ruth[7], 1570.Jean[6], 1569.Edward[5], 1558.William[4], 1512.Edward[3], 1253.Matthew[2], 1.Benjamin, Sr.[1]) was born 8 Sep 1978, the daughter of **Marshall Eugene Shepherd** and **Ruth Garland Micklem**. She married **Brian McAnich**.

ISSUE:

1574. m   i.   **Oliver Miklem McAnich**, born May 2003.

- - - - - - - - - -

1575. Elizabeth Garland[8] Shepherd (1572.Ruth[7], 1570.Jean[6], 1569.Edward[5], 1558.William[4], 1512.Edward[3], 1253.Matthew[2], 1.Benjamin, Sr.[1]) was born 17 Apr 1980, the daughter of **Marshall Eugene Shepherd** and **Ruth Garland Micklem**. She married **Daniel Grillo**.

ISSUE:

1576. f   i.   **Liliana Grillo**, born 29 Oct 2002.

- - - - - - - - - -

1577. Elizabeth Warner[6] Wilson <See pg. 158> (1569.Edward[5], 1558.William[4], 1512.Edward[3], 1253.Matthew[2], 1.Benjamin, Sr.[1]) was born 30 Aug 1930, the daughter of **Edward Ashlin Wilson** and **Ruth Ellen Garland**. Elizabeth died 26 Apr 2005 in Richmond, Virginia. She married **Claude Malcom East** 30 Jan 1953. He was born 31 Aug 1920. Claude died 18 Jan 2002.

ISSUE:

+ 1578. f   i.   **Suzanne East**, born 20 Jan 1954.

- - - - - - - - - -

1578. Suzanne[7] East (1577.Elizabeth[6], 1569.Edward[5], 1558.William[4], 1512.Edward[3], 1253.Matthew[2], 1.Benjamin, Sr.[1]) was born 20 Jan 1954, the daughter of **Claude Malcom East** and **Elizabeth Warner Wilson**. She married (1) **Gregory Mansfield Holland** 20 Sep 1981.
Suzanne married (2) **James Francis Carr** 6 Aug 1988. He was born 1 Jan 1966.

ISSUE:

1579. f   i.   **Samantha Garland Carr**, born 9 Apr 1991.

- - - - - - - - - -

1580. Sarah McLean[6] Wilson <See pg. 158> (1569.Edward[5], 1558.William[4], 1512.Edward[3], 1253.Matthew[2], 1.Benjamin, Sr.[1]) was born 26 Apr 1933, the daughter of **Edward Ashlin Wilson** and **Ruth Ellen Garland**. Sarah died 22 Aug 1999, and was buried at St. John's Church in Warsaw, Virginia. She married **John Lisanick.**[468]

ISSUE:

1581. m   i. **Mark Jeffries Lisanick.**

- - - - - - - - - - -

1584. Willis Trent⁵ Wilson <See pg. 156> (1558.William⁴, 1512.Edward³,
1253.Matthew², 1.Benjamin, Sr.¹) was born 28 Aug 1902 in Stanley Creek,
Gaston Co., North Carolina, the son of **William Henry Wilson** and **Sallie
Ashlin.** Willis died 13 Sep 1980. He married **Emily Louise Lincke** 27 Oct
1934. Emily died 1983.

ISSUE:

1585. f   i. **Christine Lincke Wilson,** born 2 Apr 1938. She married
Bennie Johnson.
+ 1586. m ii. **Willis Trent Wilson, Jr.,** born 19 Apr 1941, died 16 Feb
1996.
1588. m iii. **Maurice Lincke Wilson,** born 23 Dec 1945.

- - - - - - - - - - -

1586. Willis Trent⁶ Wilson, Jr. (1584.Willis⁵, 1558.William⁴,
1512.Edward³, 1253.Matthew², 1.Benjamin, Sr.¹) was born 19 Apr 1941, the
son of **Willis Trent Wilson** and **Emily Louise Lincke.** Willis, Jr. died
16 Feb 1996. He married **Nancy** _____; they divorced.

ISSUE:

1587. f   i. **Elizabeth Wilson.**

- - - - - - - - - - -

1589. Fielding Lewis⁵ Wilson <See pg. 156> (1558.William⁴, 1512.Edward³,
1253.Matthew², 1.Benjamin, Sr.¹) was born 14 Oct 1904 in Stanley Creek,
Gaston Co., North Carolina, the son of **William Henry Wilson** and **Sallie
Ashlin.** Fielding died 21 Jun 1965. He married **Katherine McDonald
Stoffregan** 7 Nov 1931. Katherine died 9 May 1975.

ISSUE:

+ 1590. f   i. **Anne Martin Wilson,** born 31 Dec 1934.
+ 1603. m ii. **Fielding Lewis Wilson, Jr.,** born 3 Jul 1938 <See pg. 161>.

- - - - - - - - - - -

1590. Anne Martin⁶ Wilson (1589.Fielding⁵, 1558.William⁴,
1512.Edward³, 1253.Matthew², 1.Benjamin, Sr.¹) was born 31 Dec 1934,
the daughter of **Fielding Lewis Wilson** and **Katherine McDonald
Stoffregan.** She married **Josiah Pollard Rowe, III** 16 Jun 1956.

---

[468] McLean, *Wilson Family,* 23-24.

ISSUE:
+ 1591. f   i.   **Jeanette MacDonald Rowe**, born 13 Jun 1957.
+ 1595. f   ii.   **Florence Chancellor Rowe**, born 24 May 1959.
+ 1599. f   iii.   **Sallie Ashlin Rowe**, born 14 Jun 1961.
   1602. m   iv.   **Josiah Peyton Rowe**, born 28 Apr 1972. He married **Erin Elizabeth O'Neil** 28 Oct 1994.

- - - - - - - - - -

1591. Jeanette MacDonald[7] Rowe (1590.Anne[6], 1589.Fielding[5], 1558.William[4], 1512.Edward[3], 1253.Matthew[2], 1.Benjamin, Sr.[1]) was born 13 Jun 1957, the daughter of **Josiah Pollard Rowe, III** and **Anne Martin Wilson**. She married **Nicholas John Cadwallender** 21 Jan 1984.
ISSUE:
   1592. m   i.   **Jess Bradford Cadwallender**, born 21 Jan 1985.
   1593. f   ii.   **Julia Frances Cadwallender**, born 4 Oct 1986.
   1594. f   iii.   **Mary Virginia Cadwallender**, born 21 Jun 1988.

- - - - - - - - - -

1595. Florence Chancellor[7] Rowe (1590.Anne[6], 1589.Fielding[5], 1558.William[4], 1512.Edward[3], 1253.Matthew[2], 1.Benjamin, Sr.[1]) was born 24 May 1959, the daughter of **Josiah Pollard Rowe, III** and **Anne Martin Wilson**. She married **Richard John Barnick** 13 Jun 1987.
ISSUE:
   1596. m   i.   **Andrew John Barnick**, born 29 Mar 1991.
   1597. m   ii.   **Scott Wilson Barnick**, born 29 Mar 1991.
   1598. m   iii.   **George Stanley Barnick**, born 28 Nov 1997.

- - - - - - - - - -

1599. Sallie Ashlin[7] Rowe (1590.Anne[6], 1589.Fielding[5], 1558.William[4], 1512.Edward[3], 1253.Matthew[2], 1.Benjamin, Sr.[1]) was born 14 Jun 1961, the daughter of **Josiah Pollard Rowe, III** and **Anne Martin Wilson**. She married **Raymond Rohrer Roberts, Jr.** 14 Jan 1984.
ISSUE:
   1600. m   i.   **Harrison McHaney Roberts**, born 22 Oct 1987.
   1601. f   ii.   **Katherine MacDonald Roberts**, born 7 Jan 1990.

- - - - - - - - - -

1603. Fielding Lewis[6] Wilson, Jr. <See pg. 160> (1589.Fielding[5], 1558.William[4], 1512.Edward[3], 1253.Matthew[2], 1.Benjamin, Sr.[1]) was born 3 Jul 1938, the son of **Fielding Lewis Wilson** and **Katherine McDonald Stoffregan**. He married **Bettie Brewer Beckwith** 19 Jun 1959.

ISSUE:

1604. m i. **Fielding Brewer Wilson**, born 4 Jun 1970.
+ 1605. f ii. **Sarah Ashlin Wilson**, born 12 Aug 1973.

- - - - - - - - - - -

1605. Sarah Ashlin[7] Wilson (1603.Fielding, Jr.[6], 1589.Fielding[5], 1558.William[4], 1512.Edward[3], 1253.Matthew[2], 1.Benjamin, Sr.[1]) was born 12 Aug 1973, the daughter of **Fielding Lewis Wilson, Jr.** and **Bettie Brewer Beckwith**. She married **Steven Jason Harrington** 10 Oct 1998.
ISSUE:

1606. m i. **Jayden Lewis Harrington**, born 10 Jul 2003.

- - - - - - - - - - -

1608. Elizabeth Trent "Lizzie"[4] Wilson <See pg. 149> (1512.Edward[3], 1253.Matthew[2], 1.Benjamin, Sr.[1]) was born 1 Dec 1862 in Cumberland Co., Virginia, the daughter of **Edward Wilson** and **Sarah Linton Powell**. Elizabeth died 24 Jun 1946 in Kirksville, Adair Co., Missouri, and was buried in Appleton City Cemetery, St. Clair Co., Missouri. She married (1) **Thomas Jefferson Pheasant** 9 Dec 1886 in Missouri. He was born 3 Sep 1856 in Deputy, Jefferson Co., Indiana, the son of **Charles Edward Pheasant** and **Emma Roberts**. Thomas died 22 Mar 1915 in Hudson, Bates Co., Missouri, and was buried in Appleton City Cemetery.[469]
ISSUE:

1609. f i. **Dr. Anna Lena Pheasant**, born 20 Jul 1888 in Hudson, Bates Co., Missouri. She married **Samuel Clay Mauck** 9 Aug 1911 in Hudson. He was born 21 Jul 1882 in Missouri. He was the son of **Julius Mauck** and **Ella** _____. Samuel died 18 Aug 1923 in Missouri, and was buried in Appleton City Cemetery, St. Clair Co., Missouri. Anna died 19 Jan 1982 in Lee's Summit, Jackson Co., Missouri, and was buried in Appleton City Cemetery.

+ 1610. m ii. **Bruce Thornton Pheasant**, born 12 Mar 1890, died 21 Jul 1985 <See pg. 163>.

+ 1625. f iii. **Mary Estella Pheasant**, born 25 Feb 1892, died 24 Aug 1978 <See pg. 165>.

1654. m iv. **Charles Edward Pheasant**, born 18 Sep 1895 in Hudson, Bates Co., Missouri. He married **Alma Margaret Manhalter** 1 Jun 1926 in Casper, Natrona Co., Wyoming. Charles died 10 Apr 1927 in Casper.

+ 1655. f v. **Elizabeth Wilson Pheasant**, born 23 Jul 1900, died 12 Feb

---

[469] McLean, *Wilson Family*, 24-27. Additional information from John C. Reid of Peculiar MO.

1988 <See pg. 169>.

+ 1657. m   vi.   **Thomas DeWitt Pheasant**, born 6 Mar 1902, died 1 Nov 1995 <See pg. 169>.

Elizabeth married (2) **Sylvester H. Horton** 7 Jun 1925 in El Dorado Springs, Cedar Co., Missouri. He was born 29 Dec 1860. Sylvester died 2 Jul 1926 in Otwell, Pike Co., Indiana, and was buried in the IOOF Cemetery in Otwell.

- - - - - - - - - -

1610. Bruce Thornton[5] Pheasant <See pg. 162> (1608.Elizabeth[4], 1512.Edward[3], 1253.Matthew[2], 1.Benjamin, Sr.[1]) was born 12 Mar 1890 in Hudson, Bates Co., Missouri, the son of **Thomas Jefferson Pheasant** and **Elizabeth Trent "Lizzie" Wilson**. Bruce died 21 Jul 1985 in Buffalo, Johnson Co., Wyoming, and was buried in Willow Grove Cemetery there. He married (1) **Georgia Grace Harris** 11 Jun 1919. She was born 1 Jun 1892 in Mattoon, Coles Co., Illinois. Georgia died 2 Feb 1963 in Thermopolis, Hot Springs Co., Wyoming, and was buried in Willow Grove Cemetery.[470]

ISSUE:

+ 1611. f   i.   **Josephine Davis Pheasant**, born 12 Mar 1920, died Aug 1985.
+ 1615. m   ii.   **Edward Bruce Pheasant**, born 18 Aug 1921, died 22 Oct 1966 <See pg. 164>.
+ 1623. f   iii.   **Helen Mae Pheasant**, born 7 Jan 1925, died Nov 1979 <See pg. 164>.

Bruce married (2) **Carrie East** after 1964 in Louisville, Kentucky. She was born 28 Oct 1891 in Appleton City, St. Clair Co., Missouri. Carrie died 21 Oct 1980 in Buffalo, Johnson Co., Wyoming, and was buried in Appleton City Cemetery.

- - - - - - - - - -

1611. Josephine Davis[6] Pheasant (1610.Bruce[5], 1608.Elizabeth[4], 1512.Edward[3], 1253.Matthew[2], 1.Benjamin, Sr.[1]) was born 12 Mar 1920, the daughter of **Bruce Thornton Pheasant** and **Georgia Grace Harris**. Josephine died Aug 1985 in Illinois. She married **Howard Frank Stewart** 25 Sep 1947. He was born 7 Sep 1920. Howard died Feb 1984 in Illinois.

ISSUE:

1612. f   i.   **Carol Ann Stewart**, born 5 Jun 1948.
1613. f   ii.   **Mary Ellen Stewart**.

---

[470] McLean, *Wilson Family*, 25.

1614. f   iii.   **Laurie Stewart**.

- - - - - - - - - - -

1615. Edward Bruce[6] Pheasant <See pg. 163> (1610.Bruce[5],
1608.Elizabeth[4], 1512.Edward[3], 1253.Matthew[2], 1.Benjamin, Sr.[1]) was born
18 Aug 1921, the son of **Bruce Thornton Pheasant** and **Georgia Grace
Harris**. Edward died 22 Oct 1966 in Buffalo, Johnson Co., Wyoming, and
was buried in Willow Grove Cemetery in Buffalo. He married **Lola Phyllis
Gray** 2 Nov 1947 in Buffalo. She was born 19 Aug 1927 in Buffalo, the
daughter of **Fred Gray** and **Elsie Hepp**.
ISSUE:
+ 1616. f   i.   **Elaine Sue Pheasant**, born 31 Aug 1950.
   1619. f   ii.   **Linda Kae Pheasant**, born 29 Jun 1953 in Buffalo,
                    Johnson Co., Wyoming.
+ 1620. m   iii.   **Bruce David Pheasant**, born 14 Sep 1956.

- - - - - - - - - - -

1616. Elaine Sue[7] Pheasant (1615.Edward[6], 1610.Bruce[5], 1608.Elizabeth[4],
1512.Edward[3], 1253.Matthew[2], 1.Benjamin, Sr.[1]) was born 31 Aug 1950 in
Buffalo, Johnson Co., Wyoming, the daughter of **Edward Bruce Pheasant**
and **Lola Phyllis Gray**. She married **Robert Walker**.
ISSUE:
   1617. f   i.   **Melissa Walker**.
   1618. f   ii.   **Amanda Walker**.

- - - - - - - - - - -

1620. Bruce David[7] Pheasant (1615.Edward[6], 1610.Bruce[5],
1608.Elizabeth[4], 1512.Edward[3], 1253.Matthew[2], 1.Benjamin, Sr.[1]) was born
14 Sep 1956 in Buffalo, Johnson Co., Wyoming, the son of **Edward Bruce
Pheasant** and **Lola Phyllis Gray**. He married **Wendy _____** about
1986 in Kaycee, Johnson Co., Wyoming.
ISSUE:
   1621. m   i.   **Seth Pheasant**, born about 1987 in Wyoming.
   1622. f   ii.   **Sarah Pheasant**.

- - - - - - - - - - -

1623. Helen Mae[6] Pheasant <See pg. 163> (1610.Bruce[5], 1608.Elizabeth[4],
1512.Edward[3], 1253.Matthew[2], 1.Benjamin, Sr.[1]) was born 7 Jan 1925, the
daughter of **Bruce Thornton Pheasant** and **Georgia Grace Harris**. Helen
died Nov 1979 in Denver, Colorado. She married (1) **William Vroom
Tomson** 7 Sep 1948; they divorced. He was born May 1929 in New York,
New York, the son of **John Tomson** and **Josephine Vroom**. William died

1981 in Santa Barbara, California.

ISSUE:

1624. f   i.   **Tamara Tomson**, born 1949 in Tacoma, Washington. She was adopted by her step-father and changed her name to **Tamara Kotoske**.

Helen married (2) **Roger Kotoske**.

- - - - - - - - - - -

1625. Mary Estella⁵ Pheasant <See pg. 162> (1608.Elizabeth⁴, 1512.Edward³, 1253.Matthew², 1.Benjamin, Sr.¹) was born 25 Feb 1892 in Hudson, Bates Co., Missouri, the daughter of **Thomas Jefferson Pheasant** and **Elizabeth Trent "Lizzie" Wilson**. Mary died 24 Aug 1978 in Kansas City, Jackson Co., Missouri, and was buried in Wills Cemetery in Peculiar, Cass Co., Missouri. She married **Oscar Elton Reid** 2 Mar 1917 in Nevada, Vernon Co., Missouri. He was born 26 Mar 1889 in Coleman, Cass Co., Missouri, the son of **John Reid** and **Martha Reeder**. Oscar died 21 Nov 1969 in Peculiar and was buried in Wills Cemetery.[471]

ISSUE:

+ 1626. f   i.   **Mary Elizabeth Reid**, born 22 Jan 1918.

   1638. m   ii.   **Harold Elton Reid**, born 8 Oct 1920 in Peculiar, died 1 Jan 1923 in Belton, Cass Co., Missouri, and was buried in Wills Cemetery.

+ 1639. m   iii.   **Charles Wayne Reid**, born 5 Nov 1922 <See pg. 167>.

+ 1644. m   iv.   **Robert Clay Reid**, born 13 Jun 1925 <See pg. 167>.

- - - - - - - - - - -

1626. Mary Elizabeth⁶ Reid (1625.Mary⁵, 1608.Elizabeth⁴, 1512.Edward³, 1253.Matthew², 1.Benjamin, Sr.¹) was born 22 Jan 1918 in Peculiar, Cass Co., Missouri, the daughter of **Oscar Elton Reid** and **Mary Estella Pheasant**. She married (1) **Dr. Eugene Henry Hamilton** 1 Sep 1941 in Peculiar. He was born 23 Oct 1909 in Kirksville, Adair Co., Missouri, the son of **Robert Hamilton** and **Katherine McMurry**. Eugene died 9 Oct 1975 in Joplin, Jasper Co., Missouri, and was buried in Wills Cemetery in Peculiar.

ISSUE:

+ 1627. m   i.   **Wayne Robert Hamilton**, born 19 Oct 1943 <See pg. 166>.

+ 1631. m   ii.   **Douglas MacMurry Hamilton**, born 7 Dec 1947 <See pg. 166>.

+ 1634. m   iii.   **Reid Henry Hamilton**, born 19 Nov 1956 <See pg. 166>.

   1637. f   iv.   **Mary Katherine Hamilton**, born 21 Feb 1959 in Joplin,

---

[471] McLean, *Wilson Family*, 25-26.

Missouri.

Mary married (2) **Philip Laurence Jones** May 1981 in Joplin, Jasper Co., Missouri. He was born 25 Oct 1904 in Hornsey, England, the son of **Walter Jones** and **Henrietta Miller**. Philip died 23 Mar 2000 in Lee's Summit, Jackson Co., Missouri, and was buried at Ozark Memorial in Joplin, Missouri.   - - - - - - - - - - -

1627. Wayne Robert[7] **Hamilton** <See pg. 165> (1626.Mary[6], 1625.Mary[5], 1608.Elizabeth[4], 1512.Edward[3], 1253.Matthew[2], 1.Benjamin, Sr.[1]) was born 19 Oct 1943 in Kansas City, Jackson Co., Missouri, the son of **Eugene Henry Hamilton and Mary** Elizabeth Reid. He married **Devina Georgie Baker** 11 Jul 1970 in Joplin, Missouri. She was born 21 Jul 1947 in Kansas, the daughter of **Curtis Baker** and **Jane Thomson**.

ISSUE:

1628. m   i.   **Curtis Douglas Hamilton**, born Apr 1973.
1629. m   ii. **Kyle Wayne Hamilton**, born 14 Jun 1974. He married **Jamie Lynn Habersat** 28 Oct 2000 in Raymore, Cass Co., Missouri. She was born about 1976.
1630. m   iii. **Kevin Reid Hamilton**, born 14 Jun 1974. He married **Olivia Naomi Brower** 22 Jun 1996 in Harrisonville, Cass Co., Missouri; they divorced. She was born about 1976.

- - - - - - - - - - -

1631. Douglas MacMurry[7] **Hamilton** <See pg. 165> (1626.Mary[6], 1625.Mary[5], 1608.Elizabeth[4], 1512.Edward[3], 1253.Matthew[2], 1.Benjamin, Sr.[1]) was born 7 Dec 1947 in Missouri, the son of **Eugene Henry Hamilton** and **Mary Elizabeth Reid**. He married (1) **Edith "Edie" Baker** 1968 in Joplin, Jasper Co., Missouri; they divorced. She is the daughter of **Paul Baker** and **Maxine_**.

ISSUE:

1632. m   i.   **Robert Eugene "Robby" Hamilton**, born 5 Feb 1969, died 22 Sep 2003 in Joplin, Missouri, and was buried in Osborne Memorial Park Cemetery in Joplin.
1633. f   ii. **Debby Hamilton**, born about 1970.

Douglas married (2) **Sondra Lynn Emmot** Nov 1990 in Topeka, Kansas. She was born about 1955.

- - - - - - - - - - -

1634. Reid Henry[7] **Hamilton** <See pg. 165> (1626.Mary[6], 1625.Mary[5], 1608.Elizabeth[4], 1512.Edward[3], 1253.Matthew[2], 1.Benjamin, Sr.[1]) was born 19 Nov 1956 in Joplin, Missouri, the son of **Eugene Henry Hamilton** and

Mary Elizabeth Reid. He married (1) **Sandra Jean Huba** 12 Aug 1978 in Joplin; they divorced.

ISSUE:

1635. m   i.   **David Geoffrey Hamilton**, born 27 Jun 1982.

Reid married (2) **Debra Kaye Garner** 11 Jun 1987 in Atlanta, Fulton Co., Georgia.

ISSUE:

1636. f   ii.   **Emily Ruth Hamilton**, born 3 Jan 1989 in Georgia.

- - - - - - - - - -

1639. Charles Wayne[6] Reid <See pg. 165> (1625.Mary[5], 1608.Elizabeth[4], 1512.Edward[3], 1253.Matthew[2], 1.Benjamin, Sr.[1]) was born 5 Nov 1922 in Peculiar, Cass Co., Missouri, the son of **Oscar Elton Reid** and **Mary Estella Pheasant**. He married **Marjorie Jean Chaffin** 21 May 1944 in Raymore, Cass Co., Missouri. She was born 3 Aug 1921 in Raymore, the daughter of **Wellman Chaffin** and **Mary Small**. Marjorie died 31 Mar 2003 in Peculiar, and was buried in Wills Cemetery in Peculiar.[472]

ISSUE:

1640. m   i.   **Charles Wayne Reid, II**, born 17 Jun 1945 in Kansas City, Jackson Co., Missouri.

+ 1641. m   ii.   **John Chaffin Reid**, born 17 Dec 1946.

- - - - - - - - - -

1641. John Chaffin[7] Reid (1639.Charles[6], 1625.Mary[5], 1608.Elizabeth[4], 1512.Edward[3], 1253.Matthew[2], 1.Benjamin, Sr.[1]) was born 17 Dec 1946 in Harrisonville, Cass Co., Missouri, the son of **Charles Wayne Reid** and **Marjorie Jean Chaffin**. He married **Cathleen Anne Shine** 15 Mar 1986 in Harrisonville,. She was born 31 May 1953 in Kansas City, Jackson Co., Missouri, the daughter of **Edward Shine** and **Mary O'Donnell**.

ISSUE:

1642. f   i.   **Emily Anne Reid**, born 22 Aug 1988 in Kansas City, Jackson Co., Missouri.

1643. m   ii.   **Michael John Reid**, born 28 Oct 1991 in Kansas City, Jackson Co., Missouri.

- - - - - - - - - -

1644. Dr. Robert Clay[6] Reid <See pg. 165> (1625.Mary[5], 1608.Elizabeth[4], 1512.Edward[3], 1253.Matthew[2], 1.Benjamin, Sr.[1]) was born 13 Jun 1925 in Peculiar, Cass Co., Missouri, the son of **Oscar Elton Reid** and **Mary Estella Pheasant**. He married **Dr. Elizabeth Frances "Betsy" Aub** 19 Jun

---

[472] McLean, *Wilson Family*, 26.

1954 in Belmont, Middlesex Co., Massachusetts. She was born 29 Oct 1926 in Boston, Suffolk Co., Massachusetts, the daughter of **Joseph Aub** and **Elizabeth Cope.**[473]

ISSUE:

+ 1645. m   i.   **Joseph Aub Reid**, born 13 Jan 1957.
+ 1648. f   ii. **Mary Elizabeth Reid**, born 21 Nov 1958.
+ 1651. m   iii. **Dr. Robert Clay Reid**, born 10 May 1960 <See pg. 168>.

- - - - - - - - - -

1645. Joseph Aub[7] **Reid** (1644.Robert[6], 1625.Mary[5], 1608.Elizabeth[4], 1512.Edward[3], 1253.Matthew[2], 1.Benjamin, Sr.[1]) was born 13 Jan 1957 in Boston, Suffolk Co., Massachusetts, the son of **Robert Clay Reid** and **Elizabeth Frances "Betsy" Aub**. He married **Dr. Karen Linda Shore** 6 Sep 1987 in Rockville, Montgomery Co., Maryland; they divorced. She was born about 1957, the daughter of **Morris Lawrence Shore** and **Susan_____**.

ISSUE:

1646. f   i.   **Sara Elizabeth Reid**, born 16 Jul 1990 in Massachusetts.
1647. m   ii. **Benjamin Eli Reid**, born 29 Aug 1994 in Massachusetts.

- - - - - - - - - -

1648. Mary Elizabeth[7] **Reid** (1644.Robert[6], 1625.Mary[5], 1608.Elizabeth[4], 1512.Edward[3], 1253.Matthew[2], 1.Benjamin, Sr.[1]) was born 21 Nov 1958 in Boston, Suffolk Co., Massachusetts, the daughter of **Robert Clay Reid** and **Elizabeth Frances "Betsy" Aub**. She married (1) **William Stiles "Tad" Lawrence** Jun 1985 in Saunderstown, Washington Co., Rhode Island; they divorced. He was born Jun 1957.

ISSUE:

1649. f   i.   **Katherine Reid "Kate" Lawrence**, born 13 Dec 1988.
1650. f   ii. **Jennifer Stiles Lawrence**, born 30 Jan 1991.

Mary married (2) **John Maxwell "Jack" Reynolds** 16 Oct 1999 in Lincoln, Massachusetts.

- - - - - - - - - -

1651. Dr. Robert Clay[7] **Reid** <See pg. 168> (1644.Robert[6], 1625.Mary[5], 1608.Elizabeth[4], 1512.Edward[3], 1253.Matthew[2], 1.Benjamin, Sr.[1]) was born 10 May 1960 in Massachusetts, the son of **Robert Clay Reid** and **Elizabeth Frances "Betsy" Aub**. He married **Carole Elizabeth Landisman** 18 Jun 1995 in Saunderstown, Washington Co., Rhode Island. She was born about

---

[473] McLean made a mistake about his education. Robert is a graduate of Harvard Medical School. Correction by John C. Reid of Peculiar MO.

1966, the daughter of **Mark Landisman** and **Celia** _____.
ISSUE:
1652. f   i.   **Micah Helen Reid**, born 8 Jan 1998 in Boston, Massachusetts.
1653. m   ii. **Nathaniel Clay Reid**, born 29 Sep 2000.

- - - - - - - - - -

1655. Elizabeth Wilson[5] Pheasant <See pg. 163> (1608.Elizabeth[4], 1512.Edward[3], 1253.Matthew[2], 1.Benjamin, Sr.[1]) was born 23 Jul 1900 in Hudson, Bates Co., Missouri, the daughter of **Thomas Jefferson Pheasant** and **Elizabeth Trent "Lizzie" Wilson**. Elizabeth died 12 Feb 1988 in Kansas City, Jackson Co., Missouri, and was buried in Holden Cemetery, Johnson Co., Missouri. She married **Ira Nelson Wetherill** 2 Jul 1928 in Harrisonville, Cass Co., Missouri. He was born 17 Jun 1905 in Holden, the son of **Addison Wetherill** and **Sallie Thompson**. Ira died 29 Apr 1990 in Lee's Summit, Jackson Co., Missouri, and was buried in Holden Cemetery.[474]
ISSUE:
1656. m   i.   **Ira Elton Wetherill**, born 5 Sep 1929 in Missouri, died 25 Dec 2001 in Prairie Village, Johnson Co., Kansas, and was buried in Wills Cemetery in Peculiar, Cass Co., Missouri.

- - - - - - - - - -

1657. Thomas DeWitt[5] Pheasant <See pg. 163> (1608.Elizabeth[4], 1512.Edward[3], 1253.Matthew[2], 1.Benjamin, Sr.[1]) was born 6 Mar 1902 in Hudson, Bates Co., Missouri, the son of **Thomas Jefferson Pheasant** and **Elizabeth Trent "Lizzie" Wilson**. Thomas died 1 Nov 1995 in Lakewood, Jefferson Co., Colorado. He married (1) **Ethel Pauline Henderson** 12 Dec 1929; they divorced. She was born 21 Jan 1911 in Story, Sheridan Co., Wyoming. Ethel died 29 Jan 1990, and was buried in Mountain View Cemetery in Riverton, Fremont Co., Wyoming.[475]
ISSUE:
+ 1658. m   i.   **Charles Earl Pheasant**, born 21 Oct 1930 <See pg. 170>.
  1661. m   ii. **Thomas James Pheasant**, born 19 Jul 1934 in Buffalo, Johnson Co., Wyoming.
+ 1662. m iii. **Richard Bruce Pheasant**, born 26 Aug 1938.
+ 1664. f   iv. **Ethel Katherine "Kay" Pheasant**, born 20 Sep 1945.

Thomas married (2) **Stella** _____. She was born 22 Apr 1899. Stella

---
[474] McLean, *Wilson Family*, 26.
[475] McLean, *Wilson Family*, 26-27.

died 26 Dec 1989 in Colorado.

- - - - - - - - - - -

1658. Charles Earl[6] Pheasant <See pg. 169> (1657.Thomas[5],
1608.Elizabeth[4], 1512.Edward[3], 1253.Matthew[2], 1.Benjamin, Sr.[1]) was born
21 Oct 1930 in Buffalo, Johnson Co., Wyoming, the son of **Thomas
DeWitt Pheasant** and **Ethel Pauline Henderson**.

ISSUE:

1659. f   i.   **Elizabeth Florence Pheasant**, born 9 Aug 1963 in Denver,
Colorado. She married **Donald Hugh McClelland, II**
17 Aug 1985 in Denver.

Charles married (2) **Vicki Cowan** 18 Oct 1987 in Denver.

ISSUE:

1660. f   ii.   **Catherine Ann Pheasant**, born 2 Jan 1988 in Denver.

- - - - - - - - - - -

1662. Richard Bruce[6] Pheasant (1657.Thomas[5], 1608.Elizabeth[4],
1512.Edward[3], 1253.Matthew[2], 1.Benjamin, Sr.[1]) was born 26 Aug 1938 in
Riverton, Fremont Co., Wyoming, the son of **Thomas DeWitt Pheasant**
and **Ethel Pauline Henderson**. He married **Caroll Rivard** 28 Feb 1975 in
Las Vegas, Clark Co., Nevada.

ISSUE:

1663. m   i.   **Richard Eugene Pheasant**, born 26 Nov 1970 in Tacoma,
Washington. Adopted.

- - - - - - - - - - -

1664. Ethel Katherine "Kay"[6] Pheasant (1657.Thomas[5], 1608.Elizabeth[4],
1512.Edward[3], 1253.Matthew[2], 1.Benjamin, Sr.[1]) was born 20 Sep 1945 in
Riverton, Fremont Co., Wyoming, the daughter of **Thomas DeWitt
Pheasant** and **Ethel Pauline Henderson**. She married (1) **Gary Alden
Anderson** 29 Jun 1965 in Riverton. He was born 13 Jun 1944 in Lusk,
Niobrara Co., Wyoming. Gary died 28 Oct 1988, and was buried in
Roselawn Cemetery in Ft. Collins, Larimer Co., Colorado.

ISSUE:

+ 1665. f   i.   **Cheryl Kay Anderson**, born 16 Jan 1969 <See pg. 171>.
1668. u   ii.   **Dale Alden Anderson**, born 18 Jul 1971 in Denver,
Colorado.

Ethel married (2) **Edmund LeMoyne Meeks** 9 Oct 1989. He was born
28 May 1944 in Ft. Washakie, Fremont Co., Wyoming.

- - - - - - - - - - -

1665. Cheryl Kay[7] Anderson <See pg. 170> (1664.Ethel[6], 1657.Thomas[5], 1608.Elizabeth[4], 1512.Edward[3], 1253.Matthew[2], 1.Benjamin, Sr.[1]) was born 16 Jan 1969 in Denver, Colorado, the daughter of **Gary Alden Anderson** and **Ethel Katherine "Kay" Pheasant**. She married **Joe Hall** Jul 1994 in Wyoming.

ISSUE:
1666. f   i.   **Rebecca Jo Hall,** born 14 Apr 1998.
1667. f   ii. **Kaitlyn Gari Hall,** born 18 Apr 2001.

- - - - - - - - - - -

1669. Edward C.[4] Wilson <See pg. 149> (1512.Edward[3], 1253.Matthew[2], 1.Benjamin, Sr.[1]) was born 1 Jan 1865 at "Somerset", Cumberland Co., Virginia, the son of **Edward Wilson** and **Sarah Linton Powell**. Edward died 18 Sep 1940. He married **Evalena Bennett** 14 Jun 1892.[476]

ISSUE:
1670. f   i.   **Mary Ella Wilson,** born 21 Nov 1893.
+ 1671. m   ii. **Edward Bennett Wilson,** born 11 Sep 1895, died 1986.
+ 1678. f   iii. **Evalena Linton "Lena" Wilson,** born 29 Aug 1897, died Oct 1984 <See pg. 172>.

- - - - - - - - - - -

1671. Edward Bennett[5] Wilson (1669.Edward[4], 1512.Edward[3], 1253.Matthew[2], 1.Benjamin, Sr.[1]) was born 11 Sep 1895, the son of **Edward C. Wilson** and **Evalena Bennett**. Edward died 1986. He married (1) **Nell Cox** 29 Nov 1918. Nell died 26 Apr 1923.

ISSUE:
+ 1672. f   i.   **Nell Wilson,** born 2 Jun 1920.
+ 1675. f   ii. **Barbara Wilson,** born 19 Feb 1924 <See pg. 172>.

Edward married (2) **Mary Bridges Harvell** 3 Jul 1932.

- - - - - - - - - - -

1672. Nell[6] Wilson (1671.Edward[5], 1669.Edward[4], 1512.Edward[3], 1253.Matthew[2], 1.Benjamin, Sr.[1]) was born 2 Jun 1920, the daughter of **Edward Bennett Wilson** and **Nell Cox**. She married **Phillip William Haish** 9 Sep 1942.

ISSUE:
1673. f   i.   **Marilyn Bennett Haish,** born 19 Jun 1943.
1674. m   ii. **Frederick Edward Haish,** born 11 Feb 1945.

---

[476] McLean, *Wilson Family*, 27-29.

- - - - - - - - - - -

1675. Barbara⁶ Wilson <See pg. 171> (1671.Edward⁵, 1669.Edward⁴, 1512.Edward³, 1253.Matthew², 1.Benjamin, Sr.¹) was born 19 Feb 1924, the daughter of **Edward Bennett Wilson** and **Nell Cox**. She married **John Luther Moore** 24 May 1947.

ISSUE:

1676. f   i.   **Eva Teresa Moore**, born 10 Oct 1948.
1677. f   ii.   **Deborah Lynn Moore**, born 20 Sep 1949.

- - - - - - - - - - -

1678. Evalena Linton "Lena"⁵ Wilson <See pg. 171> (1669.Edward⁴, 1512.Edward³, 1253.Matthew², 1.Benjamin, Sr.¹) was born 29 Aug 1897, the daughter of **Edward C. Wilson** and **Evalena Bennett**. Evalena died Oct 1984. She married **J. Wesley Runyan** 29 Jul 1920.

ISSUE:

1679. m   i.   **Robert Wesley Runyan**, born 30 Apr 1922. He married **Doris Langs** 18 Apr 1922. She was born in Pomona, California.
+ 1680. f   ii.   **Anita May Runyan**, born 19 Sep 1924.

- - - - - - - - - - -

1680. Anita May⁶ Runyan (1678.Evalena⁵, 1669.Edward⁴, 1512.Edward³, 1253.Matthew², 1.Benjamin, Sr.¹) was born 19 Sep 1924, the daughter of **J. Wesley Runyan** and **Evalena Linton "Lena" Wilson**. She married **Edgar O. Bryant** 5 Jan 1946.

ISSUE:

1681. m   i.   **Steven Edgar Bryant**, born 3 Oct 1947.

- - - - - - - - - - -

1682. Gallatin Trent⁴ Wilson <See pg. 149> (1512.Edward³, 1253.Matthew², 1.Benjamin, Sr.¹) was born 10 Feb 1867 at "Somerset", Cumberland Co., Virginia, the son of **Edward Wilson** and **Sarah Linton Powell**. Gallatin died 6 Oct 1926. He married **Mary Emma Frances Shelton** 26 Nov 1897. Mary died 4 Jul 1942.[477]

ISSUE:

+ 1683. m   i.   **Horace Shelton Wilson**, born 23 Feb 1899 <See pg. 173>.
+ 1687. f   ii.   **Edna Muriel Wilson**, born 29 Jul 1901.
+ 1692. f   iii. **Lelia Rose Wilson**, born 2 Mar 1904 <See pg. 173>.
1700. f   iv.   **Lois Odea Wilson**, born 3 Oct 1906.
1701. f   v.   **Lotus Loraine Wilson**, born 16 Apr 1910. She married **Finley Maxwell Reeder** 13 Apr 1940.

---

[477] McLean, *Wilson Family*, 29-31.

- - - - - - - - - - -

1683. Horace Shelton[5] Wilson <See pg. 172> (1682.Gallatin[4], 1512.Edward[3], 1253.Matthew[2], 1.Benjamin, Sr.[1]) was born 23 Feb 1899, the son of **Gallatin Trent Wilson** and **Mary Emma Frances Shelton**. He married **Beatrice Phillips** 25 May 1924.

ISSUE:
+ 1684. f   i.   **Cartha Nita Wilson**, born 8 Sep 1925.
   1686. f   ii.   **Joleen Helen Wilson**, born 1 Dec 1929. She married **Lewis Glen Fearing** 3 Sep 1948.

- - - - - - - - - - -

1684. Cartha Nita[6] Wilson (1683.Horace[5], 1682.Gallatin[4], 1512.Edward[3], 1253.Matthew[2], 1.Benjamin, Sr.[1]) was born 8 Sep 1925, the daughter of **Horace Shelton Wilson** and **Beatrice Phillips**. She married **Gordon Ira Clark** 12 May 1942.

ISSUE:
   1685. m   i.   **Terry Alan Clark**, born 6 Nov 1948.

- - - - - - - - - - -

1687. Edna Muriel[5] Wilson (1682.Gallatin[4], 1512.Edward[3], 1253.Matthew[2], 1.Benjamin, Sr.[1]) was born 29 Jul 1901, the daughter of **Gallatin Trent Wilson** and **Mary Emma Frances Shelton**. She married **Lawrence Russell Harr** 9 Nov 1924.

ISSUE:
+ 1688. f   i.   **Peggy Jean Harr**, born 26 May 1926.
   1690. f   ii.   **Thelma Rena Harr**, born 3 Nov 1928. She married **Robert Johnson** 1 Feb 1948.
   1691. f   iii.   **Helen Colette Harr**, born 10 Oct 1930.

- - - - - - - - - - -

1688. Peggy Jean[6] Harr (1687.Edna[5], 1682.Gallatin[4], 1512.Edward[3], 1253.Matthew[2], 1.Benjamin, Sr.[1]) was born 26 May 1926, the daughter of **Lawrence Russell Harr** and **Edna Muriel Wilson**. She married **James Hugh Rose**.

ISSUE:
   1689. f   i.   **Randy Lynn Rose**, born 20 Aug 1946.

- - - - - - - - - - -

1692. Lelia Rose[5] Wilson <See pg. 172> (1682.Gallatin[4], 1512.Edward[3], 1253.Matthew[2], 1.Benjamin, Sr.[1]) was born 2 Mar 1904, the daughter of **Gallatin Trent Wilson** and **Mary Emma Frances Shelton**. She married

Sykes B. Stokes 9 Jun 1929. Sykes died 13 May 1946.

ISSUE:

1693. m   i.   **Robert Trent Stokes**, born 1 Apr 1930.

1694. f   ii.   **Corrinne Marie Stokes**, born 30 Jul 1932.

1695. f   iii. **Patti Rose Stokes**, born 4 Dec 1935.

1696. f   iv. **Evelyn Muriel Stokes**, born 28 Jul 1938.

1697. m   v.   **Joe Bradley Stokes**, born 22 Oct 1939.

1698. m vi. **Sykes B. Stokes, Jr.**, born 22 Jul 1942, died 10 May 1943 in McAlester, Oklahoma.

1699. f vii. **Marjorie Sue Stokes**, born 16 Dec 1943.

- - - - - - - - - - -

1704. Mary Anna[3] Wilson <See pg. 113> (1253.Matthew[2], 1.Benjamin, Sr.[1]) was born 28 Jun 1822 at "Barter Hill", Cumberland Co., Virginia, the daughter of **Matthew Wilson** and **Elizabeth "Betsy" Trent**.[478] Mary died 11 Jul 1864 at "Bonbrook", Cumberland Co., Virginia. She married **Willis Wilson (See number 62 - pg. 15)** 26 May 1847 at "Barter Hill". He was born 15 Sep 1817 at "Bonbrook", the son of **John Park Wilson** and **Maria Willis Wilson**.[479]

ISSUE:[480]

+ 63. f   i.   **Elizabeth Trent Wilson**, born 10 Nov 1848, died 4 Jan 1875 <See pg. 17>.

  65. m   ii.   **Willis Wilson, Jr.**, born 25 Oct 1850 at "Bonbrook", Cumberland Co., Virginia, died 22 Jul 1869 at "Bonbrook". After the death of his parents, he remained in Virginia to finish his education at Hampden-Sydney. The second wife of his grandfather wrote from "Bonbrook" Jul 22, 1869 to the kin in Texas of his death.[481]

  66. f   iii.   **Maria Louisa Wilson**, born 15 Mar 1853 at "Walnut Grove", Rusk Co., Texas, died 25 Aug 1853 in Rusk Co., Texas, and was buried in Walnut Grove Cemetery.[482]

+ 67. f   iv.   **Mary Anna Wilson**, born 7 May 1855, died 12 Oct 1940 <See pg. 18>.

  85. f   v.   **Mary Isabella Wilson**, born 18 Sep 1857 at "Walnut Grove", Rusk Co., Texas, died 19 Sep 1858, and was buried in Walnut Grove Cemetery.

---

[478] Nash family, *Papers, 1734-1889*.

[479] McLean, *Wilson Family*, 14.

[480] Family Bible of Willis and Mary Anna Wilson.

[481] Letters 22 Jul 1869, 21 Aug 1934, Finley, John M., Family history research.

[482] Gregg Co. Gen. Soc., *Cemeteries*, Walnut Grove, 3:189.

+ 86. f   vi.   **Maria Willis Wilson**, born 9 Aug 1859, died 11 Jun 1947 <See pg. 21>.

169. f   vii.   **Laura Marye Wilson**, born 4 Feb 1862 at "Bonbrook", Cumberland Co., Virginia, died 15 Jun 1868 in Rusk Co., Texas.[483]

+ 170. f   viii.   **Caroline Louisa "Carrie" Wilson**, born 29 Jan 1864, died 2 Dec 1899 <See pg. 31>.

---

[483] Letter 16 Jun 1868, Finley, John M., Family history research.

CHAPTER 8

Descendants of Goodridge Wilson (1776-1849)

1707. Dr. Goodridge² Wilson <See pg. 3> (1.Benjamin, Sr.¹) was born 26 Mar 1776 at "Somerset", Cumberland Co., Virginia, the son of **Benjamin Wilson, Sr.** and **Anne Seay.**[484] Goodridge died 30 Sep 1849 at the Johnson Shoals area of the Kanawha River, Kanawha Co., Virginia (West Virginia),[485] and was buried in the family plot in the garden there. The marriage bond for Goodridge and **Elizabeth Woodson Venable** is dated 4 Nov 1802.[486] She was born 21 Nov 1784 at "Slate Hill", Prince Edward Co., Virginia, the daughter of **Nathaniel Venable** and **Elizabeth Michaux Woodson.**[487] Elizabeth died 1 Mar 1851 in Kanawha Co. and was buried in the family plot in the garden there.[488]

ISSUE:

+ 1708. f   i.   **Anne Thomas Wilson**, born 7 Dec 1806, died 28 Feb 1887 <See pg. 178>.

+ 1792. m   ii.   **Benjamin Francis Wilson**, born about 1810, died after 1882 <See pg. 190>.

+ 1806. f   iii.   **Elizabeth Woodson Wilson**, born 11 Apr 1812, died 5 May 1871 <See pg. 192>.

+ 1863. m   iv.   **Nathaniel Venable Wilson**, born before 21 Jun 1814, died 1905 <See pg. 198>.

+ 1885. m   v.   **Goodridge Alexander Wilson**, born 7 Oct 1815, died 8 Dec 1897 <See pg. 201>.

+ 2056. m   vi.   **William Venable Wilson**, born 18 Jan 1819, died 22 Jan 1908 <See pg. 219>.

+ 2130. m vii.   **Samuel Venable Wilson**, born 3 Mar 1821, died 17 Apr

---

[484] Woodson Family, *Papers, 1740-1945*, Accession 29437-41, LVA.

[485] Boddie, *Historical Southern Families*, 3:65.

[486] Prince Edward Co. VA Marriage Bonds 1754-1850. Knorr, *Marriages Prince Edward Co VA*, 84.

[487] Venable, *Venables of Virginia*, 37. The Woodson and Michaux ancestors of Elizabeth are documented in Meyer and Dorman, *Adventurers of Purse and Person*, 714. **(See Appendix pg. 312)**

[488] Boddie, *Historical Southern Families*, 3:65. In a 1940 letter, **Martha Agnes (Wilson) Watson,** giving recollections of her mother, wrote, "They were buried in the family plot there in the garden, and Mother visited the graves ... in about 1878 or 1879. ..... The house was on the banks of the Kanawha and later sold and some sort of negro school was established there." Copy from Nancy (Whitman) Santheson of Roswell NM.

1870 <See pg. 228>.

+ 2131. mviii. **James Willis Wilson**, born 3 Dec 1823, died 2 Sep 1899
<See pg. 260>.

+ 2132. f   ix. **Martha Agnes Wilson**, born 5 May 1826, died 31 Oct
1899 <See pg. 284>.

Goodridge's name is sometimes spelled Goodrich, the surname of his
grandmother. In correspondence, two of his brothers refer to him as
Goodrich, but more often the spelling Goodridge was used. He signed all
documents found to this date "G. Wilson."

Letters written in 1795 and 1796 mention his being in Philadelphia "a
student of Phisic", and in 1797 Goodridge received his M. D. degree from
the University of Pennsylvania.[489]

His 1799 Christmas letter shows warm family feeling, describing "a rousing
fire in the old house" and himself and the brothers who are "bachelors, not
from a contempt of wedlock or insensibility to the fair, but because we think
our situation too variable and uncertain for anyone's but our own happiness
to depend on".[490]

After his marriage in 1802, he purchased land on the Bush and Briery
Rivers in Prince Edward Co. and called his home "Milnwood".[491] The
house, located in present day Farmville, burned in 1919, but the residents in
1992 called their home at that location "Milnwood".[492]

Goodridge and Elizabeth were listed as members of Briery Presbyterian
Church until 1813 when they removed to the College church at Hampden-
Sydney.[493] He served on the Board of Trustees for Hampden-Sydney
College from 1803-1836. A session of the Hanover Presbytery, held in
1775 at the home of **Nathaniel Venable**, Goodridge's father-in-law; was
the beginning of the college. One of Goodridge's duties involved dealing
with "unruly" students who were "gaming" (gambling), leaving the college
during study hours without permission, "revelling and drinking" at a local

---

[489] University of Pennsylvania Archives and Records Center copies, 3 Sep 1992.

[490] McCrary, *Wilson Families ... Correspondence 1785-1849*, 63, 67, 72, 80-2,
106, 193.

[491] Prince Edward Co. VA Deed Books 13:259, 297, 432, 14:387, 15:358.

[492] *Today and Yesterday*, 251. An 1820 map of the county located in the
courthouse labels "Dr. Wilson's" location. This has been mistakenly called
"Millwood".

[493] Douglas, *Briery*, #'s 208, 213.

tavern, destroying fruit trees, and ringing the college bell.[494]

Goodridge moved his family to Kanawha Co., Virginia (West Virginia), around 1836 at Johnson Shoals on the Kanawha River down river from Charleston, buying land that had been granted to **George Washington** in 1772.[495] In 1841 he was on a committee that addressed the inequalities of representation of the "western people" in the General Assembly of Virginia.[496]

His son-in-law, Charles Woodson, wrote 25 Jan 1847 of Goodridge, his wife and youngest daughter being in St. Charles Co., Missouri.[497] The recollections of the daughter were of the boat trip from Kanawha to St. Louis where they stayed at the home of **Edward Bates**, then afterwards took the stage ride out to "Mount Airy".

After the death of Goodridge, the children deeded their inheritance of real and personal property back to their mother.[498]

- - - - - - - - - - -

1708. Anne Thomas³ Wilson <See pg. 176> (1707.Goodridge², 1.Benjamin, Sr.¹) was born 7 Dec 1806 in Prince Edward Co., Virginia, the daughter of **Goodridge Wilson** and **Elizabeth Woodson Venable**. Anne died 28 Feb 1887 at "Mount Airy", St. Charles Co., Missouri, and was buried in the family plot "Violet Hill" at "Mount Airy". She married **Charles Friend Woodson** 15 Apr 1830 at "Milnwood", Prince Edward Co., Virginia. He was born 20 Nov 1794 at Neck of Land, Chesterfield Co., Virginia, the son of **George Woodson** and **Sarah Friend**. Charles died 7 Jun 1887 at "Mount Airy" and was buried in "Violet Hill".[499]

---

[494] Henneman, "Trustees", 180. Bradshaw, *History of Hampden-Sydney College*, 15, 116-9.

[495] Kanawha Co. WV Deed Books I-J:280, L:442, M:63.

[496] *West Virginia History*, 25:283-4 (1964).

[497] Wilson, Nath'l V. *Papers, 1834-1878*, 24.

[498] Kanawha Co. WV Deed Book Q:181-4.

[499] The birth, marriage, and death information on the parents and children is found in Woodson Family Bible, Accession 30316 LVA. Boddie, *Historical Southern Families*, 3:66-7. McLean, *Wilson Family*, 39-43. Corrections of and additions to McLean and Boddie were provided by Nancy (Whitman) Santheson of Roswell NM. The cemetery is referred to as "Woodson Burying Ground" in vol 4:42 of Wiechens, *Cemeteries of St. Charles Co. MO*.

ISSUE:

1709. m   i.   **George Thomas Woodson,** born 19 Jun 1831 in Prince Edward Co., Virginia, died 8 Dec 1905 probably in St. Charles Co., Missouri, and was buried in "Violet Hill".

+ 1710. m   ii.   **Richard Goodridge Woodson,** born 6 Sep 1833, died 8 Mar 1911.

+ 1767. f   iii.   **Sarah Friend Woodson,** born 14 Oct 1836, died 14 Oct 1918 <See pg. 188>.

1775. f   iv.   **Anne Virginia Woodson,** born 7 Dec 1838 in Chesterfield Co., Virginia, died 3 Jan 1929.

1776. f   v.   **Elizabeth Venable Woodson,** born 26 Oct 1840 at Johnson Shoals, Kanawha Co., Virginia (West Virginia), died 2 Jan 1929.

+ 1777. f   vi.   **Ellen Wilson Woodson,** born 24 Nov 1842, died 26 Aug 1933 <See pg. 188>.

+ 1780. f   vii.   **Julia Bates Woodson,** born 27 Feb 1845, died 15 Apr 1910 <See pg. 189>.

+ 1788. f   viii.   **Mary Randolph Woodson,** born 10 Feb 1849, died 4 Mar 1916 <See pg. 190>.

Anne and Charles moved from Virginia to St. Charles Co., Missouri, in 1841, settling on the west end of Dardenne Prairie, building a stone dwelling which they called "Mount Airy".[500]   In a letter written by Charles from Kanawha Co. 21 Jul 1841, he asks Mr. **Robt. B. Frayser, (See pg. 284)** who married Charles' cousin, to purchase some things needed on their arrival.[501]   Anne's brother **Nat** wrote a letter 9 Nov 1841 saying, "I went to Mo with Captain Woodsons family, saw them fixed at home".[502]

They are shown with their children in the 1850 and 1860 Callaway Twp., St. Charles Co., Missouri, censuses. Charles' prestige in the community was described in an 1891 news article.[503]

- - - - - - - - - -

1710. Richard Goodridge[4] Woodson (1708.Anne[3], 1707.Goodridge[2], 1.Benjamin, Sr.[1]) was born 6 Sep 1833 at "Milnwood", Prince Edward Co., Virginia, the son of **Charles Friend Woodson** and **Anne Thomas Wilson**. Richard died 8 Mar 1911 in Dardenne, St. Charles Co., Missouri, and was

---

[500]   Drummond, *Historic Sites in St. Charles County*, 251.

[501]   Copy of letter from Watson sisters of Kirkwood MO.

[502]   McCrary, *Wilson Families ... Correspondence .... 1785-1849*, 289.

[503]   "Dardenne Prairie", from *St. Charles Cosmos*.

buried there. He married **Grace Lee** 15 Jul 1868 in Dardenne. She was
born 7 Aug 1850 in Port Jervis, Orange Co., New York, the daughter of
Philip Lee and **Nancy Jane Cunion**. Grace died 22 Feb 1936 in Dardenne
and was buried there.[504]

ISSUE:

1711. f   i.   **Gertrude G. Woodson**, born 19 Jul 1869. She married
Jerry Harper Hodnett 24 Jan 1895. Jerry died 12 Apr
1948. Gertrude died 8 Feb 1949 in St. Charles, Missouri.

+ 1712. f   ii.   **Alice Lee Woodson**, born 30 Jan 1871, died 22 Aug 1898.

1727. m   iii.   **Charles Friend Woodson**, born 23 Jul 1872, died 21 Feb
1903.

1728. m   iv.   **Tarlton Woodson**, born 3 Feb 1874. He married **Junia
Snyder** 22 Jun 1908. Tarlton died 26 Apr 1959.

+ 1729. f   v.   **Nancy Lee Woodson**, born 9 Oct 1876, died 17 Dec 1968
<See pg. 183>.

+ 1757. f   vi.   **Grace Goodridge Woodson**, born 6 May 1881, died 7 Oct
1943 <See pg. 186>.

1764. f   vii.   **Fred Lee Woodson**, born 1 Jan 1884 at "Spring Dale", St.
Charles Co., Missouri, died 19 Aug 1979.

1765. f   viii.   **Anne Thomas Woodson**, born 30 Jan 1886, died 7 Dec
1886.

1766. m   ix.   **George T. Woodson**, born 14 Aug 1889. He married
Minerva Muschaney 9 Jan 1909. George died 25 Jun
1932.

- - - - - - - - - -

1712. Alice Lee[5] Woodson (1710.Richard[4], 1708.Anne[3], 1707.Goodridge[2],
1.Benjamin, Sr.[1]) was born 30 Jan 1871 in Dardenne, St. Charles Co.,
Missouri. She was the daughter of **Richard Goodridge Woodson** and
Grace Lee. Alice died 22 Aug 1898 in Peach Orchard, Clay Co., Arkansas,
and was buried in Dardenne Presbyterian Stone Church Cemetery, St.
Charles Co., Missouri. She married **Charles Blize** 7 Sep 1892 in Dardenne.
He was born 13 Oct 1869 in Howell, St. Charles Co., Missouri. He was the
son of **John Blize** and _____ **Stewart**. Charles died 13 Jan 1947 in
Seminole, Seminole Co., Oklahoma.[505]

---

[504] Boddie, _Historical Southern Families_, 3:67. McLean, _Wilson Family_, 39-41.
Portrait and Biographical Record of St. Charles Co. MO, 154. _History of St.
Charles Co. MO_ ......, 492. Wiechens, _Cemeteries of St. Charles Co. MO_, 5:77.

[505] McLean, _Wilson Family_, 39-40. Boddie, _Historical Southern Families_, 3: 67-
69,5:43. Additional information from Nancy (Whitman) Santheson of Roswell NM
and Henrietta (McCluer) Phelps of Auxvasse MO.

ISSUE:

+ 1713. f   i.   **Nellie Grace Blize**, born 27 Mar 1895.
+ 1720. f   ii. **Hazel Blize**, born 11 Oct 1897, died 7 Aug 1964.

- - - - - - - - - - -

1713. Nellie Grace[6] Blize (1712.Alice[5], 1710.Richard[4], 1708.Anne[3], 1707.Goodridge[2], 1.Benjamin, Sr.[1]) was born 27 Mar 1895 in Peach Orchard, Clay Co., Arkansas, the daughter of **Charles Blize** and **Alice Lee Woodson**. Nellie died in Elsberry, Lincoln Co., Missouri. She married **Robert Lee Cox** 29 Nov 1919 in St. Louis, Missouri. He was born 29 Jun 1893 in Lincoln Co., Missouri, the son of **W. Sumner Cox** and **Emma Marmaduke**.

ISSUE:

1714. m   i.   **Charles Woodson Cox**, born 7 Oct 1920 in Foley, Lincoln Co., Missouri.
+ 1715. f   ii. **Marjorie Lillian Cox**, born 8 Oct 1922 .
+ 1717. m   iii. **Robert Lee Cox, Jr.**, born 25 Oct 1924.

- - - - - - - - - - -

1715. Marjorie Lillian[7] Cox (1713.Nellie[6], 1712.Alice[5], 1710.Richard[4], 1708.Anne[3], 1707.Goodridge[2], 1.Benjamin, Sr.[1]) was born 8 Oct 1922 in Foley, Lincoln Co., Missouri, the daughter of **Robert Lee Cox** and **Nellie Grace Blize**. She married **Albert Hyatt** 9 Dec 1944 in Washington, District of Columbia.

ISSUE:

1716. m   i.   **Ronald Israel Hyatt**, born 30 Nov 1946.

- - - - - - - - - - -

1717. Robert Lee[7] Cox, Jr. (1713.Nellie[6], 1712.Alice[5], 1710.Richard[4], 1708.Anne[3], 1707.Goodridge[2], 1.Benjamin, Sr.[1]) was born 25 Oct 1924 in Foley, Lincoln Co., Missouri, the son of **Robert Lee Cox** and **Nellie Grace Blize**. He married **Jean Admire Lee** 5 Jul 1952.

ISSUE:

1718. m   i.   **Stephen Robert Cox**, born 15 May 1953.
1719. f   ii. **Christine Lee Cox**, born 10 Jan 1958.

- - - - - - - - - - -

1720. Hazel[6] Blize <See pg. 181> (1712.Alice[5], 1710.Richard[4], 1708.Anne[3], 1707.Goodridge[2], 1.Benjamin, Sr.[1]) was born 11 Oct 1897 in Peach Orchard, Clay Co., Arkansas, the daughter of **Charles Blize** and **Alice Lee Woodson**. Hazel died 7 Aug 1964 in Auxvasse, Callaway Co., Missouri. She married **Henry McCluer** 21 Apr 1917 in O'Fallon, St. Charles Co.,

Missouri. He was born 16 Sep 1897 in O'Fallon, the son of **Louis McCluer** and **Jeannette Muschany Watson**. Henry died 29 Dec 1978 in Auxvasse.

ISSUE:

+ 1721. f i. **Henrietta Alice McCluer**, born 27 Jun 1919, died 18 Oct 2004 <See pg. 182>.

1726. f ii. **Doris Virginia McCluer**, born 11 Jul 1923 in Auxvasse, Callaway Co., Missouri. She married **William J. Stewart** Aug 1970 in Memphis, Shelby Co., Tennessee. He was born 27 Dec 1900. William died 11 Aug 1974 in Columbia, Boone Co., Missouri. Doris died 2 Mar 1975 in Mexico, Audrain Co., Missouri.

- - - - - - - - - - -

1721. Henrietta Alice⁷ McCluer <See pg. 182> (1720.Hazel⁶, 1712.Alice⁵, 1710.Richard⁴, 1708.Anne³, 1707.Goodridge², 1.Benjamin, Sr.¹) was born 27 Jun 1919 in Auxvasse, Callaway Co., Missouri, the daughter of **Henry McCluer** and **Hazel Blize**. Henrietta died 18 Oct 2004. She married **Richard A. Phelps** 6 Apr 1944 in Jefferson City, Cole Co., Missouri. He was born 7 Jan 1922 in Jefferson City, the son of **Julius Caesar Phelps** and **Katherine M. Kelpe**.[506]

ISSUE:

+ 1722. f i. **Doris Virginia Phelps**, born 2 Dec 1946.
+ 1724. m ii. **Richard A. Phelps, Jr.**, born 11 Feb 1948.

- - - - - - - - - - -

1722. Doris Virginia⁸ Phelps (1721.Henrietta⁷, 1720.Hazel⁶, 1712.Alice⁵, 1710.Richard⁴, 1708.Anne³, 1707.Goodridge², 1.Benjamin, Sr.¹) was born 2 Dec 1946 in Jefferson City, Cole Co., Missouri, the daughter of **Richard A. Phelps** and **Henrietta Alice McCluer**. She married **Fred E. Dugan** 8 Nov 1985; they divorced. He was the son of **Frank Dugan** and **Margaret** _____.

ISSUE:

1723. m i. **Devlin Kyle Dugan**, born 25 Sep 1985 in Columbia, Boone Co., Missouri. He married **Megan Jean Baldwin** 30 Jul 2004 in Fulton, Missouri. She was born 1986.

- - - - - - - - - - -

1724. Richard A.⁸ Phelps, Jr. (1721.Henrietta⁷, 1720.Hazel⁶, 1712.Alice⁵, 1710.Richard⁴, 1708.Anne³, 1707.Goodridge², 1.Benjamin, Sr.¹) was born 11 Feb 1948 in Jefferson City, Cole Co., Missouri, the son of **Richard A.**

---

[506] McLean, *Wilson Family*, 39-40. Boddie, *Historical Southern Families*, 3: 67-69.

Phelps and **Henrietta Alice McCluer**. He married **Jo Ann Martin** 13 May 1967 in Auxvasse, Callaway Co., Missouri. She was born 28 Feb 1948 in Mexico, Audrain Co., Missouri, the daughter of **William Martin** and **Nora Lee Luckaman**.

ISSUE:

1725. m   i.   **Eric Martin Phelps**, born 10 Dec 1970 in Rapid City, South Dakota. He married **Amber Victoria McCartney** 12 Jun 2004 in Cancun, Mexico. She was born 2 Aug 1981.

- - - - - - - - - -

1729. Nancy Lee⁵ Woodson <See pg. 180> (1710.Richard⁴, 1708.Anne³, 1707.Goodridge², 1.Benjamin, Sr.¹) was born 9 Oct 1876 in Dardenne, St. Charles Co., Missouri, the daughter of **Richard Goodridge Woodson** and **Grace Lee**. Nancy died 17 Dec 1968. She married **Robert Henry Towers** 23 Dec 1902. He was born 7 Jul 1872 in Cottlesville, St. Charles Co., Missouri. Robert died 26 Mar 1963.[507]

ISSUE:

+ 1730. f   i.   **Dorothy Berenice Towers**, born 6 Oct 1903, died 11 Aug 1980.

- - - - - - - - - -

1730. Dorothy Berenice⁶ Towers (1729.Nancy⁵, 1710.Richard⁴, 1708.Anne³, 1707.Goodridge², 1.Benjamin, Sr.¹) was born 6 Oct 1903 in St. Charles Co., Missouri, the daughter of **Robert Henry Towers** and **Nancy Lee Woodson**. Dorothy died 11 Aug 1980. She married **Scott Russell Whitman** 14 Jun 1928 in St. Charles Co. He was born 20 Jul 1904 in Cerro Gordo Co., Iowa. Scott died 23 Jan 1956.

ISSUE:

+ 1731. f   i.   **Nancy Jane Whitman**, born 18 Aug 1929.
+ 1741. m   ii.   **Robert Charles Whitman**, born 19 Sep 1932 <See pg. 185>.
+ 1750. m   iii.   **Harry Paul Whitman**, born 30 Dec 1933 <See pg. 186>.

- - - - - - - - - -

1731. Nancy Jane⁷ Whitman (1730.Dorothy⁶, 1729.Nancy⁵, 1710.Richard⁴, 1708.Anne³, 1707.Goodridge², 1.Benjamin, Sr.¹) was born 18 Aug 1929 in St. Charles, Missouri, the daughter of **Scott Russell Whitman** and **Dorothy Berenice Towers**. She married **Stephen Stanley Santheson** 22 Sep 1949 in St. Charles. He was born 12 Sep 1926 in Roswell, Chaves Co., New Mexico, the son of **Stig Sixten Santheson** and **Jessie Bernice Mapes**.

[507] McLean, *Wilson Family*, 40. Boddie, *Historical Southern Families*, 3: 68-69.

ISSUE:

+ 1732. f   i.   **Stephana Sharon Santheson**, born 6 Sep 1950 <See pg. 184>.
+ 1737. f   ii. **Ciri Ellen Santheson**, born 20 Sep 1955.

- - - - - - - - - - -

1732. Stephana Sharon[8] Santheson <See pg. 184> (1731.Nancy[7], 1730.Dorothy[6], 1729.Nancy[5], 1710.Richard[4], 1708.Anne[3], 1707.Goodridge[2], 1.Benjamin, Sr.[1]) was born 6 Sep 1950 in Roswell, Chaves Co., New Mexico, the daughter of **Stephen Stanley Santheson** and **Nancy Jane Whitman**. She married **Clay Douglas Thornton** 5 Aug 1973. He was born 27 Aug 1951.

ISSUE:

1733. m   i.   **Trent Anthony Thornton**, born 9 Jul 1974 in Highland Park, California.
+ 1734. f   ii. **Tracy Celeste Thornton**, born 17 Jun 1978.

- - - - - - - - - - -

1734. Tracy Celeste[9] Thornton (1732.Stephana[8], 1731.Nancy[7], 1730.Dorothy[6], 1729.Nancy[5], 1710.Richard[4], 1708.Anne[3], 1707.Goodridge[2], 1.Benjamin, Sr.[1]) was born 17 Jun 1978 in Pasadena, California, the daughter of **Clay Douglas Thornton** and **Stephana Sharon Santheson**. She married **Thomas Francis Bulharowski** 19 Aug 2001. He was born 24 Jul 1964 in Newport, Rhode Island.

ISSUE:

1735. m   i.   **Ryan Phillip Bulharowski**, born 16 Sep 2002 in Ventura, California.
1736. m   ii. **Ethan Patrick Bulharowski**, born 5 May 2005 in Ventura.

- - - - - - - - - - -

1737. Ciri Ellen[8] Santheson (1731.Nancy[7], 1730.Dorothy[6], 1729.Nancy[5], 1710.Richard[4], 1708.Anne[3], 1707.Goodridge[2], 1.Benjamin, Sr.[1]) was born 20 Sep 1955 in Roswell, Chaves Co., New Mexico, the daughter of **Stephen Stanley Santheson** and **Nancy Jane Whitman**. She married **William Howard Enoch** 10 Jan 1976 in Roswell. He was born 9 Feb 1954 in Roswell, the son of **Howard Enoch** and **Billie** _____.

ISSUE:

1738. m   i.   **Trevor Howard Enoch**, born 30 Oct 1979 in Las Cruces, Doña Ana Co., New Mexico. He married **Crystal Bee Armendariz** 21 Jun 2003 in Las Cruces. She was born 17 Mar 1980 in Las Cruces.
1739. f   ii. **Tiffany Lynn Enoch**, born 7 Feb 1982 in Las Cruces.

1740. m iii. **Travis Stephen Enoch**, born 12 Sep 1983 in Las Cruces.

- - - - - - - - - -

1741. Robert Charles[7] Whitman <See pg. 183> (1730.Dorothy[6],
1729.Nancy[5], 1710.Richard[4], 1708.Anne[3], 1707.Goodridge[2], 1.Benjamin,
Sr.[1]) was born 19 Sep 1932 in Dexter, Chaves Co., New Mexico, the son of
Scott Russell Whitman and **Dorothy Berenice Towers**. He married **Joan
Isabel Vollmer** 16 Feb 1957 in St. Charles, Missouri. She was born 4 Nov
1932, the daughter of **Vitalis Vollmer** and **Beatrice Klotz**. [508]

ISSUE:

+ 1742. f   i.   **Ann Frances Whitman**, born 29 Nov 1959.
+ 1745. m ii. **Ty Russell Whitman**, born 16 Mar 1963.
  1749. f iii. **Lee Christine Whitman**, born 18 Oct 1965 in St. Charles,
                 Missouri. She married **John Kirn** 14 Nov 1986 in St.
                 Charles. He was born 20 Sep 1965, the son of **Fred Kirn**
                 and **Jane Hagan**. Lee died 15 Jan 1989 in St. Charles.

- - - - - - - - - -

1742. Ann Frances[8] Whitman (1741.Robert[7], 1730.Dorothy[6],
1729.Nancy[5], 1710.Richard[4], 1708.Anne[3], 1707.Goodridge[2], 1.Benjamin,
Sr.[1]) was born 29 Nov 1959 in St. Charles, Missouri, the daughter of
Robert Charles Whitman and **Joan Isabel Vollmer**. She married **Joseph
Meuth** 27 Feb 1982 in St. Charles. He was born 7 Dec 1954 in St. Louis,
Missouri, the son of **Ivo Meuth** and **Marie Felicicchia**.

ISSUE:

1743. m   i.   **Jacob Alan Meuth**, born 4 May 1985 in St. Charles,
               Missouri.
1744. f ii.   **Nancy Joan Meuth**, born 16 Jul 1987 in Lake St. Louis, St.
               Charles Co., Missouri.

- - - - - - - - - -

1745. Ty Russell[8] Whitman (1741.Robert[7], 1730.Dorothy[6], 1729.Nancy[5],
1710.Richard[4], 1708.Anne[3], 1707.Goodridge[2], 1.Benjamin, Sr.[1]) was born
16 Mar 1963 in St. Charles, Missouri, the son of **Robert Charles Whitman**
and **Joan Isabel Vollmer**. He married **Jennifer Susan Hall** 19 Feb 1982 in
St. Charles. She was born 6 Jul 1963 in St. Louis, Missouri, the daughter of
Clarence Hall and **Estalee Wheeler**.

ISSUE:

1746. f   i.   **Crystal Leigh Whitman**, born 20 Apr 1982 in St. Louis,
               Missouri.
1747. m ii.   **Scott Russell Whitman**, born 21 May 1985 in St. Charles,

[508] McLean, *Wilson Family*, 40. Boddie, *Historical Southern Families*, 3: 69.

Missouri.

1748. f   iii.   **Sara Lee Whitman**, born 3 Nov 1991 in St. Charles.

- - - - - - - - - - -

1750. Harry Paul[7] Whitman <See pg. 183> (1730.Dorothy[6], 1729.Nancy[5], 1710.Richard[4], 1708.Anne[3], 1707.Goodridge[2], 1.Benjamin, Sr.[1]) was born 30 Dec 1933 in Dexter, Chaves Co., New Mexico, the son of **Scott Russell Whitman** and **Dorothy Berenice Towers**. He married **Carol Sue Minker** 7 Aug 1954 in St. Charles, Missouri. She was born 6 Oct 1932 in Fulton, Callaway Co., Missouri, the daughter of **Charles Minker** and **Sally Bedsworth**.

ISSUE:

+ 1751. f   i.   **Melinda Jon Whitman**, born 8 Apr 1956.
+ 1754. f   ii.   **Carmen Sue Whitman**, born 11 Aug 1959.

- - - - - - - - - - -

1751. Melinda Jon[8] Whitman (1750.Harry[7], 1730.Dorothy[6], 1729.Nancy[5], 1710.Richard[4], 1708.Anne[3], 1707.Goodridge[2], 1.Benjamin, Sr.[1]) was born 8 Apr 1956, the daughter of **Harry Paul Whitman** and **Carol Sue Minker**. She married **Stephen A. Adams** 9 Feb 1979; they divorced.

ISSUE:

1752. m   i.   **Kyle Michael Adams**, born 24 Jun 1985.
1753. m   ii.   **Ian Russell Adams**, born 8 Feb 1990.

- - - - - - - - - - -

1754. Carmen Sue[8] Whitman (1750.Harry[7], 1730.Dorothy[6], 1729.Nancy[5], 1710.Richard[4], 1708.Anne[3], 1707.Goodridge[2], 1.Benjamin, Sr.[1]) was born 11 Aug 1959 in St. Louis, Missouri, the daughter of **Harry Paul Whitman** and **Carol Sue Minker**. She married **Dr. Bret DeForest** 3 Aug 1985 in St. Charles, Missouri. He was born 24 Mar 1959 in Cape Girardeau, Missouri, the son of **Byron Neely DeForest** and **Wanda Jean Darden**.

ISSUE:

1755. f   i.   **Whitney Nicole DeForest**, born 13 Oct 1987 in Chesterfield, Missouri.
1756. m   ii.   **Aaron Drew DeForest**, born 30 Mar 1990 in Chesterfield.

- - - - - - - - - - -

1757. Grace Goodridge[5] Woodson <See pg. 180> (1710.Richard[4], 1708.Anne[3], 1707.Goodridge[2], 1.Benjamin, Sr.[1]) was born 6 May 1881, the daughter of **Richard Goodridge Woodson** and **Grace Lee**. Grace died 7 Oct 1943 in Washington, District of Columbia. She married **Brank Farris Watson (See number 1845 - pg. 197)** 27 Aug 1902. He was born 13 Jan 1880, the son of **Samuel McCluer Watson** and **Annie Pleasantia**

Ruffner. Brank died 30 Jan 1939 in Washington. [509]

ISSUE:

+ 1758. m   i.   **Quentin Durward Watson**, born 27 Jun 1903.

- - - - - - - - - -

1758. Quentin Durward[6] Watson <See pg. 197> (1757.Grace[5], 1710.Richard[4], 1708.Anne[3], 1707.Goodridge[2], 1.Benjamin, Sr.[1]) was born 27 Jun 1903 in St. Louis, Missouri, the son of **Brank Farris Watson** and **Grace Goodridge Woodson**. He married (1) **Mary Van Hoesen** 7 Apr 1928 in the Episcopal Church in Washington, District of Columbia.

ISSUE:

+ 1759. f   i.   **Fred Lee Watson**, born 24 Apr 1930, died 7 Oct 1956.

Quentin married (2) **Katherine Ham** 14 Oct 1949 in Chicago, Illinois.

ISSUE:

1763. f   ii.   **Margot Lee Watson**, born 18 Mar 1952 in Washington, District of Columbia.

- - - - - - - - - -

1759. Fred Lee[7] Watson (1758.Quentin[6], 1757.Grace[5], 1710.Richard[4], 1708.Anne[3], 1707.Goodridge[2], 1.Benjamin, Sr.[1]) was born 24 Apr 1930 in Washington, District of Columbia, the daughter of **Quentin Durward Watson** and **Mary Van Hoesen**. Fred died 7 Oct 1956 in Richmond, Virginia. She married **Forrest Wheeler Stanfield** 21 Feb 1953.[510]

ISSUE:

+ 1760. f   i.   **Anne Lee Stanfield**, born 15 Nov 1953.

- - - - - - - - - -

1760. Anne Lee[8] Stanfield (1759.Fred[7], 1758.Quentin[6], 1757.Grace[5], 1710.Richard[4], 1708.Anne[3], 1707.Goodridge[2], 1.Benjamin, Sr.[1]) was born 15 Nov 1953 at George Air Force Base, San Bernardino Co., California, the daughter of **Forrest Wheeler Stanfield** and **Fred Lee Watson**. She married **Glenn Staley** 3 Mar 1979; they divorced.

ISSUE:

1761. m   i.   **Colin David Staley**, born 5 Feb 1981 in Annapolis, Maryland.

1762. f   ii.   **Leigh Anne Staley**, born 15 Feb 1983 in Annapolis.

- - - - - - - - - -

---

[509] McLean, *Wilson Family*, 40-41. Boddie, *Historical Southern Families*, 3: 70.

[510] McLean, *Wilson Family*, 46. Boddie, *Historical Southern Families*, 3: 70-1.

1767. Sarah Friend[4] Woodson <See pg. 179> (1708.Anne[3], 1707.Goodridge[2], 1.Benjamin, Sr.[1]) was born 14 Oct 1836 in Chesterfield Co., Virginia, the daughter of **Charles Friend Woodson** and **Anne Thomas Wilson**. Sarah died 14 Oct 1918. She married **Dr. Julian Bates** 14 Oct 1858. He was born 7 Jan 1833, the son of **Edward Bates** and **Julia D. Coalter**. Julian died 20 Jul 1902 in St. Louis, Missouri. [511]

ISSUE:

+ 1768. f   i.   **Wenona Bates**, born 30 Apr 1862.
  1770. m   ii.   **Edward Bates**, born 1872, died 1899.
  1771. m   iii.   **George Woodson Bates**, born 1874, died 25 Jun 1932.
  1772. m   iv.   **Fleming Bates**, born 1877, died 1937.
  1773. m   v.   **T. Frank Bates**, born 1879, died 21 Aug 1961.
  1774. m   vi.   **John Hodgen Bates**, born 28 Nov 1882, died 1944.

Edward Bates wrote of his son Julian frequently in his diary. His entry May 18, 1859 stated, "Went with Julia to Florissant to vis't Julian and Sally. Dined with them and returned in the evening. I never saw Sally so handsome - a good family reason for it - Julian is well and his professional prospects improving - They both seem very happy. Julian got his buggy broke today, by leaving his horse standing, unhitched, while he visited a patient. The carriage, he says, is not badly hurt, but I fear the horse may be spoiled."[512]

- - - - - - - - - -

1768. Wenona[5] Bates (1767.Sarah[4], 1708.Anne[3], 1707.Goodridge[2], 1.Benjamin, Sr.[1]) was born 30 Apr 1862, the daughter of **Julian Bates** and **Sarah Friend Woodson**. She married **Rev. William McCluer** 1902.

ISSUE:

  1769. m   i.   **Samuel McCluer**, born 16 Mar 1904. He married **Ruby Robbins** 1937. Samuel died 23 Mar 1985 probably in Lafayette Co., Tennessee.

- - - - - - - - - -

1777. Ellen Wilson[4] Woodson <See pg. 179> (1708.Anne[3], 1707.Goodridge[2], 1.Benjamin, Sr.[1]) was born 24 Nov 1842 at "Mount Airy", St. Charles Co., Missouri, the daughter of **Charles Friend Woodson** and **Anne Thomas Wilson**. Ellen died 26 Aug 1933. She married **Richard Bates** 23 Mar 1863. He was born 12 Dec 1836 in Missouri, the son of **Edward Bates** and

---

[511] McLean, *Wilson Family*, 41. Boddie, *Historical Southern Families*, 3: 66. Bates, *Bates, et al*, 35.

[512] There was evidently a daughter named Edwa, who must have died young. Beale, *Diary of Edward Bates*, xv-xvi, 15, etc., 528.

Julia D. Coalter. Richard died 25 Sep 1879.[513]

ISSUE:

1778. m   i.   **Charles Woodson Bates**, born 23 Jan 1864, died 1928.

1779. f   ii.   **Anne Woodson Bates**, born 30 Nov 1866. She married **Charles Finley Hersman**. Charles died before 1914. Anne died 1948 in St. Louis, Missouri.

- - - - - - - - - -

1780. Julia Bates[4] Woodson <See pg. 179> (1708.Anne[3], 1707.Goodridge[2], 1.Benjamin, Sr.[1]) was born 27 Feb 1845 at "Mount Airy", St. Charles Co., Missouri, the daughter of **Charles Friend Woodson** and **Anne Thomas Wilson**. Julia died 15 Apr 1910. She married **Isaac Newton Stoutemyer**.[514]

ISSUE:

1781. f   i.   **Mabel Woodson Stoutemyer**, born 10 May 1877, died 17 Feb 1959.

1782. m   ii.   **Bernard Erhart "Hart" Stoutemyer**, born 27 Jan 1879. He married **Lorena Sonna**. Lorena died 1947.

+ 1783. m   iii.   **Woodson George Stoutemyer**, born 10 May 1880.

1787. m   iv.   **John Paul Stoutemyer**, born 7 Oct 1881. He married **Sallie Sabin**. John died 13 May 1960.

- - - - - - - - - -

1783. Woodson George[5] Stoutemyer (1780.Julia[4], 1708.Anne[3], 1707.Goodridge[2], 1.Benjamin, Sr.[1]) was born 10 May 1880, the son of **Isaac Newton Stoutemyer** and **Julia Bates Woodson**. He married **Emma Johnson** 14 Jun 1911. Emma died Aug 1961.

ISSUE:

+ 1784. m   i.   **James Paul Stoutemyer**.

- - - - - - - - - -

1784. James Paul[6] Stoutemyer (1783.Woodson[5], 1780.Julia[4], 1708.Anne[3], 1707.Goodridge[2], 1.Benjamin, Sr.[1]). He was the son of **Woodson George Stoutemyer** and **Emma Johnson**. He married **Beulah Rosser**.

ISSUE:

1785. m   i.   **James Rosser Stoutemyer**.

1786. m   ii.   **Paul Woodson Stoutemyer**.

- - - - - - - - - -

---

[513] McLean, *Wilson Family*, 43. Boddie, *Historical Southern Families*, 3: 66. Bates, *Bates, et al*, 35. Beale, *Diary of Edward Bates*, xvi, 286, etc.

[514] McLean, *Wilson Family*, 42. Boddie, *Historical Southern Families*, 3: 66.

1788. Mary Randolph⁴ Woodson <See pg. 179> (1708.Anne³,
1707.Goodridge², 1.Benjamin, Sr.¹) was born 10 Feb 1849 at "Mount Airy",
St. Charles Co., Missouri, the daughter of **Charles Friend Woodson** and
Anne Thomas Wilson. Mary died 4 Mar 1916. She married **William A.
Harris** 1872 in St. Charles Co., Missouri. ⁵¹⁵

ISSUE:

- 1789. m   i.   **Julian Harris**, born about 1874, died about 1877.
- 1790. m   ii.   **William Leslie Harris**, born about 1876, died about 1876.
- 1791. m iii.   **Edward Kerr Harris**, born 1880. He married **Willie
  Snyder** 1922. Edward died 1936 in St. Charles, Missouri.

- - - - - - - - - - -

1792. Dr. Benjamin Francis³ Wilson <See pg. 176> (1707.Goodridge²,
1.Benjamin, Sr.¹) was born about 1810 in Prince Edward Co., Virginia, the
son of **Goodridge Wilson** and **Elizabeth Woodson Venable**. Benjamin
died after 1882 probably in Gregg Co., Texas. He married (1) **Mary
Elizabeth Wilson** 20 Sep 1831 in Cumberland Co., Virginia. She was born
1813. She was the daughter of **Allen Wilson** and **Elizabeth Seymour
Wright**. Mary died before 1869.⁵¹⁶

ISSUE:

- + 1793. f   i.   **Anna F. Wilson**, born 1836, died before 1914 <See pg. 191>.
- 1797. f   ii.   _____ **Wilson**, born 1838.
- 1798. f iii.   _____ **Wilson**, born 1840.
- 1799. f   iv.   **Margaret Wilson**, born 1842 in Virginia, died after 1860.
- 1800. f   v.   **Mary Grace Wilson**, born 1844 in Virginia, died after
  1883 probably in Mulberry Grove Co., Crawford, Kansas.
- 1801. f   vi.   **Frances Allen "Fannie" Wilson**, born 1846 in Virginia,
  died after 1886 probably in St. Louis Co., Missouri.
- 1802. f vii.   **Susan Wilson**, born 1848 in Virginia. She married **James
  Sandridge**. Susan died before 1924.
- 1803. m viii.   **Dr. Allen Wilson**, born 1850 in Missouri, died probably in
  St Louis, Missouri.
- 1804. m   ix.   **Nathaniel Venable Wilson**, born 1852 in Missouri, died
  23 Oct 1862 in St. Charles Co., Missouri, and was buried in
  Frayser Burying Ground, St. Charles Co.⁵¹⁷
- 1805. f   x.   **Sally Carey Wilson**, born 1854 in Missouri, died 27 Oct
  1862 in St. Charles Co. and was buried in Frayser Burying

---

⁵¹⁵ McLean, _Wilson Family_, 43. Boddie, _Historical Southern Families_, 3: 67.

⁵¹⁶ McLean, _Wilson Family_, 43-4. Boddie, _Historical Southern Families_, 3: 65-6.
Elliott, _Marriages, Cumberland Co VA_, 139.

⁵¹⁷ Wiechens, _Cemeteries of St. Charles Co. MO_, 5:81.

Ground.

Benjamin was a student at Hampden-Sydney College in 1827 and received his M. D. degree from the University of Pennsylvania in 1831. As a surgeon in 1836 in Prince Edward Co., Virginia, with his father, he contributed to medical information for a Revolutionary War pension application.[518]

By 1845 he was living in Kanawha Co., Virginia (West Virginia), and in the 1850 and 1860 censuses, he is shown in St. Louis Co., Missouri, with his wife and children. His home an "old brick house on Orf Road, was built in 1857" in St. Charles Co., Missouri.[519] In 1850 he is mentioned visiting Edward Bates.[520]

He left Missouri during the Civil War; on the trip south, his wife, Mary Elizabeth, died. Benjamin married (2) **Margaret O'Neill** 3 Nov 1869 in Bossier Parish, Louisiana, where they are shown in the 1870 census. They moved to Gregg Co., Texas, by the 1880 census. Benjamin may have died by 5 Feb 1883 when his daughters gave their brother Alan power of attorney to handle their property in Gregg Co.[521]

- - - - - - - - - - -

1793. Anna F.[4] Wilson <See pg. 190> (1792.Benjamin[3], 1707.Goodridge[2], 1.Benjamin, Sr.[1]) was born 1836 in Virginia, the daughter of **Benjamin Francis Wilson** and **Mary Elizabeth Wilson**. Anna died before 1914. She married **Fleming Bates** 15 May 1857. He was born 2 Apr 1834 in Missouri, the son of **Edward Bates** and **Julia D. Coalter**. Fleming died 8 Dec 1871.[522]

ISSUE:

1794. m   i.   **Dr. Allen Cumberland Bates**, born 17 Oct 1858 in Missouri, died 14 Feb 1906.

1795. m   ii. **Benjamin W. Bates**, born 29 Jun 1863 in Missouri, died 8 Dec 1870.

1796. f   iii. **Nannie Fleming Bates**, born 31 Oct 1869 in Louisiana, died after 1924.

---

[518] Bradshaw, *History of Hampden-Sydney College*, 200. University of Pennsylvania, (accessed 7 Mar 2006). Dorman, *VA Revolutionary Pension Applications*, 50.

[519] Drummond, *Historic Sites in St. Charles County*, 249. "Dardenne Prairie".

[520] Beale, *Diary of Edward Bates*, 122.

[521] Gregg Co. TX Deed Book G:327

[522] Bates, *Bates, et al*, 35, 77.

As would be expected "Fleming and wife and child" visited in Edward
Bates' home frequently.

It is said that Fleming "grieved his father by serving in the Confederate
Army" In 1863 he had word that Fleming had been sent from Arkansas to
Mobile "in pursuit of an absconding quarter master" and that he had "the
prisoner in charge". On 14 Sep 1865 "Fleming arrived, direct from
Washington, Arks; apparently in good health .... dressed (not to my liking)
in grey frock and pantaloons".[523]

Fleming and Anna are shown with their children in the 1860 St. Louis Co.,
Missouri, census and in the 1870 Morehouse Parish, Louisiana, census. A
1924 letter written by **Charles Woodson Wilson** said that Nannie was
living in St. Louis with other kin.[524]

- - - - - - - - - - -

1806. Elizabeth Woodson[3] Wilson <See pg. 176> (1707.Goodridge[2],
1.Benjamin, Sr.[1]) was born 11 Apr 1812 at "Milnwood", Prince Edward
Co., Virginia, the daughter of **Goodridge Wilson** and **Elizabeth Woodson
Venable**.[525] Elizabeth died 5 May 1871 in Cabell, West Virginia. She
married **Charles Ruffner** 25 Sep 1844 in Kanawha Co., Virginia (West
Virginia). He was born 24 Feb 1801 in Charleston, Kanawha Co., the son of
Daniel Ruffner.[526] Charles died 22 Mar 1881 in Cabell.[527]

ISSUE:[528]

  1807. m   i.   **Charles Ruffner, II**, born 20 Feb 1846, died 1862.

\+ 1808. f   ii. **Elizabeth Venable "Lizzie" Ruffner**, died before 25 Feb
         1924.

\+ 1820. f iii. **Agnes Goodrich Ruffner**, born 20 Mar 1851, died 5 May
         1920 <See pg. 194>.

\+ 1822. f iv. **Annie Pleasantia Ruffner**, born 10 Aug 1853, died 26 Sep
         1934 <See pg. 194>.

  1862. f   v.   **Ella Nettleton Ruffner**, born 14 Jan 1856, died 1862.

---

[523] Beale, *Diary of Edward Bates*, xvi, 24, 26, 93, 319, 505.

[524] Copy from Watkins sisters of Kirkwood MO.

[525] Kanawha Co. WV Deed Book Q:182,184.

[526] West Virginia became a state in 1863. Atkinson, *History of Kanawha County*,
303.

[527] DAR - Application # 81352, Jeannette McCluer Watson.

[528] McLean, *Wilson Family*, 44-47. Boddie, *Historical Southern Families*, 3: 66,
69.

Charles also married (1) **Ann Hedrick** 26 Jun 1825. Ann died 6 Nov 1842.

- - - - - - - - - -

1808. Elizabeth Venable "Lizzie"[4] Ruffner (1806.Elizabeth[3], 1707.Goodridge[2], 1.Benjamin, Sr.[1]). She was the daughter of **Charles Ruffner** and **Elizabeth Woodson Wilson**. Elizabeth died before 25 Feb 1924. She married **Morgan W. Rider**.[529]

ISSUE:
+ 1809. f   i.   **Virginia Rider.**
+ 1813. m   ii.   **Paul Rider.**
+ 1815. m   iii. **Percy Rider.**

- - - - - - - - - -

1809. Virginia[5] Rider (1808.Elizabeth[4], 1806.Elizabeth[3], 1707.Goodridge[2], 1.Benjamin, Sr.[1]). She was the daughter of **Morgan W. Rider** and **Elizabeth Venable "Lizzie" Ruffner**. She married **Robert Largent**.

ISSUE:
+ 1810. m   i.   **John Joseph Largent.**

- - - - - - - - - -

1810. John Joseph[6] Largent (1809.Virginia[5], 1808.Elizabeth[4], 1806.Elizabeth[3], 1707.Goodridge[2], 1.Benjamin, Sr.[1]). He was the son of **Robert Largent** and **Virginia Rider**. He married **Bethel McKinney**.

ISSUE:
1811. m   i.   **John Largent**, born 1942.
1812. f   ii. **Joan Roberta Largent**, born 1943.

- - - - - - - - - -

1813. Paul[5] Rider (1808.Elizabeth[4], 1806.Elizabeth[3], 1707.Goodridge[2], 1.Benjamin, Sr.[1]). He was the son of **Morgan W. Rider** and **Elizabeth Venable "Lizzie" Ruffner**.

ISSUE:
1814. m   i.   **Morgan Rider.**

- - - - - - - - - -

1815. Percy[5] Rider (1808.Elizabeth[4], 1806.Elizabeth[3], 1707.Goodridge[2], 1.Benjamin, Sr.[1]). He was the son of **Morgan W. Rider** and **Elizabeth Venable "Lizzie" Ruffner**. He married **Lois Moore**.

ISSUE:
1816. f   i.   **Betty Rider.** She married _____ **Charlesworth.**

---

[529] McLean, *Wilson Family*, 44. Boddie, *Historical Southern Families*, 3: 69, 5:42.

1817. f   ii.   **Louise Rider.** She married _____ **Ide.**
1818. f   iii. **Marjorie Rider.** She married _____ **Butler.**
1819. f   iv.   **Pattie Rider.** She married _____ **Pooser.**

- - - - - - - - - -

1820. Agnes Goodrich[4] Ruffner <See pg. 192> (1806.Elizabeth[3], 1707.Goodridge[2], 1.Benjamin, Sr.[1]) was born 20 Mar 1851 in Charleston, Kanawha Co., Virginia (West Virginia). She was the daughter of **Charles Ruffner** and **Elizabeth Woodson Wilson.** Agnes died 5 May 1920 in Los Angeles, California. She married **Sampson Sanders Simmons** 13 Feb 1870 in Cabell Co., West Virginia. He was born 5 Nov 1843 in Cabell Co., Virginia (West Virginia).[530]

ISSUE:

1821. f   i.   **Naomi Anne Simmons.** She married **George Taylor Klipstein.**

- - - - - - - - - -

1822. Annie Pleasantia[4] Ruffner <See pg. 192> (1806.Elizabeth[3], 1707.Goodridge[2], 1.Benjamin, Sr.[1]) was born 10 Aug 1853 in Charleston, Kanawha Co., Virginia (West Virginia), the daughter of **Charles Ruffner** and **Elizabeth Woodson Wilson.** Annie died 26 Sep 1934 in St. Louis, Missouri. She married **Samuel McCluer Watson** 13 Jul 1876 in St. Charles, Missouri. He was born 13 Nov 1851 in Dardenne, St. Charles Co., Missouri, the son of **Thomas Watson** and **Nannie Campbell McCluer.** Samuel died 9 Apr 1925 in Maplewood, Missouri.[531]

ISSUE:

+ 1823. f   i.   **Constance Ruffner Watson,** born 6 Oct 1877, died 30 Dec 1956 <See pg. 195>.
+ 1845. m   ii.   **Brank Farris Watson,** born 13 Jan 1880, died 30 Jan 1939 <See pg. 197>.
  1846. f   iii. **Agnes Frayser Watson,** born 9 Mar 1882, died 18 Jan 1924.
  1847. f   iv.   **Jeannette McCluer Watson,** born 16 Jun 1884, died 1972.
  1848. f   v.   **Julia Coanza Watson,** born 30 Jul 1886, died 1 Dec 1968.
+ 1849. m   vi.   **Thomas William Watson,** born 9 Mar 1889, died 27 Feb 1941 <See pg. 197>.
  1858. f   vii. **Virginia Gauss Watson,** born 18 Feb 1891. She married

---

[530] McLean, *Wilson Family*, 44. Boddie, *Historical Southern Families*, 3: 69. DAR - Application #114487 Naomi Anne Simmons Klipstein

[531] McLean, *Wilson Family*, 44-47. Boddie, *Historical Southern Families*, 3: 69-73. Additional information from Nancy (Whitman) Santheson of Roswell NM and Henrietta (McCluer) Phelps of Auxvasse MO. Watson, *Heritage And Promise*, 198.

    Leslie E. Cleek 6 Oct 1932.

1859. m viii. **Charles Ruffner Watson**, born 30 Jul 1893. He married **Ida Allene Kallenbach** 30 Dec 1925. Charles died 11 Oct 1956.

1860. f ix. **Nannie Lucretia Watson**, born 29 Dec 1895, died 21 Jan 1937.

+ 1861. m x. **Samuel McCluer Watson, Jr.**, born 16 Feb 1898, died 27 Sep 1956 <See pg. 197>.

- - - - - - - - - - -

1823. Constance Ruffner[5] Watson <See pg. 194> (1822.Annie[4], 1806.Elizabeth[3], 1707.Goodridge[2], 1.Benjamin, Sr.[1]) was born 6 Oct 1877 in Washington, Franklin Co., Missouri, the daughter of **Samuel McCluer Watson** and **Annie Pleasantia Ruffner**. Constance died 30 Dec 1956. She married **Benjamin Martin Audrain** 10 Aug 1905.

ISSUE:

1824. f i. **Annie Elizabeth Audrain**, born 28 Jun 1906. She married **Ralph Kerr Watson** 1934.

+ 1825. m ii. **Samuel Harold Audrain**, born 24 Oct 1907.

+ 1834. f iii. **Beatrice Marguerite Audrain**, born 1909 <See pg. 196>.

1843. m iv. **Benjamin Manarre Audrain**, born 1911, died 1966.

1844. f v. **Nannie Constance Audrain**, born 31 Jan 1913, died 29 Mar 1913.

- - - - - - - - - - -

1825. Samuel Harold[6] Audrain (1823.Constance[5], 1822.Annie[4], 1806.Elizabeth[3], 1707.Goodridge[2], 1.Benjamin, Sr.[1]) was born 24 Oct 1907, the son of **Benjamin Martin Audrain** and **Constance Ruffner Watson**. He married **Jane Abbott Symons** 29 Jul 1933.

ISSUE:

+ 1826. m i. **Samuel Harold Audrain, Jr.**, born 1934.

+ 1831. m ii. **David Bruce Audrain**, born 28 Oct 1941 <See pg. 196>.

1833. f iii. **Nancy Jane Audrain**, born 25 Sep 1945. She married **Joseph Davis** 1970.

- - - - - - - - - - -

1826. Samuel Harold[7] Audrain, Jr. (1825.Samuel[6], 1823.Constance[5], 1822.Annie[4], 1806.Elizabeth[3], 1707.Goodridge[2], 1.Benjamin, Sr.[1]) was born 1934, the son of **Samuel Harold Audrain** and **Jane Abbott Symons**. He married (1) **Dottye Stewart Baird** 1958.

ISSUE:

1827. f i. **Valerie Lynn Audrain**.

1828. m   ii.   **Michael Stewart Audrain.**
1829. m   iii. **Samuel Harold Audrain, III.**

Samuel, Jr. married (2) **Dee Floyd** 1974.
ISSUE:
1830. f   iv.   **Kendra Leanne Audrain.**

- - - - - - - - - - -

1831. David Bruce[7] Audrain <See pg. 195> (1825.Samuel[6], 1823.Constance[5], 1822.Annie[4], 1806.Elizabeth[3], 1707.Goodridge[2], 1.Benjamin, Sr.[1]) was born 28 Oct 1941, the son of **Samuel Harold Audrain** and **Jane Abbott Symons.** He married **Michelle Sterr** 1971.
ISSUE:
1832. f   i.   **Yvette Michelle Audrain.**

- - - - - - - - - - -

1834. Beatrice Marguerite[6] Audrain <See pg. 195> (1823.Constance[5], 1822.Annie[4], 1806.Elizabeth[3], 1707.Goodridge[2], 1.Benjamin, Sr.[1]) was born 1909, the daughter of **Benjamin Martin Audrain** and **Constance Ruffner Watson.** She married **Samuel Ebbert Clippard** 1930.
ISSUE:
+ 1835. f   i.   **Katherine Elizabeth Clippard**, born 5 Sep 1931.
+ 1839. f   ii. **Joyce Ann Clippard**, born 18 Sep 1942.

- - - - - - - - - - -

1835. Katherine Elizabeth[7] Clippard (1834.Beatrice[6], 1823.Constance[5], 1822.Annie[4], 1806.Elizabeth[3], 1707.Goodridge[2], 1.Benjamin, Sr.[1]) was born 5 Sep 1931, the daughter of **Samuel Ebbert Clippard** and **Beatrice Marguerite Audrain.** She married **Matthew Pierce Matheny, III** 1952.
ISSUE:
1836. f   i.   **Susan Veronica Matheny.**
1837. m   ii. **Matthew Pierce Matheny, IV.**
1838. m   iii. **Kendall Clippard Matheny.**

- - - - - - - - - - -

1839. Joyce Ann[7] Clippard (1834.Beatrice[6], 1823.Constance[5], 1822.Annie[4], 1806.Elizabeth[3], 1707.Goodridge[2], 1.Benjamin, Sr.[1]) was born 18 Sep 1942, the daughter of **Samuel Ebbert Clippard** and **Beatrice Marguerite Audrain.** She married **Leslie Thomas McKnelly** 1963.
ISSUE:
1840. m   i.   **Leslie Thomas McKnelly, Jr.**
1841. f   ii. **Karen Tanya McKnelly.**

1842. f   iii.   **Sharon Lynette McKnelly.**

- - - - - - - - - - -

1845. Brank Farris[5] Watson <See pg. 194> (1822.Annie[4], 1806.Elizabeth[3], 1707.Goodridge[2], 1.Benjamin, Sr.[1]) was born 13 Jan 1880, the son of **Samuel McCluer Watson** and **Annie Pleasantia Ruffner.** Brank died 30 Jan 1939 in Washington, District of Columbia. He married **Grace Goodridge Woodson (See number 1757 - pg. 186)** 27 Aug 1902. She was born 6 May 1881, the daughter of **Richard Goodridge Woodson** and **Grace Lee.**

ISSUE:

+ 1758. m   i.   **Quentin Durward Watson,** born 27 Jun 1903 <See pg. 187>.

- - - - - - - - - - -

1849. Thomas William[5] Watson <See pg. 194> (1822.Annie[4], 1806.Elizabeth[3], 1707.Goodridge[2], 1.Benjamin, Sr.[1]) was born 9 Mar 1889, the son of **Samuel McCluer Watson** and **Annie Pleasantia Ruffner.** Thomas died 27 Feb 1941. He married **Grace B. Bissland** 14 Jun 1920.

ISSUE:

1850. f   i.   **Irene Hope Watson,** born 19 Nov 1922.
1851. m   ii.   **William Ruffner Watson,** born 1926, died about 1930.
+ 1852. m   iii.   **Thomas William Watson, Jr.,** born 22 Jan 1934.

- - - - - - - - - - -

1852. Thomas William[6] Watson, Jr. (1849.Thomas[5], 1822.Annie[4], 1806.Elizabeth[3], 1707.Goodridge[2], 1.Benjamin, Sr.[1]) was born 22 Jan 1934, the son of **Thomas William Watson** and **Grace B. Bissland.** He married (1) **Flora Armbruster.**

ISSUE:

1853. f   i.   **Heather Ann Watson.**
1854. f   ii.   **Sally Denise Watson.**
1855. m   iii.   **Bruce Andrew Watson.**
1856. f   iv.   **Karen Elizabeth Watson.**

Thomas, Jr. married (2) **Ellen** _____.

ISSUE:

1857. f   v.   **Jennifer Mary Watson.**

- - - - - - - - - - -

1861. Samuel McCluer[5] Watson, Jr. <See pg. 195> (1822.Annie[4], 1806.Elizabeth[3], 1707.Goodridge[2], 1.Benjamin, Sr.[1]) was born 16 Feb 1898, the son of **Samuel McCluer Watson** and **Annie Pleasantia Ruffner.**

Samuel, Jr. died 27 Sep 1956. He married **Martha Agnes Wilson (See number 1130 - pg. 268)** 1929 probably in St. Charles Co., Missouri. She was born 30 Oct 1899, the daughter of **Charles Woodson Wilson** and **Julia Bentley Frayser**.

ISSUE:

1131. f	i.	**Julia Margaret Watson**.
1132. f	ii.	**Sally Ann Watson**.
1133. f	iii.	**Mary Watson**, married with two daughters and one son.
+ 1137. f	iv.	**Martha Agnes Watson** <See pg. 269>.
1143. m	v.	**Samuel McCluer Watson, III**.

- - - - - - - - - - -

1863. Nathaniel Venable[3] Wilson <See pg. 176> (1707.Goodridge[2], 1.Benjamin, Sr.[1]) was born before 21 Jun 1814 in Prince Edward Co., Virginia, the son of **Goodridge Wilson** and **Elizabeth Woodson Venable**. Nathaniel died 1905 probably in Kanawha Co., West Virginia. He married **Elizabeth "Betsy" Ruffner** 30 Jul 1835 in Kanawha Co., West Virginia. She was born 1815 in Kanawha Co., Virginia (West Virginia), the daughter of **Daniel Ruffner**. Elizabeth died after 5 Jul 1891.[532]

ISSUE:

+ 1864. f	i.	**Kate Wilson**, born before 4 Aug 1836 <See pg. 199>.
1866. m	ii.	**Daniel Wilson**, born 1838 in Charleston, Kanawha Co., Virginia (West Virginia).
+ 1867. f	iii.	**Elizabeth "Bettie" Wilson**, born 1840 <See pg. 199>.
1877. f	iv.	**Annie Wilson**, born 1842 in Charleston. She married _____ **Allemong**. Annie died after 1924 probably in Kanawha Co.
+ 1878. f	v.	**Virginia Wilson**, born 1844 <See pg. 200>.
+ 1880. f	vi.	**Wilhemina "Willie" Wilson**, born 1847, died after 1924 <See pg. 200>.
1883. m	vii.	**Nathaniel Wilson, Jr.**, born 1849 in Charleston, died after 1924 probably in Kanawha Co.
1884. m	viii.	**James Wilson**, born about 1851 in Charleston.

Nathaniel's birth is mentioned in a letter his uncle wrote in 1814, "Goodrich a second son". His father wrote from Farmville 25 Jan 1836, then from Charleston to Nat "on Buster's Farm" 4 Aug 1836, with advice concerning stock and crops, sending "love to Betsey & the Chick". This land had been

---

[532] McLean, *Wilson Family*, 44. Boddie, *Historical Southern Families*, 3:66. Swango, *Early Kanawha County Marriage Records*, Part II, 7.

owned by Claudius Buster.[533]

Nat wrote a letter to his cousin in Kentucky in 1841 concerning a salt shipment. Two 1844 letters from Nat's brothers, Ben and Goodridge, mention his involvement in the salt business, which was started by his Ruffner in-laws.[534]   His family is listed in the 1840 and 1850 Kanawha Co. censuses, his occupation, saltmaker.

Betsey wrote in her diary of her memories of the family and the area in 1876 and 1890.[535]

- - - - - - - - - - -

1864. Kate[4] Wilson <See pg. 198> (1863.Nathaniel[3], 1707.Goodridge[2], 1.Benjamin, Sr.[1]) was born before 4 Aug 1836 in Charleston, Kanawha Co., Virginia (West Virginia), the daughter of **Nathaniel Venable Wilson** and **Elizabeth "Betsy" Ruffner**. She married **Phillip Noyes** before 1892.
ISSUE:
1865. m   i.   **Wilson Noyes,** born in Charleston, Kanawha Co., West Virginia.

- - - - - - - - - - -

1867. Elizabeth "Bettie"[4] Wilson <See pg. 198> (1863.Nathaniel[3], 1707.Goodridge[2], 1.Benjamin, Sr.[1]) was born 1840 in Charleston, Kanawha Co., Virginia (West Virginia), the daughter of **Nathaniel Venable Wilson** and **Elizabeth "Betsy" Ruffner**. She married **Charles C. Lewis** 1864 in Kanawha Co. He was born 15 Apr 1839 in Kanawha Co., the son of **John Dickenson Lewis** and **Ann Dickenson**. Charles died 1882.[536]
ISSUE:
1868. m   i.   **John D. Lewis,** born about 1865 in Charleston, Kanawha Co., West Virginia.
+ 1869. m   ii.   **Charles Cameron Lewis, Jr.,** born 1867.
+ 1871. f   iii.   **Virginia Lewis,** born about 1870 <See pg. 200>.
1874. f   iv.   **Josephine Lewis.**
1875. f   v.   **Ann Lewis.**
1876. m   vi.   **Goodrich Lewis.**

---

[533] 1814 and 1841 letters, McCrary, *Wilson Families ... Correspondence .... 1785-1849,* 168-9,289. 1836 and 1844 letters, Wilson, Nath'l V. *Papers, 1834-1878.* Kanawha Co. WV Deed Book I-J:280.
[534] *Virginia Magazine of History and Biography,* 101:532-4 (1993).
[535] Trotter, "Glimpse of Charleston".
[536] Hale, *History of the Great Kanawha Valley,* 2:189-190.

- - - - - - - - - - -

1869. Charles Cameron[5] Lewis, Jr. (1867.Elizabeth[4], 1863.Nathaniel[3], 1707.Goodridge[2], 1.Benjamin, Sr.[1]) was born 1867 in Charleston, Kanawha Co., West Virginia, the son of **Charles C. Lewis** and **Elizabeth "Bettie" Wilson**. He married **Laura Payne** before 1891 in Charleston, Kanawha Co., West Virginia.

ISSUE:
1870. m   i.   **Cameron Lewis**, born 16 Aug 1890 in Charleston.

- - - - - - - - - - -

1871. Virginia[5] Lewis <See pg. 199> (1867.Elizabeth[4], 1863.Nathaniel[3], 1707.Goodridge[2], 1.Benjamin, Sr.[1]) was born about 1870 in Charleston, Kanawha Co., West Virginia, the daughter of **Charles C. Lewis** and **Elizabeth "Bettie" Wilson**. She married **Charles Stacy** before 1891 in Charleston.

ISSUE:
1872. m   i.   _____ **Stacy**, born before 4 Jan 1892 in Charleston.
1873. m   ii.   _____ **Stacy**, born before 4 Jan 1892 in Charleston.

- - - - - - - - - - -

1878. Virginia[4] Wilson <See pg. 198> (1863.Nathaniel[3], 1707.Goodridge[2], 1.Benjamin, Sr.[1]) was born 1844 in Charleston, Kanawha Co., Virginia (West Virginia), the daughter of **Nathaniel Venable Wilson** and **Elizabeth "Betsy" Ruffner**. She married _____ **Hall** before 1892.

ISSUE:
1879. f   i.   **Elizabeth Hall**, born in Charleston.

- - - - - - - - - - -

1880. Wilhemina "Willie"[4] Wilson <See pg. 198> (1863.Nathaniel[3], 1707.Goodridge[2], 1.Benjamin, Sr.[1]) was born 1847 in Charleston, Kanawha Co., Virginia (West Virginia), the daughter of **Nathaniel Venable Wilson** and **Elizabeth "Betsy" Ruffner**. Wilhemina died after 1924 probably in Cincinnati, Ohio. She married _____ **Rooke** before 1892.[537]

ISSUE:
+ 1881. f   i.   **Elizabeth Rooke**.

- - - - - - - - - - -

1881. Elizabeth[5] Rooke (1880.Wilhemina[4], 1863.Nathaniel[3], 1707.Goodridge[2], 1.Benjamin, Sr.[1]). She was the daughter of _____ **Rooke** and **Wilhemina "Willie" Wilson**. She married _____ **Trotter**.

---

[537] 1924 letter. Copy from Watkins sisters of Kirkwood MO.

ISSUE:

1882. f   i.   **Margret G. Trotter**.

- - - - - - - - - - -

1885. Dr. Goodridge Alexander[3] Wilson <See pg. 176> (1707.Goodridge[2], 1.Benjamin, Sr.[1]) was born 7 Oct 1815 in Prince Edward Co., Virginia, the son of **Goodridge Wilson** and **Elizabeth Woodson Venable**. Goodridge died 8 Dec 1897 in Dallas, Texas. He married **Margaret Nicholas Cabell Reid** 7 Nov 1837. She was born 25 Feb 1816, the daughter of **William Shields Reid** and **Clementine Venable**. Margaret died Feb 1887 in Granville Co., North Carolina, and was buried in the Wilson Family Cemetery at "Somerset", Granville Co., North Carolina.[538]

ISSUE:

+ 1886. m   i.   **William Reid Wilson**, born 22 Feb 1839, died 8 Dec 1897
                    <See pg. 202>.

 1951. f   ii.   **Elizabeth Woodson Wilson**, born 11 Jun 1840, died
                    17 Mar 1910, and was buried at the Wilson Family
                    Cemetery.

 1952. f   iii.   **Clementine Reid Wilson**, born 18 Aug 1842, died 10 Jan
                    1931 and was buried in the Wilson Family Cemetery.

 1953. f   iv.   **Mary Grace Wilson**, born 11 Feb 1844, died 13 Jan 1931
                    and was buried in the Wilson Family Cemetery.

 1954. f   v.   **Margaret Ringgold Wilson**, born 25 Aug 1846, died
                    9 May 1875 and was buried in the Wilson Family
                    Cemetery.

 1955. f   vi.   **Nannie Thomas Wilson**, born 4 Apr 1848. She married
                    Archie H. Gregory. Nannie died 8 Jun 1937 and was
                    buried in the Wilson Family Cemetery.

+ 1956. m   vii.   **Goodridge Wilson**, born 6 Nov 1849, died 13 Oct 1933
                    <See pg. 208>.

+ 2028. f viii.   **Ellen Scott Wilson**, born 17 Nov 1851, died 29 May 1914
                    <See pg. 217>.

In Jan 1834, Goodridge wrote from Hampden-Sydney to his brother at "Milnwood, Pr. Edward Va. .....there is a report afloat that you have a notion of passing the parable to a gal very shortly .... Nat - think before you further go. Think that you are endeavouring to involve yourself into all the mazes of a matrimonial state.... from hearing the sentiments expressed by

---

[538] McLean, *Wilson Family*, 47-57. Boddie, *Historical Southern Families*, 3:66. Blackwood, "Somerset" - Wilson Family Cemetery. Additions and corrections on this family were provided by Samuel J. and Marguerite F. (Morton) Blackwood of Clearwater FL.

yourself about an unmarried man being free from the danger of being broke." Goodridge received his A B degree there in 1834 and his M. D. degree from the University of Pennsylvania in 1837.[539]

He wrote a letter in 1844 from Clarkesville (Mecklenburg Co.) naming his fourth child and mentioning his brother **William** living nearby. In Jan 1852 he wrote from Richmond where he lamented being away from his family, then another in Jun 1852 about the division of their parents' estate. Goodridge was an elder in the Clarksville Church from 1840 until he removed to Richmond in 1851.[540]

Before the Civil War, Goodridge and his family moved to Granville Co., North Carolina, where their home was called "Somerset". This is where McLean visited with two daughters, Clementine and Grace.[541]

- - - - - - - - - - -

1886. Dr. William Reid[4] Wilson <See pg. 201> (1885.Goodridge[3], 1707.Goodridge[2], 1.Benjamin, Sr.[1]) was born 22 Feb 1839 at "Wheatland", Mecklenburg Co., Virginia, the son of **Goodridge Alexander Wilson** and **Margaret Nicholas Cabell Reid**. William died 8 Dec 1897. He married (1) **Josephine Scott Morton** 15 May 1862 in Richmond, Virginia.[542]

ISSUE:

+ 1887. f   i.   **Mary Tazewell Wilson**, born 15 Mar 1864, died 7 Nov 1938 <See pg. 203>.
  1907. m   ii.   **Goodridge Alexander Wilson**, born about 1865.
  1908. f   iii. **Margaret Reid Wilson**, born 17 May 1869, died 18 Jan 1935, and was buried in the Wilson Family Cemetery at "Somerset", Granville Co., North Carolina.
  1909. f   iv.   **Emma Morton Wilson**.
+ 1910. f   v.   **Bessie Woodson Wilson**, born about 1873, died Apr 1948 <See pg. 205>.
+ 1914. m vi.   **William Ringgold Wilson**, born 21 Sep 1876 <See pg. 205>.
  1922. f vii. **Josephine Scott Wilson**.
+ 1923. f viii. **Kate Goodridge Wilson**, born 7 Dec 1881 <See pg. 206>.
  1931. m ix.   **Samuel Reid Wilson**, born 3 May 1884, died May 1885.

[539] Wilson, Nath'l V. *Papers, 1834-1878*. University of Pennsylvania Archives and Records Center copies, 3 Sep 1992.

[540] Wilson, Nath'l V. *Papers, 1834-1878*. Presbyterian Church, 177.

[541] *Oxford (NC) Ledger*, 9 Jan 1978. McLean, *Wilson Family*, 5, 6, 53, 54.

[542] McLean, *Wilson Family*, 47-53. Handbook of Texas Online, "WILSON, WILLIAM REID", (accessed 8 Mar 2006).

William married (2) **Bettie Thomas** 9 Jan 1889.

ISSUE:

+ 1932. m   x.   **John Thomas Wilson,** born 7 Oct 1889 <See pg. 207>.
+ 1937. m   xi.   **Cabell Flournoy Wilson,** born 8 Oct 1892 <See pg. 207>.
+ 1939. f   xii.   **Annie Thomas Wilson,** born 22 Feb 1894 <See pg. 208>.
+ 1948. f xiii.   **Clement Reid Wilson,** born 8 Nov 1894, died 25 Oct 1927
                         <See pg. 208>.

- - - - - - - - - -

1887. Mary Tazewell[5] Wilson <See pg. 202> (1886.William[4],
1885.Goodridge[3], 1707.Goodridge[2], 1.Benjamin, Sr.[1]) was born 15 Mar
1864, the daughter of **William Reid Wilson** and **Josephine Scott Morton**.
Mary died 7 Nov 1938 and was buried in Tranquility Cemetery, Granville
Co., North Carolina. She married **Joseph William Morton** 1889. He was
born 1 Jan 1859, the son of **Joseph Morton** and **Anne Eliza Daniel**. Joseph
died 11 Jun 1936 and was buried in Tranquility Cemetery.[543]

ISSUE:

+ 1888. m   i.   **William Wilson Morton,** born 6 Jun 1890.
+ 1890. f   ii.   **Anne Eliza Morton,** born 22 Mar 1892 <See pg. 204>.
  1897. f   iii.   **Josephine Scott Morton,** born 8 Jan 1895, died 15 Jun
                         1942, and was buried in Tranquility Cemetery.
  1898. m   iv.   **Tazewell Norvell Morton,** born 16 Nov 1896, died 26 Oct
                         1918 in France, and was buried in Tranquility Cemetery.
+ 1899. m   v.   **Nathaniel Venable Morton,** born 9 Oct 1898, died 28 Nov
                         1979 <See pg. 204>.
+ 1901. f   vi.   **Margaret Reid Morton,** born 18 Nov 1900 <See pg. 205>.
  1904. f vii.   **Elizabeth Watkins Morton,** born 16 Aug 1903. She
                         married (1) **R. G. Bradley.** R. G. died 1940. Elizabeth
                         married (2) **Garland S. May.**
  1905. m viii.   **Goodridge Alexander Morton,** born 29 Oct 1905, died
                         18 Jul 1949, and was buried in Tranquility Cemetery.
  1906. m ix.   **Douglas Reid Morton,** born 1907, died about 1907,and
                         was buried in Tranquility Cemetery.

- - - - - - - - - -

1888. William Wilson[6] Morton (1887.Mary[5], 1886.William[4],
1885.Goodridge[3], 1707.Goodridge[2], 1.Benjamin, Sr.[1]) was born 6 Jun 1890
at "Level Green", Granville Co., North Carolina, the son of **Joseph
William Morton** and **Mary Tazewell Wilson.** He married **Frances Wilson**

---

[543] McLean, *Wilson Family*, 48-50. Watkins, *Thomas Watkins of Chickahominy*,
20. Blackwood, Tranquility Cemetery.

Campbell 25 Jun 1930.[544]

ISSUE:

1889. f   i. **Frances Wilson Morton,** born 4 Jul 1931.

- - - - - - - - - - -

1890. Anne Eliza[6] Morton <See pg. 203> (1887.Mary[5], 1886.William[4], 1885.Goodridge[3], 1707.Goodridge[2], 1.Benjamin, Sr.[1]) was born 22 Mar 1892 at "Level Green", Granville Co., North Carolina, the daughter of **Joseph William Morton** and **Mary Tazewell Wilson**. She married **Louie McGhee Simpson** 6 Jun 1922 at "Level Green".

ISSUE:

+ 1891. f   i. **Mary E. Simpson,** born 15 Mar 1923.
  1893. f   ii. **Jo M. Simpson,** born 24 Aug 1924.
  1894. m   iii. **Louis McGhee Simpson, Jr.,** born 24 Mar 1926.
  1895. m   iv. **William Venable Simpson,** born 21 Apr 1928.
  1896. m   v. **John Alva Simpson,** born 11 Jul 1931.

- - - - - - - - - - -

1891. Mary E.[7] Simpson (1890.Anne[6], 1887.Mary[5], 1886.William[4], 1885.Goodridge[3], 1707.Goodridge[2], 1.Benjamin, Sr.[1]) was born 15 Mar 1923, the daughter of **Louie McGhee Simpson** and **Anne Eliza Morton**. She married **Robert Newton Taylor** 9 Jun 1948. He was born 9 Apr 1920. Robert died 16 Jun 1993 and was buried in Tranquility Cemetery, Granville Co., North Carolina.

ISSUE:

1892. f   i. **Elizabeth Ann Taylor,** born 12 May 1949.

- - - - - - - - - - -

1899. Nathaniel Venable[6] Morton <See pg. 203> (1887.Mary[5], 1886.William[4], 1885.Goodridge[3], 1707.Goodridge[2], 1.Benjamin, Sr.[1]) was born 9 Oct 1898, the son of **Joseph William Morton** and **Mary Tazewell Wilson**. Nathaniel died 28 Nov 1979, and was buried in Tranquility Cemetery, Granville Co., North Carolina. He married **Florine Wright** 4 Jan 1930. She was born 3 Mar 1904. Florine died 9 Apr 1973 and was buried in Tranquility Cemetery. [545]

Florine also married (1) _____ **Cook.**

ISSUE:

1900. f   i. **Miriam Christine Cook,** born 1920, died 1983.

- - - - - - - - - - -

---

[544] McLean, *Wilson Family*, 48.

[545] McLean, *Wilson Family*, 49.

1901. Margaret Reid[6] Morton <See pg. 203> (1887.Mary[5], 1886.William[4], 1885.Goodridge[3], 1707.Goodridge[2], 1.Benjamin, Sr.[1]) was born 18 Nov 1900, the daughter of **Joseph William Morton** and **Mary Tazewell Wilson**. She married (1) **E. L. Cowan** 1926.

ISSUE:

1902. f   i.   **Margaret Virginia Cowan**, born 23 Jan 1927.

1903. m   ii.   **Joseph William Cowan**, born 12 Jul 1929.

Margaret married (2) **Alexander Doane Cromartie**.

- - - - - - - - - - -

1910. Bessie Woodson[5] Wilson <See pg. 202> (1886.William[4], 1885.Goodridge[3], 1707.Goodridge[2], 1.Benjamin, Sr.[1]) was born about 1873, the daughter of **William Reid Wilson** and **Josephine Scott Morton**. Bessie died Apr 1948 in Celo, North Carolina. She married **Thomas Vance Kirk** 13 Jun 1894. [546]

ISSUE:

+ 1911. m   i.   **William Wilson Kirk**, born 12 Mar 1895.

- - - - - - - - - - -

1911. William Wilson[6] Kirk (1910.Bessie[5], 1886.William[4], 1885.Goodridge[3], 1707.Goodridge[2], 1.Benjamin, Sr.[1]) was born 12 Mar 1895, the son of **Thomas Vance Kirk** and **Bessie Woodson Wilson**. He married **Harriet Seymour**.

ISSUE:

1912. f   i.   **Lillian Elizabeth Kirk**, born in Jacksonville, Florida. She married **John Pilkington**.

1913. f   ii.   **Harriet Vance Kirk**, born in Jacksonville. She married **Richard Crago**.

- - - - - - - - - - -

1914. William Ringgold[5] Wilson <See pg. 202> (1886.William[4], 1885.Goodridge[3], 1707.Goodridge[2], 1.Benjamin, Sr.[1]) was born 21 Sep 1876, the son of **William Reid Wilson** and **Josephine Scott Morton**. He married **Kate Bransford**.

ISSUE:

+ 1915. m   i.   **William Reid Wilson**, born 29 Jul 1911.

+ 1917. m   ii.   **Joseph Bransford Wilson**, born 29 Jun 1913 <See pg. 206>.

+ 1919. f   iii.   **Katherine Morton Wilson**, born 2 Sep 1915 <See pg. 206>.

- - - - - - - - - - -

---

[546] McLean, *Wilson Family*, 50.

1915. William Reid[6] Wilson (1914.William[5], 1886.William[4], 1885.Goodridge[3], 1707.Goodridge[2], 1.Benjamin, Sr.[1]) was born 29 Jul 1911, the son of **William Ringgold Wilson** and **Kate Bransford**. He married **Marjorie Christian** Nov 1948. William died 14 Dec 2005 in Austin, Texas.[547]   ISSUE:
  1916. m i. **William Reid Wilson, Jr.**, born 13 Nov 1949.

- - - - - - - - - - -

1917. Joseph Bransford[6] Wilson <See pg. 205> (1914.William[5], 1886.William[4], 1885.Goodridge[3], 1707.Goodridge[2], 1.Benjamin, Sr.[1]) was born 29 Jun 1913, the son of **William Ringgold Wilson** and **Kate Bransford**. He married **Dottie Simmons**.
                       ISSUE:
  1918. m i. **Joseph Bransford Wilson, Jr.**, born 19 Apr 1947.

- - - - - - - - - - -

1919. Katherine Morton[6] Wilson <See pg. 205> (1914.William[5], 1886.William[4], 1885.Goodridge[3], 1707.Goodridge[2], 1.Benjamin, Sr.[1]) was born 2 Sep 1915, the daughter of **William Ringgold Wilson** and **Kate Bransford**. She married **Ralph Smith**.
                       ISSUE:
  1920. m i. **Ralph Wilson Smith**, born 14 May 1945.
  1921. f ii. **Shirley Katherine Smith**, born 30 Dec 1946.

- - - - - - - - - - -

1923. Kate Goodridge[5] Wilson <See pg. 202> (1886.William[4], 1885.Goodridge[3], 1707.Goodridge[2], 1.Benjamin, Sr.[1]) was born 7 Dec 1881, the daughter of **William Reid Wilson** and **Josephine Scott Morton**. She married **Charles H. Taggart**.
                       ISSUE:
  1924. m i. **William Wilson Taggart**, born 5 Nov 1911. He married **Nadine Wells**.
+ 1925. f ii. **Martha Morton Taggart**, born 17 Oct 1917.
  1928. f iii. **Esther Rose Taggart**, born 2 Jun 1921.
+ 1929. m iv. **Charles Laurence Taggart**, born 15 Sep 1923 <See pg. 207>.

- - - - - - - - - - -

1925. Martha Morton[6] Taggart (1923.Kate[5], 1886.William[4], 1885.Goodridge[3], 1707.Goodridge[2], 1.Benjamin, Sr.[1]) was born 17 Oct

---

[547] McLean, *Wilson Family*, 51. Obituary, http://obit.wcfish.com/obit_display.cgi?id=272465&listing=All, (accessed 8 Mar 2006).

1917, the daughter of **Charles H. Taggart** and **Kate Goodridge Wilson**.
She married **Langdon Todd Merrill**.

ISSUE:

1926. f   i.   **Judith Merrill**, born 20 Apr 1943.

1927. m   ii.   **John Reid Merrill**, born 19 Sep 1947.

- - - - - - - - - -

1929. Charles Laurence[6] Taggart <See pg. 206> (1923.Kate[5],
1886.William[4], 1885.Goodridge[3], 1707.Goodridge[2], 1.Benjamin, Sr.[1]) was
born 15 Sep 1923, the son of **Charles H. Taggart** and **Kate Goodridge
Wilson**. He married **Vivian Tuthill**.

ISSUE:

1930. f   i.   **Vivian Lynne Taggart**, born 26 Sep 1948.

- - - - - - - - - -

1932. John Thomas[5] Wilson <See pg. 203> (1886.William[4],
1885.Goodridge[3], 1707.Goodridge[2], 1.Benjamin, Sr.[1]) was born 7 Oct 1889,
the son of **William Reid Wilson** and **Bettie Thomas**. He married **Mildred
Symes**. [548]

ISSUE:

+ 1933. f   i.   **Lilburn Elizabeth Wilson**, born 8 Apr 1913.

- - - - - - - - - -

1933. Lilburn Elizabeth[6] Wilson (1932.John[5], 1886.William[4],
1885.Goodridge[3], 1707.Goodridge[2], 1.Benjamin, Sr.[1]) was born 8 Apr 1913,
the daughter of **John Thomas Wilson** and **Mildred Symes**. She married
Robert C. Walker.

ISSUE:

1934. f   i.   **Mildred Sharon Walker**, born 8 Apr 1941.

1935. f   ii.   **Lilburn Dale Walker**, born 27 Nov 1943.

1936. m   iii.   **Robert Cleveland Walker**, born 2 Mar 1947.

- - - - - - - - - -

1937. Cabell Flournoy[5] Wilson <See pg. 203> (1886.William[4],
1885.Goodridge[3], 1707.Goodridge[2], 1.Benjamin, Sr.[1]) was born 8 Oct 1892,
the son of **William Reid Wilson** and **Bettie Thomas**. He married **Leone
Paulk**.

ISSUE:

1938. f   i.   **Jere Wilson**.

- - - - - - - - - -

---

[548] McLean, *Wilson Family*, 52.

1939. Annie Thomas⁵ Wilson <See pg. 203> (1886.William⁴, 1885.Goodridge³, 1707.Goodridge², 1.Benjamin, Sr.¹) was born 22 Feb 1894, the daughter of **William Reid Wilson** and **Bettie Thomas**. She married **Rae Skillern**.

ISSUE:
+ 1940. f   i.   **Bettie Skillern**, born 23 Dec 1916.
+ 1944. f   ii. **Nancy Rae Skillern**, born 31 Jul 1920.
  1947. f   iii. **Jean Skillern**, born 24 Dec 1928.

- - - - - - - - - -

1940. Bettie⁶ Skillern (1939.Annie⁵, 1886.William⁴, 1885.Goodridge³, 1707.Goodridge², 1.Benjamin, Sr.¹) was born 23 Dec 1916, the daughter of **Rae Skillern** and **Annie Thomas Wilson**. She married **Sam Leake**.

ISSUE:
  1941. m   i.   **Sam Skillern Leake**, born 9 Oct 1941.
  1942. m   ii. **David Hobson Leake**, born 13 Sep 1943.
  1943. m   iii. **John Wilson Leake**, born 25 Dec 1948.

- - - - - - - - - -

1944. Nancy Rae⁶ Skillern (1939.Annie⁵, 1886.William⁴, 1885.Goodridge³, 1707.Goodridge², 1.Benjamin, Sr.¹) was born 31 Jul 1920, the daughter of **Rae Skillern** and **Annie Thomas Wilson**. She married **Andreas Korn**.

ISSUE:
  1945. m   i.   **Rae Skillern Korn**, born 1 Nov 1944.
  1946. f   ii. **Annie Elizabeth Korn**, born 24 May 1948.

- - - - - - - - - -

1948. Clement Reid⁵ Wilson <See pg. 203> (1886.William⁴, 1885.Goodridge³, 1707.Goodridge², 1.Benjamin, Sr.¹) was born 8 Nov 1894, the son of **William Reid Wilson** and **Bettie Thomas**. Clement died 25 Oct 1927. He married **Andie Newton**. [549]

ISSUE:
  1949. m   i.   **Clement Reid Wilson, Jr.**, born 1925.
  1950. m   ii. **John Thomas Wilson**, born Sep 1927. He married **Nancy Marion Davis**.

- - - - - - - - - -

1956. Goodridge⁴ Wilson <See pg. 201> (1885.Goodridge³, 1707.Goodridge², 1.Benjamin, Sr.¹) was born 6 Nov 1849, the son of **Goodridge Alexander Wilson** and **Margaret Nicholas Cabell Reid**. Goodridge died 13 Oct 1933 and was buried in the Wilson Family Cemetery at "Somerset", Granville

---

[549] McLean, *Wilson Family*, 53.

Co., North Carolina. He married **Margaret Goodridge Frayser (See number 2134 - pg. 285)** 15 May 1888. She was born 7 Oct 1861 in Dardenne Twp, St. Charles Co., Missouri. She was the daughter of **Robert Bentley Frayser** and **Martha Agnes Wilson**. Margaret died 17 Jan 1931 at "Somerset" and was buried in the Wilson Family Cemetery there.[550]

ISSUE:

1957. m   i.   **Robert Bentley Wilson**, born 10 Apr 1889, died 3 May 1976, and was buried in the Wilson Family Cemetery.

+ 1958. m   ii.   **Goodridge Alexander Wilson**, born 16 Apr 1890, died 3 Mar 1959.

+ 1969. f   iii. **Agnes Frayser Wilson**, born 6 Nov 1892, died 8 Sep 1975 <See pg. 210>.

1985. m   iv.   **Charles Julian Wilson**, born 13 Jun 1895. He married **Rachel Howard**. She was born 13 May 1898, died 13 Jan 1966, and was buried in the Wilson Family Cemetery at "Somerset", Granville Co., North Carolina. Julian died 11 Sep 1983, and was buried in the Wilson Family Cemetery.[551]

+ 1986. m   v.   **William Reid Wilson**, born 28 Apr 1898 <See pg. 212>.

+ 2018. f   vi.   **Marguerite Rochet Wilson**, born 24 Sep 1902, died 4 Jun 1986 <See pg. 215>.

- - - - - - - - - -

1958. Goodridge Alexander[5] Wilson <See pg. 285> (1956.Goodridge[4], 1885.Goodridge[3], 1707.Goodridge[2], 1.Benjamin, Sr.[1]) was born 16 Apr 1890, the son of **Goodridge Wilson** and **Margaret Goodridge Frayser**. Goodridge died 3 Mar 1959, and was buried in Smithfield, North Carolina. He married **Irwin Stark**. Irwin died 3 Feb 1960 and was buried in Smithfield.

ISSUE:

+ 1959. f   i.   **Isabel Frayser Wilson**, born 26 Nov 1917, died 5 Sep 1974.

+ 1966. m   ii.   **Edwin Bentley Wilson**, born 1 Apr 1921 <See pg. 210>.

- - - - - - - - - -

1959. Isabel Frayser[6] Wilson (1958.Goodridge[5], 1956.Goodridge[4], 1885.Goodridge[3], 1707.Goodridge[2], 1.Benjamin, Sr.[1]) was born 26 Nov 1917, the daughter of **Goodridge Alexander Wilson** and **Irwin Stark**. Isabel died 5 Sep 1974. She married **Noah Hunter Leggett** 16 Feb 1946.

---

[550] McLean, *Wilson Family*, 56-7. Blackwood, "Somerset" - Wilson Family Cemetery.

[551] *Oxford (NC) Ledger*, 9 Jan 1978.

Noah died Apr 1997.
ISSUE:

+ 1960. m   i. **John Goodrich Leggett**, born 2 Oct 1948, died 11 Jan 1991 <See pg. 210>.
+ 1963. f   ii. **Margaret Irwin Leggett**, born 28 Jun 1950 <See pg. 210>.
  1965. f   iii. **Susan Isabel Leggett**, born 2 Aug 1954. She married **Kenneth Cattrell** 1992.

- - - - - - - - - - -

1960. John Goodrich[7] Leggett <See pg. 210> (1959.Isabel[6], 1958.Goodridge[5], 1956.Goodridge[4], 1885.Goodridge[3], 1707.Goodridge[2], 1.Benjamin, Sr.[1]) was born 2 Oct 1948, the son of **Noah Hunter Leggett** and **Isabel Frayser Wilson**. John died 11 Jan 1991. He married **Diane Landry** 9 Apr 1977.
ISSUE:

  1961. m   i. **Charles Hunter Leggett**, born 30 Jun 1978 in Athens, Georgia. He married **Erin _____** 29 Jun 2002.
  1962. m   ii. **Justin Garner Leggett**, born 7 Jul 1981.

- - - - - - - - - - -

1963. Margaret Irwin[7] Leggett <See pg. 210> (1959.Isabel[6], 1958.Goodridge[5], 1956.Goodridge[4], 1885.Goodridge[3], 1707.Goodridge[2], 1.Benjamin, Sr.[1]) was born 28 Jun 1950, the daughter of **Noah Hunter Leggett** and **Isabel Frayser Wilson**. She married **Eugene Edward Staats** 2 Aug 1980.
ISSUE:

  1964. m   i. **Christopher John Staats**, born 13 Jan 1984.

- - - - - - - - - - -

1966. Edwin Bentley[6] Wilson <See pg. 209> (1958.Goodridge[5], 1956.Goodridge[4], 1885.Goodridge[3], 1707.Goodridge[2], 1.Benjamin, Sr.[1]) was born 1 Apr 1921, the son of **Goodridge Alexander Wilson** and **Irwin Stark**. He married **Joan Pyke**.[552]
ISSUE:

  1967. f   i. **Linda Joan Wilson**.
  1968. f   ii. **Julia Rachel Wilson**.

- - - - - - - - - - -

1969. Agnes Frayser[5] Wilson <See pg. 209, 285> (1956.Goodridge[4], 1885.Goodridge[3], 1707.Goodridge[2], 1.Benjamin, Sr.[1]) was born 6 Nov

---

[552] McLean, *Wilson Family*, 57. Additional information from Joan (Pyke) Wilson of Takoma Park MD.

1892, the daughter of **Goodridge Wilson** and **Margaret Goodridge Frayser.** Agnes died 8 Sep 1975. She married **Leslie Longstreet Mason, Sr.** 27 Nov 1920 at "Somerset", Granville Co., North Carolina. He was born 18 Feb 1890, died 22 Dec 1976.

ISSUE:

+ 1970. m   i. **William Wilson Mason**, born 5 Oct 1921.
+ 1973. m ii. **Leslie Longstreet Mason, Jr.**, born 8 Dec 1926 <See pg. 211>.

- - - - - - - - - - -

1970. William Wilson[6] Mason (1969.Agnes[5], 1956.Goodridge[4], 1885.Goodridge[3], 1707.Goodridge[2], 1.Benjamin, Sr.[1]) was born 5 Oct 1921 in Logan, West Virginia, the son of **Leslie Longstreet Mason, Sr.** and **Agnes Frayser Wilson**. He married **Katherine Johnson** 16 Jul 1949 in Charleston, West Virginia. She was born 10 Dec 1921 in Nashville, Tennessee.

ISSUE:

+ 1971. m   i. **John Mark Mason**, born 30 Sep 1961.

- - - - - - - - - - -

1971. John Mark[7] Mason (1970.William[6], 1969.Agnes[5], 1956.Goodridge[4], 1885.Goodridge[3], 1707.Goodridge[2], 1.Benjamin, Sr.[1]) was born 30 Sep 1961 in Greensboro, North Carolina, the son of **William Wilson Mason** and **Katherine Johnson**. He married **Donna Stepnick** 13 Jan 1996. She was born 15 Jul 1963.

ISSUE:

1972. m   i. **John Matthew Mason**, born 4 Dec 2000.

- - - - - - - - - - -

1973. Judge Leslie Longstreet[6] Mason, Jr. <See pg. 211> (1969.Agnes[5], 1956.Goodridge[4], 1885.Goodridge[3], 1707.Goodridge[2], 1.Benjamin, Sr.[1]) was born 8 Dec 1926, the son of **Leslie Longstreet Mason, Sr.** and **Agnes Frayser Wilson**. He married **Helen Hope Chiles**. She was born 23 Nov 1928.

ISSUE:

+ 1974. f   i. **Rebecca Lee Mason**, born 28 Oct 1959.
  1977. f ii. **Elizabeth Ann Mason**, born 27 Jan 1961.
+ 1978. m iii. **Chiles Bentley Mason**, born 16 Jul 1963 <See pg. 212>.
+ 1982. f iv. **Mary Margaret Mason**, born 5 Feb 1965 <See pg. 212>.

- - - - - - - - - - -

1974. Rebecca Lee[7] Mason (1973.Leslie, Jr.[6], 1969.Agnes[5], 1956.Goodridge[4], 1885.Goodridge[3], 1707.Goodridge[2], 1.Benjamin, Sr.[1]) was born 28 Oct 1959, the daughter of **Leslie Longstreet Mason, Jr.** and **Helen Hope Chiles**. She married **William Towne Baker** 8 Jun 1991 in the Glebe, Powhatan Co., Virginia. He was born 9 Jun 1960.

ISSUE:

1975. m   i.   **Ford Baker**, born about 1996.
1976. m   ii.   **Grey Baker**, born about 2000.

- - - - - - - - - -

1978. Chiles Bentley[7] Mason <See pg. 211> (1973.Leslie, Jr.[6], 1969.Agnes[5], 1956.Goodridge[4], 1885.Goodridge[3], 1707.Goodridge[2], 1.Benjamin, Sr.[1]) was born 16 Jul 1963, the son of **Leslie Longstreet Mason, Jr.** and **Helen Hope Chiles**. He married **Leslie Abbot Hume** 26 Jun 1993. She was born 14 Jul 1968.

ISSUE:

1979. m   i.   **Reilly Mason**, born about 1995.
1980. f   ii.   **Chiles Bentley Mason, Jr.**, born about 1997.
1981. m   iii. **Reid Mason**, born about 1999.

- - - - - - - - - -

1982. Mary Margaret[7] Mason <See pg. 211> (1973.Leslie, Jr.[6], 1969.Agnes[5], 1956.Goodridge[4], 1885.Goodridge[3], 1707.Goodridge[2], 1.Benjamin, Sr.[1]) was born 5 Feb 1965, the daughter of **Leslie Longstreet Mason, Jr.** and **Helen Hope Chiles**. She married **Tom Davidson Evans**.

ISSUE:

1983. m   i.   **Davis Evans**, born about 1998.
1984. m   ii.   **Mason Evans**, born about 2000.

- - - - - - - - - -

1986. William Reid[5] Wilson <See pg. 209, 285> (1956.Goodridge[4], 1885.Goodridge[3], 1707.Goodridge[2], 1.Benjamin, Sr.[1]) was born 28 Apr 1898, the son of **Goodridge Wilson** and **Margaret Goodridge Frayser**. He married **Helen Windish** 19 Sep 1925. [553]

ISSUE:

+ 1987. f   i.   **Helen Louise Wilson**, born 8 Sep 1928.
+ 2003. f   ii.   **Carolyn Margaret Wilson**, born 15 Mar 1931 <See pg. 214>.

- - - - - - - - - -

1987. Helen Louise[6] Wilson (1986.William[5], 1956.Goodridge[4], 1885.Goodridge[3], 1707.Goodridge[2], 1.Benjamin, Sr.[1]) was born 8 Sep 1928

---

[553] McLean, *Wilson Family*, 57.

in Chicago, Illinois, the daughter of **William Reid Wilson** and **Helen Windish**. She married **Kenneth James Tolley** 6 May 1950 in Lakewood, Ohio. He was born 12 Mar 1925 in Cleveland, Ohio.

ISSUE:
+ 1988. f   i.   **Gale Louise Tolley**, born 14 Dec 1953.
+ 1993. m   ii.   **Reid James Tolley**, born 13 Jul 1957 .
+ 1996. f   iii.   **Lynn Ellen Tolley**, born 14 May 1959.

- - - - - - - - - -

1988. Gale Louise[7] Tolley (1987.Helen[6], 1986.William[5], 1956.Goodridge[4], 1885.Goodridge[3], 1707.Goodridge[2], 1.Benjamin, Sr.[1]) was born 14 Dec 1953 in Lakewood, Ohio, the daughter of **Kenneth James Tolley** and **Helen Louise Wilson**. She married **Thomas Scott Cole, Jr.** 21 Aug 1976 in Fairview Park, Ohio. He was born 10 Nov 1954 in Fairview Park, Ohio.
ISSUE:
+ 1989. f   i.   **Lindsey Ann Cole**, born 8 Oct 1979.
  1991. m   ii.   **Steven Thomas Cole**, born 2 Oct 1982 in Fairview Park, Ohio.
  1992. f   iii.   **Sarah Elizabeth Cole**, born 18 Feb 1985 in Columbus, Ohio.

- - - - - - - - - -

1989. Lindsey Ann[8] Cole (1988.Gale[7], 1987.Helen[6], 1986.William[5], 1956.Goodridge[4], 1885.Goodridge[3], 1707.Goodridge[2], 1.Benjamin, Sr.[1]) was born 8 Oct 1979 in Columbus, Ohio, the daughter of **Thomas Scott Cole, Jr.** and **Gale Louise Tolley**. She married **Greg Cozzens** 12 Jun 2004 in Dublin, Ohio.
ISSUE:
  1990. m   i.   **Thomas Allen Cozzens**, born 26 Apr 2005.

- - - - - - - - - -

1993. Reid James[7] Tolley (1987.Helen[6], 1986.William[5], 1956.Goodridge[4], 1885.Goodridge[3], 1707.Goodridge[2], 1.Benjamin, Sr.[1]) was born 13 Jul 1957 in Fairview Park, Ohio, the son of **Kenneth James Tolley** and **Helen Louise Wilson**. He married **Lori Stromer** 3 Jan 1981 in Hastings, Nebraska. She was born 8 Nov 1959 in Hastings.
ISSUE:
  1994. m   i.   **Zachary Reid Tolley**, born 31 Jan 1985 in Lincoln, Nebraska.
  1995. m   ii.   **Benjamin Scott Tolley**, born 23 Aug 1987 in N. Canton, Ohio.

- - - - - - - - - -

1996. Lynn Ellen[7] Tolley (1987.Helen[6], 1986.William[5], 1956.Goodridge[4], 1885.Goodridge[3], 1707.Goodridge[2], 1.Benjamin, Sr.[1]) was born 14 May 1959 in Fairview Park, Ohio, the daughter of **Kenneth James Tolley** and **Helen Louise Wilson**. She married **William Gary George** 16 Aug 1980 in Fairview Park. He was born 25 Sep 1957 in Cleveland, Ohio.

ISSUE:

1997. m   i.   **Collin David George**, born 18 Jun 1984 in Columbus, Ohio.

1998. f   ii.   **Meridith Grace George**, born 8 Feb 1986 in Portland, Maine.

1999. m   iii.   **Andrew William George**, born 3 Jan 1988 in Silver Spring, Maryland.

2000. f   iv.   **Elspeth Hope George**, born 28 Oct 1989 in Silver Spring.

2001. m   v.   **Thomas Nathaniel George**, born 7 Aug 1991 in Silver Spring.

2002. f   vi.   **Grace Elizabeth George**, born 29 May 1993 in Asheville, North Carolina.

- - - - - - - - - -

2003. Carolyn Margaret[6] Wilson <See pg. 212> (1986.William[5], 1956.Goodridge[4], 1885.Goodridge[3], 1707.Goodridge[2], 1.Benjamin, Sr.[1]) was born 15 Mar 1931 in Chicago, Illinois, the daughter of **William Reid Wilson** and **Helen Windish**. She married **Jack Holt Jones** 20 Dec 1952 in Lakewood, Ohio. He was born 7 Nov 1930 in Cleveland, Ohio.

ISSUE:

+ 2004. m   i.   **Thomas Reid Jones**, born 14 Jul 1955.

+ 2008. f   ii.   **Karen Sue Jones**, born 5 Aug 1956.

+ 2011. m   iii.   **Robert William Jones**, born 28 Jan 1958 <See pg. 215>.

+ 2014. m   iv.   **William David Jones**, born 25 Jan 1959 <See pg. 215>.

- - - - - - - - - -

2004. Thomas Reid[7] Jones (2003.Carolyn[6], 1986.William[5], 1956.Goodridge[4], 1885.Goodridge[3], 1707.Goodridge[2], 1.Benjamin, Sr.[1]) was born 14 Jul 1955 in Williamsburg, Virginia, the son of **Jack Holt Jones** and **Carolyn Margaret Wilson**. He married **Nancy Satava** 14 Jul 1976 in Hudson, Ohio. She was born Apr 1953.

ISSUE:

2005. m   i.   **Scott Thomas Jones**, born 17 Oct 1978 in Columbus, Ohio.

2006. m   ii.   **Michael Reid Jones**, born 7 Mar 1982 in Columbus.

2007. m iii.   **Gregory William Jones**, born 31 Jul 1984 in Columbus.

- - - - - - - - - -

2008. Karen Sue[7] Jones (2003.Carolyn[6], 1986.William[5], 1956.Goodridge[4], 1885.Goodridge[3], 1707.Goodridge[2], 1.Benjamin, Sr.[1]) was born 5 Aug 1956 in Lakewood, Ohio, the daughter of **Jack Holt Jones** and **Carolyn Margaret Wilson**. She married **William Joseph Everal** 28 Nov 1981 in Ann Arbor, Michigan. He was born 14 May 1954.
ISSUE:
2009. f   i.   **Carrie Elyse Everal**, born 15 Oct 1983 in Ann Arbor, Michigan.
2010. m ii.   **Jeffery William Everal**, born 20 Mar 1985 in Ann Arbor.

- - - - - - - - - -

2011. Robert William[7] Jones <See pg. 214> (2003.Carolyn[6], 1986.William[5], 1956.Goodridge[4], 1885.Goodridge[3], 1707.Goodridge[2], 1.Benjamin, Sr.[1]) was born 28 Jan 1958 in Lakewood, Ohio, the son of **Jack Holt Jones** and **Carolyn Margaret Wilson**. He married **Peggy Sue Russell** 16 Oct 1982 in Williamsburg, Virginia.
ISSUE:
2012. m i.   **Robert Len Jones**, born 20 Jul 1985 in Williamsburg, Virginia.
2013. f ii.   **Rebecca Jones**, born 10 Mar 1987 in Williamsburg.

- - - - - - - - - -

2014. William David[7] Jones <See pg. 214> (2003.Carolyn[6], 1986.William[5], 1956.Goodridge[4], 1885.Goodridge[3], 1707.Goodridge[2], 1.Benjamin, Sr.[1]) was born 25 Jan 1959 in Lakewood, Ohio, the son of **Jack Holt Jones** and **Carolyn Margaret Wilson**. He married **Lisa Talbot** in Williamsburg, Virginia.
ISSUE:
2015. m i.   **Brian Wilson Jones**, born 2 May 1990 in Williamsburg, Virginia.
2016. m ii.   **Paul Reed Jones**, born 7 Nov 1992 in Williamsburg.
2017. f iii.   **Melanie Jones**, born 5 Jun 1994 in Williamsburg.

- - - - - - - - - -

2018. Marguerite Rochet[5] Wilson <See pg. 209, 285> (1956.Goodridge[4], 1885.Goodridge[3], 1707.Goodridge[2], 1.Benjamin, Sr.[1]) was born 24 Sep 1902 at "Somerset", Granville Co., North Carolina, the daughter of **Goodridge Wilson** and **Margaret Goodridge Frayser**. Marguerite died 4 Jun 1986 in Harrisonburg, Virginia, and was buried in Tranquility

Cemetery, Granville Co. She married **Joe Baird Morton, Sr.** 7 Oct 1926 in Stovall, Granville Co. He was born 1 Dec 1898 in Granville Co., the son of **James Thomas Morton** and **Frances Crichton Daniel.** Joe, Sr. died 10 Dec 1940 in Oxford, Granville Co., and was buried in Tranquility Cemetery.[554]

ISSUE:

+ 2019. m   i.   **Joe Baird Morton, Jr.,** born 27 Jul 1929.
+ 2025. f   ii. **Marguerite Frances Morton,** born 10 Aug 1934.

- - - - - - - - - -

2019. Joe Baird[6] Morton, Jr. (2018.Marguerite[5], 1956.Goodridge[4], 1885.Goodridge[3], 1707.Goodridge[2], 1.Benjamin, Sr.[1]) was born 27 Jul 1929 in Granville Co., North Carolina, the son of **Joe Baird Morton, Sr.** and **Marguerite Rochet Wilson.** He married **Patricia Gaston** 6 Apr 1953 in Houston, Texas. She was born 26 Aug 1932.

ISSUE:

2020. m   i.   **Lawrence Raymond Morton,** born 26 Sep 1957 in Charlotte, North Carolina.
2021. m   ii. **Richard Bentley Morton,** born 3 Jan 1960 in Richmond, Virginia, died 4 Jan 1960 in Richmond.
+ 2022. m   iii. **Richard Francis Morton,** born 5 Jun 1964.

- - - - - - - - -

2022. Richard Francis[7] Morton (2019.Joe, Jr.[6], 2018.Marguerite[5], 1956.Goodridge[4], 1885.Goodridge[3], 1707.Goodridge[2], 1.Benjamin, Sr.[1]) was born 5 Jun 1964 in Richmond, Virginia, the son of **Joe Baird Morton, Jr.** and **Patricia Gaston.** He married **Ellen Prescott Pendleton** 8 Jul 1995 in Richmond. She was born 19 May 1965 in Richmond.

ISSUE:

2023. f   i.   **Julia Baird Morton,** born 1 May 1999 in Richmond.
2024. m   ii. **Brian Douglas Morton,** born 27 Mar 2001 in Richmond.

- - - - - - - - - -

2025. Marguerite Frances[6] Morton (2018.Marguerite[5], 1956.Goodridge[4], 1885.Goodridge[3], 1707.Goodridge[2], 1.Benjamin, Sr.[1]) was born 10 Aug 1934 in Granville Co., North Carolina, the daughter of **Joe Baird Morton, Sr.** and **Marguerite Rochet Wilson.** She married **Samuel Joyner Blackwood** 23 Dec 1954 in Oxford, North Carolina. He was born 30 Apr 1933 in Durham, North Carolina, the son of **Samuel Craig Blackwood** and **Laura Anna Joyner.**

---

[554] McLean, *Wilson Family,* 57. Blackwood, Tranquility Cemetery.

ISSUE:

2026. m   i.   **Joe Morton Blackwood**, born 12 Jul 1956 in Wiesbaden, Germany. He married (1) **Janet Louise Bohling** 14 Sep 1978 in California. She was born 21 Sep 1944. Joe married (2) **Angela Hope Wapner** 29 Feb 1996. She was born 19 Apr 1956.

2027. f   ii.   **Diane Joyner Blackwood**, born 16 Mar 1961 in Raleigh, Wake Co., North Carolina. She married **Wesley Royce Elsberry** 23 Jun 1984 in Clearwater, Pinellas Co., Florida. He was born 23 Jan 1960 in Lakeland, Florida.

- - - - - - - - - - -

2028. Ellen Scott[4] Wilson <See pg. 201> (1885.Goodridge[3], 1707.Goodridge[2], 1.Benjamin, Sr.[1]) was born 17 Nov 1851, the daughter of **Goodridge Alexander Wilson** and **Margaret Nicholas Cabell Reid**. Ellen died 29 May 1914, and was buried in the Wilson Family Cemetery at "Somerset", Granville Co., North Carolina. She married **James Nathaniel Daniel**. He was born 4 Jul 1849, the son of **James Beverly Daniel** and **Jane Elizabeth Reade**. James died 9 Jul 1922, and was buried in the Wilson Family Cemetery.[555]

ISSUE:

+ 2029. m   i.   **William Goodridge Daniel**.

+ 2034. f   ii.   **Jean Reid Daniel**, died 11 Apr 1949.

+ 2037. f   iii.   **Margaret Reid Daniel**, born 25 Jan 1887 <See pg. 218>.

   2044. m   iv.   **Norvell Watkins Daniel**, born 25 Sep 1889, died 5 Mar 1924, and was buried in the Wilson Family Cemetery.

   2045. m   v.   **James Venable Daniel**. He married **Agnes Daniel**.

   2046. f   vi.   **Nellie Wilson Daniel**, born 1 Jul 1893, died 11 Sep 1944 in Florida, and was buried in the Wilson Family Cemetery.

+ 2047. m   vii.   **Edward Abbott Daniel** <See pg. 219>.

- - - - - - - - - - -

2029. William Goodridge[5] Daniel (2028.Ellen[4], 1885.Goodridge[3], 1707.Goodridge[2], 1.Benjamin, Sr.[1]). He was the son of **James Nathaniel Daniel** and **Ellen Scott Wilson**. He married **Virginia Fyfe**.

ISSUE:

   2030. f   i.   **Elizabeth Daniel**.

   2031. f   ii.   **Virginia Daniel**.

+ 2032. f   iii.   **Margaret Ellen Daniel**.

---

[555] McLean, *Wilson Family*, 54-6. Blackwood, "Somerset" - Wilson Family Cemetery.

- - - - - - - - - - -

2032. Margaret Ellen[6] Daniel (2029.William[5], 2028.Ellen[4], 1885.Goodridge[3], 1707.Goodridge[2], 1.Benjamin, Sr.[1]). She was the daughter of **William Goodridge Daniel** and **Virginia Fyfe**. She married **Charles Butler**.

ISSUE:

2033. m   i.   **Terry Butler**.

- - - - - - - - - - -

2034. Jean Reid[5] Daniel (2028.Ellen[4], 1885.Goodridge[3], 1707.Goodridge[2], 1.Benjamin, Sr.[1]). She was the daughter of **James Nathaniel Daniel** and **Ellen Scott Wilson**. Jean died 11 Apr 1949. She married **Henry S. Garnett**.

ISSUE:

+ 2035. m   i.   **Henry S. Garnett, Jr.**.

- - - - - - - - - - -

2035. Henry S.[6] Garnett, Jr. (2034.Jean[5], 2028.Ellen[4], 1885.Goodridge[3], 1707.Goodridge[2], 1.Benjamin, Sr.[1]). He was the son of **Henry S. Garnett** and **Jean Reid Daniel**. He married **Jane Welch**.

ISSUE:

2036. m   i.   **James Daniel Garnett**, born 23 Mar 1948.

- - - - - - - - - - -

2037. Margaret Reid[5] Daniel <See pg. 217> (2028.Ellen[4], 1885.Goodridge[3], 1707.Goodridge[2], 1.Benjamin, Sr.[1]) was born 25 Jan 1887, the daughter of **James Nathaniel Daniel** and **Ellen Scott Wilson**. She married **Hep McGhee Stovall**.

ISSUE:

2038. m   i.   **Hep McGhee Stovall, Jr.**, born 1 Feb 1908, died 19 Sep 1935 in Pittsburgh, Pennsylvania.
2039. m   ii. **James Daniel Stovall**, born 11 Sep 1911. He married **Joanne Marie Stayer**.
+ 2040. m   iii. **Edward Stewart Stovall**, born 11 Feb 1914.
2042. m   iv. **John Beverly Stovall**, born 9 Jun 1921, died 4 Apr 1922.
2043. m   v.   **William Norvell Stovall**, born 14 Aug 1924. He married **Elouise Mayrant Cuthbert**.

- - - - - - - - - - -

2040. Edward Stewart[6] Stovall (2037.Margaret[5], 2028.Ellen[4], 1885.Goodridge[3], 1707.Goodridge[2], 1.Benjamin, Sr.[1]) was born 11 Feb 1914, the son of **Hep McGhee Stovall** and **Margaret Reid Daniel**. He married **Elizabeth Massengill**.

ISSUE:

2041. f   i.   **Ellen Scott Stovall**, born 16 Sep 1941.

- - - - - - - - - -

2047. Edward Abbott[5] Daniel <See pg. 217> (2028.Ellen[4], 1885.Goodridge[3], 1707.Goodridge[2], 1.Benjamin, Sr.[1]). He was the son of **James Nathaniel Daniel** and **Ellen Scott Wilson**. He married **Annie Sizemore**.

ISSUE:

+ 2048. f   i.   **Ellen Scott Daniel**, born 18 Dec 1920.
+ 2052. f   ii.   **Nannie Wilson Daniel**, born 19 May 1923.
   2054. f   iii.   **Martha Anderson Daniel**, born 18 Apr 1925. She married **John Haddow Cornwell** 2 Sep 1945.
   2055. m   iv.   **Edward Abbott Daniel, Jr.**, born 27 May 1929.

- - - - - - - - - -

2048. Ellen Scott[6] Daniel (2047.Edward[5], 2028.Ellen[4], 1885.Goodridge[3], 1707.Goodridge[2], 1.Benjamin, Sr.[1]) was born 18 Dec 1920, the daughter of **Edward Abbott Daniel** and **Annie Sizemore**. She married **James Cecil Kiser** 18 Nov 1941.

ISSUE:

2049. f   i.   **Nancy Elizabeth Kiser**, born 3 Oct 1942.
2050. m   ii.   **James Edward Kiser**, born 31 Mar 1944.
2051. m   iii.   **John Taise Kiser**, born 3 May 1946.

- - - - - - - - - -

2052. Nannie Wilson[6] Daniel (2047.Edward[5], 2028.Ellen[4], 1885.Goodridge[3], 1707.Goodridge[2], 1.Benjamin, Sr.[1]) was born 19 May 1923, the daughter of **Edward Abbott Daniel** and **Annie Sizemore**. She married **Albert Joseph Lipsius** 30 Dec 1945.

ISSUE:

2053. f   i.   **Daniel Lynne Lipsius**, born 15 Feb 1948.

- - - - - - - - - -

2056. Rev. William Venable[3] Wilson <See pg. 176> (1707.Goodridge[2], 1.Benjamin, Sr.[1]) was born 18 Jan 1819 at "Milnwood", Prince Edward Co., Virginia, the son of **Goodridge Wilson** and **Elizabeth Woodson Venable**. William died 22 Jan 1908 in Lynchburg, Virginia, and was buried in the Presbyterian Cemetery in Lynchburg, Virginia. He married **Grace Ann Wilson** 8 Nov 1843 at "Woodville", Cumberland Co., Virginia. She was born 22 Nov 1816 in Virginia, the daughter of **Judge Daniel Allen Wilson** and **Ann Rebecca Macon**. Grace died 17 Sep 1901 in Lynchburg, Virginia, and was buried in the Presbyterian Cemetery.[556]

ISSUE:[557]

2057. f   i.   **Cornelia Emily Wilson**, born 30 Oct 1844, died 23 Jun 1848.

+ 2058. f   ii.   **Elizabeth Goodridge Wilson**, born 27 Sep 1846.

2078. m iii. **Daniel Allen Wilson**, born 8 Oct 1848, died 25 Jan 1865, and was buried in the Wilson Family Cemetery at "Somerset", Granville Co., North Carolina.[558]

+ 2079. m iv. **Goodridge Alexander Wilson**, born 5 Oct 1850, died 11 Jun 1934 <See pg. 222>.

2100. m v. **Samuel Graham Wilson**, born 14 Jun 1852. He married (1) **Sarah Pauline**. Samuel married (2) **Felixiana Pauline** before 1891.

2101. m vi. **William Venable Wilson, Jr.**, born 22 Apr 1854 in Petersburg, Virginia. He married **Nellie Buford**. William, Jr. died after 1924.[559] In a book written in 1915, he was said to have possession of the Woodson musket that is now on display at the Virginia Historical Society in Richmond. The family story is that this gun was used to protect the Woodson family in the massacre of 1644 in Virginia. **(See pg. 314)**

+ 2102. m vii. **Robert Cowan Wilson**, born 26 Feb 1856, died 25 Sep 1942 <See pg. 224>.

2129. f viii. **Grace Ann Macon Wilson**, born 2 Jan 1860.

William attended Hampden-Sydney from 1832-1835 and then the Union Theological Seminary, which at that time was located in Prince Edward Co. He served at the Clarksville Presbyterian Church in Mecklenburg Co., Virginia, from 1847-1852 and many other places as described in his obituary, which was published in the 29 Jan 1908 issue of the *Christian Observer*.[560]

- - - - - - - - - - -

[556] McLean, *Wilson Family*, 58-62. Boddie, *Historical Southern Families*, 3:66.

[557] Family Bible copy obtained by Maurice Leach from Margaret Potts 1994. Additional information from Williams Wilson of Charleston SC and Suzanne (Greene) Seyfried of Midvale UT.

[558] Blackwood, "Somerset" - Wilson Family Cemetery.

[559] *Virginia Biography, History of Virginia*, 5:46. Woodson, *Woodsons and Their Connections*, 22.

[560] Hampden-Sydney, *General Catalogue*. Presbyterian Church, 178. Obituary, Woodson Family, *Papers, 1778-1908*, Mss1 W8687a 33-36, VHS.

2058. Elizabeth Goodridge⁴ Wilson (2056.William³, 1707.Goodridge², 1.Benjamin, Sr.¹) was born 27 Sep 1846, the daughter of **William Venable Wilson** and **Grace Ann Wilson**. She married **A. J. Sale** 1869 in Marion, Virginia.[561]

ISSUE:
+ 2059. f   i.   **Daniel Allen Wilson Sale**, died 1923.
  2061. f   ii.   **Grace O'Neal Sale**.
+ 2062. m iii. **William Goodridge Sale**, died 1943.
+ 2075. m iv. **John Graham Sale**, died 1940 <See pg. 222>.

- - - - - - - - - - -

2059. Daniel Allen Wilson⁵ Sale (2058.Elizabeth⁴, 2056.William³, 1707.Goodridge², 1.Benjamin, Sr.¹). He was the son of **A. J. Sale** and **Elizabeth Goodridge Wilson**. Daniel died 1923 probably in Virginia. He married **Ruth Herr**.

ISSUE:
  2060. f   i.   **Ruth Wilson Sale**.

- - - - - - - - - - -

2062. William Goodridge⁵ Sale (2058.Elizabeth⁴, 2056.William³, 1707.Goodridge², 1.Benjamin, Sr.¹). He was the son of **A. J. Sale** and **Elizabeth Goodridge Wilson**. William died 1943. He married **Annie Belle Sackett**.

ISSUE:
+ 2063. f   i.   **Elizabeth Goodridge Sale**.
+ 2066. f   ii.   **Louise Moseley Sale**.
+ 2068. m iii. **William Goodridge Sale, Jr.**.

- - - - - - - - - - -

2063. Elizabeth Goodridge⁶ Sale (2062.William⁵, 2058.Elizabeth⁴, 2056.William³, 1707.Goodridge², 1.Benjamin, Sr.¹). She was the daughter of **William Goodridge Sale** and **Annie Belle Sackett**. She married **Johnson McRee**.

ISSUE:
  2064. m   i.   **Johnson McRee, Jr.**, born 3 Jun 1923. He married **Elizabeth Johnson** 22 Oct 1949.
  2065. m   ii.   **Goodridge McRee**, born 11 Jun 1930.

- - - - - - - - - - -

2066. Louise Moseley⁶ Sale (2062.William⁵, 2058.Elizabeth⁴, 2056.William³, 1707.Goodridge², 1.Benjamin, Sr.¹). She was the daughter

---
[561] McLean, *Wilson Family*, 58-9.

of **William Goodridge Sale** and **Annie Belle Sackett**. She married **George Gage DeLoach** Sep 1927.

ISSUE:

2067. f   i.   **Louise Sackett DeLoach**, born 30 Jan 1931.

- - - - - - - - - -

2068. William Goodridge⁶ Sale, Jr. (2062.William⁵, 2058.Elizabeth⁴, 2056.William³, 1707.Goodridge², 1.Benjamin, Sr.¹). He was the son of **William Goodridge Sale** and **Annie Belle Sackett**. He married **Ann Anderson**.

ISSUE:

2069. f   i.   **Ann Goodridge Sale**, born 18 Jun 1930.
2070. f   ii.   **Grace Wilson Sale**, born 12 Dec 1932.
2071. f   iii.   **Jane Lewis Sale**, born 19 Jun 1937.
2072. m   iv.   **William Goodridge Sale, III**, born 21 Aug 1940.
2073. m   v.   **Merriwether Anderson Sale**, born 3 Aug 1942.
2074. f   vi.   **Nell Graham Sale**, born 24 Apr 1946.

- - - - - - - - - -

2075. John Graham⁵ Sale <See pg. 221> (2058.Elizabeth⁴, 2056.William³, 1707.Goodridge², 1.Benjamin, Sr.¹). He was the son of **A. J. Sale** and **Elizabeth Goodridge Wilson**. John died 1940 in Welch, West Virginia. He married **Nellie Quinn**.

ISSUE:

2076. f   i.   **Evelyn Sale**. She married **William Howard**.
2077. m   ii.   **John Graham Sale, Jr.**

- - - - - - - - - -

2079. Rev. Goodridge Alexander⁴ Wilson <See pg. 220> (2056.William³, 1707.Goodridge², 1.Benjamin, Sr.¹) was born 5 Oct 1850 in Clarksville, Virginia, the son of **William Venable Wilson** and **Grace Ann Wilson**. Goodridge died 11 Jun 1934 in Lexington, Virginia. He married **Fanny Pryor Campbell** 18 Oct 1877 in Hampden-Sydney, Prince Edward Co., Virginia. She was born 24 Aug 1857, the daughter of **Thomas H. Campbell** and **Fannie F. Pryor**. Fanny died 24 Jul 1938 in Lexington.[562]

ISSUE:

2080. f   i.   **Fanny Campbell Wilson**, born 17 Sep 1878, died 11 Aug 1879.
2081. m   ii.   **William Venable Wilson**, born 9 Oct 1879, died 19 Oct 1882.
2082. m   iii.   **Thomas Campbell Wilson**, born 5 Mar 1882, died May

---

[562] McLean, *Wilson Family*, 60-62.

1927.

+ 2083. f iv. **Grace Ann Wilson**, born 12 Feb 1884.

2089. m v. _____ **Wilson**, born 1 Apr 1886, died 1 Apr 1886.

+ 2090. m vi. **Goodrich Alexander Wilson, Jr.**, born 15 Jul 1887, died 17 May 1976.

2094. f vii. **Margaret Elizabeth Wilson**, born 25 Sep 1889.

2095. f viii. **Theodorrick Pryor Wilson**, born 24 Feb 1892, died Mar 1937.

2096. f ix. **Jacquelin Campbell Wilson**, born 21 Apr 1895, died 15 Aug 1896.

+ 2097. m x. **Daniel Allen Wilson**, born 27 Jun 1898 <See pg. 224>.

2099. f xi. **Ellen Garrett Wilson**, born 29 Mar 1900. She married **R. Lee Chambliss**.

- - - - - - - - - - -

2083. Grace Ann[5] Wilson (2079.Goodridge[4], 2056.William[3], 1707.Goodridge[2], 1.Benjamin, Sr.[1]) was born 12 Feb 1884, the daughter of **Goodridge Alexander Wilson** and **Fanny Pryor Campbell**. She married **James E. Bosworth**.

ISSUE:

+ 2084. f i. **Fanny Campbell Bosworth**.

+ 2087. m ii. **Elam Withrow Bosworth**, born 23 Apr 1921.

- - - - - - - - - - -

2084. Fanny Campbell[6] Bosworth (2083.Grace[5], 2079.Goodridge[4], 2056.William[3], 1707.Goodridge[2], 1.Benjamin, Sr.[1]). She was the daughter of **James E. Bosworth** and **Grace Ann Wilson**. She married **George Gilliam**.

ISSUE:

2085. f i. **Fanny Campbell Gilliam**, born 26 Sep 1943.

2086. f ii. **Ellen Bland Gilliam**, born 6 Apr 1947.

- - - - - - - - - - -

2087. Elam Withrow[6] Bosworth (2083.Grace[5], 2079.Goodridge[4], 2056.William[3], 1707.Goodridge[2], 1.Benjamin, Sr.[1]) was born 23 Apr 1921, the son of **James E. Bosworth** and **Grace Ann Wilson**. He married **Stella Scott**.

ISSUE:

2088. m i. **David Christopher Bosworth**, born 8 Nov 1945.

- - - - - - - - - - -

2090. Rev. Goodrich Alexander[5] Wilson, Jr. (2079.Goodridge[4], 2056.William[3], 1707.Goodridge[2], 1.Benjamin, Sr.[1]) was born 15 Jul 1887 in Mount Clinton, Virginia, the son of **Goodridge Alexander Wilson** and **Fanny Pryor Campbell**. Goodrich, Jr. died 17 May 1976 in Richmond, Virginia, and was buried in Knollkreg Memorial Park in Abingdon, Virginia. He married (1) **Margaret Holmes Taylor** 27 Jun 1917 in City Point, Prince George Co., Virginia. Margaret died 1958.[563]

ISSUE:

2091. f   i.   **Ellen Meade Wilson**, born 25 Dec 1918. She married **Volney Howard Campbell** 28 Nov 1942. Ellen died probably in Brookhaven Co., Mississippi.

+ 2092. f   ii.   **Margaret Holmes Wilson**, born 29 Jul 1923.

Goodrich, Jr. married (2) **Virginia Taylor Drew** 21 Jun 1961 in Richmond, Virginia.

A memorial to Goodrich, condensed from the minutes of Highlands Presbytery meeting 13 Oct 1977, is written as part of a collection articles that had been written by him.[564]

- - - - - - - - - - -

2092. Margaret Holmes[6] Wilson (2090.Goodrich, Jr.[5], 2079.Goodridge[4], 2056.William[3], 1707.Goodridge[2], 1.Benjamin, Sr.[1]) was born 29 Jul 1923, the daughter of **Goodrich Alexander Wilson, Jr.** and **Margaret Holmes Taylor**. She married **Embree William Potts, Jr.**

ISSUE:

2093. f   i.   **Margaret Holmes Potts**, born 1 Jun 1944.

- - - - - - - - - - -

2097. Daniel Allen[5] Wilson <See pg. 223> (2079.Goodridge[4], 2056.William[3], 1707.Goodridge[2], 1.Benjamin, Sr.[1]) was born 27 Jun 1898, the son of **Goodridge Alexander Wilson** and **Fanny Pryor Campbell**. He married **Jennie Dawson**.

ISSUE:

2098. f   i.   **Margaret Elizabeth Wilson**, born 23 Mar 1925.

- - - - - - - - - - -

2102. Robert Cowan[4] Wilson <See pg. 220> (2056.William[3], 1707.Goodridge[2], 1.Benjamin, Sr.[1]) was born 26 Feb 1856 in Moorefield,

---

[563] McLean, *Wilson Family*, 61. Additional information from James and Jean (Wilson) Micklem of Hopewell VA.

[564] *Southwest Corner.*

Hardy Co., Virginia (West Virginia), the son of **William Venable Wilson** and **Grace Ann Wilson**. Robert died 25 Sep 1942 in Belton, Cass Co., Missouri. He married **Frances Lee Scott** 1 Sep 1886 in Belton. She was born 13 Sep 1862 in Lee's Summit, Missouri. She was the daughter of **George Washington Scott** and **Susan March**. Frances died 2 Oct 1944 in Belton.[565]

ISSUE:

+ 2103. m   i.   **George Scott Wilson**, born 23 Jan 1889, died 21 Jul 1970.
+ 2118. f   ii.   **Grace March Wilson**, born 5 Mar 1892 <See pg. 227>.
+ 2123. f   iii. **Susan Ella Wilson**, born 11 Mar 1894, died 1 Feb 1978 <See pg. 227>.
+ 2127. f   iv.   **Margaret Lucy Wilson**, born 30 Sep 1897 <See pg. 228>.

Robert and his brother **Samuel** did some land speculation in West Texas from 1886-1895, but they apparently returned and/or stayed in Cass Co., Missouri.[566]

- - - - - - - - - - -

2103. George Scott[5] Wilson (2102.Robert[4], 2056.William[3], 1707.Goodridge[2], 1.Benjamin, Sr.[1]) was born 23 Jan 1889 in Belton, Cass Co., Missouri, the son of **Robert Cowan Wilson** and **Frances Lee Scott**. Scott died 21 Jul 1970 in Washington, DC, and was buried in Belton Cemetery. He married **Sue Clark Williams** 2 Jun 1923 in Boonville, Missouri. She was born 15 Apr 1896 in Boonville, the daughter of **William Muir Williams** and **Jessie Evans**. Sue died 21 May 1999 in Lee's Summit, Missouri.[567]

ISSUE:

+ 2104. m   i.   **Williams Wilson**, born 4 Feb 1928.
+ 2114. f   ii.   **Sue Scott Wilson**, born 5 Nov 1929 <See pg. 226>.

- - - - - - - - - - -

2104. Williams[6] Wilson (2103.George[5], 2102.Robert[4], 2056.William[3], 1707.Goodridge[2], 1.Benjamin, Sr.[1]) was born 4 Feb 1928 in St. Louis, St. Louis Co., Missouri, the son of **George Scott Wilson** and **Sue Clark Williams**. He married **Nathalie Gray** 26 Mar 1951 in Charleston, South Carolina. She was born 30 Oct 1927 in Charleston, the daughter of **James B. Gray** and **Annie Laurie Williams**.

---

[565] McLean, *Wilson Family*, 62. *Belton, Missouri Centennial*, 27F.

[566] Nolan Co. TX Deed Books F:212, 256, 394, 611-2.,I:52, 607. Fisher Co. TX Deed Books 5:366, 7:111, 7:407, 7:491. *Belton, Missouri Centennial*, 27F.

[567] *Belton, Missouri Centennial*, 27F, 28F. Additional information from Williams Wilson of Charleston SC.

ISSUE:
+ 2105. m   i.   **John Scott Wilson**, born 20 Aug 1954.
   2107. f   ii.   **Sue Ann Wilson**, born 15 Nov 1955 in Charleston.
   2108. f   iii.   **Mary Elizabeth Wilson**, born 26 Apr 1957 in Charleston.
+ 2109. f   iv.   **Ruth Edna Wilson**, born 26 Sep 1962.
+ 2111. f   v.   **Jessie Evans Wilson**, born 4 Nov 1966.

- - - - - - - - - - -

2105. John Scott[7] Wilson (2104.Williams[6], 2103.George[5], 2102.Robert[4], 2056.William[3], 1707.Goodridge[2], 1.Benjamin, Sr.[1]) was born 20 Aug 1954 in Charleston, South Carolina, the son of **Williams Wilson** and **Nathalie Gray**. He married **Courtney Smith** 27 Nov 1992 in Dallas, Texas. She was born 8 Dec 1954 in Ft. Worth, Tarrant Co., Texas.
ISSUE:
   2106. m   i.   **John Scott Wilson**.

- - - - - - - - - - -

2109. Ruth Edna[7] Wilson (2104.Williams[6], 2103.George[5], 2102.Robert[4], 2056.William[3], 1707.Goodridge[2], 1.Benjamin, Sr.[1]) was born 26 Sep 1962 in Charleston, South Carolina, the daughter of **Williams Wilson** and **Nathalie Gray**. She married **Bruce Fuller** 20 Apr 1996 in Ft. Sill, Oklahoma. He was born 15 Aug 1960 in Alaska. He is the son of **Kenneth Fuller** and **Dorothy** _____.
ISSUE:
   2110. f   i.   **Audrey Fuller**.

- - - - - - - - - - -

2111. Jessie Evans[7] Wilson (2104.Williams[6], 2103.George[5], 2102.Robert[4], 2056.William[3], 1707.Goodridge[2], 1.Benjamin, Sr.[1]) was born 4 Nov 1966 in Charleston, South Carolina, the daughter of **Williams Wilson** and **Nathalie Gray**. She married **Andrew Chan** 21 Jun 1997 in Charleston. He was born 18 Aug 1963, the son of **Paul Chan** and **Felicia** _____.
ISSUE:
   2112. f   i.   **Natalie Chan**.
   2113. f   ii.   **Angela Chan**.

- - - - - - - - - - -

2114. Sue Scott[6] Wilson <See pg. 225> (2103.George[5], 2102.Robert[4], 2056.William[3], 1707.Goodridge[2], 1.Benjamin, Sr.[1]) was born 5 Nov 1929 in St. Louis, Missouri, the daughter of **George Scott Wilson** and **Sue Clark Williams**. She married **Arnold Eversull** 28 Jul 1951 in Kansas City, Missouri.

ISSUE:

2115. f   i.   **Susan Elizabeth Eversull**, born 15 Sep 1953 in Kansas City.

2116. f   ii. **Mary Margaret Eversull**, born 8 Oct 1955 in Kansas City. She married **Don Emory**.

2117. m   iii. **Hubert Arnold Eversull, Jr.**, born 29 May 1960 in Kansas City.

- - - - - - - - - - -

2118. Grace March⁵ Wilson <See pg. 225> (2102.Robert⁴, 2056.William³, 1707.Goodridge², 1.Benjamin, Sr.¹) was born 5 Mar 1892 in Belton, Missouri, the daughter of **Robert Cowan Wilson** and **Frances Lee Scott**. She married **John Van Brunt, Jr.** 2 Jun 1920 in Belton.⁵⁶⁸

ISSUE:

+2119. f   i.   **Margaret Macon Van Brunt**.

- - - - - - - - - - -

2119. Margaret Macon⁶ Van Brunt (2118.Grace⁵, 2102.Robert⁴, 2056.William³, 1707.Goodridge², 1.Benjamin, Sr.¹). She was the daughter of **John Van Brunt, Jr.** and **Grace March Wilson**. She married **Julian W. Rymar** 11 Dec 1954.

ISSUE:

2120. f   i.   **Ann Mackall Rymar**.

2121. f   ii. **Grace Macon Rymar**.

2122. f   iii. **Margaret Gibson Rymar**.

- - - - - - - - - - -

2123. Susan Ella⁵ Wilson <See pg. 225> (2102.Robert⁴, 2056.William³, 1707.Goodridge², 1.Benjamin, Sr.¹) was born 11 Mar 1894 in Belton, Missouri, the daughter of **Robert Cowan Wilson** and **Frances Lee Scott**. Susan died 1 Feb 1978 in Mexico, Missouri. She married **Dr. Lynn B. Greene** 3 Dec 1919 in Belton.⁵⁶⁹

ISSUE:

+2124. f   i.   **Suzanne Lee Greene**, born 10 Jul 1923.

- - - - - - - - - - -

2124. Suzanne Lee⁶ Greene (2123.Susan⁵, 2102.Robert⁴, 2056.William³, 1707.Goodridge², 1.Benjamin, Sr.¹) was born 10 Jul 1923 in Kansas City, Missouri, the daughter of **Lynn B. Greene** and **Susan Ella Wilson**. She

---

⁵⁶⁸ *Belton, Missouri Centennial*, 27F, 28F, 77-8.

⁵⁶⁹ *Belton, Missouri Centennial*, 28F. Additional information from Suzanne (Greene) Seyfried of Midvale UT.

married **William E. Seyfried** 1949 in Columbia, Missouri.

ISSUE:

2125. f   i.   **Lynda Seyfried**.

2126. m   ii.   **Paul Seyfried**.

- - - - - - - - - - -

2127. Margaret Lucy[5] Wilson <See pg. 225> (2102.Robert[4], 2056.William[3], 1707.Goodridge[2], 1.Benjamin, Sr.[1]) was born 30 Sep 1897 in Belton, Missouri, the daughter of **Robert Cowan Wilson** and **Frances Lee Scott**. She married **Richard L. Dunlap** 12 Apr 1923 in Belton.[570]

ISSUE:

2128. f   i.   **Frances Scott Dunlap**.

- - - - - - - - - - -

2130. Samuel Venable[3] Wilson <See pg. 177> (1707.Goodridge[2], 1.Benjamin, Sr.[1]) was born 3 Mar 1821 in Prince Edward Co., Virginia, the son of **Goodridge Wilson** and **Elizabeth Woodson Venable**. Samuel died 17 Apr 1870 in Poplar Bluff, Butler Co., Missouri, and was buried in Wilson/Rose Hill Cemetery, Butler Co.[571] He married **Sarah Cox Meredith (See number 707 - pg. 99)** 2 Dec 1843 in Kanawha Co., Virginia (West Virginia). She was born 21 Jan 1821 probably in Buckingham Co., Virginia. She was the daughter of **John Meredith** and **Ann Seay Wilson**.[572]

ISSUE:

+ 708. m   i.   **James Meredith Wilson**, born 23 Sep 1845, died 14 Dec 1933 <See pg. 229>.

765. m   ii.   **Goodridge Wilson**, born 24 Dec 1847 in Virginia. He married **Mary "Mollie" Willis Trent (See number 662 - pg. 94, 100)**. She was born 1843. She was the daughter of **James Wilson Trent** and **Ann Wilson "Nannie" Meredith**. Goodridge died 8 Nov 1870 in Butler Co., Missouri, and was buried in Wilson/Rose Hill Cemetery, Butler Co., Missouri.

+ 766. m   iii.   **Samuel Venable Wilson**, born 4 Jun 1850, died 27 Feb 1935 <See pg. 235>.

+ 795. m   iv.   **Robert Faris Wilson**, born 3 Nov 1852, died 15 Feb 1937 <See pg. 238>.

+ 838. f   v.   **Anne "Nancy" Meredith Wilson**, born 2 Jun 1855, died

---

[570] *Belton, Missouri Centennial*, 28F.

[571] Hanks, "Wilson/ Rose Hill" Cemetery (accessed 10 Mar 2006).

[572] McLean, *Wilson Family*, 62-86. Boddie, *Historical Southern Families*, 3:66, 73-4. DAR - Meredith Family Bible.

16 Sep 1901 <See pg. 240>.

+ 903. m vi.   **Benjamin Francis Wilson**, born Nov 1857, died after 26 Mar 1919 <See pg. 247>.

918. f vii.   **Hetty Meredith Wilson**, born 9 Nov 1860, died 26 Nov 1870 in Butler Co., and was buried in Wilson/Rose Hill Cemetery.

+ 919. f viii. **Elizabeth Venable "Bessie" Wilson**, born 14 Mar 1864, died 22 Mar 1927 <See pg. 249>.

+ 1070. f ix.   **Sarah Stonewall Wilson**, born 27 May 1865, died 11 Nov 1951 <See pg. 259>.

Samuel was a graduate of Washington College in Lexington, Virginia, (now Washington and Lee University), the matriculation list for the session beginning September 1ˢᵗ 1838 showing his father as G. Wilson at Post office "Charleston Va".[573]

He along with his brothers and sisters deeded the property they inherited at their father's death to their mother.[574] Samuel is shown with his family in the 1850 St. Louis Co., Missouri, census.

In April of 1850 he wrote from Ellisville, Missouri, to his sister in Kanawha. His brother wrote a letter 25 Aug 1853 saying, "Sam talks of selling his place and going off to the prairie country.[575] The family records show him in southern Missouri. He was probably one of the brothers that left the St. Louis area during the Civil War.

- - - - - - - - - -

708. James Meredith⁴ Wilson <See pg. 99, 228> (2130.Samuel³, 1707.Goodridge², 1.Benjamin, Sr.¹) was born 23 Sep 1845 in Kanawha Co., Virginia (West Virginia), the son of **Samuel Venable Wilson** and **Sarah Cox Meredith**. James died 14 Dec 1933 in Dardenne, St. Charles Co., Missouri. He married **Mary Frances "Fanny" Combs** 22 Sep 1870 in Cane Creek, Butler Co., Missouri. She was born 14 Dec 1854 in Lexington, Kentucky, daughter of **Rev. Wm. Ryan Combs** and **Catherin Orr**. Fanny died 28 Mar 1926 in St. Charles, Missouri. The family is shown in the 1880 St. Charles Co., Missouri, census.[576]

[573] Washington and Lee University, *Catalogue*, 90.

[574] Kanawha Co. WV Deed Book Q:182, 184.

[575] Copies of letters from Watson sisters, Kirkwood MO.

[576] McLean, *Wilson Family*, 63. Boddie, *Historical Southern Families*, 3:74. Watson, *Heritage And Promise*, 177-180.

ISSUE:

709. f   i.   **Hettie Meredith Wilson**, born 19 Aug 1871 in Missouri. She married **Bernard Chenoweth**. Bernard died in Syracuse, Kansas.

+ 710. m   ii.   **William Combs Wilson**, born 10 Aug 1873.

+ 715. f   iii.   **Sarah Agnes Wilson**, born 24 Oct 1875 <See pg. 231>.

+ 723. f   iv.   **Elizabeth Venable Wilson**, born 25 Mar 1877 <See pg. 231>.

+ 734. m   v.   **John Meredith Wilson**, born 7 Oct 1882 <See pg. 232>.

746. m   vi.   **James M. Wilson, Jr.**, born in Missouri.

+ 747. f   vii.   **Mary Fanny Wilson**, born 17 Feb 1885, died 12 Dec 1948 <See pg. 233>.

+ 751. f   viii.   **Martha Viola Wilson**, born 7 Jan 1888 <See pg. 234>.

+ 763. m   ix.   **James Venable Wilson**, born 2 Aug 1898 <See pg. 235>.

- - - - - - - - - - -

710. Dr. William Combs[5] Wilson (708.James[4],2130.Samuel[3], 1707.Goodridge[2], 1.Benjamin, Sr.[1]) was born 10 Aug 1873 in Cane Creek, Butler Co., Missouri, the son of **James Meredith Wilson** and **Mary Frances "Fanny" Combs**. He married **Carrie H. Watson** 9 Oct 1902 in O'Fallon, St. Charles Co., Missouri, the daughter of **Thomas Watson, Jr.** and **Ada E. M. Harris**. [577]

ISSUE:

711. m   i.   **Clifford Combs Wilson**, born 1903 in Missouri and died there 18 Apr 1905.

712. m   ii.   **Gordon Goodridge Wilson**, born 16 Apr 1908 in Missouri. He married **Margaret E. Chamberlain**.

+ 713. f   iii.   **Catherine H. Wilson**, born 16 Apr 1908.

A news article found in the vertical files at the St. Charles Missouri Historical Society Archives showed William still a practicing osteopathic physician at age 92.

- - - - - - - - - - -

713. Catherine H.[6] Wilson (710.William[5], 708.James[4], 2130.Samuel[3], 1707.Goodridge[2], 1.Benjamin, Sr.[1]) was born 16 Apr 1908 in Missouri, the daughter of **William Combs Wilson** and **Carrie H. Watson**. She married **Andrew McGaffin**.

ISSUE:

714. m   i.   **James Farr McGaffin**, born 22 Sep 1935 in China.

---

[577] McLean, *Wilson Family*, 63. Boddie, *Historical Southern Families*, 3:74. Watson, *Heritage And Promise*,178.

- - - - - - - - - -

715. Sarah Agnes⁵ Wilson <See pg. 230> (708.James⁴, 2130.Samuel³, 1707.Goodridge², 1.Benjamin, Sr.¹) was born 24 Oct 1875 in Missouri, the daughter of **James Meredith Wilson** and **Mary Frances "Fanny" Combs**. Sarah died probably in Calloway Co., Missouri. She married **Harry Hatcher** in 1897.[578]

ISSUE:
+ 716. m   i.   **Frank Meredith Hatcher**, born 7 Dec 1901.
  719. m ii.   **Robert Lee Hatcher**, born 19 May 1905. He married **Ora Lee Joyce** 19 Jul 1941. Robert died 2 Feb 1949 probably in Wyoming.
  720. m iii. **James H. Hatcher**, born 10 May 1907, died 15 Oct 1927.
+ 721. m iv. **Harold W. Hatcher**, born 10 Apr 1909.

- - - - - - - - - -

716. Frank Meredith⁶ Hatcher (715.Sarah⁵, 708.James⁴, 2130.Samuel³, 1707.Goodridge², 1.Benjamin, Sr.¹) was born 7 Dec 1901, the son of **Harry Hatcher** and **Sarah Agnes Wilson**. He married **Ruth Clement** 1 May 1926.

ISSUE:
  717. f   i.   **Sarah Ann Hatcher**, born 12 Oct 1934.
  718. f ii.   **Hettie L. Hatcher**, born 26 Jul 1941.

- - - - - - - - - -

721. Harold W.⁶ Hatcher (715.Sarah⁵, 708.James⁴, 2130.Samuel³, 1707.Goodridge², 1.Benjamin, Sr.¹) was born 10 Apr 1909, the son of **Harry Hatcher** and **Sarah Agnes Wilson**. He married **Gretchen Tate** 15 Oct 1933.

ISSUE:
  722. f   i.   **Juanita Hatcher**, born 13 Dec 1938.

- - - - - - - - - -

723. Elizabeth Venable⁵ Wilson <See pg. 230> (708.James⁴,2130.Samuel³, 1707.Goodridge², 1.Benjamin, Sr.¹) was born 25 Mar 1877 in Missouri, the daughter of **James Meredith Wilson** and **Mary Frances "Fanny" Combs**. She married **Dr. John Franklin Bumpus** 30 Jul 1908. John died 19 Apr 1939.[579]

ISSUE:
+ 724. f   i.   **Evelyn Bumpus**, born 10 Oct 1910.
+ 728. m ii.   **John Franklin Bumpus, Jr.**, born 28 Jul 1912 <See pg. 232>.

---

[578] McLean, *Wilson Family*, 64. Boddie, *Historical Southern Families*, 3:74.

[579] McLean, *Wilson Family*, 64-5. Boddie, *Historical Southern Families*, 3:74.

+ 732. f   iii.   **Frances Katherine Bumpus**, born 15 Mar 1916 <See pg. 232>.

- - - - - - - - - - -

724. Evelyn[6] Bumpus (723.Elizabeth[5], 708.James[4],2130.Samuel[3], 1707.Goodridge[2], 1.Benjamin, Sr.[1]) was born 10 Oct 1910, the daughter of **John Franklin Bumpus** and **Elizabeth Venable Wilson**. She married **Nelson Salters** 16 Jun 1936.

ISSUE:
725. m   i.   **John Joseph Salters**, born 6 Jun 1937.
726. f   ii.   **Dianne Wilson Salters**, born 30 Sep 1941.
727. f   iii. **Donna Katherine Salters**, born 3 Aug 1945.

- - - - - - - - - - -

728. John Franklin[6] Bumpus, Jr. <See pg. 231> (723.Elizabeth[5], 708.James[4], 2130.Samuel[3], 1707.Goodridge[2], 1.Benjamin, Sr.[1]) was born 28 Jul 1912, the son of **John Franklin Bumpus** and **Elizabeth Venable Wilson**. He married **Margaret Morris** 13 Dec 1937.

ISSUE:
729. m   i.   **John Franklin Bumpus, III**, born 19 Apr 1940.
730. f   ii.   **Dallas Elizabeth Bumpus**, born 20 Jul 1942.
731. f   iii. **Mary L. Bumpus**, born 20 Jul 1945.

- - - - - - - - - - -

732. Frances Katherine[6] Bumpus <See pg. 232> (723.Elizabeth[5], 708.James[4], 2130.Samuel[3], 1707.Goodridge[2], 1.Benjamin, Sr.[1]) was born 15 Mar 1916, the daughter of **John Franklin Bumpus** and **Elizabeth Venable Wilson**. She married **A. C. Payne** 6 May 1942.

ISSUE:
733. f   i.   **Sharon Lee Payne**, born 24 Aug 1943.

- - - - - - - - - - -

734. John Meredith[5] Wilson <See pg. 230> (708.James[4],2130.Samuel[3], 1707.Goodridge[2], 1.Benjamin, Sr.[1]) was born 7 Oct 1882 in Missouri, the son of **James Meredith Wilson** and **Mary Frances "Fanny" Combs**. He married **Mabel Watson** 25 Jan 1906. She was the daughter of **Thomas Watson, Jr.** and **Ada E. M. Harris**. Mabel died 23 Mar 1942. [580]

ISSUE:
+ 735. f   i.   **Alma M. Wilson**, born 15 Jan 1907.
+ 740. f   ii.   **Ruth Meredith Wilson**, born 3 Nov 1901 <See pg. 233>.

---

[580] McLean, *Wilson Family*, 65-6. Boddie, *Historical Southern Families*, 3:74. Watson, *Heritage And Promise*, 177-8.

742. m   iii.   **John B. Wilson**, born 5 Feb 1915. He married **Carolyn Hunter** 10 Apr 1942.[581]

+ 743. m   iv.   **James L. Wilson**, born 5 Feb 1915.

- - - - - - - - - -

735. Alma M.[6] Wilson (734.John[5], 708.James[4],2130.Samuel[3], 1707.Goodridge[2], 1.Benjamin, Sr.[1]) was born 15 Jan 1907, daughter of **John Meredith Wilson** and **Mabel Watson**. She married **Ivan Lay** 1932.

ISSUE:

736. m   i.   **Carroll Dean Lay**, born 25 Jul 1933.
737. m   ii.   **Mack Gerald Lay**, born 22 Nov 1938.
738. f   iii.   **Helen Gean Lay**, born 22 Nov 1938.
739. m   iv.   **Rae Derald Lay**, born 1 Aug 1947.

- - - - - - - - - -

740. Ruth Meredith[6] Wilson <See pg. 232> (734.John[5], 708.James[4], 2130.Samuel[3], 1707.Goodridge[2], 1.Benjamin, Sr.[1]) was born 3 Nov 1901, the daughter of **John Meredith Wilson** and **Mabel Watson**. She married **Charles A. Garner**.

ISSUE:

741. f   i.   **Margaret C. Garner**, born 9 Feb 1945.

- - - - - - - - - -

743. James L.[6] Wilson (734.John[5], 708.James[4],2130.Samuel[3], 1707.Goodridge[2], 1.Benjamin, Sr.[1]) was born 5 Feb 1915, the son of **John Meredith Wilson** and **Mabel Watson**. He married **Dessie Dillard** May 1942.

ISSUE:

744. f   i.   **Judith Ann Wilson**, born 9 Jun 1944.
745. m   ii.   **Robert Wilson**, born 9 Jan 1946.

- - - - - - - - - -

747. Mary Fanny[5] Wilson <See pg. 230> (708.James[4],2130.Samuel[3], 1707.Goodridge[2], 1.Benjamin, Sr.[1]) was born 17 Feb 1885 in Missouri, the daughter of **James Meredith Wilson** and **Mary Frances "Fanny" Combs**. Mary died 12 Dec 1948 probably in Springdale Co., Arkansas. She married **George Muschaney**. [582]

ISSUE:

748. m   i.   **Eugene Muschaney**, born 12 Dec 1912. He married **Mary Hutchinson** 4 Jun 1946.

---

[581]   Watson, *Heritage And Promise*, 178, 186-7.

[582]   McLean, *Wilson Family*, 66. Boddie, *Historical Southern Families*, 3:74.

+ 749. m   ii.   **George Venable Muschaney**, born 17 Feb 1919.

- - - - - - - - - - -

749. George Venable[6] Muschaney (747.Mary[5], 708.James[4], 2130.Samuel[3], 1707.Goodridge[2], 1.Benjamin, Sr.[1]) was born 17 Feb 1919, the son of **George Muschaney** and **Mary Fanny Wilson**. He married **Elizabeth Hutchinson** 23 Dec 1945.
ISSUE:
750. f   i.   **Mary Jean Muschaney**, born 6 May 1948.

- - - - - - - - - - -

751. Martha Viola[5] Wilson <See pg. 230> (708.James[4], 2130.Samuel[3], 1707.Goodridge[2], 1.Benjamin, Sr.[1]) was born 7 Jan 1888 in Missouri, the daughter of **James Meredith Wilson** and **Mary Frances "Fanny" Combs**. She married **Henry Yates** 1909. [583]
ISSUE:
+ 752. m   i.   **Herschel Wilson Yates**, born 1910.
+ 755. f   ii. **Mary Frances Yates**.
+ 758. m   iii. **Joseph Orville Yates**.
  760. m   iv. **James Wilson Yates**.
  761. m   v.   **Thomas Yates**.
  762. f   vi. **Martha Jane Yates**.

- - - - - - - - - - -

752. Herschel Wilson[6] Yates (751.Martha[5], 708.James[4], 2130.Samuel[3], 1707.Goodridge[2], 1.Benjamin, Sr.[1]) was born 1910, the son of **Henry Yates** and **Martha Viola Wilson**. He married **Gertrude Wilson**.
ISSUE:
753. m   i.   **Herschel Wilson Wilson, Jr.**, born 1937.
754. m   ii. **Marshall Wilson**, born 1940.

- - - - - - - - - - -

755. Mary Frances[6] Yates (751.Martha[5], 708.James[4], 2130.Samuel[3], 1707.Goodridge[2], 1.Benjamin, Sr.[1]). She was the daughter of **Henry Yates** and **Martha Viola Wilson**. She married **Francis McGuire**.
ISSUE:
756. m   i.   **Francis Joseph McGuire**, born 1935.
757. m   ii. **Franklin H. McGuire**, born 1938.

- - - - - - - - - - -

---

[583] McLean, *Wilson Family*, 67. Boddie, *Historical Southern Families*, 3:74.

758. Joseph Orville[6] Yates (751.Martha[5], 708.James[4], 2130.Samuel[3], 1707.Goodridge[2], 1.Benjamin, Sr.[1]). He was the son of **Henry Yates** and **Martha Viola Wilson**. He married **Marguerite De Large**.

ISSUE:

759. f   i.   **Julianne Yates**, born Sep 1946.

- - - - - - - - - - -

763. James Venable[5] Wilson <See pg. 230> (708.James[4], 2130.Samuel[3], 1707.Goodridge[2], 1.Benjamin, Sr.[1]) was born 2 Aug 1898 in Missouri, the son of **James Meredith Wilson** and **Mary Frances "Fanny" Combs**. He married **Hazel McCormick**. [584]

ISSUE:

764. m   i.   **McCormick Venable Wilson**, born 29 Sep 1926.

- - - - - - - - - - -

766. Samuel Venable[4] Wilson <See pg. 99, 228> (2130.Samuel[3], 1707.Goodridge[2], 1.Benjamin, Sr.[1]) was born 4 Jun 1850 in Missouri, the son of **Samuel Venable Wilson** and **Sarah Cox Meredith**. Samuel died 27 Feb 1935, and was buried in Colfax Cemetery, Van Zandt Co., Texas. He married **Martha "Mattie" Batterton**. She was born 27 Mar 1852. Martha died 8 Oct 1926, and was buried in Colfax Cemetery.[585]

ISSUE:

+ 767. m   i.   **John Howard Wilson**, born 16 Dec 1876, died 4 Jan 1958.

773. f   ii.   **Fannie B. Wilson**, born 14 Sep 1878, died 7 Jan 1905, and was buried in Colfax Cemetery.

+ 774. m   iii.   **Goodridge Batterton Wilson**, born 13 Jul 1880 <See pg. 236>.

776. m   iv.   **Benjamin Felix Wilson**, born 1882. He married **Lucy Schwab** 1945.

777. f   v.   **Sarah M. "Sadie" Wilson**, born 31 Jan 1884, died 22 Jan 1966, and was buried in Colfax Cemetery.

+ 778. m   vi.   **Samuel Watson Wilson**, born 22 Feb 1887 <See pg. 236>.

+ 785. f   vii.   **Helen Ashmore Wilson**, born 1891 <See pg. 237>.

- - - - - - - - - - -

767. John Howard[5] Wilson (766.Samuel[4], 2130.Samuel[3], 1707.Goodridge[2], 1.Benjamin, Sr.[1]) was born 16 Dec 1876, the son of **Samuel Venable Wilson** and **Martha "Mattie" Batterton**. John died 4 Jan 1958, and was buried in Colfax Cemetery, Van Zandt Co., Texas. He married **Helen Fern Nelson** 21 Jul 1914 in McPherson, Kansas. She was

---

[584] McLean, *Wilson Family*, 67-68. Boddie, *Historical Southern Families*, 3:74.

[585] McLean, *Wilson Family*, 68-70. Boddie, *Historical Southern Families*, 3:74. Curry, *Colfax Cemetery*, 14.

born 20 Jan 1887. Helen died 30 Aug 1971, and was buried in Colfax Cemetery.[586]

ISSUE:

+ 768. f   i.   **Jean Wilson**, born 2 Jun 1915.
   771. f   ii.   **Ann Meredith Wilson**, born 22 May 1918, died 2 Oct 1943, and was buried in Colfax Cemetery.
   772. f   iii.   **Frances Fern Wilson**, born 19 May 1921. She married **Wheeler W. Jackson** 30 Dec 1945.

- - - - - - - - - - -

768. Jean[6] Wilson (767.John[5], 766.Samuel[4], 2130.Samuel[3], 1707.Goodridge[2], 1.Benjamin, Sr.[1]) was born 2 Jun 1915, the daughter of **John Howard Wilson** and **Helen Fern Nelson**. She married **F. T. Tunnell** 1 Aug 1942.

ISSUE:

   769. f   i.   **Joan Frances Tunnell**, born 7 Oct 1945.
   770. m   ii.   **Forrest Truman Tunnell**, born 9 Jun 1949.

- - - - - - - - - - -

774. Goodridge Batterton[5] Wilson <See pg. 235> (766.Samuel[4], 2130.Samuel[3], 1707.Goodridge[2], 1.Benjamin, Sr.[1]) was born 13 Jul 1880, the son of **Samuel Venable Wilson** and **Martha "Mattie" Batterton**. He married **Mary Jourdan**.

ISSUE:

   775. f   i.   **Mary Claire Wilson**, born 1920.

- - - - - - - - - - -

778. Samuel Watson[5] Wilson <See pg. 235> (766.Samuel[4], 2130.Samuel[3], 1707.Goodridge[2], 1.Benjamin, Sr.[1]) was born 22 Feb 1887, the son of **Samuel Venable Wilson** and **Martha "Mattie" Batterton**. He married **Lucille Sherrard** 1918. [587]

ISSUE:

+ 779. m   i.   **Bernard T. Wilson**, born 1919.
+ 782. m   ii.   **Jerry Batterton Wilson**, born 1921.
   784. f   iii.   **Marjorie Anita Wilson**, born 1924.

- - - - - - - - - - -

779. Bernard T.[6] Wilson (778.Samuel[5], 766.Samuel[4], 2130.Samuel[3], 1707.Goodridge[2], 1.Benjamin, Sr.[1]) was born 1919, the son of **Samuel Watson Wilson** and **Lucille Sherrard**. His spouse has not been identified.

---

[586] McLean, *Wilson Family*, 68. Curry, *Colfax Cemetery*, 14.

[587] McLean, *Wilson Family*, 69.

ISSUE:
780. f   i.   **Melody Wilson**, born 1943.
781. m   ii.   **Jerry Batterton Wilson**, born 1948.

- - - - - - - - - -

782. Jerry Batterton[6] Wilson (778.Samuel[5], 766.Samuel[4], 2130.Samuel[3], 1707.Goodridge[2], 1.Benjamin, Sr.[1]) was born 1921, the son of **Samuel Watson Wilson** and **Lucille Sherrard**. His spouse has not been identified.
ISSUE:
783. m   i.   _____ **Wilson**, born 1948.

- - - - - - - - - -

785. Helen Ashmore[5] Wilson <See pg. 235> (766.Samuel[4], 2130.Samuel[3], 1707.Goodridge[2], 1.Benjamin, Sr.[1]) was born 1891, the daughter of **Samuel Venable Wilson** and **Martha "Mattie" Batterton**. She married **Albert W. Rainey**.
ISSUE:
+ 786. m   i.   **Gordon W. Rainey**.
+ 789. m   ii.   **Frank Rainey**.
  792. f   iii.   **Ruth Helen Rainey**, born 1914. She married **Frank Nayer** 1946.
+ 793. m   iv.   **Albert Gerald "Jerry" Rainey**, born 1926 <See pg. 238>.

- - - - - - - - - -

786. Gordon W.[6] Rainey (785.Helen[5], 766.Samuel[4], 2130.Samuel[3], 1707.Goodridge[2], 1.Benjamin, Sr.[1]). He was the son of **Albert W. Rainey** and **Helen Ashmore Wilson**. He married **Doris Briggs**.[588]
ISSUE:
787. f   i.   **Doris Lynn Rainey**, born 1944.
788. m   ii.   **Hal Wilson Rainey**, born 16 Oct 1948.

- - - - - - - - - -

789. Frank[6] Rainey (785.Helen[5], 766.Samuel[4], 2130.Samuel[3], 1707.Goodridge[2], 1.Benjamin, Sr.[1]). He was the son of **Albert W. Rainey** and **Helen Ashmore Wilson**. He married **Dorene Hill**.
ISSUE:
790. f   i.   **Frances Annette Rainey**, born 1933.
791. f   ii.   **Dorothy Lee Rainey**, born 1938.

- - - - - - - - - -

---

[588] McLean, *Wilson Family*, 69-70.

793. Albert Gerald "Jerry"⁶ Rainey <See pg. 237> (785.Helen⁵, 766.Samuel⁴, 2130.Samuel³, 1707.Goodridge², 1.Benjamin, Sr.¹) was born 1926, the son of **Albert W. Rainey** and **Helen Ashmore Wilson**. He married **Ruby Ashley** 1946.

ISSUE:

794. f   i.   **Joan Rainey**, born 11 Jun 1949.

- - - - - - - - - -

795. Robert Faris⁴ Wilson <See pg. 99, 228> (2130.Samuel³, 1707.Goodridge², 1.Benjamin, Sr.¹) was born 3 Nov 1852 in Missouri, the son of **Samuel Venable Wilson** and **Sarah Cox Meredith**. Robert died 15 Feb 1937, and was buried in Colfax Cemetery, Van Zandt Co., Texas. He married **Georgia Ann Combs**. She was born 19 Jul 1857 in Kentucky, daughter of **Rev. Wm. Ryan Combs** and **Catherin Orr**. Georgia died 10 Feb 1936, and was buried in Colfax Cemetery.[589]

ISSUE:

+ 796. f   i.   **Roberta Wilson**, born 1879.
  803. m   ii.   **Samuel Venable Wilson**, born 28 Jan 1882, died 28 May 1912, and was buried in Colfax Cemetery.
+ 804. f   iii. **Ellen Bates "Nell" Wilson**, born 1884 <See pg. 239>.
  810. m   iv.   **Charles Wilson**, born 11 Sep 1887, died 22 Jan 1928 in Colfax, Van Zandt Co., Texas, and was buried in Colfax Cemetery.
  811. f   v.   **Grace Wilson**, born 1889.
+ 812. m   vi.   **Robert Farris Wilson**, born 14 Aug 1892, died 10 May 1924 <See pg. 240>.

Robert is shown with his family in the 1880 St. Charles Co., Missouri, census. He and his brother **Benjamin** registered brands in Fisher Co., Texas in 1888. Robert and his wife sold land there in 1893 and in 1902 bought land in Van Zandt Co.[590]

- - - - - - - - - -

796. Roberta⁵ Wilson (795.Robert⁴, 2130.Samuel³, 1707.Goodridge², 1.Benjamin, Sr.¹) was born 1879 in Missouri, the daughter of **Robert Faris Wilson** and **Georgia Ann Combs**. She married **H. Cathey Fite** 1908. He

---

[589] McLean, *Wilson Family*, 70-71. Boddie, *Historical Southern Families*, 3:74. Curry, *Colfax Cemetery*, 14.

[590] Fisher Co. TX Marks and Brands:288, Deed Book 7:249. Van Zandt Co. TX Deed Book 72:389.

was born 1866 in North Carolina. [591]

ISSUE:

+ 797. m   i.   **Robert Wilson Fite.**
+ 800. f   ii.   **Anna Grace Fite.**

- - - - - - - - - - -

797. Robert Wilson[6] Fite (796.Roberta[5], 795.Robert[4], 2130.Samuel[3], 1707.Goodridge[2], 1.Benjamin, Sr.[1]). He was the son of **H. Cathey Fite** and **Roberta Wilson**. He married **Lois Oliver**.

ISSUE:

798. m   i.   **Robert Wilson Fite, Jr.**
799. m   ii.   **James W. Fite.**

- - - - - - - - - - -

800. Anna Grace[6] Fite (796.Roberta[5], 795.Robert[4], 2130.Samuel[3], 1707.Goodridge[2], 1.Benjamin, Sr.[1]). She was the daughter of **H. Cathey Fite** and **Roberta Wilson**. She married **Dougan Camper**.

ISSUE:

801. m   i.   **Larry Don Camper**, born 1942.
802. f   ii.   **Dianne Camper**, born 1944.

- - - - - - - - - - -

804. Ellen Bates "Nell"[5] Wilson <See pg. 238> (795.Robert[4], 2130.Samuel[3], 1707.Goodridge[2], 1.Benjamin, Sr.[1]) was born 1884. She was the daughter of **Robert Faris Wilson** and **Georgia Ann Combs**. She married **Walter Smith**. He was born 1882.[592]

ISSUE:

805. f   i.   **Matilda "Tillie" Smith**, born 1910. She married **Calvin Wallis**. Matilda died 1990.
806. f   ii.   **Lula May Smith**, born Oct 1915. She married (1) **Edward F. Stuard**; they divorced. Lula married (2) **Lawrence Alouise Greenwell** 1963.
807. m   iii. **Farris W. Smith**. He married **Rose Marie Wittkuhns**.
+ 808. m   iv.   **Charles Edward Smith**.

- - - - - - - - - - -

808. Charles Edward[6] Smith (804.Ellen[5], 795.Robert[4], 2130.Samuel[3], 1707.Goodridge[2], 1.Benjamin, Sr.[1]). He was the son of **Walter Smith** and **Ellen Bates "Nell" Wilson**. He married **Betty Rose Haley**.

---

[591] McLean, *Wilson Family*, 70-71.

[592] McLean, *Wilson Family*, 71. Additional information from May (Smith) Greenwell of Terrell TX.

ISSUE:

809. f   i.   **Betty Ellen Smith**, born 1947.

- - - - - - - - - - -

812. Robert Farris[5] Wilson <See pg. 238> (795.Robert[4], 2130.Samuel[3], 1707.Goodridge[2], 1.Benjamin, Sr.[1]) was born 14 Aug 1892, the son of **Robert Faris Wilson** and **Georgia Ann Combs**. Farris died 10 May 1924, and was buried in Colfax Cemetery, Van Zandt Co., Texas. He married **Birdie Eulacia Tunnell** 19 Mar 1919. She was born 1898, the daughter of **Commodore Tunnell** and **Rebecca Rusk**. Birdie died 1980 and was buried in Colfax Cemetery.[593]

ISSUE:

+ 813. f   i.   **Bobbye Rebecca Wilson**, born 31 Dec 1919.

Birdie also married (2) **Samuel Willis Wilson (See number 1072 - pg. 270)** 26 Oct 1926.

If I recorded the memories of May Greenwell correctly, Robert had tuberculosis; his father built a little house in the yard for him, where he lived for three years. They boiled things and carted food there. People visited to cheer him, but they left cheered instead.

- - - - - - - - - - -

813. Bobbye Rebecca[6] Wilson (812.Robert[5], 795.Robert[4], 2130.Samuel[3], 1707.Goodridge[2], 1.Benjamin, Sr.[1]) was born 31 Dec 1919 in Colfax, Van Zandt Co., Texas, the daughter of **Robert Farris Wilson** and **Birdie Eulacia Tunnell**. She married **Clem Smith** 6 Jun 1942 in San Antonio, Texas. Clem died 17 Dec 1988.

ISSUE:

814. f   i.   **Teresa Rebecca Smith**, born 28 Jan 1953 in San Antonio.
815. m   ii.   **Sanford Wayne Smith**, born 23 Jan 1956 in Dallas, Texas, died 24 Jan 1956 in Dallas, and was buried in Colfax Cemetery, Van Zandt Co., Texas.

- - - - - - - - - - -

838. Anne "Nancy" Meredith[4] Wilson <See pg. 99, 229> (2130.Samuel[3], 1707.Goodridge[2], 1.Benjamin, Sr.[1]) was born 2 Jun 1855 in St. Louis Co., Missouri, the daughter of **Samuel Venable Wilson** and **Sarah Cox Meredith**. Nancy died 16 Sep 1901 and was buried in Sparkman Cemetery in Cane Creek, Butler Co., Missouri. She married **Rev. Thaddeus Holmes Sparkman** 16 Oct 1877. He was born 16 Oct 1852 in Giles Co., Tennessee,

---

[593] McLean, *Wilson Family*, 71. Curry, *Colfax Cemetery*, 14.

the son of **William Williams Sparkman** and **Elizabeth Jane Fitzgerald**. Thaddeus died 11 May 1932, and was buried in Sparkman Cemetery.[594]

ISSUE:

+ 839. f   i.   **Georgia Meredith Sparkman**, born 2 Aug 1878.

   845. m   ii.   **Venable William Sparkman**, born 13 May 1881, died 29 Jul 1891.

+ 846. f   iii.   **Sarah Elizabeth Sparkman**, born 15 Jan 1883, died 20 Jun 1928 <See pg. 242>.

   851. f   iv.   **Jennie J. Sparkman**, born 23 Sep 1884. She married **James A. Johnston** 20 Jun 1910.

+ 852. f   v.   **Lee Fanning Sparkman**, born 5 Sep 1886, died 1944 <See pg. 243>.

+ 860. m   vi.   **Robert Holmes Sparkman**, born 7 Nov 1888 <See pg. 243>.

+ 867. f   vii.   **Nancy Hetty Lavinia Sparkman**, born 3 Nov 1890 <See pg. 244>.

+ 879. m viii.   **Rothwell Mayfield Sparkman**, born 27 Jan 1893 <See pg. 245>.

+ 891. m   ix.   **Francis Wilson "Frank" Sparkman**, born 17 Mar 1895, died 22 Mar 1941 <See pg. 246>.

   902. f   x.   **Mildred Lois Sparkman**, born 11 Feb 1897. She married **Harry R. Kneeland** 1920.

Thaddeus also married (1) **Elizabeth Azalee Adams** 1872. She was born 29 Feb 1856. Elizabeth died 1873.

Thaddeus also married (3) **Elizabeth Rushing** 31 Dec 1902. Elizabeth died 20 Jun 1918.

Thaddeus also married (4) **Lillie Tillis** 1920.

- - - - - - - - - - -

839. Georgia Meredith[5] Sparkman (838.Anne[4], 2130.Samuel[3], 1707.Goodridge[2], 1.Benjamin, Sr.[1]) was born 2 Aug 1878, the daughter of **Thaddeus Holmes Sparkman** and **Anne "Nancy" Meredith Wilson**. She married **Charles A. Freer** 16 Oct 1902.[595]

ISSUE:

+ 840. f   i.   **Avice Meredith Freer**, born 1906, died 1928.

+ 843. f   ii.   **Eleanor Iris Freer**, born 1914.

- - - - - - - - - - -

---

[594] McLean, *Wilson Family*, 73-78. Hanks, *Sparkman Cemetery*, (accessed 15 Dec 2005). "Butler Co. MO, Sparkman Cemetery", (accessed 19 Mar 2006). Additional information from Patricia (Sparkman) Thomas.

[595] McLean, *Wilson Family*, 73.

840. Avice Meredith⁶ Freer (839.Georgia⁵, 838.Anne⁴, 2130.Samuel³, 1707.Goodridge², 1.Benjamin, Sr.¹) was born 1906, the daughter of **Charles A. Freer** and **Georgia Meredith Sparkman**. Avice died 1928. She married **Elmer Rexford Shobert** 1926.

ISSUE:
841. m   i.   **Charles Elmer Shobert**, born 1927.
842. f   ii. **Sarah Ann Shobert**, born 1927.

- - - - - - - - - -

843. Eleanor Iris⁶ Freer (839.Georgia⁵, 838.Anne⁴, 2130.Samuel³, 1707.Goodridge², 1.Benjamin, Sr.¹) was born 1914,the daughter of **Charles A. Freer** and **Georgia Meredith Sparkman**. She married **James Ross Hoggan** 1937.

ISSUE:
844. f   i.   **Judith Louise Hoggan**, born 1943.

- - - - - - - - - -

846. Sarah Elizabeth⁵ Sparkman <See pg. 241> (838.Anne⁴, 2130.Samuel³, 1707.Goodridge², 1.Benjamin, Sr.¹) was born 15 Jan 1883, the daughter of **Thaddeus Holmes Sparkman** and **Anne "Nancy" Meredith Wilson**. Sarah died 20 Jun 1928. She married **William L. Lindsay** 2 Jun 1904 in Long Beach, California. [596]

ISSUE:
+ 847. m   i.   **Roger William Lindsay**, born 15 Jan 1907.
+ 849. m   ii. **James Carrol Lindsay**, born 27 Oct 1911.

- - - - - - - - - -

847. Roger William⁶ Lindsay (846.Sarah⁵, 838.Anne⁴, 2130.Samuel³, 1707.Goodridge², 1.Benjamin, Sr.¹) was born 15 Jan 190, the son of **William L. Lindsay** and **Sarah Elizabeth Sparkman**. He married **Margaret Horgan** 16 Feb 1934 in New York, New York.

ISSUE:
848. f   i.   **Elizabeth Ann Lindsay**, born 18 Aug 1937.

- - - - - - - - - -

849. James Carrol⁶ Lindsay (846.Sarah⁵, 838.Anne⁴, 2130.Samuel³, 1707.Goodridge², 1.Benjamin, Sr.¹) was born 27 Oct 1911, son of **William L. Lindsay** and **Sarah Elizabeth Sparkman**. He married **Mary Jane Myers** 5 Jun 1938.

ISSUE:
850. m   i.   **William James Lindsay**, born 10 Dec 1942.

---

[596] McLean, *Wilson Family*, 73-74.

- - - - - - - - - - -

852. Lee Fanning⁵ Sparkman <See pg. 241> (838.Anne⁴, 2130.Samuel³, 1707.Goodridge², 1.Benjamin, Sr.¹) was born 5 Sep 1886, the daughter of **Thaddeus Holmes Sparkman** and **Anne "Nancy" Meredith Wilson**. Lee died 1944. She married **Dr. Grover C. Wallis** 1909.

ISSUE:

+ 853. m   i.   **Charles Sparkman Wallis**, born 1911.
+ 856. f   ii.   **Nancy Marie Wallis**, born 1924.

- - - - - - - - - - -

853. Charles Sparkman⁶ Wallis (852.Lee⁵, 838.Anne⁴, 2130.Samuel³, 1707.Goodridge², 1.Benjamin, Sr.¹) was born 1911, the son of **Grover C. Wallis** and **Lee Fanning Sparkman**. He married **Verla Nadine Roberts** 1942.[597]

ISSUE:

854. m   i.   **Charles Sparkman Wallis, II**, born 1943.
855. m   ii.   **Edward Gene Wallis**, born 1945.

- - - - - - - - - - -

856. Nancy Marie⁶ Wallis (852.Lee⁵, 838.Anne⁴, 2130.Samuel³, 1707.Goodridge², 1.Benjamin, Sr.¹) was born 1924, the daughter of **Grover C. Wallis** and **Lee Fanning Sparkman**. She married **Dr. Spencer Hebron Brown**.[598]

ISSUE:

857. m   i.   **Spencer Hebron Brown, II**, born 1941.
858. f   ii.   **Nancy Lee Brown**, born 1943.
859. m   iii.   **Earl Harold Brown**, born 1947.

- - - - - - - - - - -

860. Robert Holmes⁵ Sparkman <See pg. 241> (838.Anne⁴, 2130.Samuel³, 1707.Goodridge², 1.Benjamin, Sr.¹) was born 7 Nov 1888 in Poplar Bluff, Missouri, the son of **Thaddeus Holmes Sparkman** and **Anne "Nancy" Meredith Wilson**. He married **Elizabeth James** 1916. [599]

ISSUE:

861. m   i.   **James Robert Sparkman**, born 1916. He married **Mabelle Burleigh** 1945.
+ 862. m   ii.   **Donald Joseph Sparkman**, born 1919 .
864. f   iii.   **Geneva Marie Sparkman**, born 1920. She married **James S. Trummell**.

---

[597] McLean, *Wilson Family*, 74.

[598] McLean, *Wilson Family*, 74-75.

[599] McLean, *Wilson Family*, 75.

865. m   iv.   **Laddie Dale Sparkman**, born 1922.
866. m   v.   **Lee Holmes Sparkman**, born 1925.

- - - - - - - - - - -

862. Donald Joseph[6] Sparkman (860.Robert[5], 838.Anne[4], 2130.Samuel[3], 1707.Goodridge[2], 1.Benjamin, Sr.[1]) was born 1919, the son of **Robert Holmes Sparkman** and **Elizabeth James**. He married **Clara Kirkendall** 1945.
                            ISSUE:
863. f   i.   **Clara Kay Sparkman**, born 1946.

- - - - - - - - - - -

867. Nancy Hetty Lavinia[5] Sparkman <See pg. 241> (838.Anne[4], 2130.Samuel[3], 1707.Goodridge[2], 1.Benjamin, Sr.[1]) was born 3 Nov 1890, the daughter of **Thaddeus Holmes Sparkman** and **Anne "Nancy" Meredith Wilson**. She married **William Sparkman** 25 Dec 1910.[600]
                            ISSUE:
+ 868. f   i.   **Nancy Janice Sparkman**, born 28 Oct 1911, died 15 Feb 1939.
+ 871. f   ii.   **Katherine Lois Sparkman**, born 3 Mar 1913.
+ 874. f iii.   **Vivian Marie Sparkman**, born 8 Sep 1914.
+ 877. f   iv.   **Zadah Lucille Sparkman**, born 18 Jan 1916 <See pg. 245>.

- - - - - - - - - - -

868. Nancy Janice[6] Sparkman (867.Nancy[5], 838.Anne[4], 2130.Samuel[3], 1707.Goodridge[2], 1.Benjamin, Sr.[1]) was born 28 Oct 1911, the daughter of **William Sparkman** and **Nancy Hetty Lavinia Sparkman**. Nancy died 15 Feb 1939. She married **Jay Pollard** 1932.[601]
                            ISSUE:
869. f   i.   **Shirley Jean Pollard**, born 2 Mar 1933.
870. m   ii.   **James Meredith Pollard**, born 22 Aug 1935.

- - - - - - - - - - -

871. Katherine Lois[6] Sparkman (867.Nancy[5], 838.Anne[4], 2130.Samuel[3], 1707.Goodridge[2], 1.Benjamin, Sr.[1]) was born 3 Mar 1913, the daughter of **William Sparkman** and **Nancy Hetty Lavinia Sparkman**. She married **William H. Kurz** 5 Apr 1936.
                            ISSUE:
872. f   i.   **Patricia Elizabeth Kurz**, born 3 Dec 1937.
873. f   ii.   **Vivian Janice Kurz**, born 30 Jul 1940.

---

[600] McLean, *Wilson Family*, 75-76.

[601] McLean, *Wilson Family*, 76.

- - - - - - - - - -

874. Vivian Marie⁶ Sparkman (867.Nancy⁵, 838.Anne⁴, 2130.Samuel³, 1707.Goodridge², 1.Benjamin, Sr.¹) was born 8 Sep 1914, the daughter of **William Sparkman** and **Nancy Hetty Lavinia Sparkman**. She married **Elmer Kurz** 5 Apr 1936.

ISSUE:
- 875. f   i.   **Nancy Lavinia Kurz**, born 16 Jan 1937.
- 876. f   ii.   **Geraldine Marie Kurz**, born 5 May 1944.

- - - - - - - - - -

877. Zadah Lucille⁶ Sparkman <See pg. 244> (867.Nancy⁵, 838.Anne⁴, 2130.Samuel³, 1707.Goodridge², 1.Benjamin, Sr.¹) was born 18 Jan 1916, the daughter of **William Sparkman** and **Nancy Hetty Lavinia Sparkman**. She married **Robert Jackson Leach** 26 Feb 1943. [602]

ISSUE:
- 878. m   i.   **Robert Sparkman Leach**, born 15 Sep 1945.

- - - - - - - - - -

879. Rothwell Mayfield⁵ Sparkman <See pg. 241> (838.Anne⁴, 2130.Samuel³, 1707.Goodridge², 1.Benjamin, Sr.¹) was born 27 Jan 1893, the son of **Thaddeus Holmes Sparkman** and **Anne "Nancy" Meredith Wilson**. He married **Gertrude Edna Sneed** 1915. [603]

ISSUE:
- + 880. f   i.   **Margaret Nancy Sparkman**, born 1917.
- + 883. f   ii.   **Velma Frances Sparkman**, born 1921.
- + 885. f   iii. **Kathleen Inez Sparkman**, born 1923 <See pg. 246>.
-   889. m   iv.   **Venable Mayfield Sparkman**, born 1924.
-   890. f   v.   **Doris Mae Sparkman**, born 1926. She married **Theodore Dean Emery** 1946.

- - - - - - - - - -

880. Margaret Nancy⁶ Sparkman (879.Rothwell⁵, 838.Anne⁴, 2130.Samuel³, 1707.Goodridge², 1.Benjamin, Sr.¹) was born 1917, the daughter of **Rothwell Mayfield Sparkman** and **Gertrude Edna Sneed**. She married **William Raleigh Galey** 1942.

ISSUE:
- 881. m   i.   **William Raleigh Galey, II**, born 1943.
- 882. m   ii.   **Joe Richard Galey**, born 1945.

---

[602] McLean, *Wilson Family*, 76.

[603] McLean, *Wilson Family*, 76-77.

- - - - - - - - - - -

883. Velma Frances[6] Sparkman (879.Rothwell[5], 838.Anne[4], 2130.Samuel[3], 1707.Goodridge[2], 1.Benjamin, Sr.[1]) was born 1921, the daughter of **Rothwell Mayfield Sparkman** and **Gertrude Edna Sneed**. She married **Walter Earl Forsythe** 1944.

ISSUE:
884. f   i.   **Frances Jean Forsythe**, born 1946.

- - - - - - - - - - -

885. Kathleen Inez[7] Sparkman <See pg. 245> (879.Rothwell[6], 838.Anne[5], 2130.Samuel[3], 1707.Goodridge[2], 1.Benjamin, Sr.[1]) was born 1923, the daughter of **Rothwell Mayfield Sparkman** and **Gertrude Edna Sneed**. She married **James Andrew Johns** 1939.[604]

ISSUE:
886. f   i.   **Dorma Frances Johns**, born 1940.
887. m   ii.   **Jimmie Fred Johns**, born 1942.
888. m   iii.   **Albert Paul Johns**, born 1944.

- - - - - - - - - - -

891. Francis Wilson "Frank"[5] Sparkman <See pg. 241> (838.Anne[4], 2130.Samuel[3], 1707.Goodridge[2], 1.Benjamin, Sr.[1]) was born 17 Mar 1895, the son of **Thaddeus Holmes Sparkman** and **Anne "Nancy" Meredith Wilson**. Frank died 22 Mar 1941. He married **Jennie Faye Doty** Oct 1917 in Springfield, Missouri.[605]

ISSUE:
+ 892. m   i.   **Frank William Sparkman, Jr.**, born 5 Aug 1920.
+ 895. m   ii.   **Jack Billy Sparkman**, born 28 Feb 1922.
+ 898. m   iii.   **Robert Eugene Sparkman**, born 22 Jan 1929 <See pg. 247>.
  901. m   iv.   **Raymond Thad Sparkman**, born 1930.

- - - - - - - - - - -

892. Frank William[6] Sparkman, Jr. (891.Francis[5], 838.Anne[4], 2130.Samuel[3], 1707.Goodridge[2], 1.Benjamin, Sr.[1]) was born 5 Aug 1920, the son of **Francis Wilson "Frank" Sparkman** and **Jennie Faye Doty**. He married **Luella Jane Hubbard** 1946.

ISSUE:
893. f   i.   **Winona Jane Sparkman**, born 6 Aug 1947.
894. m   ii.   **Frank William Sparkman, III**, born 9 Aug 1948.

---

[604] McLean, *Wilson Family*, 77.

[605] McLean, *Wilson Family*, 77-78. His name became Frank William Sparkman when he joined the army in 1913.

- - - - - - - - - -

895. Jack Billy[6] Sparkman (891.Francis[5], 838.Anne[4], 2130.Samuel[3], 1707.Goodridge[2], 1.Benjamin, Sr.[1]) was born 28 Feb 1922, the son of **Francis Wilson "Frank" Sparkman** and **Jennie Faye Doty**. He married **Elsie Ruth Brown** 5 Mar 1939.

ISSUE:

896. f   i.   **Carroll Fay Sparkman**, born 15 Jun 1944.

897. f   ii. **Margaret Ellen Sparkman**, born 22 Sep 1947.

- - - - - - - - - -

898. Robert Eugene[6] Sparkman <See pg. 246> (891.Francis[5], 838.Anne[4], 2130.Samuel[3], 1707.Goodridge[2], 1.Benjamin, Sr.[1]) was born 22 Jan 1929, the son of **Francis Wilson "Frank" Sparkman** and **Jennie Faye Doty**. He married **Jeanne Osborn** 1946.[606]

ISSUE:

899. f   i.   **Linda Joyce Sparkman**, born 1947.

900. m   ii. **Robert Eugene Sparkman**, born 18 May 1948.

- - - - - - - - - -

903. Benjamin Francis[4] Wilson <See pg. 99, 229> (2130.Samuel[3], 1707.Goodridge[2], 1.Benjamin, Sr.[1]) was born Nov 1857 in Missouri, the son of **Samuel Venable Wilson** and **Sarah Cox Meredith**. Benjamin died after 26 Mar 1919 probably in Prairie Grove Co., Arkansas. He married **Nancy Meredith Wilson (See number 1148 - pg. 276)** 1889. She was born 11 Jul 1864 in Navarro Co., Texas, the daughter of **James Willis Wilson** and **Mary Hetty Meredith**. Nancy died after 1928 probably in Prairie Grove Co., Arkansas.[607]

ISSUE:

904. m   i.   **Richard Venable Wilson**, born 29 Nov 1889.

+ 905. m ii. **Gus Scruggs Wilson**, born 15 Mar 1893, died about 1981 <See pg. 248>.

910. f   iii. **Mary Hettie Wilson**, born 1 Aug 1895, died probably in Prairie Grove Co., Arkansas.

+ 911. m iv. **William McNaught Wilson**, born 8 Dec 1897 <See pg. 248>.

+ 916. m v. **James Willis Wilson**, born 14 Jan 1905, died 24 Jan 1993 <See pg. 248>.

Benjamin registered brands in Fisher Co., Texas, in 1888 and 1891. In 1886 he was awarded 80 acres of land there which he and his wife sold in 1894 for "7 head of mules" valued at $480. In the same year they bought

---

[606] McLean, *Wilson Family*, 78.

[607] McLean, *Wilson Family*, 72-73.

land in Van Zandt Co., Texas.[608]

The 1900 and 1910 Van Zandt Co., Texas, censuses list the family and state that they have been married 11 and 21 years respectively.

A letter written by kin Mar 26, 1919 says, "Bro Bens health is not good he has heart trouble & Sis Nan wants to move away some where".[609]   Since Nan is shown living in Prairie Grove, Arkansas, in her brother's 1928 obituary, Ben may have died there.

- - - - - - - - - - -

905. Gus Scruggs[5] Wilson <See pg. 247, 276> (903.Benjamin[4], 2130.Samuel[3], 1707.Goodridge[2], 1.Benjamin, Sr.[1]) was born 15 Mar 1893, the son of **Benjamin Francis Wilson** and **Nancy Meredith Wilson**. Gus died about 1981. He married **Grace Skaggs** 1927. [610]
                                 ISSUE:
906. m   i.   **John Wilson**, born 1 Aug 1928.
907. m   ii. **Joe Mack Wilson**, born 1937.
908. f   iii. **Hope Augusta Wilson**, born 1940.
909. f   iv. **Helen Geneva Wilson**, born 1947.

- - - - - - - - - - -

911. William McNaught[5] Wilson <See pg. 247, 276> (903.Benjamin[4], 2130.Samuel[3], 1707.Goodridge[2], 1.Benjamin, Sr.[1]) was born 8 Dec 1897, the son of **Benjamin Francis Wilson** and **Nancy Meredith Wilson**. He married **Gertrude Collins** 1935.
                                 ISSUE:
912. f   i.   **Katherine Louise Wilson**, born 21 Nov 1937.
913. f   ii. **Virginia Lee Wilson**, born 20 Feb 1939.
914. f   iii. **Nancy Carolyn Wilson**, born 30 Aug 1940.
915. f   iv. **Martha Elaine Wilson**, born 9 Jun 1943.

- - - - - - - - - - -

916. James Willis[5] Wilson <See pg. 247, 276> (903.Benjamin[4],2130.Samuel[3], 1707.Goodridge[2], 1.Benjamin, Sr.[1]) was born 14 Jan 1905, the son of **Benjamin Francis Wilson** and **Nancy Meredith Wilson**. James died

---

[608]   Fisher Co. TX Marks and Brands:288, 295, Deed Book 7:370.   Van Zandt Co. TX Deed Book 49:597.

[609]   Look, *Family history*.

[610]   McLean, *Wilson Family*, 72.

24 Jan 1993 in Van Zandt Co., Texas. He married **Zula Anderson**.[611]
ISSUE:
917. m   i.   **Lawrence Eugene Wilson**, born 29 Oct 1928.

- - - - - - - - - -

919. Elizabeth Venable "Bessie"[4] Wilson <See pg. 99, 229> (2130.Samuel[3], 1707.Goodridge[2], 1.Benjamin, Sr.[1]) was born 14 Mar 1864 in St. Louis Co., Missouri, the daughter of **Samuel Venable Wilson** and **Sarah Cox Meredith**. Elizabeth died 22 Mar 1927 probably in Poplar Bluff, Butler Co., Missouri, and was buried in Sparkman Cemetery in Cane Creek, Missouri. She married **John Elonzo Sparkman** 24 Jan 1886 in Butler Co., Missouri. He was born 13 May 1860, the son of **William Williams Sparkman** and **Elizabeth Jane Fitzgerald**. John died 10 Jun 1948 in Cane Creek, Missouri, and was buried in Sparkman Cemetery. [612]
ISSUE:
+ 920. f   i.   **Edith Wilson Sparkman**, born 26 Aug 1886.
+ 930. f   ii. **Sarah Grace Sparkman**, born 20 Oct 1888 <See pg. 250>.
+ 972. f   iii. **Pearl Sparkman**, born 16 Jun 1891 <See pg. 253>.
+ 1014. f   iv. **Hettie Meredith Sparkman**, born 2 Dec 1894, died 20 Jan 1968 <See pg. 255>.
+ 1042. m   v.   **John Edwin Sparkman**, born 1897 <See pg. 257>.
  1050. m   vi. **Samuel Wilson Sparkman**, born 22 Jul 1900, died 29 Feb 1920.
+ 1051. f   vii. **Mabel Abigail Sparkman**, born 9 Feb 1903, died 19 Mar 1987 <See pg. 258>.
+ 1064. m viii. **Charles Norman Sparkman**, born 13 Oct 1906 <See pg. 258>.

- - - - - - - - - -

920. Edith Wilson[5] Sparkman (919.Elizabeth[4], 2130.Samuel[3], 1707.Goodridge[2], 1.Benjamin, Sr.[1]) was born 26 Aug 1886, the daughter of **John Elonzo Sparkman** and **Elizabeth Venable "Bessie" Wilson**. She married **R. Frank Black** 25 Dec 1907.

ISSUE:[613]
921. m   i.   **Robert F. Black, Jr.**, born 1909.

---

[611] McLean, *Wilson Family*, 73. Van Zandt Co. TX Register of Deaths, 24:38.

[612] McLean, *Wilson Family*, 79-84. Butler Co. MO Marriage Book D-298-2 (1:296). Hanks, *Sparkman Cemetery*, (accessed 15 Dec 2005). Additional information from Karen (Crites) Look and Patricia (Sparkman) Thomas.

[613] McLean, *Wilson Family*, 79. Look, *Family history*, includes a large collection of letters written from ca 1909-1927.

+ 922. m   ii.   **Paul Wilson Black**, born before 2 Aug 1912.
  924. m   iii. **John David Black**, died 26 Nov 1915.
  925. f   iv.   **Helen Black**.
  926. m   v.   **Roger Black**, born 1 Feb 1916.
  927. f   vi.   **Ruth Black**, born before 4 Oct 1917.
  928. m vii. **Joseph T. Black**.
  929. m viii. **William Black**.

- - - - - - - - - -

922. Paul Wilson [6] Black (920.Edith[5], 919.Elizabeth[4], 2130.Samuel[3], 1707.Goodridge[2], 1.Benjamin, Sr.[1]) was born before 2 Aug 1912, the son of **R. Frank Black** and **Edith Wilson Sparkman**. His spouse has not been identified.

ISSUE:[614]
  923. f   i.   **Sharon Black**. She married _____ **Parnell**.

- - - - - - - - - -

930. Sarah Grace[5] Sparkman <See pg. 249> (919.Elizabeth[4], 2130.Samuel[3], 1707.Goodridge[2], 1.Benjamin, Sr.[1]) was born 20 Oct 1888, the daughter of **John Elonzo Sparkman** and **Elizabeth Venable "Bessie" Wilson**. She married **Chester Herschel Boyers** 23 Feb 1909.[615]

ISSUE:
+ 931. f   i.   **Elizabeth Vernetta "Bessie" Boyers**, born 7 Jan 1910, died 23 Jan 1965.
+ 935. f   ii.   **Alma Irene Boyers**, born 16 Sep 1911.
+ 939. f   iii. **Ruth S. Boyers**, born 21 Sep 1913 <See pg. 251>.
  945. f   iv.   **Hildegard Boyers**, born 11 Dec 1915, died 28 Jan 1920.
+ 946. f   v.   **Mabel Kate Boyers**, born 7 Sep 1918 <See pg. 251>.
+ 950. m   vi.   **Robert James Boyers**, born 26 Apr 1921 <See pg. 251>.
+ 954. f   vii. **Grace LaNell Boyers**, born 22 Aug 1923 <See pg. 252>.
+ 956. f viii. **Imogene Boyers**, born 20 Apr 1926 <See pg. 252>.
+ 960. m   ix.   **Chester Herschel Boyers, Jr.**, born 19 Mar 1929 <See pg. 252>.
+ 968. f   x.   **Peggy Joan Boyers**, born 9 Sep 1932 <See pg. 252>.

- - - - - - - - - -

931. Elizabeth Vernetta "Bessie"[6] Boyers (930.Sarah[5], 919.Elizabeth[4], 2130.Samuel[3], 1707.Goodridge[2], 1.Benjamin, Sr.[1]) was born 7 Jan 1910, the daughter of **Chester Herschel Boyers** and **Sarah Grace Sparkman**.

---

[614] Additional information from Sharon (Black) Parnell.

[615] McLean, *Wilson Family*, 79-80.

Elizabeth died 23 Jan 1965. She married **Cole Miller** 10 May 1934.

ISSUE:

932. m   i.   **George Robert Miller.**
933. m   ii.   **Jerry Cole Miller.**
934. m   iii. **Paul David Miller.**

- - - - - - - - - -

935. Alma Irene[6] Boyers (930.Sarah[5], 919.Elizabeth[4], 2130.Samuel[3], 1707.Goodridge[2], 1.Benjamin, Sr.[1]) was born 16 Sep 1911, the daughter of **Chester Herschel Boyers** and **Sarah Grace Sparkman**. She married **Raymond Frederick Harloff** 6 Aug 1933.

ISSUE:

936. f   i.   **Carol Sue Harloff.**
937. m   ii.   **Dennis Ray Harloff.**
938. m   iii. **Michael Lee Harloff.**

- - - - - - - - - -

939. Ruth S.[6] Boyers <See pg. 250> (930.Sarah[5], 919.Elizabeth[4], 2130.Samuel[3], 1707.Goodridge[2], 1.Benjamin, Sr.[1]) was born 21 Sep 1913, the daughter of **Chester Herschel Boyers** and **Sarah Grace Sparkman**. She married **John Allen Thurman** 1 Apr 1933.

ISSUE:

940. m   i.   **John Allen Thurman, Jr.**
941. m   ii.   **Gordon Boyers Thurman.**
942. m   iii. **Kenneth Ray Thurman.**
943. f   iv.   **Ruth Marie Thurman.**
944. f   v.   **Phyllis Ann Thurman.**

- - - - - - - - - -

946. Mabel Kate [6] Boyers <See pg. 250> (930.Sarah[5], 919.Elizabeth[4], 2130.Samuel[3], 1707.Goodridge[2], 1.Benjamin, Sr.[1]) was born 7 Sep 1918, the daughter of **Chester Herschel Boyers** and **Sarah Grace Sparkman**. She married **Ralph Sanford Epps** 24 Jun 1939.

ISSUE:

947. f   i.   **Judith Ann Epps.**
948. m   ii.   **Richard Ralph Epps.**
949. f   iii. **Janet Kay Epps.**

- - - - - - - - - -

950. Robert James[6] Boyers <See pg. 250> (930.Sarah[5], 919.Elizabeth[4], 2130.Samuel[3], 1707.Goodridge[2], 1.Benjamin, Sr.[1]) was born 26 Apr 1921, the son of **Chester Herschel Boyers** and **Sarah Grace Sparkman**. He married **Mary Helen Seirowski** 2 Aug 1953.

ISSUE:

951. m   i.   **Robert James Boyers, Jr.**
952. f   ii.   **Mary Nella Boyers.**
953. f   iii. **Grace Annette Boyers.**

- - - - - - - - - -

954. Grace LaNell[6] Boyers <See pg. 250> (930.Sarah[5], 919.Elizabeth[4], 2130.Samuel[3], 1707.Goodridge[2], 1.Benjamin, Sr.[1]) was born 22 Aug 1923, the daughter of **Chester Herschel Boyers** and **Sarah Grace Sparkman**. She married **Garland Stanley Kumpe** 21 Jun 1944.

ISSUE:

955. m   i.   **Wayne Norris Kumpe.**

- - - - - - - - - -

956. Imogene[6] Boyers <See pg. 250> (930.Sarah[5], 919.Elizabeth[4], 2130.Samuel[3], 1707.Goodridge[2], 1.Benjamin, Sr.[1]) was born 20 Apr 1926, the daughter of **Chester Herschel Boyers** and **Sarah Grace Sparkman**. She married **Leonard Orrill Taylor** 2 Jun 1946.

ISSUE:

957. f   i.   **Linda Jean Taylor.**
958. m   ii.   **Leonard Orrill Taylor, Jr.**
959. f   iii. **Lisa Adele Taylor.**

- - - - - - - - - -

960. Chester Herschel[6] Boyers, Jr. <See pg. 250> (930.Sarah[5], 919.Elizabeth[4], 2130.Samuel[3], 1707.Goodridge[2], 1.Benjamin, Sr.[1]) was born 19 Mar 1929, the son of **Chester Herschel Boyers** and **Sarah Grace Sparkman**. He married **Elizabeth Lackey** 30 Sep 1948.

ISSUE:

961. m   i.   **Chester Herschel Boyers, III.**
962. m   ii.   **Charles Edwin Boyers.**
963. f   iii. **Julie Ann Boyers.**
964. m   iv.   **Tommy Joe Boyers.**
965. m   v.   **Raymond Allen Boyers.**
966. m   vi.   **Ronald Bruce Boyers.**
967. f   vii. **Susan Elizabeth Boyers.**

- - - - - - - - - -

968. Peggy Joan[6] Boyers <See pg. 250> (930.Sarah[5], 919.Elizabeth[4], 2130.Samuel[3], 1707.Goodridge[2], 1.Benjamin, Sr.[1]) was born 9 Sep 1932, the daughter of **Chester Herschel Boyers** and **Sarah Grace Sparkman**.

She married **Richard Newel Dickison** 26 Apr 1952.

ISSUE:

969. m   i. **Richard Newel Dickison, Jr.**
970. f   ii. **Peggy Lynn Dickison.**
971. m iii. **Ronald Craig Dickison.**

- - - - - - - - - - -

972. Pearl⁵ Sparkman <See pg. 249> (919.Elizabeth⁴, 2130.Samuel³, 1707.Goodridge², 1.Benjamin, Sr.¹) was born 16 Jun 1891, the daughter of **John Elonzo Sparkman** and **Elizabeth Venable "Bessie" Wilson**. She married **James Earl Houts** 1 Nov 1911.⁶¹⁶

ISSUE:

+ 973. m   i. **James Earl Houts, Jr.**, born 1912.
+ 981. f   ii. **Mavis Kate Houts**, born 17 Dec 1914.
+ 987. m iii. **Venable Meredith Houts**, born 1916 <See pg. 254>.
  992. f   iv. **Ina Louise Houts**, born 9 Mar 1919, died 20 May 1924.
+ 993. f   v. **Betty Jo Houts**, born 16 Apr 1921, died 17 Jan 1939 <See pg. 254>.
+ 995. f   vi. **Elizabeth Annette Houts**, born 1923 <See pg. 254>.
+ 1002. m vii. **Samuel Paul Houts**, born 1925 <See pg. 255>.
+ 1005. f viii. **Irma Louise Houts**, born 1927 <See pg. 255>.
+ 1009. m ix. **Farris Lee Houts**, born 1930 <See pg. 255>.
+ 1011. m x. **John Caroll Houts**, born 20 May 1932 <See pg. 255>.

- - - - - - - - - - -

973. James Earl⁶ Houts, Jr. (972.Pearl⁵, 919.Elizabeth⁴, 2130.Samuel³, 1707.Goodridge², 1.Benjamin, Sr.¹) was born 1912, the son of **James Earl Houts** and **Pearl Sparkman**. He married **Jennie Buchanan** 17 Dec 1932 in Butler Co., Missouri.

ISSUE:

974. f   i. **Alma Juanita Houts**, born 22 Oct 1933.
975. m ii. **James Earl Houts, III**, born 23 Mar 1936.
976. m iii. **Orville Houts**, born 27 Apr 1937.
977. m iv. **Wendell Ray Houts**, born 30 Jul 1940.
978. f   v. **Wanda Fay Houts**, born 30 Jul 1940.
979. m vi. **Jerry Norman Houts**, born 6 Nov 1943.
980. f vii. **Jo Ann Houts**, born 6 Nov 1943.

- - - - - - - - - - -

---

⁶¹⁶ McLean, *Wilson Family*, 80-1. Corrections and additions from Karen Look, citing correspondence with Irma (Houts) Epps.

981. Mavis Kate⁶ Houts (972.Pearl⁵, 919.Elizabeth⁴, 2130.Samuel³, 1707.Goodridge², 1.Benjamin, Sr.¹) was born 17 Dec 1914, the daughter of **James Earl Houts** and **Pearl Sparkman**. She married **George B. Greer** 1 Jan 1933.

ISSUE:

982. m   i.   **David Earl Greer**, born 30 Mar 1934.
983. f   ii.   **Mavis Marie Greer**, born 9 Sep 1935.
984. f   iii.   **Pearl V. Greer**, born 23 Mar 1937.
985. f   iv.   **Betty Jean Greer**, born 16 Mar 1941.
986. m   v.   **George Roger Greer**.

- - - - - - - - - -

987. Venable Meredith⁶ Houts <See pg. 253> (972.Pearl⁵, 919.Elizabeth⁴, 2130.Samuel³, 1707.Goodridge², 1.Benjamin, Sr.¹) was born 1916, the son of **James Earl Houts** and **Pearl Sparkman**. He married **Gladys Goss** 17 May 1942 in London, England.

ISSUE:

988. m   i.   **Bruce Lee Houts**, born 11 Jul 1944 in England.
989. m   ii.   **William Godfrey Houts**, born 23 Jun 1947.
990. m   iii.   **Venable Jo Houts**.
991. f   iv.   **Mabel Houts**.

- - - - - - - - - -

993. Betty Jo⁶ Houts <See pg. 253> (972.Pearl⁵, 919.Elizabeth⁴, 2130.Samuel³, 1707.Goodridge², 1.Benjamin, Sr.¹) was born 16 Apr 1921, the daughter of **James Earl Houts** and **Pearl Sparkman**. Betty died 17 Jan 1939. Her spouse has not been identified.

ISSUE:

994. f   i.   **Patricia Ann Houts**.

- - - - - - - - - -

995. Elizabeth Annette⁶ Houts <See pg. 253> (972.Pearl⁵, 919.Elizabeth⁴, 2130.Samuel³, 1707.Goodridge², 1.Benjamin, Sr.¹) was born 1923, the daughter of **James Earl Houts** and **Pearl Sparkman**. She married **Marvin L. Atwood**.[617]

ISSUE:

996. m   i.   **Teddy Lee Atwood**.
997. m   ii.   **Dan Atwood**.
998. f   iii.   **Lynn Atwood**, died 1957.
999. f   iv.   **Mary Atwood**.
1000. f   v.   **Donna Atwood**.

---

[617] McLean, *Wilson Family*, 81-82.

1001. m vi. **Steve Atwood.**

- - - - - - - - - -

1002. Samuel Paul[6] Houts <See pg. 253> (972.Pearl[5], 919.Elizabeth[4], 2130.Samuel[3], 1707.Goodridge[2], 1.Benjamin, Sr.[1]) was born 1925, the son of **James Earl Houts** and **Pearl Sparkman**. He married **Betty Hughel** 12 Nov 1949 in Detroit, Michigan.

ISSUE:

1003. f   i. **Paula Houts.**
1004. f   ii. **Deborah Houts.**

- - - - - - - - - -

1005. Irma Louise[6] Houts <See pg. 253> (972.Pearl[5], 919.Elizabeth[4], 2130.Samuel[3], 1707.Goodridge[2], 1.Benjamin, Sr.[1]) was born 1927, the daughter of **James Earl Houts** and **Pearl Sparkman**. She married **Grady Epps** 6 Jun 1950.

ISSUE:

1006. m   i. **David Epps.**
1007. m   ii. **Donald Epps.**
1008. f   iii. **Janis Epps.**

- - - - - - - - - -

1009. Farris Lee[6] Houts <See pg. 253> (972.Pearl[5], 919.Elizabeth[4], 2130.Samuel[3], 1707.Goodridge[2], 1.Benjamin, Sr.[1]) was born 1930, the son of **James Earl Houts** and **Pearl Sparkman**. He married **Doris Brown** 4 Jul 1951 in California.

ISSUE:

1010. m   i. **Jeffrey Houts.**

- - - - - - - - - -

1011. John Caroll[6] Houts <See pg. 253> (972.Pearl[5], 919.Elizabeth[4], 2130.Samuel[3], 1707.Goodridge[2], 1.Benjamin, Sr.[1]) was born 20 May 1932, the son of **James Earl Houts** and **Pearl Sparkman**. He married **Marie Sampson** 6 Jun 1952 in California.

ISSUE:

1012. f   i. **Cherylann Houts.**
1013. f   ii. **Cindy Houts.**

- - - - - - - - - -

1014. Hettie Meredith[5] Sparkman <See pg. 249> (919.Elizabeth[4], 2130.Samuel[3], 1707.Goodridge[2], 1.Benjamin, Sr.[1]) was born 2 Dec 1894, the daughter of **John Elonzo Sparkman** and **Elizabeth Venable "Bessie"**

Wilson. Hettie died 20 Jan 1968. She married **Byrd F. Boyers** 6 Mar 1915. He was born 22 Nov 1892. Byrd died 16 Jul 1981.[618]

ISSUE:

+ 1015. f   i.   **Virginia Boyers**, born 4 Sep 1916.
   1019. f   ii.   **Ruth Ann Boyers**, born 16 Aug 1918, died 10 Oct 1945.
+ 1020. f   iii.   **Dorothy Elizabeth Boyers**, born 8 Feb 1921.
   1025. m   iv.   **Benjamin Francis Boyers**, born 8 Sep 1923. He married **Mary David**.
+ 1026. f   v.   **Mildred Delores Boyers**, born 23 Aug 1926.
+ 1030. f   vi.   **Betty Jean Boyers**, born 11 Sep 1930 <See pg. 257>.
+ 1037. m   vii.   **Meredith Ray Boyers**, born 7 May 1936 <See pg. 257>.

- - - - - - - - - - -

1015. Virginia[6] Boyers (1014.Hettie[5], 919.Elizabeth[4], 2130.Samuel[3], 1707.Goodridge[2], 1.Benjamin, Sr.[1]) was born 4 Sep 1916, the daughter of **Byrd F. Boyers** and **Hettie Meredith Sparkman**. She married **Deo Hadley Crites** 20 Feb 1935.

ISSUE:

   1016. f   i.   **Carroll Sue Crites**.
   1017. f   ii.   **Karen Louise Crites**.
   1018. m   iii.   **Donnell Harrison Crites**.

- - - - - - - - - - -

1020. Dorothy Elizabeth[6] Boyers (1014.Hettie[5], 919.Elizabeth[4], 2130.Samuel[3], 1707.Goodridge[2], 1.Benjamin, Sr.[1]) was born 8 Feb 1921, the daughter of **Byrd F. Boyers** and **Hettie Meredith Sparkman**. She married **Theodore Dowd** Dec 1943.

ISSUE:

   1021. f   i.   **Sandy Dowd**.
   1022. m   ii.   **Larry Dowd**.
   1023. f   iii.   **Debra Dowd**.
   1024. m   iv.   **Teddy Dowd**.

- - - - - - - - - - -

1026. Mildred Delores[6] Boyers (1014.Hettie[5], 919.Elizabeth[4], 2130.Samuel[3], 1707.Goodridge[2], 1.Benjamin, Sr.[1]) was born 23 Aug 1926 the daughter of **Byrd F. Boyers** and **Hettie Meredith Sparkman**. She married **Harry Worley** 26 Nov 1942.

ISSUE:

   1027. f   i.   **Sharon Worley**.
   1028. u   ii.   **Cleon Worley**.

---

[618] McLean, *Wilson Family*, 82.

1029. f   iii.   **Marilyn Worley.**

- - - - - - - - - - -

1030. Betty Jean[6] Boyers <See pg. 256> (1014.Hettie[5], 919.Elizabeth[4], 2130.Samuel[3], 1707.Goodridge[2], 1.Benjamin, Sr.[1]) was born 11 Sep 1930, the daughter of **Byrd F. Boyers** and **Hettie Meredith Sparkman**. She married **John Webb**.

ISSUE:
1031. m   i.   **Gary Webb.**
1032. f   ii.   **Zoeanna Webb.**
1033. m   iii.   **John Webb.**
1034. m   iv.   **Phillip Webb.**
1035. m   v.   **Jeffrey Webb.**
1036. m   vi.   **Christopher Webb.**

- - - - - - - - - - -

1037. Meredith Ray[6] Boyers <See pg. 256> (1014.Hettie[5], 919.Elizabeth[4], 2130.Samuel[3], 1707.Goodridge[2], 1.Benjamin, Sr.[1]) was born 7 May 1936, the son of **Byrd F. Boyers** and **Hettie Meredith Sparkman**. He married **Ella Jean White**.

ISSUE:
1038. f   i.   **Cindy Boyers.**
1039. m   ii.   **Steve Boyers.**
1040. f   iii.   **Michelle Boyers.**
1041. u   iv.   **LaVan Boyers.**

- - - - - - - - - - -

1042. John Edwin[5] Sparkman <See pg. 249> (919.Elizabeth[4], 2130.Samuel[3], 1707.Goodridge[2], 1.Benjamin, Sr.[1]) was born 1897, the son of **John Elonzo Sparkman** and **Elizabeth Venable "Bessie" Wilson**. He married **Vera Kunz** 1920.[619]

ISSUE:
1043. m   i.   **John Edwin Sparkman, III.**
1044. f   ii.   **Norma Irene Sparkman.**
1045. m   iii.   **Kenneth L. Sparkman.**
1046. m   iv.   **Meredith Sparkman.**
1047. f   v.   **Marie Ann Sparkman.**
1048. m   vi.   **Robert Francis Sparkman.**
1049. f   vii.   **Carol Jean Sparkman.**

The family letters between Edwin's sister and others speak of the time he

---

[619] McLean, *Wilson Family*, 82-3. Look, *Family history*.

was in the service during Word War I, some proud of his enlistment, others regretting his decision to join the effort. Edwin, having grown up on a farm, wrote to his sister 18 Mar 1818, "I haven't touched an animal for over three weeks except a cat." On 24 Jun 1918 his mother wrote to a daughter, "About our Red Cross ... knitting and sewing, we have made 23 garments & bandages .... bed shirts for wounded soldiers." 11 Sep 1918, Edwin wrote, "This war is not going to last much longer, the Germans are getting weaker every day ...". The Armistice was signed 11 Nov 1918.

- - - - - - - - - - -

1051. Mabel Abigail⁵ Sparkman <See pg. 249> (919.Elizabeth⁴, 2130.Samuel³, 1707.Goodridge², 1.Benjamin, Sr.¹) was born 9 Feb 1903, the daughter of **John Elonzo Sparkman** and **Elizabeth Venable "Bessie" Wilson**. Mabel died 19 Mar 1987. She married **Clarence D. Crites** 1 Apr 1923. He was born 26 Feb 1885. Clarence died 30 Nov 1933. *⁶²⁰*
ISSUE:
1052. f i. **Mary Bess Crites**.
1053. m ii. **Joe David Crites**.
1054. m iii. **Carl Ray Crites**.
1055. m iv. **John Oliver Crites**.
+ 1056. m v. **Charles Dayton Crites**, born 1931.

- - - - - - - - - - -

1056. Charles Dayton⁶ Crites (1051.Mabel⁵, 919.Elizabeth⁴, 2130.Samuel³, 1707.Goodridge², 1.Benjamin, Sr.¹) was born 1931, the son of **Clarence D. Crites** and **Mabel Abigail Sparkman**. He married **Marcia Ann Heil** 9 Jan 1952. She was born 1932.
ISSUE:
1057. m i. **Richard Ray Crites**, born 1952.
1058. m ii. **John Clarence Crites**, born 1954, died 1954.
1059. f iii. **Karen Renee Crites**, born 1955. She married **Alson Look**.
1060. f iv. **Cynthia Leah Crites**, born 1956.
1061. m v. **David Eric Crites**, born 1959.
1062. f vi. **Nancy Ann Crites**, born 1961.
1063. f vii. **Susan Elizabeth Crites**, born 1963.

- - - - - - - - - - -

1064. Charles Norman⁵ Sparkman <See pg. 249> (919.Elizabeth⁴, 2130.Samuel³, 1707.Goodridge², 1.Benjamin, Sr.¹) was born 13 Oct 1906, the son of **John Elonzo Sparkman** and **Elizabeth Venable "Bessie"**

---

⁶²⁰ McLean, *Wilson Family*, 83.

Wilson. He married **Martha E. Finney** in 1927.[621]

ISSUE:

1065. f   i.   **Elizabeth Sparkman.**
1066. m ii. **Charles Norman Sparkman, Jr.**
1067. m iii. **Samuel Paul Sparkman.**
1068. f   iv. **Myra Louise Sparkman.**
1069. m v. **David Glenn Sparkman.**

- - - - - - - - - -

1070. Sarah Stonewall[4] Wilson <See pg. 100> (2130.Samuel[3], 1707.Goodridge[2], 1.Benjamin, Sr.[1]) was born 27 May 1865 in Missouri, the daughter of **Samuel Venable Wilson** and **Sarah Cox Meredith**. Sarah died 11 Nov 1951 in Van Zandt Co., Texas, and was buried in Colfax Cemetery, Van Zandt Co. She married **Nathaniel Venable Wilson (See number 1146 - pg. 269)** 1889. He was born 5 Nov 1859 in St. Louis, Missouri, the son of **James Willis Wilson** and **Mary Hetty Meredith**. Nathaniel died 24 Jun 1911 in Ben Wheeler, Van Zandt Co., Texas, and was buried in Colfax Cemetery.[622]

ISSUE:

1071. m   i.   **Thomas Francis Wilson**, born May 1890 in Texas, died 6 Feb 1933 in Dallas, Texas, and was buried in Colfax Cemetery, Van Zandt Co., Texas.
+ 1072. m ii. **Samuel Willis Wilson**, born 28 Oct 1892, died 17 May 1976 <See pg. 270>.
+ 1073. m iii. **Woodville Bates Wilson**, born 16 Oct 1894, died 8 Feb 1958 <See pg. 273>.
1079. f   iv. **Ellen Trent Wilson**, born Dec 1896 in Texas. She married **Paul Ford** in Guatemala. Paul also married (2) **June** _____.
+ 1080. f v. **Sarah "Sallie" Wilson**, born 8 Mar 1899, died 15 Jul 1951 <See pg. 274>.
+ 1086. f vi. **Janette Wilson** <See pg. 275>.
1087. f vii. **Mary Lucille Wilson**, born 1904, died 1914, and was buried in Colfax Cemetery.
+ 1088. m viii. **Nathaniel Venable Wilson, II**, born 2 Mar 1909, died 26 Jun 1983 <See pg. 275>.

- - - - - - - - - -

[621] McLean, *Wilson Family*, 84.

[622] McLean, *Wilson Family*, 84-6. Curry, *Colfax Cemetery*, 14. . Geddie, *Colfax*, 131-3. Additional information from Imogene (Beggs) Wilson.

2131. James Willis³ Wilson <See pg. 177> (1707.Goodridge², 1.Benjamin, Sr.¹) was born 3 Dec 1823 at "Milnwood", Prince Edward Co., Virginia, the son of **Goodridge Wilson** and **Elizabeth Woodson Venable**. James died 2 Sep 1899 in St. Charles, Missouri, and was buried in Frayser Burying Ground in St. Charles Co. He married **Mary Hetty Meredith (See number 1094 - pg. 101)** 25 Feb 1847 in Kanawha Co., Virginia (West Virginia). She was born 28 Feb 1828 in Buckingham Co., Virginia. She was the daughter of **John Meredith** and **Ann Seay Wilson**.*⁶²³*

ISSUE:*⁶²⁴*

+ 1095.m   i.   **John Meredith Wilson**, born 22 Feb 1848, died before 1926 <See pg. 263>.

  1102. f   ii.   **Julia Bates Wilson**, born 2 Dec 1850 in St. Louis, Missouri, died after 1870.

+ 1103. f   iii.   **Margaret Virginia Wilson**, born 6 Jul 1852, died 5 Jun 1925 <See pg. 264>.

+ 1111. m   iv.   **Charles Woodson Wilson**, born 5 Aug 1854, died 16 Apr 1926 <See pg. 265>.

  1144. f   v.   **Elizabeth Venable Wilson**, born 4 May 1856 in Franklin Co., Missouri, died 17 May 1857 in Franklin Co.

  1145. m   vi.   **Willis Wilson**, born 19 Feb 1858 in Franklin Co., died 12 May 1862.

+ 1146. m vii.   **Nathaniel Venable Wilson**, born 5 Nov 1859, died 24 Jun 1911 <See pg. 269>.

  1147. m viii.   **Goodridge Wilson**, born 12 Oct 1861 at "Thornhill", St. Louis Co., Missouri, died Dec 1928 in West Plains, Howell Co., Missouri, and was buried in Evergreen Cemetery in Howell Co.*⁶²⁵*

+ 1148. f   ix.   **Nancy Meredith Wilson**, born 11 Jul 1864, died after 1928 <See pg. 276>.

  1149. f   x.   **Mary Hetty "Polly" Wilson**, born 26 Sep 1866 in Rapides Parish, Louisiana, died 19 Feb 1932 in Howell Co., Missouri, and was buried in Blue Mound Cemetery in Howell Co.*⁶²⁶*

  1150. m xi.   **James W. Wilson**, born 26 Sep 1866 in Rapides Parish,

---

⁶²³ McLean, *Wilson Family*, 86-8. Boddie, *Historical Southern Families*, 3:65-6, 5:43-4. Kanawha Co. WV Marriage Records. DAR - Meredith Family Bible. Wiechens, *Cemeteries of St. Charles Co. MO*, 5:81.

⁶²⁴ "Old notebook" gives children's birth dates and places. Copy from Watson sisters of Kirkwood MO.

⁶²⁵ Obituary for Goodrich Wilson, probably from a West Plains newspaper.

⁶²⁶ Death certificate #4484, Missouri State Board of Health, Bureau of Vital Statistics, Jefferson MO. *Howell County, Missouri, Cemeteries, 1795-1987*, 57-8.

Louisiana. He married **Alice W. Clark** 7 Nov 1925 in
Howell Co., Missouri. James died 1939 in West Plains,
Howell Co., and was buried in Blue Mound Cemetery.[627]

+ 1151. m xii.   **Samuel Venable Wilson**, born 27 Mar 1868, died 12 Aug
1951 <See pg. 276>.

James' family moved from Prince Edward Co., Virginia, to the Johnson
Shoals area down river from Charleston, West Virginia, when he was about
13 years old. He was a graduate of Washington College in Lexington,
Virginia, (now Washington and Lee University), the matriculation list for
the session beginning September 1ˢᵗ 1841 showing his father as Dr.
Goodridge Wilson at Post office "Charleston Kanawha.". In 1843-44 he
took the first course at Transylvania medical school, and he was a medical
graduate of the University of Pennsylvania, listed at the public
commencement 4 Apr 1845.[628]

He wrote to his sister, **Agnes**, 15 Oct 1845 from Loutre Island, Missouri,
saying he had begun "to stick up my cards", that he thought his situation
good, except that he felt solitary and alone, his eldest sister living 40 miles
away. He spoke of plans to visit Kanawha in 18 months (which nearly
coincides with his marriage date). One of his medical books was inscribed
"J. W. Wilson, Loutre Island, Mo, May 28ᵗʰ 1846." On March of 1847
James and his new wife Het wrote from Kanawha to his sister, who was on
a family visit in St. Charles, Missouri.[629]

By Nov 1848 James apparently selected the city of St. Louis as the best
place to practice his profession. He wrote to his brother of the reports of
cholera on the increase from the south. In Feb 1849 it had reached St.
Louis; in June **Edward Bates** wrote in his diary of his admiration of "my
talented young friend, Dr. James W. Wilson" in his treatment of cholera.[630]
James' letter to his sister 28 May 1849 told of the problem with cholera and
his loss of property from the St. Louis fire, saving his clothes and books.
James and his wife and son are listed in the 1850 St. Louis 4ᵗʰ Ward census.
In the St. Louis Directory for the year 1854-5, he is listed for his business

---

[627] Howell Co. MO Marriage Records index book pg. 97, No. 222.

[628] Washington and Lee University, *Catalogue*, 96. Transylvania University,
Lexington KY. University of Pennsylvania, (accessed 22 Mar 2006).

[629] Copy of letter from Watson sisters of Kirkwood MO. Medical book owned by
Patti Sue (Thomas) McCrary of Gulf Shores AL.

[630] "St. Louis News", *Missouri Historical Society Bulletin*, 6:78.

address and another city address.[631]   In 1859 and 1860, Edward Bates mentioned several visits with Dr. J. W. Wilson in his diary.[632]

James had land transactions in Franklin Co., Missouri from 1855 to 1859, and the family is shown in the 1860 census in Bonhomme Township, St. Louis Co., in which "Thornhill" is located and is the place Hetty's mother is said to have died in 1856 and son Goodridge born in 1861. **Frederick Bates**, the future husband of Hetty's sister, **Lavinia**, who is listed with them on that census, is listed in the neighboring household.[633]

The family stories tell of James leaving Missouri during the Civil War for the safety of his family, although his eldest and youngest sisters and families and his second eldest son and family remained in St. Charles Co., Missouri. An account says "he served in the Confederate Army as a surgeon". James had a daughter, born in Navarro Co., Texas in 1864; family stories say he traveled between, Missouri and Texas, "carrying a buggy load of gold for a buggy load of quinine". A diary notes that on "Oct. 24, 1864 .... a Confederate Quartermaster" was "in town, and that Corsicana (Navarro Co.) was being made a depot for government supplies." In 1865 in Van Zandt Co., agents of the county priced quinine at $6.00 per bottle and used the proceeds to feed indigent families of soldiers. Years later, when James was passing through Starrville in Smith Co., Texas, with his son, he said he had been there before. [634]

After the Civil War, James joined other of his kin in Louisiana.   At the Louisiana State Seminary near Alexandria, Louisiana, the beginning of Louisiana State University, James W. Wilson, M. D., is listed on the Academic Board as acting surgeon from Mar 1st to June 30th, 1866. The Register dated June 30, 1867 names him as an officer, surgeon, and on the Academic Board as professor of Anatomy and Physiology. Three of his sons were enrolled as cadets for that session. A proposed medical curriculum was abandoned, so the family moved north. They were in Bossier Parish in 1868 for the birth of their youngest son.[635]

---

[631] Wilson, Nath'l V. *Papers, 1834-1878*. "Great St. Louis Fire of 1849", (accessed 10 Mar 2006). Copy of letter from Watson sisters of Kirkwood MO.

[632] Beale, *Diary of Edward Bates*, 29, 46, 47, 93, 94.

[633] Franklin Co. MO Deed Books M:160, O:678-9, Q:.367-8 Obituary of Goodridge Wilson says he was born at "Thornhill Place".

[634] Fleming, *LSU*, 133. Putman, *Navarro County History*, 1:94. Mills, *History of Van Zandt County*, 159.

[635] *Official Register .... La. State Seminary*. Fleming, *LSU*, 133. 20 Jun 1866

(continued...)

In the 1870 census the family is listed at South Point post office, Washington Township, Franklin Co., Missouri. A letter from South Point written by Hetty, before the date of the census, mentions their stop in Cape Girardeau. She describes their house at South Point, 16 rooms, 150 yards from the railroad depot and about the same distance from the Missouri River. In a later letter, she invites kin to "come to Franklin".[636]

The 1880 Missouri census shows the family in Chalk Level, St. Clair Co., Missouri. In 1886, son Charles bought land in Fisher Co., Texas and told his family they could have it, if they could "make a go of it".[637] Mary Hetty died there. Her son remembers hauling rocks to put on her grave. She was later moved to the Germany plot in Sweetwater cemetery in Nolan Co. They didn't succeed in farming, so most of the family moved to Van Zandt Co., Texas. James returned to St. Charles, Missouri to live with his son Charles until his death.

- - - - - - - - - -

1095. John Meredith[4] Wilson <See pg. 101, 260> (2131.James[3], 1707.Goodridge[2], 1.Benjamin, Sr.[1]) was born 22 Feb 1848 in Kanawha Co., Virginia(West Virginia), the son of **James Willis Wilson** and **Mary Hetty Meredith**. John died before 1926. He married **Bettie Cooper** about 1872 probably in Louisiana.

ISSUE:[638]

1096. m i. **James Nathaniel Wilson**, born 7 May 1873 in Louisiana.
1097. f ii. **Hettie Meredith Wilson**, born 25 Nov 1878 in Missouri.
1098. f iii. **Agnes Frayser Wilson**, born 16 Dec 1879.
1099. f iv. **Pattie Cooper Wilson**, born 15 Mar 1881.
1100. f v. **Bettie Wilson**, born 22 Feb 1883.
1101. f vi. **Lavinia John Wilson**, born 31 Jan 1887.

John is shown in the 1850 and 1860 censuses with his parents. He is listed as a cadet from 1866 to 1868 at the Louisiana State Seminary, where his

---

[635] (...continued)
issue of (Alexandria) *Louisiana Democrat.* 1924 letter by C. W. Wilson.
[636] Copy of letters from Watson sisters of Kirkwood MO.
[637] Fisher Co. TX Deed Book 1:260.
[638] A document dated 29 Nov 1887, found in the papers of Charles Woodson Wilson in files at the St. Charles Historical Society, lists the children of "Jno M. Wilson & Bettie Wilson" with birth dates and physical descriptions, signed by Bettie Wilson, attested to by C. W. Wilson, along with notes referring to travel between Arkansas and Missouri.

father was a professor and surgeon.[639] In an 1870 letter that his mother
wrote, she stated that he was recuperating from an illness at his uncle **Ben**'s
home in Bossier Parish, Louisiana,, and in 1872 she wrote of his doing
surveying there and in adjacent parishes.[640] He apparently married in
Louisiana, had their first child, then moved to Missouri. The family is
listed in the 1880 Henry Co., Missouri, census.

- - - - - - - - - - -

1103. Margaret Virginia⁴ Wilson <See pg. 101, 260> (2131.James³,
1707.Goodridge², 1.Benjamin, Sr.¹) was born 6 Jul 1852 in St. Louis,
Missouri, the daughter of **James Willis Wilson** and **Mary Hetty Meredith**.
M. Virginia (as her descendants say she called herself) died 5 Jun 1925 in
Appleton City, Missouri. She married **James Gardner Coffin, Jr.** 4 Nov
1879 in Ohio, St. Clair Co., Missouri. He was born 23 Apr 1848 in
Allegheny City, Pennsylvania, the son of **James Gardner Coffin** and
Isabella Catherine Anderson. James, Jr. died 17 Dec 1927 in Appleton
City.[641]
ISSUE:

 1104. f   i.   **Margaret V. Coffin**, born 7 Jan 1886, died 7 Jan 1886.
+ 1105. f   ii. **Isabella Catherine Coffin**, born 24 May 1891, died 4 Feb
                1950.

- - - - - - - - - - -

1105. Isabella Catherine⁵ Coffin (1103.Margaret⁴, 2131.James³,
1707.Goodridge², 1.Benjamin, Sr.¹) was born 24 May 1891 in Ohio, St.
Clair Co., Missouri, the daughter of **James Gardner Coffin, Jr.** and
Margaret Virginia Wilson. Isabella died 4 Feb 1950 in Appleton City,
Missouri. She married **Earl Lowe Schryver** 25 Dec 1913 in Appleton City.
He was born 12 Nov 1891 in Glendive, Montana, the son of **Joseph
Schryver** and **Esther Lowe**. Earl died 1935 in Santa Rosa, California.
ISSUE:

 1106. m   i.   **Joseph James Schryver**, born 2 Sep 1914 in Silvis,
                Illinois. He married **Lessie Mae Stevens** 9 Jun 1942 in St.
                Louis, Missouri. Lessie died Jul 1974. Joe died 3 Jan
                1986.
+ 1107. f   ii. **Virginia Wilson Schryver**, born 14 Nov 1916.

- - - - - - - - - - -

---
[639] *Official Register .... La. State Seminary*, 8.
[640] Copies of letters from Watson sisters, Kirkwood MO.
[641] McLean, *Wilson Family*, 87. Additional information from Virginia W.
(Schryver) Aydelotte.

1107. Virginia Wilson⁶ Schryver (1105.Isabella⁵, 1103.Margaret⁴, 2131.James³, 1707.Goodridge², 1.Benjamin, Sr.¹) was born 14 Nov 1916 in Appleton City, Missouri, the daughter of **Earl Lowe Schryver** and **Isabella Catherine Coffin**. She married **J. Robert Aydelotte** 27 Oct 1940. He was born 10 Jan 1918 in Ft. Scott, Kansas, the son of **James B. Aydelotte** and **Gertrude Canatsey**.

ISSUE:
+ 1108. m   i.   **James Edward Aydelotte**, born 20 Aug 1946.
  1110. m   ii. **Kevin Robert Aydelotte**, born 19 Feb 1949 in Bridgeport, Connecticut. He married **Janell Oksoon Kim** 13 Dec 1986 in Honolulu, Hawaii. She was born 5 Sep 1957, the daughter of **Sung Bok Kim** and **Katherine Youngsoon**.

- - - - - - - - - -

1108. James Edward⁷ Aydelotte (1107.Virginia⁶, 1105.Isabella⁵, 1103.Margaret⁴, 2131.James³, 1707.Goodridge², 1.Benjamin, Sr.¹) was born 20 Aug 1946 in Philadelphia, Pennsylvania, the son of **J. Robert Aydelotte** and **Virginia Wilson Schryver**. He married **Holly Elaine Francke** 12 Oct 1974 in Milwaukee, Wisconsin,. She was born 9 Dec 1947 in Milwaukee, the daughter of **Elmer George Francke** and **Elaine J. Bromley**.

ISSUE:
  1109. m   i.   **James Christopher Aydelotte**, born 2 May 1976 in Milwaukee, Wisconsin.

- - - - - - - - - -

1111. Charles Woodson⁴ Wilson <See pg. 101, 260> (2131.James³, 1707.Goodridge², 1.Benjamin, Sr.¹) was born 5 Aug 1854 in St. Louis Co., Missouri, the son of **James Willis Wilson** and **Mary Hetty Meredith**. Charles died 16 Apr 1926 in St. Charles, Missouri, and was buried in Oak Grove Cemetery, St. Charles Co., Missouri.⁶⁴² He married **Julia Bentley Frayser (See number 2133 - pg. 284)** 10 Oct 1888. She was born 1 Nov 1858 at "Elmwood", St. Charles Co., Missouri, the daughter of **Robert Bentley Frayser** and **Martha Agnes Wilson**. Julia died 24 Jun 1940 in St. Charles and was buried in Oak Grove Cemetery.⁶⁴³

ISSUE:
+ 1112. m   i.   **James Willis Wilson**, born 18 Jul 1889, died 30 Jul 1939 <See pg. 266>.

---

⁶⁴² McLean, *Wilson Family*, 86-7. Boddie, *Historical Southern Families*, 5:43-4. Additional information from Julia Watson of Kirkwood MO. Wiechens, *Cemeteries of St. Charles Co. MO*, 2:105, 166.
⁶⁴³ *St. Charles Cosmos-Monitor* June 26, 1940. Johnson, *Obituaries, St. Charles County Missouri*.

   1121. m   ii.   **Robert Frayser Wilson**, born 11 Mar 1892, died 4 Oct 1965 in Kirkwood, Missouri, and was buried in Oak Grove Cemetery.

+ 1122. m iii.   **Bates Frayser Wilson**, born 21 Dec 1895, died 29 Jan 1980 <See pg. 267>.

   1129. m iv.   **Charles Woodson Wilson, Jr.**, born Nov 1897, died 2 Aug 1963 in Temple, Texas, and was buried in Oak Grove Cemetery.

+ 1130. f   v.   **Martha Agnes Wilson**, born 30 Oct 1899, died 26 Dec 1971 <See pg. 268>.

Charles was a cadet at Louisiana State Seminary in 1867.[644]   His occupation is stated as "Lawyer" in the 1880 St. Charles, Missouri, census in the household of his future mother-in-law and wife. He is listed as a lawyer also in St. Charles city directories. In 1886 he bought land in West Texas, which his father and siblings checked out.

In 1924 he wrote a letter to kin in Virginia giving many details of his generation and the one above him. His obituary tells of the family history, of his law practice, and lists his surviving brothers, sisters, wife and children.[645]

- - - - - - - - - -

1112. James Willis⁵ Wilson <See pg. 265, 285> (1111.Charles⁴, 2131.James³, 1707.Goodridge², 1.Benjamin, Sr.¹) was born 18 Jul 1889 in St. Charles, Missouri, the son of **Charles Woodson Wilson** and **Julia Bentley Frayser**. Willis died 30 Jul 1939 in South Charleston, West Virginia, and was buried in Oak Grove Cemetery, St. Charles Co., Missouri. He married **Rosalie Prevost Watkins**. She was born 17 May 1887 in St. Charles, Missouri, the daughter of **James Allen Watkins** and **Hattie Rebecca Purkitt**. Rose died 19 Nov 1971 in Akron, Ohio.[646]

ISSUE:

+ 1113. m   i.   **Charles Woodson Wilson, III**, born 20 Nov 1924.

- - - - - - - - - -

---

[644] *Official Register .... La. State Seminary*, 8.

[645] Fisher Co. TX Deed Book 1:260. *St. Charles Cosmos-Monitor* April 17, 1926. Johnson, *Obituaries, St. Charles County Missouri*.

[646] McLean, *Wilson Family*, 86-7. Boddie, *Historical Southern Families*, 5:43-4. Watkins, *Tearin' Through the Wilderness* , 165-7. Additional information from James Willis Wilson of St. Catherines, Ontario.

1113. Charles Woodson[6] Wilson, III (1112.James[5], 1111.Charles[4], 2131.James[3], 1707.Goodridge[2], 1.Benjamin, Sr.[1]) was born 20 Nov 1924 in Columbus, Ohio, the son of **James Willis Wilson** and **Rosalie Prevost Watkins**. He married **Martha Ann Moore** 1948. She was born 5 Jun 1927 in South Charleston, West Virginia, the daughter of **Walter Graham Moore** and **Macel Riley**. Martha died May 2002 in Akron, Ohio.

ISSUE:

+ 1114. m   i.   **James Willis Wilson**, born 29 Nov 1951.
  1117. f   ii.   Daughter
  1118. f   iii.   Daughter
+ 1119. m   iv.   **Robert Woodson Wilson**, born 20 Aug 1960.

- - - - - - - - - -

1114. James Willis[7] "Will" Wilson (1113.Charles, III[6], 1112.James[5], 1111.Charles[4], 2131.James[3], 1707.Goodridge[2], 1.Benjamin, Sr.[1]) was born 29 Nov 1951 in St. Louis, Missouri, the son of **Charles Woodson Wilson, III** and **Martha Ann Moore**. He married **Elizabeth Pamela Spear** 27 Jul 1973. She was born 4 Dec 19 in Toronto, Ontario, Canada.

ISSUE:

  1115. f   i.   **Olivia Rose Wilson**, born 17 Aug 1979 in Toronto.
  1116. m   ii.   **Charles Robert Wilson**, born 20 Jan 1984 in Toronto.

- - - - - - - - - -

1119. Robert Woodson[7] Wilson (1113.Charles, III[6], 1112.James[5], 1111.Charles[4], 2131.James[3], 1707.Goodridge[2], 1.Benjamin, Sr.[1]) was born 20 Aug 1960, the son of **Charles Woodson Wilson, III** and **Martha Ann Moore**. He married **Robin Mains**.

ISSUE:

  1120. m   i.   **Alexander Roman Wilson**.

- - - - - - - - - -

1122. Bates Frayser[5] Wilson <See pg. 266, 285> (1111.Charles[4], 2131.James[3], 1707.Goodridge[2], 1.Benjamin, Sr.[1]) was born 21 Dec 1895, the son of **Charles Woodson Wilson** and **Julia Bentley Frayser**. Bates died 29 Jan 1980 in Houston, Texas. He married **Margaret Gillespie**. She was born 23 Mar 1895. Margaret died 15 Feb 1980.[647]

ISSUE:

+ 1123. f   i.   **Margaret Gillespie Wilson**, born 29 Aug 1924, died 18 May 2002.

---

[647] McLean, *Wilson Family*, 87. Boddie, *Historical Southern Families*, 5:44. Additional information from Mary Anne (Kopecky) Ludwick.

- - - - - - - - - - -

1123. Margaret Gillespie⁶ Wilson (1122.Bates⁵, 1111.Charles⁴, 2131.James³, 1707.Goodridge², 1.Benjamin, Sr.¹) was born 29 Aug 1924, the daughter of **Bates Frayser Wilson** and **Margaret Gillespie**. Margaret died 18 May 2002 in Houston, Texas. She married (1) **Robert Cocherell**.

ISSUE:

1124. f   i.   **Cathleen Cocherell**, born 18 Jun 1946. She married **Paul Rhine**.

Margaret married (2) **Roy Kopecky**. He was born 24 Apr 1923. Roy died Dec 2001.

ISSUE:

1125. f   ii.   **Mary Anne Kopecky**, born 15 Feb 1950. She married _____ **Ludwick**; they divorced.

+ 1126. f   iii.   **Linda Susan Kopecky**.

- - - - - - - - - - -

1126. Linda Susan⁷ Kopecky (1123.Margaret⁶, 1122.Bates⁵, 1111.Charles⁴, 2131.James³, 1707.Goodridge², 1.Benjamin, Sr.¹) was born 2 Oct 1951, the daughter of **Roy Kopecky** and **Margaret Gillespie** Wilson. She married **R. Darryl Stanley**.

ISSUE:

1127. f   i.   **Kacy Lea Stanley**, born 7 Feb 1976. She married **Chadrick Arnold**. Their son, **Christian Daniel Arnold**, was born 6 Jan 2005.

1128. f   ii.   **April Ann Stanley**, born 14 Sep 1978. She married **Jason Sebesta**.

- - - - - - - - - - -

1130. Martha Agnes⁵ Wilson <See pg. 266, 285> (1111.Charles⁴, 2131.James³, 1707.Goodridge², 1.Benjamin, Sr.¹) was born 30 Oct 1899 in St. Charles, Missouri, the daughter of **Charles Woodson Wilson** and **Julia Bentley Frayser**. (Martha) Agnes died 26 Dec 1971 in St. Louis, Missouri, and was buried in Old Dardenne Cemetery, St. Charles Co., Missouri. She married **Samuel McCluer Watson, Jr. (See number 1861 - pg. 197)** 28 Aug 1929 at her family home in St. Charles. He was born 16 Feb 1898 near Howell, St. Charles Co., the son of **Samuel McCluer Watson** and **Annie Pleasantia Ruffner**. Samuel, Jr. died 27 Sep 1956[648] in Callaway Co.,

---

[648] McLean, *Wilson Family*, 87, 47. Boddie, *Historical Southern Families*, 5:44. Watson, *Heritage And Promise*, 184-5, 199-200. Additional family information

(continued...)

Missouri, and was buried in Old Dardenne Cemetery.

ISSUE:

1131. f   i.   **Julia Margaret Watson.**
1132. f   ii.   **Sally Ann Watson.**
1133. f   iii.   **Mary Watson**, married with two daughters and one son.
+ 1137. f   iv.   **Martha Agnes Watson.**
1143. m   v.   **Samuel McCluer Watson, III.**

- - - - - - - - - -

1137. Martha Agnes[6] Watson (1130.Martha[5], 1111.Charles[4], 2131.James[3], 1707.Goodridge[2], 1.Benjamin, Sr.[1]) is the daughter of **Samuel McCluer Watson, Jr.** and **Martha Agnes Wilson**. She married **Kent Stuart Hornberger** 1967.

ISSUE:

+ 1138. m   i.   **Kent Stuart Hornberger, Jr..**
+ 1141. m   ii.   **Robert Samuel Hornberger.**

- - - - - - - - - -

1138. Kent Stuart[7] Hornberger, Jr. (1137.Martha[6], 1130.Martha[5], 1111.Charles[4], 2131.James[3], 1707.Goodridge[2], 1.Benjamin, Sr.[1]). He is the son of **Kent Stuart Hornberger** and **Martha Agnes Watson**. He married **Tammy Pinell.**

ISSUE:

1139. f   i.   **Rebecca Grace Hornberger.**
1140. m   ii.   **Joseph Kent Hornberger.**

- - - - - - - - - -

1141. Robert Samuel[7]Hornberger (1137.Martha[6], 1130.Martha[5], 1111.Charles[4], 2131.James[3], 1707.Goodridge[2], 1.Benjamin, Sr.[1]). He is the son of **Kent Stuart Hornberger** and **Martha Agnes Watson**. He married **Kristie Pomrening.**

ISSUE:

1142. m   i.   **Samuel Kent Hornberger.**

- - - - - - - - - -

1146. Nathaniel Venable[4] Wilson <See pg. 102, 260> (2131.James[3], 1707.Goodridge[2], 1.Benjamin, Sr.[1]) was born 5 Nov 1859 in St. Louis, Missouri, the son of **James Willis Wilson** and **Mary Hetty Meredith**. Nathaniel died 24 Jun 1911 in Ben Wheeler, Van Zandt Co., Texas, and was

---

[648] (...continued)
from her daughters.

buried in Colfax Cemetery, Van Zandt Co., Texas. He married **Sarah Stonewall Wilson (See number 1070 - pg. 259)** 1889. She was born 27 May 1865 in Missouri, the daughter of **Samuel Venable Wilson** and **Sarah Cox Meredith.**[649]

ISSUE:

1071. m   i.   **Thomas Francis Wilson**, born May 1890 in Texas, died 6 Feb 1933 in Dallas, Texas, and was buried in Colfax Cemetery.

+ 1072. m   ii.   **Samuel Willis Wilson**, born 28 Oct 1892, died 17 May 1976.

+ 1073. m   iii.   **Woodville Bates Wilson**, born 16 Oct 1894, died 8 Feb 1958 <See pg. 273>.

1079. f   iv.   **Ellen Trent Wilson**, born Dec 1896 in Texas. She married **Paul Ford** in Guatemala. Paul also married (2) June _____.

+ 1080. f   v.   **Sarah "Sallie" Wilson**, born 8 Mar 1899, died 15 Jul 1951 <See pg. 274>.

+ 1086. f   vi.   **Janette Wilson** <See pg. 275>.

1087. f   vii.   **Mary Lucille Wilson**, born 1904, died 1914, and was buried in Colfax Cemetery.

+ 1088. m viii.   **Nathaniel Venable Wilson, II**, born 2 Mar 1909, died 26 Jun 1983 <See pg. 275>.

Although Nat has no land records in Nolan and Fisher Counties, Texas, it appears that he went to the area around 1888 with his father, mother, a sister, some brothers and cousins.[650] His son Samuel Willis was born in Sweetwater in 1892, and the 1900 and 1910 Van Zandt Co., Texas, censuses show an 1889 marriage. A family story states that Nat and his cousin **Ben** went to Texas and swapped housekeepers, Nat marrying Ben's sister **Sarah** and cousin Ben marrying Nat's sister **Nan**. Nat moved to Van Zandt Co. by 1894.[651]

- - - - - - - - - - -

1072. Samuel Willis⁵ Wilson <See pg. 259> (1146.Nathaniel⁴, 2131.James³, 1707.Goodridge², 1.Benjamin, Sr.¹) was born 28 Oct 1892 in Sweetwater, Nolan Co., Texas, the son of **Nathaniel Venable Wilson** and **Sarah Stonewall Wilson**. Samuel died 17 May 1976 in Colfax, Van Zandt Co., Texas, and was buried in Colfax Cemetery, Van Zandt Co., Texas. He

---

[649] McLean, *Wilson Family*, 84, 87. Watson, *Heritage And Promise*, 180. Curry, *Colfax Cemetery*, 14. Additional information from Imogene (Beggs) Wilson.

[650] Fisher Co. TX Deed Books 1:260, 7:407.

[651] Van Zandt Co. TX Deed Book 49:597.

married **Birdie Eulacia Tunnell** 26 Oct 1926. She was born 1898, the daughter of **Commodore Tunnell** and **Rebecca Rusk**. Birdie died 1980, and was buried in Colfax Cemetery.

ISSUE:

+ 816. m   i.   **Samuel Willis Wilson, Jr.**, born 31 Oct 1929.
+ 827. m   ii.   **Donald Glenn Wilson**, born 27 Aug 1932 <See pg. 272>.

Birdie also married (1) Robert Farris Wilson **(See number 812 - pg. 240)** 19 Mar 1919.

- - - - - - - - - - -

816. Samuel Willis⁶ Wilson, Jr.> (1072. Samuel⁵, 1146.Nathaniel⁴, 2131.James³, 1707.Goodridge², 1.Benjamin, Sr.¹) was born 31 Oct 1929 in Colfax, Van Zandt Co., Texas, the son of **Samuel Willis Wilson** and **Birdie Eulacia Tunnell**. He married **Ida Imogene Beggs** 24 Apr 1948 in Colfax.

ISSUE:

+ 817. f   i.   **Carolyn Ann Wilson**, born 11 Jun 1952.
+ 821. f   ii.   **Mary Louise Wilson**, born 14 May 1956, died 29 Dec 2003 .
+ 824. f   iii.   **Sarah Lea Wilson**, born 10 Dec 1959 <See pg. 272>.

- - - - - - - - - - -

817. Carolyn Ann⁷ Wilson (816.Samuel, Jr.⁶, 1072. Samuel⁵, 1146.Nathaniel⁴, 2131.James³, 1707.Goodridge², 1.Benjamin, Sr.¹) was born 11 Jun 1952 in Pasadena, Harris Co., Texas, the daughter of **Samuel Willis Wilson, Jr.** and **Ida Imogene Beggs**. She married **Jon Dale Green** 23 Jun 1973 in Clear Lake City, Harris Co., Texas.

ISSUE:

+ 818. f   i.   **Rachel Lynn Green**, born 4 Oct 1976.
  820. m   ii.   **Benjamin Wilson Green**, born 16 Jan 1979 in Ft. Worth, Tarrant Co., Texas.

- - - - - - - - - - -

818. Rachel Lynn⁸ Green (817.Carolyn⁷, 816.Samuel, Jr.⁶, 1072. Samuel⁵, 1146.Nathaniel⁴, 2131.James³, 1707.Goodridge², 1.Benjamin, Sr.¹) was born 4 Oct 1976 in Houston, Harris Co., Texas, the daughter of **Jon Dale Green** and **Carolyn Ann Wilson**. She married **Matthew Lynn Miller** 22 Dec 2000 in Clear Lake City, Harris Co., Texas.

ISSUE:

  819. m   i.   **Jonathan Matthew Miller**, born 5 Jun 2003 in Lawrence, Kansas.

- - - - - - - - - - -

821. Mary Louise[7] Wilson (816.Samuel, Jr.[6], 1072. Samuel[5], 1146.Nathaniel[4],2131.James[3], 1707.Goodridge[2], 1.Benjamin, Sr.[1]) was born 14 May 1956 in Ft. Worth, Tarrant Co., Texas, the daughter of **Samuel Willis Wilson, Jr.** and **Ida Imogene Beggs**. Mary died 29 Dec 2003. She married **Donald Mark Delwood** 23 Jun 1979 in Clear Lake City, Harris Co., Texas.

ISSUE:

822. m   i.   **Daniel Mark Delwood**, born 14 May 1985 in Columbia, Boone Co., Missouri.

823. f   ii.   **Christine Marie Delwood**, born 20 Jul 1987 in Columbia.

- - - - - - - - - - -

824. Sarah Lea[7] Wilson <See pg. 271> (816.Samuel, Jr.[6], 1072. Samuel[5], 1146.Nathaniel[4], 2131.James[3], 1707.Goodridge[2], 1.Benjamin, Sr.[1]) was born 10 Dec 1959 in Ft. Worth, Tarrant Co., Texas, the daughter of **Samuel Willis Wilson, Jr.** and **Ida Imogene Beggs**. She married **Jeffrey Dale Coffman** 21 May 1983 in Houston, Harris Co., Texas.

ISSUE:

825. m   i.   **Matthew Bradley Coffman**, born 10 Dec 1990 in Dallas, Texas.

826. f   ii.   **Grace Elizabeth Coffman**, born 22 Mar 1994 in Plano, Texas.

- - - - - - - - - - -

827. Donald Glenn[6] Wilson <See pg. 271> (1072. Samuel[5], 1146.Nathaniel[4], 2131.James[3], 1707.Goodridge[2], 1.Benjamin, Sr.[1]) was born 27 Aug 1932 in Colfax, Van Zandt Co., Texas, the son of **Samuel Willis Wilson** and **Birdie Eulacia Tunnell**. He married (1) **Veneta Ruth Davis** 20 Dec 1952 in Grand Saline, Van Zandt Co., Texas. Veneta died 26 Aug 1973.

ISSUE:

+ 828. f   i.   **Deborah Lynn Wilson**, born 28 Nov 1953.

+ 830. f   ii.   **Donna Marie Wilson**, born 6 Apr 1955.

+ 832. f   iii.   **Terry Denise Wilson**, born 20 Apr 1961 <See pg. 273>.

+ 836. f   iv.   **Sherry Diane Wilson**, born 20 Apr 1961.

- - - - - - - - - - -

828. Deborah Lynn[7] Wilson (827.Donald[6], 1072. Samuel[5], 1146.Nathaniel[4], 2131.James[3], 1707.Goodridge[2], 1.Benjamin, Sr.[1]) was born 28 Nov 1953 in Topeka, Kansas, the daughter of **Donald Glenn Wilson** and **Veneta Ruth Davis**. She married **David Cantu** in San Antonio, Texas; they divorced.

ISSUE:

829. m   i.   **David Christopher Cantu**, born 12 Oct 1976 in San
                Antonio.

- - - - - - - - - - -

830. Donna Marie[7] Wilson (827.Donald[6], 1072. Samuel[5], 1146.Nathaniel[4],
2131.James[3], 1707.Goodridge[2], 1.Benjamin, Sr.[1]) was born 6 Apr 1955 in
San Antonio, Texas, the daughter of **Donald Glenn Wilson** and **Veneta
Ruth Davis**. She married **Andrew Stiegemeier** in Ohio; they divorced.

ISSUE:

831. u   i.   **Andrew James Stiegemeier**, born 10 Aug 1978 in Ohio.

- - - - - - - - - - -

832. Terry Denise[7] Wilson <See pg. 272> (827.Donald[6], 1072. Samuel[5],
1146.Nathaniel[4], 2131.James[3], 1707.Goodridge[2], 1.Benjamin, Sr.[1]) was born
20 Apr 1961 in San Antonio, Texas, the daughter of **Donald Glenn Wilson**
and **Veneta Ruth Davis**. She married (1) **J. R. "Happy" Krezdorn** in San
Antonio, Texas; they divorced.

ISSUE:

833. m   i.   **Wilson Lee Krezdorn**, born 15 Oct 1980.
834. f   ii.   **Kristen Celeste Krezdorn**, born 5 Jan 1983.

Terry married (2) **Stephen Garrett Martin** 14 May 1988 in Canton, Van
Zandt Co., Texas; they divorced.

ISSUE:

835. f   iii.   **Amanda Nicole Martin**, born 21 Oct 1989.

- - - - - - - - - - -

836. Sherry Diane[7] Wilson (827.Donald[6], 1072. Samuel[5], 1146.Nathaniel[4],
2131.James[3], 1707.Goodridge[2], 1.Benjamin, Sr.[1]) was born 20 Apr 1961 in
San Antonio, Texas, the daughter of **Donald Glenn Wilson** and **Veneta
Ruth Davis**. She married **George C. Clayton** in San Antonio, Texas.

ISSUE:

837. f   i.   **Lori Michelle Clayton**, born 10 Dec 1985.

- - - - - - - - - - -

1073. Woodville Bates[5] Wilson <See pg. 259, 270> (1146.Nathaniel[4],
2131.James[3], 1707.Goodridge[2], 1.Benjamin, Sr.[1]) was born 16 Oct 1894 in
Texas, the son of **Nathaniel Venable Wilson** and **Sarah Stonewall
Wilson**. Woodville died 8 Feb 1958 in Edom, Van Zandt Co., Texas, and
was buried in Colfax Cemetery, Van Zandt Co., Texas. He married **Viola
Belle Gee** 19 Jun 1916 in Edom, Van Zandt Co., Texas. She was born

15 Jan 1898. Viola died and was buried in Colfax Cemetery. [652]
ISSUE:
1074. m   i.   **James Willis Wilson**, born 1918. He married **Lucy Ann St. Lawrence**.
1075. f   ii.   **Thelma Wilson**. She married **Gaylord Brocket**.
+ 1076. f   iii.   **Pansy Fay "Pat" Wilson** <See pg. 274>.

A letter written 4 Jul 1916 described the wedding of Woodville and Viola, "in their buggies that is the Texas style".[653]

- - - - - - - - - - -

1076. Pansy Fay "Pat"[6] Wilson <See pg. 274> (1073.Woodville[5], 1146.Nathaniel[4], 2131.James[3], 1707.Goodridge[2], 1.Benjamin, Sr.[1]). She was the daughter of **Woodville Bates Wilson** and **Viola Belle Gee**. She married (1) **Carroll Price** in Alice, Texas.
ISSUE:
1077. f   i.   **Marilyn Price**.
1078. m   ii.   **Glenn Richard Price**.

Pansy married (2) _____ **Mayfield**.

- - - - - - - - - - -

1080. Sarah "Sallie"[5] Wilson <See pg. 259, 270> (1146.Nathaniel[4], 2131.James[3], 1707.Goodridge[2], 1.Benjamin, Sr.[1]) was born 8 Mar 1899, the daughter of **Nathaniel Venable Wilson** and **Sarah Stonewall Wilson**. Sarah died 15 Jul 1951 and was buried in Colfax Cemetery, Van Zandt Co., Texas. She married **Percy Blackwell**. He was born 24 Nov 1897 in Texas, the son of **Charles H. Blackwell** and **Mary E. "Bettie" Berry**. Percy died and was buried in Colfax Cemetery. [654]
ISSUE:
+ 1081. f   i.   **Lucile Fern Blackwell**, born 1921.
+ 1083. f   ii.   **Sallie Patricia Blackwell**, born 1923 <See pg. 275>.
1085. m   iii.   **Charles Percy Blackwell**, born 1930.

Percy also married (2) **Janette Wilson (See number 1086)** after 1951. She was the daughter of **Nathaniel Venable Wilson** and **Sarah Stonewall Wilson**.

---

[652] McLean, *Wilson Family*, 84-5. Curry, *Colfax Cemetery*, 14.
[653] Look, *Family history*.
[654] McLean, *Wilson Family*, 85. Curry, *Colfax Cemetery*, 16.

- - - - - - - - - -

1081. Lucile Fern[6] Blackwell (1080.Sarah[5], 1146.Nathaniel[4], 2131.James[3], 1707.Goodridge[2], 1.Benjamin, Sr.[1]) was born 1921, the daughter of **Percy Blackwell** and **Sarah "Sallie" Wilson**. She married **Osborn Amburg**.

ISSUE:

1082. f   i.   **Carole Lynn Amburg**, born 1947.

- - - - - - - - - -

1083. Sallie Patricia[6] Blackwell <See pg. 274> (1080.Sarah[5], 1146.Nathaniel[4], 2131.James[3], 1707.Goodridge[2], 1.Benjamin, Sr.[1]) was born 1923, the daughter of **Percy Blackwell** and **Sarah "Sallie" Wilson**. She married **Charles Schleuter**.

ISSUE:

1084. f   i.   **Sallie Ann Schleuter**, born 1945.

- - - - - - - - - -

1086. Janette[5] Wilson <See pg. 259, 270> (1146.Nathaniel[4], 2131.James[3], 1707.Goodridge[2], 1.Benjamin, Sr.[1]). She was the daughter of **Nathaniel Venable Wilson** and **Sarah Stonewall Wilson**. She married **Percy Blackwell** after 1951. He was born 24 Nov 1897 in Texas, the son of **Charles H. Blackwell** and **Mary E. "Bettie" Berry**. Percy died and was buried in Colfax Cemetery, Van Zandt Co., Texas.

Percy also married (1) **Sarah "Sallie" Wilson (See number 1080)**. She was born 8 Mar 1899, the daughter of **Nathaniel Venable Wilson** and **Sarah Stonewall Wilson**.

- - - - - - - - - -

1088. Nathaniel Venable[5] Wilson, II <See pg. 259, 270> (1146.Nathaniel[4], 2131.James[3], 1707.Goodridge[2], 1.Benjamin, Sr.[1]) was born 2 Mar 1909, the son of **Nathaniel Venable Wilson** and **Sarah Stonewall Wilson**. Nathaniel, II died 26 Jun 1983, and was buried at Rose Hill in Memorial Park, California. He married **Thelma _____**.

ISSUE:

1089. m   i.   **Neil Wilson**, born 1944.

Nathaniel, II had 1 stepchild:

1090. m   ii. **Wayne Sackett**. He was the son of _____ **Sackett** and **Thelma _____**.

- - - - - - - - - -

1148. Nancy Meredith[4] Wilson <See pg. 260> 2131.James[3], 1707.Goodridge[2], 1.Benjamin, Sr.[1]) was born 11 Jul 1864 in Navarro Co., Texas, the daughter of **James Willis Wilson** and **Mary Hetty Meredith**. Nancy died after 1928 probably in Prairie Grove, Arkansas. She married **Benjamin Francis Wilson (See number 903 - pg. 247)** 1889. He was born Nov 1857 in Missouri, the son of **Samuel Venable Wilson** and **Sarah Cox Meredith**.[655]

ISSUE:

904. m   i.   **Richard V. Wilson**, born 29 Nov 1889.

+ 905. m   ii.   **Gus Scruggs Wilson**, born 15 Mar 1893, died about 1981 <See pg. 248>.

910. f   iii.   **Mary Hettie Wilson**, born 1 Aug 1895, died probably in Prairie Grove.

+ 911. m   iv.   **William McNaught Wilson**, born 8 Dec 1897 <See pg. 248>.

+ 916. m   v.   **James Willis Wilson**, born 14 Jan 1905, died 24 Jan 1993 <See pg. 248>.

"Aunt Nan" was a favorite of her nieces, who enjoyed her clean house, books, and most of all, her personality. One niece remembered being impressed as a girl that the well was inside in a porch, so you didn't have to go outside to get water.

- - - - - - - - - -

1151. Samuel Venable[4] Wilson <See pg. 102, 261> (2131.James[3], 1707.Goodridge[2], 1.Benjamin, Sr.[1]) was born 27 Mar 1868 in Bossier Parish, Louisiana, the son of **James Willis Wilson** and **Mary Hetty Meredith**. Samuel died 12 Aug 1951 in Van Zandt Co., Texas, and was buried in Prairie Springs Cemetery in Ben Wheeler, Van Zandt Co., Texas. He married **Lena Alice Germany** 24 Jan 1899 in Van Zandt Co. She was born 28 Oct 1878 in Ben Wheeler, the daughter of **Nathan Alexander "Alex" Germany** and **Anna Jeanette Turney**. Lena died 9 Oct 1971 in Van, Van Zandt Co., Texas, and was buried in Prairie Springs Cemetery. [656]

ISSUE

+ 1152. m   i.   **Charles Julian Wilson**, born 27 Oct 1899, died 30 Jan 1960 <See pg. 277>.

1154. m   ii.   **Edwin Allen Wilson**, born 26 Feb 1902 in Ben Wheeler. He married **Mary Rebecca Tunnell** 6 Sep 1939 in Beaumont, Texas,. She was born 13 Apr 1903, the daughter of **Commodore Tunnell** and **Rebecca Rusk**. Mary died 25 Sep 1984 in Tyler, Smith Co., Texas, and was buried in

---

[655] McLean, *Wilson Family*, 88. 1928 obituary of brother.

[656] McLean, *Wilson Family*, 87-8. Germany Family Bible.

Colfax Cemetery, Van Zandt Co., Texas. Edwin died 24 Sep 1992 in Tyler and was buried in Colfax Cemetery. (My uncle Ed is the person that inspired me to do family history. I realized that his memories needed to be captured; therefore many of the family stories come from interviews with him. He, his brother Jake, and his sisters Annette, Marj, and Hettie told me of their memories told them by their father that helped me reconstruct much of their grandfather's story. PSM)

+ 1155. f   iii.   **Lillie Annette Wilson**, born 11 Oct 1904, died 14 Jan 1999 <See pg. 278>.

+ 1175. f   iv.   **Marjorie Frances Wilson**, born 5 Dec 1909 <See pg. 280>.

+ 1184. f   v.   **Mary Hettie Wilson**, born 26 Oct 1915 <See pg. 282>.

+ 1193. m   vi.   **Eugene Venable "Jake" Wilson**, born 1 Oct 1919 <See pg. 283>.

It has been told in family stories that as a young man, Sam spent some time in Oklahoma Territory with cousin **Bates Frayser** living in a dugout and that he went to California to help on his Aunt **Lavinia**'s farm.

In the late 1880's, his parents and some of his siblings went to Fisher Co., Texas where his brother **Charles** had purchased land. On 11 Feb 1890, Charles W. Wilson of the City & County of St. Charles, Missouri deeded Sam an undivided half of section 20, Block Y. Farming was unsuccessful on the land, so after Sam went to Van Zandt Co. and married, he, his wife Lena, and his brother Charles and his wife Julia sold the property.[657]

On 19 Oct 1900 Sam bought land located at the headwaters of the Neches River. He sold this to a cousin and had several other land transactions in the county, finally settling in 1906 where he lived until his death.[658]

- - - - - - - - - -

1152. Charles Julian[5] Wilson <See pg. 276> (1151.Samuel[4], 2131.James[3], 1707.Goodridge[2], 1.Benjamin, Sr.[1]) was born 27 Oct 1899 in Ben Wheeler, Van Zandt Co., Texas, the son of **Samuel Venable Wilson** and **Lena Alice Germany**. Julian died 30 Jan 1960 in Freeport, Brazoria Co., Texas, and was buried in Peach Point Cemetery, Brazoria Co., Texas. He married **Martha Estelle Hall** 17 Aug 1926 in Freeport. She was born 31 May 1902.

---

[657] Fisher Co. TX Deed Books 5:162, 17:207.

[658] Van Zandt Co. TX Deed Books 65:459, 72:534, 86:1.

Estelle died 21 Nov 1978.[659]
ISSUE:
1153. m   i.   **Charles Julian Wilson, Jr.**, born 26 Jul 1934 in Freeport. He married **N. June Dominy** 19 Nov 1963.

- - - - - - - - - -

1155. Lillie Annette[5] Wilson <See pg. 277> (1151.Samuel[4], 2131.James[3], 1707.Goodridge[2], 1.Benjamin, Sr.[1]) was born 11 Oct 1904 in Colfax, Van Zandt Co., Texas, the daughter of **Samuel Venable Wilson** and **Lena Alice Germany**. Annette died 14 Jan 1999 in Walnut Creek, California, and was buried in Brazoria Cemetery, Brazoria Co., Texas. She married **Richard Frank Thomas** 22 May 1929 in Humble, Harris Co., Texas. He was born 30 Oct 1904 in Monahans, Ward Co., Texas, the son of **Elwood Davis Thomas** and **Myrtle Brandon**. Frank died 7 Sep 1972 in New Orleans, Louisiana, and was buried in Brazoria Cemetery.[660]
ISSUE:
+ 1156. m   i.   **Richard Frank Thomas, Jr.**, born 3 Aug 1930.
  1165. m   ii.   **Jerry Eugene Thomas**, born 6 May 1932 in Freeport, Brazoria Co., Texas, died 30 Sep 1952 in Houston, Harris Co., Texas, and was buried in Forest Park Cemetery in Houston.
+ 1166. f   iii.   **Patti Sue Thomas**, born 9 Jun 1936 <See pg. 279>.
  1174. f   iv.   **Marjory Ann Thomas**, born 4 Sep 1941 in New Orleans, Louisiana.

- - - - - - - - - -

1156. Richard Frank[6] Thomas, Jr. (1155.Annette[5], 1151.Samuel[4], 2131.James[3], 1707.Goodridge[2], 1.Benjamin, Sr.[1]) was born 3 Aug 1930 in Freeport, Brazoria Co., Texas, the son of **Richard Frank Thomas** and **Lillie Annette Wilson**. He married **Catherine Conant** 2 Jun 1960 in Santa Fe, New Mexico. She was born 3 Sep 1931 in St. Louis, Missouri, the daughter of **Paul Huffman Conant** and **Georgia Dale Saltzman**.
ISSUE:
+ 1157. m   i.   **Evan Thomas**, born 18 Apr 1961 <See pg. 279>.
+ 1161. f   ii.   **Ellen Thomas**, born 25 Sep 1963 <See pg. 279>.

- - - - - - - - - -

---

[659] McLean, *Wilson Family*, 87-8. Germany Family Bible. Additional information from Charles Wilson Jr.

[660] McLean, *Wilson Family*, 88. Germany Family Bible. Additional information from her children and grandchildren.

1157. Evan[7] Thomas <See pg. 278> (1156.Richard, Jr.[6], 1155.Annette[5], 1151.Samuel[4], 2131.James[3], 1707.Goodridge[2], 1.Benjamin, Sr.[1]) was born 18 Apr 1961 in Los Alamos, New Mexico, the son of **Richard Frank Thomas, Jr.** and **Catherine Conant**. He married **Victoria Geralyn "Vicky" Mena** 18 Mar 1989 in Boulder, Colorado. She was born 17 Aug 1967 in Fullerton, California, the daughter of **Carlos "Chuck" Mena** and **Susan Clare Cartmell**.

ISSUE:

1158. f   i.   **Alicia Marie Thomas**, born 8 Sep 1989 in Boulder, Colorado.

1159. m   ii.   **Wyatt Adam Thomas**, born 7 Nov 1991 in Boulder.

1160. m   iii.   **Michael Charles Mena**, born 10 Aug 1987 in Denver, Colorado, the son of **Joseph Cobb** and **Victoria Geralyn "Vicky" Mena**.

- - - - - - - - - - -

1161. Ellen[7] Thomas <See pg. 278> (1156.Richard, Jr.[6], 1155.Annette[5], 1151.Samuel[4], 2131.James[3], 1707.Goodridge[2], 1.Benjamin, Sr.[1]) was born 25 Sep 1963 in Los Alamos, New Mexico, the daughter of **Richard Frank Thomas, Jr.** and **Catherine Conant**. She married **Brian Keith McDonald** 24 Jul 1991 in San Jose, California. He was born 16 Jan 1965 in Kansas City, Missouri, the son of **Keith Wheeler McDonald** and **Linda Sue King**.

ISSUE:

1162. m   i.   **Colin Thomas McDonald**, born 25 Jul 1996 in Columbus, Ohio.

1163. m   ii.   **Connor Lawson McDonald**, born 22 Jul 1998 in Arlington, Texas.

1164. f   iii.   **Courtney Catherine McDonald**, born 19 Aug 2000 in Arlington.

- - - - - - - - - - -

1166. Patti Sue[6] Thomas <See pg. 278> (1155.Annette[5], 1151.Samuel[4], 2131.James[3], 1707.Goodridge[2], 1.Benjamin, Sr.[1]) was born 9 Jun 1936 in Freeport, Brazoria Co., Texas, the daughter of **Richard Frank Thomas** and **Lillie Annette Wilson**. She married (1) **Robert Rodney Foil** 21 Jan 1959 in New Orleans, Louisiana; they divorced. He was born 12 Aug 1934 in Bogalusa, Washington Parish, Louisiana, the son of **Earl Odell Foil** and **Rosa A. Green**.

ISSUE:

+ 1167. m   i.   **Jerry Thomas Foil**, born 9 Nov 1959.

+ 1170. f   ii.   **Allison Foil**, born 29 Dec 1961 <See pg. 280>.

Patti Sue married (2) **Paul Forest McCrary** 4 Aug 1987 in Clearwater, Pinellas Co., Florida. He was born 27 Jun 1926 in Birdville, Tarrant Co., Texas, the son of **Paul Forest McCrary, Sr.** and **Mettie Dickie**. Paul died 23 Jun 2002 in Pensacola, Escambia Co., Florida, and was buried in Moore Memorial Gardens in Arlington, Texas.

- - - - - - - - - - -

1167. Jerry Thomas[7] Foil (1166.Patti Sue[6], 1155.Annette[5], 1151.Samuel[4], 2131.James[3], 1707.Goodridge[2], 1.Benjamin, Sr.[1]) was born 9 Nov 1959 in Baton Rouge, East Baton Rouge Parish, Louisiana, the son of **Robert Rodney Foil** and **Patti Sue Thomas**. He married **Elvia Estella Esparza** 7 May 1981 in Houston, Harris Co., Texas. She was born 27 Sep 1958 in Mercedes, Hidalgo Co., Texas,. She is the adopted daughter of **José Irineo Torres Esparza** and **Dominga Treviño**.   She is the biological daughter of **Maria Isabel Gonzalez**.

ISSUE:

1168. f   i.   **Cheryl Marie Foil**, born 7 Jun 1987 in Palo Alto, Santa Clara Co., California.

1169. f   ii.   **Valerie Rose Foil**, born 19 Dec 1990 in Palo Alto.

- - - - - - - - - - -

1170. Allison[7] Foil <See pg. 279> (1166.Patti Sue[6], 1155.Annette[5], 1151.Samuel[4], 2131.James[3], 1707.Goodridge[2], 1.Benjamin, Sr.[1]) was born 29 Dec 1961 in Homer, Claiborne Parish, Louisiana., the daughter of **Robert Rodney Foil** and **Patti Sue Thomas**. She married **James Nixon Cryan** 18 Jun 1987 in Staten Island, New York. He was born 7 Feb 1958 in Trenton, Mercer Co., New Jersey, the son of **James Edward Cryan** and **Marjorie Elaine Nixon**.

ISSUE:

1171. f   i.   **Abigail Foil Cryan**, born 25 Jan 1991 in Princeton, Mercer Co., New Jersey.

1172. f   ii.   **Phoebe Nixon Cryan**, born 16 Aug 1992 in Princeton.

1173. f   iii.   **Martha Marjorie Cryan**, born 26 Mar 1998 in Princeton.

- - - - - - - - - - -

1175. Marjorie Frances[5] Wilson <See pg. 277> (1151.Samuel[4], 2131.James[3], 1707.Goodridge[2], 1.Benjamin, Sr.[1]) was born 5 Dec 1909 in Grand Saline, Van Zandt Co., Texas, the daughter of **Samuel Venable Wilson** and **Lena Alice Germany**. Marjorie died 6 Nov 2005 and was buried in Prairie Springs Cemetery in Ben Wheeler, Van Zandt Co., Texas. She married **John Earl Braden** 21 Feb 1936. He was born 17 Apr 1907 in Rosebud, Texas, the son of **Adam Braden** and **Vivia Knox**. Earl died 18 Dec 1999 in

Houston, Texas and was buried in Prairie Springs Cemetery.[661]

ISSUE:

+ 1176. m   i.   **Wilson Earl Braden**, born 12 Mar 1943. Adopted.
+ 1178. m   ii. **John Alan Braden**, born 9 Feb 1945 <See pg. 281>.

- - - - - - - - - - -

1176. Wilson Earl[6] Braden (1175.Marjorie[5], 1151.Samuel[4], 2131.James[3], 1707.Goodridge[2], 1.Benjamin, Sr.[1]) was born 12 Mar 1943 in Houston, Texas. He is the adopted son of **John Earl Braden** and **Marjorie Frances Wilson**. He married (1) **Dianne Theriot**.

ISSUE:

1177. f   i.   **Elise Braden**, born 29 Jun 1970 in Houston, Texas.

Wilson married (2) **Jan Gandt**.
Wilson married (3) **Tracey Anderson**.

- - - - - - - - - - -

1178. John Alan[6] Braden <See pg. 281> (1175.Marjorie[5], 1151.Samuel[4], 2131.James[3], 1707.Goodridge[2], 1.Benjamin, Sr.[1]) was born 9 Feb 1945 in Houston, Harris Co., Texas, the son of **John Earl Braden** and **Marjorie Frances Wilson**. He married **Leilani Darlene Fowler** 9 Dec 1972 in Houston. She was born 30 Aug 1945 in Fornfelt, Missouri, the daughter of **Clemo Irving Fowler** and **Alma Belle Snider**.

ISSUE:

1179. f   i.   **Meredith Michelle Braden**, born 28 Dec 1974 in Houston, Texas.
+ 1180. f   ii. **Alana Darlene Braden**, born 28 May 1979.

- - - - - - - - - - -

1180. Alana Darlene[7] Braden (1178.John[6], 1175.Marjorie[5], 1151.Samuel[4], 2131.James[3], 1707.Goodridge[2], 1.Benjamin, Sr.[1]) was born 28 May 1979 in Houston, Texas, the daughter of **John Alan Braden** and **Leilani Darlene Fowler**. She married **William Thomas Jordan** 10 Jun 1995 in Spring, Texas.

ISSUE:

1181. m   i.   **Jeffrey Thomas Jordan**, born 14 Dec 1995 in Houston, Texas.
1182. m   ii.   **David Alan Jordan**, born 17 May 1997 in Tomball, Texas.
1183. m   iii. **Nicholas Adam Jordan**, born 1 Mar 2001 in Tomball.

---

[661] McLean, *Wilson Family*, 88. Germany Family Bible. Additional information from her children.

- - - - - - - - - - - -

1184. Mary Hettie[5] Wilson <See pg. 277> (1151.Samuel[4], 2131.James[3], 1707.Goodridge[2], 1.Benjamin, Sr.[1]) was born 26 Oct 1915 in Grand Saline, Van Zandt Co., Texas, the daughter of **Samuel Venable Wilson** and **Lena Alice Germany**. She married (1) **Ivan "Ike" Preston Fleming** 25 Jun 1937 in Grand Saline. He was born 27 Jan 1908 in Callahan Co., Texas, the son of **Fred Fronie Fleming** and **Kathryn Loveless**. Ike died 14 Nov 1964 in Gladewater, Texas, and was buried in Big Sandy, Texas.[662]

ISSUE:

+ 1185. f   i.   **Carol Ann Fleming**, born 16 Aug 1940 <See pg. 282>.

Mary married (2) **Onie Lee Lumpkin** 17 Jun 1969 in Houston, Texas. He was born 3 Aug 1905 in Kennard, Houston Co., Texas.

Onie also married (1) **Ruby Gladys Brown**. She was born 11 Sep 1912 in Hartman, Arkansas.

- - - - - - - - - - - -

1185. Carol Ann [6] Fleming <See pg. 282> (1184.Mary[5], 1151.Samuel[4], 2131.James[3], 1707.Goodridge[2], 1.Benjamin, Sr.[1]) was born 16 Aug 1940 in Mount Vernon, Franklin Co., Texas, the daughter of **Ivan Preston Fleming** and **Mary Hettie Wilson**. She married **Donald Lee Lumpkin** 27 Dec 1958 in Big Sandy, Texas. He was born 20 Aug 1933 in Overton, Texas, the son of **Onie Lee Lumpkin** and **Ruby Gladys Brown**.

ISSUE:

1186. m   i.   **Steven Lee Lumpkin**, born 10 Sep 1960 in El Dorado, Arkansas. He married **Mana Rodalyn Ramo Daguio** 29 Jul 1995 in Kihei, Maui, Hawaii. She was born 11 Nov 1972 in Ilocos Norte, Philippines, the daughter of **Edison Bumagat Daguio, Sr.** and **Eufrecinia Ramo**.

+ 1187. m   ii.   **John Fleming Lumpkin**, born 27 Feb 1963.

1191. f   iii.   **Kathryn Ann Lumpkin**, born 27 Apr 1966 in El Dorado, Arkansas. She married **Rodman Crawford Johnson** 13 Oct 2001 in Houston, Texas. He was born 24 Oct 1962 in Caracas, Venezuela, the son of **Rodman Taylor Johnson** and **Winifred Jane Kay**.

- - - - - - - - - - - -

1187. John Fleming[7] Lumpkin (1185.Carol[6], 1184.Mary[5], 1151.Samuel[4], 2131.James[3], 1707.Goodridge[2], 1.Benjamin, Sr.[1]) was born 27 Feb 1963 in

---

[662] McLean, *Wilson Family*, 88. Germany Family Bible. Additional information from her daughter.

El Dorado, Arkansas, the son of **Donald Lee Lumpkin** and **Carol Ann Fleming**. He married **Janet Lynn Austin** 28 May 1985 in Austin, Texas. She was born 8 Dec 1960 in Oklahoma City, Oklahoma, the daughter of **Thomas Howard Austin** and **Jean Masters**.

ISSUE:

1188. m   i.   **John Fleming Lumpkin, II**, born 8 Apr 1986 in Austin, Texas.

1189. f   ii.   **Lauren Austin Lumpkin**, born 17 Feb 1989 in Austin.

1190. m iii.   **Samuel Jeffrey Lumpkin**, born 29 Jan 1997 in Austin.

- - - - - - - - - - -

1193. Eugene Venable "Jake"[5] Wilson <See pg. 277> (1151.Samuel[4], 2131.James[3], 1707.Goodridge[2], 1.Benjamin, Sr.[1]) was born 1 Oct 1919 in Grand Saline, Van Zandt Co., Texas, the son of **Samuel Venable Wilson** and **Lena Alice Germany**. He married **Rae Annette Egbert** 23 Jun 1948 in Alamagordo, New Mexico. She was born 3 Jan 1923 in Grand Saline, Van Zandt Co., Texas, the daughter of **Rae Allen Egbert** and **Loula Souwell**. Rae died 15 Jan 2004 in Lewes, Delaware, and was buried in Grand Saline, Van Zandt Co., Texas.[663]

ISSUE:

1194. f   i.   **Tim Stanton Wilson**, born 23 Dec 1943, daughter of Rae by a prior marriage.

+ 1195. m   ii.   **Eugene Allen Wilson**, born 4 Nov 1949.

Jake served in World War II and gives an interesting commentary on his experiences.[664]

- - - - - - - - - - -

1195. Eugene Allen[6] Wilson (1193.Eugene[5], 1151.Samuel[4], 2131.James[3], 1707.Goodridge[2], 1.Benjamin, Sr.[1]) was born 4 Nov 1949 in Houston, Harris Co., Texas, the son of **Eugene Venable "Jake" Wilson** and **Rae Annette Egbert**. He married **Genevieve McGuiness** 18 May 1984 in Wallingford, Pennsylvania,. She was born 16 Aug 1953, the daughter of **Edgar Joseph McGuiness** and **Margaret Guilday**.

ISSUE:

1196. m   i.   **Colin McGuiness Wilson**, born 18 May 1986 in Milford, Delaware.

1197. f   ii.   **Margaret Skylar Wilson**, born 10 Dec 1990 in Milford.

---

[663] McLean, *Wilson Family*, 88. Germany Family Bible. Additional information from Jake and Rae (Egbert) Wilson.

[664] Wilson, Eugene V. "The Ninth Air Force from the Beginning", (accessed 3 Apr 2006).

- - - - - - - - - - -

2132. Martha Agnes³ Wilson <See pg. 177> (1707.Goodridge², 1.Benjamin, Sr.¹) was born 5 May 1826 at "Milnwood", Prince Edward Co., Virginia, the daughter of **Goodridge Wilson** and **Elizabeth Woodson Venable**. Martha died 31 Oct 1899 in St. Charles Co., Missouri, and was buried in Frayser Burying Ground, St. Charles Co. She married **Robert Bentley Frayser** 3 Feb 1858 at "Mt Airy", St. Charles Co. He was born 4 Aug 1805 in Cumberland Co., Virginia, the son of **Robert Frayser** and **Elizabeth Walton**. Robert died 27 Oct 1875 in Elmwood, St. Charles Co., Missouri, and was buried in Frayser Burying Ground.[665]

ISSUE:

+ 2133. f   i.   **Julia Bentley Frayser,** born 1 Nov 1858, died 24 Jun 1940.
+ 2134. f   ii.   **Margaret Goodridge Frayser,** born 7 Oct 1861, died 17 Jan 1931 <See pg. 285>.

Robert also married (1) **Maria Virginia Spears** 1 Jan 1836 in St. Charles Co., Missouri. She was born 24 Mar 1809, the daughter of **John Spears** and **Margaret Maria Bates**. Maria died 1855.

ISSUE:

2135. m   iii.   **Robert Henry Frayser,** born 30 Oct 1836, died 1 May 1855, and was buried in Frayser Burying Ground, St. Charles Co., Missouri.
2136. f   iv.   **Ann Eliza Frayser,** born 1845, died 1919.
2137. m   v.   **Edward Bates Frayser,** born 5 Mar 1849. He married (1) **Mary E. Vann**. Mary died after 24 Jan 1898 in Oklahoma. Edward married (2) **Yucca Lydia Clark**. Edward died 1929.

- - - - - - - - - - -

2133. Julia Bentley⁴ Frayser (2132.Martha³, 1707.Goodridge², 1.Benjamin, Sr.¹) was born 1 Nov 1858 at "Elmwood", St. Charles Co., Missouri, the daughter of **Robert Bentley Frayser** and **Martha Agnes Wilson**. Julia died 24 Jun 1940 in St. Charles, Missouri, and was buried in Oak Grove Cemetery, St. Charles Co.[666] She married **Charles Woodson Wilson (See number 1111 - pg. 265)** 10 Oct 1888. He was born 5 Aug 1854 in St. Louis Co., Missouri, the son of **James Willis Wilson** and **Mary**

---

[665] McLean, *Wilson Family,* 89. Boddie, *Historical Southern Families,* 5:42-3. Bates, *Bates, et al,* 74. McElhiney, *Gone But Not Forgotten,* 80-1. Additional information from Watson sisters of Kirkwood MO.

[666] *St. Charles Cosmos-Monitor* June 26, 1940. Johnson, *Obituaries, St. Charles County Missouri.*

Hetty Meredith.

ISSUE:

+ 1112. m   i.   **James Willis Wilson,** born 18 Jul 1889, died 30 Jul 1939 <See pg. 266>.

  1121. m   ii. **Robert Frayser Wilson,** born 11 Mar 1892, died 4 Oct 1965 in Kirkwood, Missouri, and was buried in Oak Grove Cemetery.

+ 1122. m   iii. **Bates Frayser Wilson,** born 21 Dec 1895, died 29 Jan 1980 <See pg. 267>.

  1129. m   iv. **Charles Woodson Wilson, Jr.,** born Nov 1897, died 2 Aug 1963 in Temple, Texas, and was buried in Oak Grove Cemetery.

+ 1130. f   v.   **Martha Agnes Wilson,** born 30 Oct 1899, died 26 Dec 1971 <See pg. 268>.

- - - - - - - - - -

2134. Margaret Goodridge[4] Frayser <See pg. 284> (2132.Martha[3], 1707.Goodridge[2], 1.Benjamin, Sr.[1]) was born 7 Oct 1861 in Dardenne Twp, St. Charles Co., Missouri, the daughter of **Robert Bentley Frayser** and **Martha Agnes Wilson**. Margaret died 17 Jan 1931 at "Somerset", Granville Co., North Carolina, and was buried in the Wilson Family Cemetery at "Somerset", Granville Co., North Carolina. She married **Goodridge Wilson (See number 1956 - pg. 208)** 15 May 1888,. He was born 6 Nov 1849, the son of **Goodridge Alexander Wilson** and **Margaret Nicholas Cabell Reid.**

ISSUE:

  1957. m   i.   **Robert Bentley Wilson,** born 10 Apr 1889, died 3 May 1976, and was buried in the Wilson Family Cemetery.

+ 1958. m   ii. **Goodridge Alexander Wilson,** born 16 Apr 1890, died 3 Mar 1959 <See pg. 209>.

+ 1969. f   iii. **Agnes Frayser Wilson,** born 6 Nov 1892, died 8 Sep 1975 <See pg. 210>.

  1985. m   iv. **Charles Julian Wilson,** born 13 Jun 1895. He married **Rachel Howard.** She was born 13 May 1898. Rachel died 13 Jan 1966, and was buried in the Wilson Family Cemetery at "Somerset", Granville Co., North Carolina. Julian died 11 Sep 1983, and was buried in the Wilson Family Cemetery.[667]

+ 1986. m   v.   **William Reid Wilson,** born 28 Apr 1898 <See pg. 212>.

+ 2018. f   vi. **Marguerite Rochet Wilson,** born 24 Sep 1902, died 4 Jun 1986 <See pg. 215>.

---

[667] *Oxford (NC) Ledger,* 9 Jan 1978.

CHAPTER 9

Descendants of Martha Wilson (1778-1849)

2138. Martha² Wilson <See pg. 3> (1.Benjamin, Sr.¹) was born 1 Jun 1778 at "Somerset", Cumberland Co., Virginia, the daughter of **Benjamin Wilson, Sr.** and **Anne Seay.**[668] Martha died before 22 Apr 1849 in Rockingham Co., North Carolina. She married **James Aiken** 12 Feb 1816 in Cumberland Co., Virginia.[669] He was born about 1766. James died before May 1859 in Rockingham Co.[670]

ISSUE:

+ 2139. f   i.   **Mary Hays Aiken**, born about 1818 <See pg. 288>.
+ 2142. m   ii.   **Benjamin Wilson Aiken**, born 1822, died after 12 Jun 1851 <See pg. 288>.,

James also married (1) Betsey Womack.

ISSUE:

2146. m   iii.   **James Aiken**, born about 1805, the son of **James Aiken** and **Betsey Womack.** He died before 19 May 1829 in Pittsylvania Co., Virginia. In his 1827 will, "James Aiken of Pittsylvania Co. heretofore of Co. of Cumberland", named his sister Mary Hays, "beloved little brother Benjamin Wilson", and his brother George Lacy Aiken.[671]

2147. m   iv.   **George Lacy Aiken**, born about 1810, the son of **James Aiken** and **Betsey Womack.** He married **Lucy J. Dillaird** 3 Jul 1837 in Rockingham Co., North Carolina.[672]

Cumberland Presbyterian Church records show James Aiken clerk pro tem at an 1817 session. In 1827 they applied for a "certificate of membership and dismission".[673]

They are shown in the 1830 and 1840 Rockingham Co., North Carolina, censuses. James' 1849 will named his second wife, Martha deceased, their daughter Martha H., wife of William Mebane, and grandchildren Anne

---

[668] Woodson Family, *Papers, 1740-1945*, Accession 29437-41, LVA.

[669] Elliott, *Marriages, Cumberland Co VA*, 7.

[670] Webster, *Rockingham Co NC Will Abstracts*, 73 (C:294).

[671] Cumberland Co. VA Will Book 8:793.

[672] Ingmire, *Rockingham Co .... Marriage Records*, 1.

[673] Cumberland Presbyterian Church, Accession 20080, LVA, 49, 50, 62, 122.

Mebane, Martha Mebane, their son Benjamin W. Aiken and his daughter
Martha. He also named his first wife Betsey Womack and their son George
L. Aiken.

- - - - - - - - - - -

2139. Mary Hays³ Aiken <See pg. 287> (2138.Martha², 1.Benjamin, Sr.¹) was
born about 1818, the daughter of **James Aiken** and **Martha Wilson**. She
married **William N. Mebane** 8 May 1840 in Rockingham Co., North
Carolina.[674]

ISSUE:
2140. f   i.   **Ann Mebane**, born before 22 Apr 1849.
2141. f   ii. **Martha Mebane**, born before 22 Apr 1849.

- - - - - - - - - - -

2142. Benjamin Wilson³ Aiken <See pg. 287> (2138.Martha², 1.Benjamin,
Sr.¹) was born 1822 in Cumberland Co., Virginia, the son of **James Aiken**
and **Martha Wilson**. Benjamin died after 12 Jun 1851 in Rockingham Co.,
North Carolina. He married **Jane R. Carter** 10 Jan 1846 in Rockingham
Co.[675] She was born 1823 in North Carolina. Jane died after 12 Jun 1851.

ISSUE:
2143. f   i.   **Martha A. Aiken**, born 1847 in North Carolina.
+ 2144. m   ii. **Archibald M. Aiken**, born 1848.

Benjamin is listed with his family in the 1850 census of Rockingham Co.,
North Carolina. His wife Jane was executor of his 1851 will.[676]

- - - - - - - - - - -

2144. Judge Archibald M.⁴ Aiken (2142.Benjamin³, 2138.Martha²,
1.Benjamin, Sr.¹) was born 1848 in North Carolina, the son of **Benjamin
Wilson Aiken** and **Jane R. Carter**. He married **Mary Ella Yates**.

ISSUE:
2145. m   i.   **Archibald M. Aiken**, born 12 Feb 1888 in Danville,
                 Virginia, died 27 Nov 1971 in Danville, Virginia.[677]

Archibald Sr. is listed in the 1880 Pittsylvania Co. Virginia, census, age 30,
occupation, city judge.

---

[674] Ingmire, *Rockingham Co ... Marriage Records*, 47.
[675] Ingmire, *Rockingham Co ... Marriage Records*, 1.
[676] Webster, *Rockingham Co NC Will Abstracts*, 60 (C:126).
[677] "Archibald Murphey Aiken", (accessed 18 Mar 2006).

APPENDIX

The following prayer book, will, and Bibles, are not indexed nor footnoted for corrections.

Prayer book of Anne (Seay) Wilson (1735-1814) [678]

Benjamin Wilson born January 6th 1733.
Anne Wilson born March 6th 1735.
Mary Wilson (their daughter) born Dec 23rd 1754.
Elizabeth Wilson   do   born October 17th 1756.
Willis Wilson their son born April 22nd 1758.
Benjamin Wilson   do   Oct 24th 1759.
Anne Wilson   daughter born Sept 10th 1762.
James Wilson   son   February 6th 1765.
Mason Wilson   daughter born Dec 21st 1768.
Samuel Wilson   son   March 30th 1770.
Mathew Wilson   son   March 25th 1772.
Alexander Wilson son   April 1st 1774.
Goodridge Wilson   son   March 26th 1776.
Martha Wilson daughter   June 1st 1778.
Unita Wilson daughter Feb 22, 1783.

Will of Benjamin Wilson (1733-1814)

Written 1 Feb 1812[679] and proved on Nov 28, 1814[680]

In the name of God, amen, Benjamin Wilson of Cumberland
now nearly four score years old tho of sound and disposing
mind makes and declares this his last will & testament.
My soul is resigned to the bountifull Grace with a firm
trust of a happy resurrection thro my mercifull Redeemer.
Of the property with which we have been blessed & of that
of which we are now possessed I give & dispose to my aged
wife for life
To son Benjamin I give Jim, Abby, & Charles

---

[678] "Register of the Family of Benjamin and Anne (Seay) Wilson of Summerset Cumberland County Virginia" copied from the "Prayer Book owned by Anne Wilson wife of Benjamin now in the possession of Anne Meredith Sparkman daughter of Samuel V. Wilson who was the son of Goodridge Wilson". Woodson Family, *Papers, 1740-1945*, Accession 29437-41, LVA.

[679] Will of Benjamin Wilson, LVA.

[680] Cumberland Co. VA Order Book 1811-15, p. 464.

To son Samuel I give Mongo, Melley & Charles
To son Matthew I give Samson, Necy, Mary & children
To son Alexander I give Moses, Phillis & Arreanna
To son Goodrich I give Sam, Cate & Tom
To daughter Mason I give Will, Amy, Daphne, & her children
To daughter Martha I give Mat, Archer, ...
To Daughter Unity I give Phil .....John, Fan..& Cl..
To granddaughter Hobson I give Aggy & her children & Bob (to be ....
To granddaughter Maria Willis I give Leddy
To granddaughter Ann daughter of James I give Ned
To my sons Willis & James I assign by debt & interest due
from James Meredith in satisfaction their debts & accounts.
All the rest of my property both real & personal except
a negro boy Davy son of Anny) I give & devise to my
sons Willis, James, Samuel, & Goodrich who are hereby appointed my executors, who, the surviving or qualifying
part of whom are directed to di-
vide the same by sale of other ways or by both means
among all my children or their legal representatives
including grand daughter Hobson. - And I do further direct
that proportion of my residuary estate which shall
be so alloted to my son Alexander together with the said
negroe boy Davy be secured in trust by my executors
to my sons Benjamin, James & Goodrich to the ... annually
of son Alexander or his legal representatives in ....
I consider an inventory of my estate sufficient without
an appraisement & require no security of my
executors to the ... part of whom or all of qualify
to allow two Lbs?6c ... .. the amount of my estate
... settled & divided. In witness whereof I hereunto
set my hand and affix my seal this 1st Feby 1812
....
& ...... in presence of
George W Jones   Ben: Wilson (Seal)
Thomas Bradley
Smith Criddle

I do direct that my executors heretofore named
in this my will sel my land being 870...
acres for the payments of my debts to son Samuel witness my hand
& seal this 20 day of September 1814

Teste

Paul C Venable   Ben: Wilson (seal)
Thomas Nixon
....

Cumberland November Court 1814
This last will and testament of Benjamin Wilson deceased was exhibited in
court and proved by Thomas Bradley one of the witnesses
thereto. And on the motion of Willis Wilson, James Wilson,
Goodrich Wilson, and Samuel Wilson the executors named in
said will who made oath according to law, certificate is granted
them for obtaining probate thereof in due form they haveing
entered into bond according to law. and at a Court held for the
said county the 28th day of Nov 1814

Bible of Willis Wilson (1758-1822)[681]

This genealogy contains the most accurate account of his ancestor that has
come to the knowledge of the writer, Willis Wilson.

James Wilson, the emigrant from the Island of Great Britain, intermarried
with a Miss Willis, and settled in Princess Anne County, Virginia, at, or
near, the Poplar Grove. He raised numerous family of sons and daughters.
John, the eldest, is understood to have early moved up the Chesapeake Bay,
and most likely settled on the waters of the Potomac. Solomon and Willis
intermarried in the neighborhood of their birth and raised large families of
children.

Samuel, the 3rd son, intermarried with a Miss Mason, and died in Norfolk,
Va., about the year 1710, leaving his wife pregnant, who bore him a son
named Willis, who came into the care of his uncle, Solomon Wilson. He
was a clerk to one of the County Courts of that section of country. Willis
having been instructed in the art of Navigation, which was a favorite pursuit
of the family, made himself, what at that day was termed, a sea captain. In
his voyage up the James River he became acquainted with Miss Elizabeth
Goodridge, with whom he intermarried about the year 1732, and had, or
left, an only son named Benjamin, born the 26th of Dec. 1733, at or near the
mouth of the Chickahominy River — the paternal estate of his grand father,
Benjamin Goodridge, who left two daughters, Elizabeth, the wife of Willis

---

[681] This document was found in a Wilson file from the Francis M. Manning History
Room at Martin Community College in Williamston NC. This account is very
similar to *VA. Mag. Hist.* 25:199-200.

Wilson, - and the wife of Samuel Boush of Norfolk.

Willis Wilson died in 1740, a member of the house of Burgesses. His son, Benjamin, being disappointed in the enjoyment of his patrimonial estate from Father and Mother, she having married a second husband, transferred his interest with her own to him.

His Great uncle, Solomon (who raised his father) had dissipated what belonged to him, so that Benjamin had very slender means, with which, he moved, at a very early age, and settled on the Willis River, in the County of Cumberland, about the year 1750.

He intermarried with Anne Seay, daughter of James Seay of a Huguenot family, from the waters of York River, and had issue seven sons and six daughters. Their names: Mary, Elizabeth, Willis, Benjamin, Anne, James, Mason, Samuel, Matthew, Alexander, Goodridge, Martha and Unity.

Benjamin Wilson died on the 27th of October, 1814. Anne, his wife, died on the 26th of April, 1814, having lived together man and wife upwards of sixty years, the wife being about one year the younger. This is the end of the record made by Col. Willis Wilson in his family Bible.

The seven sons and six daughters of Benjamin and Anne Wilson: Mary married a Mr. Mumford. Willis, a widow Black, whose maiden name was Elizabeth Trent. Benjamin moved to Kentucky and married Barbara Bullock and reared a large family in Woodford Co. James married Sarah Cox, in Buckingham Co., Va. and raised three daughters – Mary, Nancy and Sally. Mason married James Meredith, and raised four children, John, James, Anne and Martha. Matthew married Elizabeth Trent, and reared a large family. Goodrich married Elizabeth Venable, and raised six sons and three daughters. Martha married George Aiken, and raised two children, Mary Mebane and Ben Wilson who is the father of Judge Archibald M. Aiken, of Danville, Va.

Mary Mumford died leaving an infant daughter, Mary, who was raised at her Grandfather Wilson's. She married John Hobson, of Powhatan co., and raised a large family of sons and daughters. The children of Benjamin who never married were Elizabeth, Anne, Samuel and Alexander, and Unity who was called Hitty.

This record was made by Willis Wilson (the son of Benjamin and Anne his wife) in his family Bible. The said Willis Wilson died in Bonbrook, his residence, in Cumberland Co., Va. Feb 10th 1822. Said Record was copied by Elizabeth Wilson, daughter of Matthew, and sent to Rev. William V. Wilson, who is the son of Goodridge Wilson, and was copied by his sister, M. A. Frayser.

Meredith Family Bible

Located in the patriot file for Benjamin Wilson, at the library of the Daughters of the American Revolution, National Society. Washington DC.

****

page 677 Family Record
Marriages:

John Meredith was born the 4th of May 1793 & was married to Ann Wilson the 6th day of October 1815, who was born the 7th day of March 1791.

James W. Trent and Nancy W. Meredith were married June 1st 1843.

Samuel V. Wilson and Sarah Cox Meredith were married December 2nd 1843.

James Willis Wilson and Mary Hetty Meredith were married February 25th 1847.

****

page 678 Family Record
Births:

James Wilson Meredith was born the 27th of July A. D. 1816.

William Alexander Meredith 16th December 1818

Sarah Cox Meredith January 21st A. D. 1821

Samuel Meredith November 23rd 1822

Benjamin Meredith November 24th 1824

Nancy Meredith April 16th 1826

Mary Hetty Meredith February 28th 1828

Margaret Virginia Meredith February 17th 1830

John Meredith 24th day of September 1832

Lavinia Meredith May 6th 1834

Elizabeth Meredith March 18th 1837

****

page 679 Family Record
Deaths:

Died at one o'clock Sept 17th 1856. Ann Meredith. My mother.

Sarah Cox Wilson died Dec 9th 1867. Samuel V. Wilson her husband died April 17th 1870 in Butler Co. Mo.

Mary Hetty Wilson died July 17th 1891 in Fisher Co. Texas. James Willis Wilson died Sept 2nd 1899.

James Wilson Meredith died the 2nd of March 1818.

William Alexander Meredith died 16th March 1820.

Samuel Meredith died 15 Decr. 1823.

Benjamin Meredith died the 4th of April 1825.

John Meredith died the 7th of October 1832.

Margaret Virginia Meredith died 25th of June 1833.

Elizabeth Meredith died 10th day of May 1838.

John Meredith the father died 26th day of May 1846.

James S. Wilson father of Ann Meredith died 5th day of June 1847.

Family Bible of Willis and Mary Anna Wilson

Record of our Family by Maria Willis (Wilson) Finley[682]
(These pencil notes were written by Maria Willis Wilson, when in her late seventies or early eighties. Since the Births section corresponds exactly to a copy from the original family Bible, it can be assumed that the marriages and deaths were also copied from the Bible.)

MARRIAGES

Willis Wilson & Mary Anna Wilson were married the 26th of May 47 at Barterhill in Cumberland Co. , Va.

Dr. Joseph H. Trent & Elizabeth Trent Wilson were married on the 29th Jan. 1874 in Rusk Co., Tex. by Rev. Dr. Marshall.

Dr. P. J. Mitchell & M. A. Wilson were married on 30th Oct. 1879 in Gregg Co. Tex. by Rev. James Wiggins.

W. B. Mitchell & M. W. Wilson were married on 19th July, 1887 in Longview by Rev. J. W. Sexton.

F. A. Glenn & C. L. Wilson were married on 17 Oct 1883 in Longview, Texas by Rev. J. DeWitt Burkhead.

BIRTHS

Willis Wilson son of John P. & Maria W. Wilson was born at Bonbrook, Cumberland Co. Va. Sept.15th, 1817

Mary Anna Wilson, daughter of Matt & Elizabeth Wilson was born at Barterhill, Cumberland Co. Va. June, 1823.

Elizabeth Trent Wilson, daughter of the above, was born in the cty of Marshall, Miss. Nov. 10th 1848.

Willis Wilson was born at Bonbrook Oct. 25th, 1850

Maria Louise was born in Texas March 15th, 1853.

Mary Anna Wilson was born in Rusk Co. Tex. May 7th, 1855.

---

[682] Copy from John M. Finley of Austin TX.

Mary Isabella Wilson was born in Tex. Sept. 18th, 1857.

Maria Willis Wilson was born in Tex. Aug. 9th, 1859.

Laura Marye Wilson was born at Bonbrook Feb. 4th, 1862.

Caroline Louisa Wilson was born at Bonbrook Jan. 29th, 1864, was baptized by Rev. Wm. S. Thompson on the day of her mother's burial.

Mitchells
Mary Preston Mitchell, daughter of P. J. & M. A. Mitchell was born at Walnut Grove , Gregg Co., Tex., Mar. 6th, 1881

Wm. Gardiner Mitchell, son of P. J. & M. A. Mitchell, was born at Walnut Grove, Gregg Co., Texas, March 23rd, 1885.

Dr. P. J. Mitchell, son of P. J. & Ann Mitchell, was born at Warrenton, Ala. Sept. 25, 1851.

W. B. Mitchell, son of the above, was born at Warrenton, Ala. Oct.30th, 1858.

Trent
William Henry Trent, son of Dr. Joseph H. Trent & Elizabeth Trent Wilson, was born in Prairieville, Kaufman Co.,Texas Dec. 21st, 1874.

Glenn
Laura Orr Glenn, daughter of F. A. & C. L. Glenn was born in Longview Tex. Nov. 15, 1884.

Mary Anna Glenn, daughter of F. A. & C. L. Glenn was born in Henrietta Tex. Feb 8th, 1888.

Elizabeth Wilson Glenn, daughter of the above, was born in Huntsville Tex Feb. 17th, 1891

John & Louise Glenn, twin children of the above, were born at Walnut Grove, Gregg Co. Tex Sept 4th 1894

Frank and Carrie Glenn, twin children of the above, were born at San Angelo Tex. on 6 Oct 1897.

DEATHS

Maria Louisa died Aug. 25th, 1853

Mary Isabella died Sept. 12th, 1858

Mary Anna Wilson, the mother, died at Bonbrook July 11th, 1864

Willis Wilson, the father, died at Bonbrook Dec. 1st, 1865

Laura Marye Wilson died at Walnut Grove, Rusk Co. Tex June 15th, 1868

Willis Wilson Jr. died at Bonbrook, Cumb. Co. Va. July 22nd 1869.

Elizabeth Trent Wilson, wife of Dr. Joseph H Trent, died in Prairieville, Kaufmann Co. Texas, Jan. 4th, 1875.

Wm. Henry Trent, son of Dr. J. H. & Elizabeth Trent died in Prairieville July 9th, 1875

J. H. Trent M. D. died Aug. 5th, 1876

Dr. P. J. Mitchell died Sept. 27, 1885 in Longview, Tex

W. B. Mitchell died at Walnut Grove, Sept. 30th, 1887

Willis A. Wilson, son of Matthew Wilson, died at Walnut Grove, Rusk Co. Tex. Oct. 1st, 1866.

William W. Wilson , son of Jno. P. Wilson, died at Walnut Grove, Oct. 1st, 1875.

Laura Orr Glenn died in Longview June 1st, 1885

Maria Willis (Wilson) Finley (1859-1947) - Family History Memories

("Willis Wilson Finley preamble: 'I am copying from a script, partly dictated and partly in the handwriting of my mother, Mrs. O. A. Finley - nee Maria Willis Wilson.' " Copy from John M. Finley of Austin TX. The names in this document are not indexed. PSM)

My father, Willis Wilson, and my mother, Mary Anna, and three other families came from near Richmond, Va., in 1850 or 51 and settled near what is now Longview, Texas. I was born in 1859 and my parents went back to Va. in the spring of 1860 for medical treatment for my father and for a visit. A steamer on the Mississippi River on which we were traveling caught fire and a kind and courageous Irishman held a rope between his teeth and swam ashore; thus enabling men on the shore to draw the boat to the bank just in time that all escaped with their lives but <u>no baggage</u>. At this time, I was a babe in arms.

The Civil War came on in 1861, lasting till 1865, so that my parents could not return to Texas. My two younger sisters, Laura, who died at 6 years of age, and Carrie were born at Bonbrook in Cumberland County, our home, where my parents died during the war. At the time of my parents death, there were seven girls and one boy, who was named Willis and was the next to the oldest child.

We were orphans on a large home in Va. and want for food and older people to keep us, made it necessary for us to return to our home in Texas. My mother's maiden sister, Elizabeth Trent Wilson (Aunt Bettie) lived in Mo. with her bachelor brother Goodrich. My mother's family had known Att. Gen. Bates of the Northern Army at college, who obtained a pass signed by Pres. Lincoln for Aunt Bettie, that she might come to Virginia for us. The Glenns still have this pass.

Finally she and my father's only brother, Uncle William, brought us back to our Texas home. My brother remained in Va. to finish his education for the ministry but died a year or two later in Va.

When we arrived in Texas, I was able for the 1st time in my life to eat all I desired. (I mentioned this to show the want in Va. during the war.) I was about 6 years of age then. How little we children dreamed of the sacrifice my Aunt Bettie and Uncle William made leaving the culture and friends in Va. and living in the backwoods of E. Texas. Uncle William was highly cultured and even read his testament in Greek, a fact that made Dick, his negro body servant, very proud. Dick would relate in a highly pleased manner, that " De officers dat come in Marse Willum's tent cain't do noth'in wid his book" (The book was a new testament in Greek.)

The other Virginian families who came to Texas with my father had settled within a ten mile radius, part being two or three miles away. In later years I had some intimate associations with members of these families, but we saw very little of our few neighbors and passed our time as best we could in out-of-door amusements of which my Uncle highly approved. We went fishing in a nearby branch with fish hooks made of bent pins. We hunted rabbits in the woods with our grey hound dog, Ring, who chased them into hollow logs, and we pulled them out. Blackberries, walnuts, hickory nuts were abundant in the woods and we always had fun gathering them with negro children as helpers and playmates. There was also a gentle old horse which we rode. And so the years passed until I was 12 or 13 when my Uncle Calvin came from Va. with his bride to visit us. During these years we had lived in the rooms my father had built for temporary use when we first came to Texas, intending to build a permanent house later. While Uncle Calvin was with us, Uncle William had him direct the building of a house after the Va. style of architecture of our old home. U. Calvin's 1st child, Annie V. Wilson was born while he was with us in 1871, & she is now a missionary in China for 32 years.

After completing the house, they, with my sister Anna, went back to Va. leaving Carrie and me at home without companionship of children of our age in the neighborhood.

Of course, there were few books, just dry history and no magazines and I suppose a newspaper and no schools near enough to attend. My oldest sister had taught me up to this time when I was 12 or 13, when she married and left home (Elizabeth Trent). From this time until I was sixteen, Carrie & I spent the time as best we could.

We loved our oldest sister (Eliz. Trent). We called her "Sister" as both older sister & mother, as she was about grown when I first begin to remember her. She married a first coz., Dr. Joe Trent, whom we knew and loved. They went to Prairieville to live, & in time his parents came to live with them. In time a baby boy was born to them about Xmas & we were so happy over it. The more so because it was a boy. Till then, was only one boy in our family of 8, & he died so young.

About seven weeks after he was born one cold winter night, Uncle Wm. was lying down before a good fire on a blanket with a chair turned down to rest on. I was lying on one side of him & Carrie on the other, & he was about to begin to tell us the tales he had told us so often that he said all he had to do was to open his mouth and the tales would pour out, but this shows how good he was helping us to pass our time as we had no books for young folk to help us pass the time.

While lying there before the fire so happy about sister's baby boy, there was a Hello all at the front gate. It was a telegram saying that Sister had died that morn which grieved us so much. Then all thru the spring Aunt Bettie intended letting Carrie or me go to see the baby, but she could not spare us both at the same time, & it was hard for her to decide which should go first

& leave the other so miserable, that when the baby was about 6 mos old, he died & we only saw him when they brought him home to bury him. His father's parents had taken care of him after his mother's death as they were living with their son, my sister's husband.

Mary Anna (Wilson) Mitchell (1855-1940), 1934 letter

(This was a letter to Willis Wilson Finley of Ft. Worth TX from his Aunt Anna near Longview TX. Copy from John M. Finley of Austin TX. It has not been indexed nor footnoted for corrections. PSM)

Aug 21st, 1934

Willis Wilson of Bonbrook, Cumberland Co., Va. was eighteen when he went with Washington to the relief of Boston. He became an Officer, later a member of the Cincinnati Club. He married Mrs. Elizabeth Black (nee Trent). They only had one child, Maria Willis , who was educated in Lexington, Va. There she met John Park Wilson from Berkeley County, West Va. , a Scot Irish Presbyterian who was attending Washington College. She had another admirer, Mr. Bates, who became an Attorney General in the Federal Army. She married John Park Wilson in 1814, her parents persuaded him to live at Bonbrook. In 1815, she gave birth to twin boys, Wm. & Willis. Willis died in infancy, in 1817, she gave birth to another son, who was named Willis (my father). She died when he was five months old. Grandpa traveled in Europe for some time. Willis, Sr., who was guardian for his younger brother, Mathew. His wife was guardian for her niece, Elizabeth Trent. In time these two married, raised ten children. Mother was one of the ten. You see my parents were near kin to each other. When father was 15, Grandpa married Elizabeth Trent, first cousin both to mother's mother and father's mother.

The oldest son to this marriage was John Park Wilson, Jr. He was at V M I (Virginia Military Academy) when the Civil War broke out & served under Jackson, came out a major.

The next child was Maria Willis, married Lawrence S Marye,

then Mary married Dr. Wm. Fuqua, raised one child, Lawrence.

Next, John Calvin married Annie Randolf Vaughn, (parents of Miss K V Wilson in China, Bessie McLaughlin; Gay, Mrs. Edward Currie).

Henry Joseph came next. Married Louisa Harrison Gay, kin to him both of
my parents. He left one son, Henry Harrison, who died last year leaving
three children and his mother. Seems to have accomplished more than I ever
knew one person could do.

My brother, Willis Wilson 3rd., graduated from Hmpden-Sydney College in
the late 60s, father 39- uncle 37.

Uncle Wm., Captain Wm. W Wilson, never married, raised us. He had
wealth & leisure & literary tastes, was a living encyclopedia, read Latin &
Greek with as much ease as English. He kept Dick, his body servant in the
Civil War, lived as long as he believed. Dick used to tell us lots about
Marse Wm.; said "de common soldiers didn't come to Marse Wm.'s tent,
dess de big orsifers, an dey couldn't do nothin wid Marse Wm. lil black
book no moren I could. De pick it up en say who book diss? I say hit's
Marse Wm.'s. Suh, uh, uh, dey have to put it down." He read his Greek
testament in his private reading as long as he lived. I think Aunt Maria
managed to get hold of it & donate it to somebody she thought would
appreciate it.

Aunt Maria evidently had no hope that any of the Texas raised rabble
appreciating it. She also wanted to put that Certificate of Membership in the
Cincinnati Club in a museum at Washington, I told her it would not do any
good in Washington. I am the only member of the family who presumed to
say her 'nay'.

John Hampden, the youngest of father's half brothers married in Crocket, a
descendent of those Swiss folk who kept the faith through the dark ages.
They raised two children, Willis Wilson . Was with a firm in Houston with
shipping interests, last I heard of him, the daughter was married & lived at
New Waverly. Don't know the name. His wife died years ago. The last I
heard of him, he was in Richmond. Somehow his Texas children didn't fit in
with his Va. ....., as Mr. Joekle said people raised there don't make the
Texas grade.

Uncle John's son was named Willis too, became a Presbyterian preacher.

Father's half sisters and brothers were devoted to him.

Mother had a nephew, Wm. Henry Wilson, who was a Presbyterian
preacher. He married Mrs. (Sallie Ashlin) McLean, sister in law to the
father of the preacher by that name in Dallas. He left three children, the last
I heard of them, the mother had employment, the children @ home in a

home & school at Fredericksberg, Va.

Mother's home was at Barter Hill. Her mother had a brother, Alexander Trent, (who) married Miss Elizabeth Randolf, who raised one daughter, Julie who married Taylor Grey of Richmond. She had a sister, Anna, who married Jack Page at Union Hill. One of their daughters, Harriet (Cousin Hallie) married Coupland Randolf, had several sons, one daughter, Mary Randolph. She never married, was in Richmond, last I heard of her.

I am writing all of this because you may run across some of them, Aunt Anna.

(Jack) Page had two sons. John had one son, Wiley became an Episcopal preacher, Edward had two girls, two boys. Nannie my dub(?) married Tribble, went to Baltimore. Mary married a son of Uncle Thomas Trent, grandma's brother, who lives with three German women. Cousin Caroline, Louisa, Elize de Ende someway connected with grandma. Uncle Thomas fell heir to their home.

I wish you could read some notes by Henry H Wilson, who died last year, telling of prominent men he has met, named Wilson. The given names are so like those we know, they must be kin of my gr grandfather.

Henry's mother Lou sold a lot of the Bonbrook books, the house was full of them. The Scott's commentary, with our genealogy on the flyleaf, was one of then. My greatgrandfather wrote it. When I was there in the early 70s, Grandma said you would value this & none the less for being in my hand writing, that is the copy I have. Hope you can understand this rigmarole.

sig Aunt Anna

NOTE: This page followed the letter proper. JMF

I am copying from records left by my grandfather, Willis Wilson of Bonbrook, also from father's stepmother, his brother Capt. Wm. W Wilson, & his half sister, Maria Willis Wilson, namesake of father's mother, who married who married Col. Lawrence Marye of Fredericksberg, Va.

I am Mary Anna Wilson, Jr. married Dr. P J Mitchell, Oct.30, 1879, raised two children. Mary born in March, 1881, Wm. Gardiner born on March 23rd., 1885.

{John Park Wilson's genealogy} - John Wilson, of either Berk's or Chester County Penn Scotch -Irish Presbyterian (the first of the line to come to this

country was James Wilson in 1619 from either Co. Down or Antrim.)
Married Mrs. Isabelle Daniel (then Kennedy). She was either sister or
daughter of Captain Samuel Kennedy, who fought under General Wayne
and was the first man over the breast works at Stony Point.

There were three sons born to them. Michael, Jacob & Wm. M. Wm. M
married Mary Park, daughter of Samuel Park & a Miss Ripey, who was the
daughter of a Miss Patterson from the south if Ireland, was Scotch or Irish.
Mary Park was know(n) as pretty Polly Park because of her great beauty.
Wm. M settled at German Town, Berkley Co. , W Va., engaged successfully
in the mercantile business. There were seven children born to them of
whom John Park was 3rd child second son. He was educated at Washington
College, Lexington, Va. He met in Lexington, Maria Willis Wilson of
Bonbrook, Cumberland Co. , who also was educated in Lexington.

John Park Wilson (1790-1871), Family from Second Marriage

John Park Wilson (see pg. 13) married (2) **Elizabeth Woodson Trent**
17 Oct 1832 at "Auburn", Cumberland Co., Virginia.[683] She was born
13 Sep 1807 at "Auburn", Cumberland Co., Virginia, the daughter of
Stephen Woodson Trent and **Elizabeth Bassett Coupland**.[684] Elizabeth
died 27 Aug 1888 possibly at "Burleigh Hall", Cumberland Co., Virginia,
and was buried at "Bonbrook", Cumberland Co., Virginia.[685]
ISSUE:[686]

+ 185. m iv. **John Park Wilson, Jr.**, born 16 Sep 1833.
  189. f   v.   **Maria Willis Wilson**, born 24 May 1835 at "Bonbrook",
                Cumberland Co., Virginia. She married **Lawrence
                Slaughter Marye** 8 Jun 1858. He was born Oct 1834 in
                Fredericksburg, Virginia, the son of **John Lawrence
                Marye, Sr.** and **Ann Maria Burton**. Maria died 5 Jul
                1910. Her many letters to and regarding her niece of the
                same name give a vivid picture of life in Virginia after the

---

[683] Elliott, *Marriages, Cumberland Co. VA*, 139.

[684] Trent Family Bible Record, Accession 25300, LVA.

[685] Letter 1 Sep 1888, Finley, John M., Family history research. WPA - Bonbrook
Cemetery CUM86.

[686] Brown, *Genealogy .... Wilson*. Wilson, Henry H., John Park Wilson notes.
Census records, Cumber land Co. VA 1850, 1860, 1870.

Civil War.[687]
- 190. f vi. **Isabella Caroline Wilson**, born 1837, died 1838.
- 191. f vii. **Elizabeth Trent Wilson**, born 1838, died 1843.
- + 192. f viii. **Mary Coe Wilson**, born 19 Oct 1840 <See pg. 304>.
- 208. f ix. **Anna Harrison Wilson**, born 1843, died 1844.
- + 209. m x. **John Calvin Wilson**, born 14 Nov 1845, died after 31 Aug 1922 <See pg. 305>.
- + 228. m xi. **Henry Joseph Wilson**, born 11 Jan 1848, died 22 Oct 1884 <See pg. 307>.
- + 230. m xii. **John Hampden Wilson**, born 3 Jul 1853, died after 21 Nov 1932 <See pg. 308>.

- - - - - - - - - - -

185. John Park[4] Wilson, Jr. was born 16 Sep 1833, the son of **John Park Wilson** and **Elizabeth Woodson Trent**. He married **Elizabeth Inskip Gibson** about 1860, the daughter of **David Gibson**. Elizabeth died Jun 1884.[688]

ISSUE:
- 186. m i. **Isaac Gibson Wilson**, born 7 Jan 1863, died 22 Jul 1864, and was buried at "Bonbrook", Cumberland Co., Virginia.[689]
- 187. m ii. **Willis Sherrard Wilson**, born 29 Jan 1867.
- 188. f iii. **Anne Van Meter Wilson**, born 18 May 1869.

- - - - - - - - - - -

192. Mary Coe[4] Wilson <See pg. 304> was born 19 Oct 1840 at "Bonbrook", Cumberland Co., Virginia, the daughter of **John Park Wilson** and **Elizabeth Woodson Trent**. She married **William Fuqua** before 20 Nov 1881.[690] He was born 18 Oct 1823, the son of **Joseph Fuqua** and **Ann Lipscomb**. William died 12 Jul 1897 at Mount Ida, Buckingham Co., Virginia, and was buried at Cumberland Presbyterian Church, Cumberland Co., Virginia. [691]

---

[687] Finley, John M., Family history research. MS1744, Jones Memorial Library, Lynchburg VA.

[688] Brown, *Genealogy .... Wilson.*

[689] WPA - Bonbrook Cemetery CUM86.

[690] 1881 Nov 20 letter, 1887 letters written from Burleigh Hall. An 1851 letter stated that Mr. Leitch gave $16/acre for land at Broomfield for Dr. Fuqua. Finley, John M., Family history research.

[691] *Cumb Co. VA and Its People*, 2nd Supplement, 86-90.

ISSUE:
193. m   i.   **Lawrence M. Fuqua**, born 15 Mar 1883, died after 21 Nov 1932. He married **Alice Rangely** in Lynchburg, Virginia. .
195. f   ii. **Mary Willis Fuqua**, born Oct 1885, died after 27 Jan 1890.

William also married (1) **Elizabeth Langhorne Leitch** 1 Dec 1846 in Trinity Presbyterian Church, Buckingham Co., Virginia. She was born 20 Sep 1828 in Buckingham Co., Virginia, the daughter of **William Leitch** and **Mary Ann Langhorne**. Elizabeth died 29 Apr 1877 in Buckingham Co., Virginia.

- - - - - - - - - -

209. John Calvin[4] Wilson <See pg. 304> was born 14 Nov 1845 at "Bonbrook", Cumberland Co., Virginia, the son of **John Park Wilson** and **Elizabeth Woodson Trent**.[692] Calvin died after 31 Aug 1922 probably in Richmond, Virginia. He married **Ann Randolph Vaughan** 21 Sep 1870. She was born 10 Oct 1847 and may have been the daughter of **John Meriwether Vaughan** and **Sally Gay**.[693] Ann died 20 Jun 1894.

Calvin was an 1866 alumnus of Hampden-Sydney College in Prince Edward Co., Virginia.[694] After his marriage, Calvin and his wife visited **William W. Wilson, Elizabeth T. Wilson** and the orphan children of **Willis Wilson** in Gregg Co., Texas. While there, he directed "the building of a house after the Va. style of architecture"[695] as requested in Willis Wilson's will. Calvin evidently considered staying , buying land there, but returned to Virginia. His wife wrote to Elizabeth in Texas in 1875 about "the sad news of our dear brother's death". In William W. Wilson's will he appointed his cousin Elizabeth and brother Calvin executors. In 1922 Calvin wrote from Richmond, enclosing a letter written by one of his three daughters, Annie, Bessie and Gay, who were missionaries in China.[696]

ISSUE:[697]
210. f   i.   **Annie V. "Dare" Wilson**, born 1871 in Texas.

---

[692] Brown, *Genealogy .... Wilson.*
[693] Hall, "Payne Data", 5:252.
[694] Hampden-Sydney, *General Catalogue.*
[695] Finley, Maria, Family history memories.
[696] Letters 18 Mar 1922, 11 Nov 1932, 1 Apr 1938. Finley, John M., Family history research.
[697] The 1880 Cumberland Co. VA census and the 1900 Henrico Co. VA census list the children.

+ 211. f   ii.   **Pocahontas Gay Wilson**, born 9 Mar 1873, died 1948.
  217. m   iii.   **John P. Wilson**, born Mar 1875 in Virginia. He married
                   Lucille Jordan. John died after 11 Oct 1943.
  218. f   iv.   **Elizabeth "Peachy" Wilson**, born 1877 in Cumberland
                   Co., Virginia, died before 8 Jul 1947.
  219. m   v.   **John Merriwether Wilson**, born 1880, died 1881.
  220. m   vi.   **William C. Wilson**, born 1883 in Virginia.
  221. m vii.   **Julian M. Wilson**, born Nov 1885 in Virginia.
+ 222. f viii.   **Elizabeth "Bessie" Wilson**, born Jun 1889 <See pg. 301>.
+ 225. f   ix.   **Gay R. Wilson**, born Jun 1890 <See pg. 307>.

- - - - - - - - - - -

211. Pocahontas Gay⁵ Wilson was born 9 Mar 1873 at "Bonbrook",
Cumberland Co., Virginia, the daughter of **John Calvin Wilson** and **Ann
Randolph Vaughan**.[698] Pocahontas died 1948. She married **Richard
Cunningham Wight** 1 Nov 1897 in Richmond, Virginia. He was born
20 Aug 1873 in Goochland Co., Virginia, the son of **William Washington
Wight** and **Arianna P. Cunningham**. [699]

ISSUE:

  212. f   i.   **Ariane Randolph Wight**, born 17 Sep 1899.
  213. f   ii.   **Pocahontas Wilson "Poky" Wight**, born 8 Nov 1904. She
                   married **Richard Edmunds**. Pocahontas died 1999.
  214. f   iii.   **Elizabeth Trent "Bessie" Wight**, born 17 Jul 1907. She
                   married _____ **Brown**. Bessie was a secretary to John
                   D. Rockefeller, Jr., in Williamsburg, Virginia, during the
                   restoration of Colonial Williamsburg from 1933-1936 and
                   later in his New York Office.[700]
  215. m   iv.   **Richard Cunningham Wight, Jr.**, born 26 May 1910.
  216. f   v.   **Virginia Matoaka "Ginny" Wight**, born 10 Mar 1913.
                   She married _____ **Lamb**.

An interesting 1995 video recording of interviews with "Poky", "Bessie",
"Ginny" and Robert Coles Edmunds, where they speak of family memories
and their relationship to Pocahontas, can be seen at the library at the
Virginia Historical Society in Richmond.[701]

---

[698] Brown, _Genealogy .... Wilson_.

[699] _Virginia Biography, History of Virginia_, 4:227. Finley, John M., Family history
research.

[700] Catalog entry for Brown, Elizabeth Trent Wight, _Papers, 1931-1953._, Mss1
B8128 a, Virginia Historical Society, Richmond.

[701] _Pocahontas: Her True Story._ London: BBC, 1995. Mss16 p7505 a, Virginia

(continued...)

- - - - - - - - - -

222. Elizabeth "Bessie"[5] Wilson was born Jun 1889 in Virginia, the daughter of **John Calvin Wilson** and **Ann Randolph Vaughan**. She married **Wilfred McLauchlin**. [702]

ISSUE:

223. f   i.   **Elizabeth Trent "Bettie" McLauchlin**.
224. f   ii. **Anne Randolph McLauchlin**.

- - - - - - - - - -

225. Gay R.[5] Wilson <See pg. 306> was born Jun 1890 in Virginia, the daughter of **John Calvin Wilson** and **Ann Randolph Vaughan**. She married **Edward "Ed" Currie**.[703]

ISSUE:

226. m   i.   **David Currie**.
227. f   ii. **Anne Currie**.

- - - - - - - - - -

228. Henry Joseph[4] Wilson <See pg. 304> was born 11 Jan 1848 at "Bonbrook", Cumberland Co., Virginia, the son of **John Park Wilson** and **Elizabeth Woodson Trent**. Henry died 22 Oct 1884 at "Bonbrook", Cumberland Co., Virginia, and was buried at "Bonbrook. He married **Lucy Harrison Gay**. She was born 1853 in Virginia. She may have been the daughter of **Peterfield Gay**. Lucy died after 1934.

ISSUE:[704]

229. m   i.   **Henry Harrison Wilson**, born 1882 in Virginia. He
               married **Eliza Lily Tyler** 1915. Henry died 1933.[705]

The sale of "Bonbrook" was rather complicated. It was inherited by William and Willis Wilson, grandsons of Willis Wilson. Willis deeded his moiety to his brother William. William, in his will, specified that proceeds be used to pay a debt.   In 1881 in response to a lawsuit regarding the debt, Henry J. Wilson purchased the property. After his death in 1884, notes on the property being left unpaid, the trustee sold the property to Henry's widow and Miss Bettie C. Gay (probably her sister). They sold "Bonbrook"

---

[701] (...continued)
Historical Society, Richmond.

[702] Letters 8 Jul 1947, 11 Apr 1938. Finley, John M., Family history research.

[703] Finley, Maria, Family history memories.

[704] Wilson, Henry H., John Park Wilson notes.

[705] Wilson, Henry H. *Papers, 1922-1925*, catalog entry gives dates, marriage.

in 1888.[706]

- - - - - - - - - - -

230. John Hampden⁴ Wilson <See pg. 304> was born 3 Jul 1853 at "Bonbrook", Cumberland Co., Virginia, the son of **John Park Wilson** and **Elizabeth Woodson Trent**. John died after 11 Nov 1932. He married **Mannie Joekle** in Crockett, Texas.[707]

ISSUE:

    231. m   i. **Willis Wilson**.

Hampden was listed with his father in the 1860 and 1870 Cumberland Co., Virginia censuses, but he was in Texas by 1875. He was postmaster at Iron Bridge, Gregg Co. Texas, in 1876 and 1885, named guardian of his nieces in 1879, and had married Mannie by 1884.

[706] Cumberland Co. VA Will Books 7:105, 13:647, Deed Books 26:438, 32:281, 34:354, 35:69.

[707] Phillips, *Gregg Co. Postoffices*. Gregg Co. TX Probate Minutes "B"- File 50 pages 161, 162 and 164, 165. Letters 8 Nov, 1875, 5 May 1885, 11 Nov 1932. Finley, John M., Family history research.

Some old home places of Wilson families in Virginia

(Not all names in the following home places are indexed.)

Some of the old home places were reported on by the Works Progress Administration Historical Inventory Project, which was sponsored during the depression by the Virginia Conservation Commission under the direction of its Division of History. Each report was given a county code and number, such as CUM86. Copies of these can be downloaded from the web site for the Library of Virginia, Virginia Historical Inventory. The reports were compiled in 1936 and 1937 and give the best information found by the authors at that time. County court records and other documents correct and update the data concerning some owners and dates.

A tour through the counties of Cumberland, Buckingham and Prince Edward can be done in a relatively short time, the distance from the little town of Cumberland to Farmville being less than 20 miles. In Cumberland Co., some of the local roads have both a name and a number. I made visits to the area in 1992 and 1994. County maps are available at the Virginia Department of Transportation in Richmond (http://www.virginiadot.org/comtravel/MAPs-default.asp) and possibly at the county court houses.

Cumberland Co.

Barter Hill home and cemetery.[708]
See Matthew Wilson (1772-1833).
Directions: Just north of Cumberland on US Hwy 60, turn north on Road 622 (Trents Mill Road), then turn left on Road 627 (Barter Hill Road). The original house burned around 1850, and the house reported on was built around the original chimneys in 1858. Pictures of Wilson grave markers for Matthew's wife Betsey and son Edward were made by John Reid in 1993. A clause in a deed excluded a portion of the property for the cemetery.[709]

---

[708] WPA - Barter Hill CUM114. McCrary, *Cumberland County ... Historical Inventory*, 2-3 (an error in this entry refers to Will Book 6:556, which should be Deed Book 6:556).
[709] Cumberland Co. VA Deed Book 28:667-8.

Bonbrook and Bonbrook Cemetery.[710]
See Willis Wilson (1758-1822).
Directions: Just north of Cumberland on US Hwy 60, turn north on Road
622 (Trents Mill Road), right on Road 623 (Sugar Fork Road), left on 696
(Bonbrook Road).
In 1992 Mr. Ray Watson was the owner; the name Bonbrook was on the
mailbox. Mr. Watson maintained the cemetery which was excluded in a
deed selling the property.[711] He verified on a map the locations of the other
Cumberland Co. places.

Somerset site.[712]
See Benjamin Wilson Sr. (1733-1814).
Directions: Just north of Cumberland on US Hwy 60, turn north on Road
622 (Trents Mill Road) , right on Road 623 (Sugar Fork Road), left on 696
(Bonbrook Road), right on 671 (Summerset Road), right on 672 (Sports
Lake Road).
In 1992 the son of Mr. Ray Watson (see Bonbrook) had a poultry farm
where Somerset had been located.

Buckingham Co.

Clay Bank.[713]
See James Wilson (1765-1847).
Directions: From Cumberland take US Hwy 60 west past the Buckingham
Co. line. Road 626 is the first road north. Clay Bank is located at the
junction of 626 and 624. There was a stone inscribed "Clay Bank" at the
entrance to the property in 1994.
There are several errors in the WPA report, because the author did not
realize the property was located in both Buckingham Co., where the
courthouse burned in 1869, and in Cumberland Co., where several deeds
were recorded. In 1994 the owners were Patrick and Virginia Bowe. They
have done a beautiful job of restoring and maintaining the original home,
while making it a comfortable place to rear their son Clay.

---

[710] WPA - Bonbrook CUM121. WPA - Bonbrook Cemetery CUM86. McCrary,
Cumberland County ... Historical Inventory, 4-5.

[711] Cumberland Co. VA Deed Book 35:69.

[712] McCrary, *Cumberland County ... Historical Inventory*, 47.

[713] WPA - Clay Bank BU288. McCrary, *Cumberland County ... Historical
Inventory*, 11.

Prince Edward Co.

Milnwood.[714]
See Goodridge Wilson (1776-1849).
Directions: Off US Hwy 15 on the south side of Farmville there is an area called Milnwood. Turn left on Milnwood Road.
In 1992 the owners of the home at 1001 Milnwood Road were S. R. or Gordon Smith, who said the original house burned in 1919.

Poplar Hill.[715]
See Richard Woodson (1706-1773).
Directions: South of Farmville on US Hwy 15, turn left on a road before Road 646. (My notes are uncertain about the road.)
An impressive house, built well after the Woodson occupancy, is at the site now. I was told that the original Woodson house was a frame house behind the present home. In 1992 the property was owned by Nelson Bolt and his mother.

Slate Hill.[716]
See Nathaniel Venable (1733-1804).
There are pictures of the original home on the Library of Virginia web site. Historical marker, VA-F66 Slate Hill Plantation, is located on US Hwy 15.
Directions: Travel south of Farmville on US Hwy 15 to Worsham, which is southeast of Hampden-Sydney. Continue on 15 down a long hill, cross a bridge and turn right at the first drive.
In 1994 the owners of the property were Ken and Dolly Worthy. The home was reported in 1936 as being in a dilapidated condition, but still standing. In 1994 the home was gone, but evidence of its location was apparent near the family cemetery.

---

[714] *Today and Yesterday*, 251.

[715] *Today and Yesterday*, 251.

[716] WPA - Slate Hill PE10. *Today and Yesterday*, 259-260.

Ancestors of Elizabeth Woodson Venable (1754-1851)
(See pg. 176)

Venable to Powhatan Indians

Elizabeth Woodson Venable, born 1784 at "Slate Hill", Prince Edward County, Virginia, was the daughter of **Nathaniel Venable** (1733-1804) and **Elizabeth Michaux Woodson** (1740-1791). She married **Goodridge Wilson** (1776-1849).[717]

Nathaniel Venable married Elizabeth Michaux Woodson in Prince Edward Co., Virginia, in 1755, His father-in-law, **Richard Woodson**, gave them the land that they built a home on and called "Slate Hill".[718]

Nathaniel wrote a genealogy of the Venable Family 25 Dec 1790, which gives the following information of his grandparents and parents: **Abraham Venable** married a widow who was a daughter of _____**Lewis**. They had a son, **Abraham Venable**, who was born 22 Mar 1700 and married **Martha Davis**, daughter of **Nathaniel Davis** of Hanover county.[719]

There are several traditions of the Davis line to the Powhatan Indians. I will speculate on one line giving possible dates of birth.

The father of Martha Davis (1705-) has been called Nathaniel (Nathaniel Venable's genealogy) and **Robert** (1680-) by another Venable genealogist.[720]

The father of Nathaniel Davis was **Nathaniel Davis** (1650 -), who married **Elizabeth Hughes**, a daughter of **John Hughes**, an Indian trader.

Trader John Hughes (1620-) married **Nicketti**, the daughter of **Opechancanough** and **Cleopatra**.

In the Council and general court records of Virginia in 1641 **Thomas Rolfe** (1616-), the son of **Pocahontas**, asked to visit his aunt Cleopatra and

---

[717] Venable, *Venables of Virginia*, 37. She gives transcriptions of court documents and excerpts from other references.

[718] WPA - Slate Hill PE10. *Today and Yesterday*, 259-260.

[719] *Genealogies, Wm. & Mary Quarterly*, 5:308.

[720] Venable, *Venables of Virginia*, 14.

kinsman, Opechancanough.[721]

An article, "Powhatan and Opechancanough", published in 1957 in the *Radford Review*, a publication of Radford College in Virgina, was written by "Katherine H. Hillman (nee Katherine Nicketti Hayes), a descendant of Opechancanough, through his daughter, the Princess Nicketti".

The acknowledged expert on the Powhatan Indians is Helen C. Rountree, who has published several books on the subject.

Woodson to 1644 Indian Massacre and to Jesse James

Elizabeth Woodson Venable (1784-1851) was the daughter of **Nathaniel Venable** (1733-1804) and **Elizabeth Michaux Woodson** (1740-1791).

Elizabeth Michaux Woodson was born 6 Jun 1740, the daughter of **Richard Woodson** (1706-1773) and **Anne Madeleine Michaux** (1710-1796). The Woodson property in Prince Edward County Virginia was called "Poplar Hill".[722]

Well after Elizabeth's marriage to Nathaniel Venable, during the Revolutionary War, she saved property at "Slate Hill", and perhaps her husband, from the troops of **Banastre Tarleton**, who were out to destroy "stores of corn and provisions". One family story says that Elizabeth stored their food supplies in tobacco hogsheads and placed them at the door of the tobacco barns in full view, a ploy which evidently worked.[723] Another story is that men were to be taken prisoner, that Nathaniel was able to hide, and when Elizabeth refused to reveal his location, Tarleton stormed through the house and slashed the portrait of Nathaniel Venable.

Richard Woodson was the son of **Richard Woodson** (1662-1717) and **Ann Smith**, who lived on the north side of the James River in Henrico County Virginia. Richard the younger acquired land further south.[724]

Richard Woodson the elder was the son of **Robert Woodson** (1634-1707)

---

[721] *Virginia Magazine of History and Biography*, 13:394-5.

[722] *Today and Yesterday*, 251.

[723] Eggleston, *Historic Slate Hill*, 14-5. Eggleston, "The Huguenot Abraham Michaux and Descendants", 46:77-8. Venable, *Venables of Virginia*, 27.

[724] Woodson, *Woodsons and Their Connections*, 25-6, 34. Venable, *Venables of Virginia*, 25, 30-5.

and **Elizabeth Ferris**.

Robert Woodson was the son of **John Woodson** (1586-1644) and **Sarah Winston?** (1600-1660).

John and Sarah Woodson were first listed in the 1623 muster at Flowerdew Hundred on the James River.[725] By the 1624 muster, they were at Piersey's Hundred up river, and sometime after that they settled at Curles, Henrico County. In the 1644 Indian Massacre John was killed while away from home. The story is told that Col. **Thomas Ligon**, a surveyor in Henrico County (and related to another Wilson line), was nearby when the Indians were attacking the Woodson home. Using an eight foot, muzzle loading gun, braced on a tree notch, he killed seven Indians. During the attack, Sarah hid her son John under a "wash tub" and son Robert in a "tater hole". When two Indians descended inside the chimney, Sarah defended herself by using a pot of boiling water and a roasting spit. The Woodson gun was said to have had the name Ligon etched in the stock. It has been refurbished somewhat and is now on display in the museum at the Virginia Historical Society in Richmond. **(See pg. 220)** [726]

During a visit in 1992 with a docent at Flowerdew Hundred on the James River, she directed me to further information on the family of John Woodson and told me of the Woodson link to Jesse James, who descended from **Benjamin Woodson** (1666-1723), son of Robert Woodson (1634-1707) and Elizabeth Ferris. Jesse's middle name was Woodson. There is much myth and truth written about the lives of **Frank James** (1843-1915) and his **brother Jesse Woodson James** (1847-1882) and Jesse's death. **John C. Reid** of Peculiar, Missouri, attended Jesse's third funeral in 1995.[727]

---

[725] Hotten:169-172.

[726] Davis, *Tidewater Virginia Families*, 399-406. Meyer and Dorman, *Adventurers of Purse and Person*, 22-3, 356, 708-714. Woodson, *Woodsons and Their Connections*, 21-35. Ligon, *Ligon Family and Connections*, 306-318.

[727] Phillip W. Steele, *Jesse and Frank James, The Family History*. Ron Hansen, The *Assassination of Jesse James by the Coward Robert Ford*. Carol (Fleming) Lumpkin, "The mother of Jesse James: A vital character", a book review of *Mamaw*, by Susan Dodd, in the *Houston Chronicle* 9 Oct 1988. Marilyn Goza Longobardi, editor of *Woodson Watcher plus Allied Lines*, Vol. 1 No. 3.

Michaux to Huguenot

Elizabeth Woodson Venable (1784-1851) was the daughter of **Nathaniel Venable** (1733-1804) and **Elizabeth Michaux Woodson** (1740-1791). In 1759 Nathaniel Venable was clerk of the vestry of St. Patrick Parish of the Church of England in Prince Edward County.

Elizabeth Michaux Woodson was born 6 Jun 1740, the daughter of **Richard Woodson** (1706-1773) and **Anne Madeleine Michaux** (1710-1796). In 1759 Richard Woodson was a vestryman of St. Patrick Parish. [728]

Anne Madeleine Michaux was the daughter of **Abraham Michaux** (1672-1717) and **Suzanne Rochet** (1667-1744). Her religious background was Huguenot. Anne is somewhat given credit for the "decline of Episcopacy" and the growth of the Presbyterian church in the Prince Edward County area. Quoting a letter to Bishop Meade, "Her strong character and devoted piety appear to have made an indelible impression on such of them as had the happiness to know her. And this it was, I believe, that gave them a respect not only for religion in general, but a bias toward that particular type of Protestantism of which she was so brilliant an ornament." [729]

Abraham Michaux was the son of **Jacob Michaux** and **Anne Severin**, baptized 23 Feb 1672 in Sedan, France. He followed his father to Amsterdam, was received as a member of the Walloon-French church there on 28 Jan 1691 and married Suzanne Rochet there 13 Jul 1692.

Suzanne Rochet was the daughter of **Jean Rochet** and **Marie Trufet**, baptized 13 Apr 1667 in Sedan, France. A family tradition says that the family, being French Protestant/Huguenot and being persecuted after the Revocation of the Edict of Nantes in 1685, sent Suzanne, hidden in a hogshead on a boat with an understanding sea captain, down the Meuse River from Sedan to sisters in Holland. Communications between her father in France and family in Holland referred to her as "the little nightcap".

Abraham and Suzanne (Rochet) Michaux went from Holland, where four of their children were born, to London in 1702, and by 1705 were settling in Virginia on the south side of the James River, which at that time was part of

---

[728] St. Patrick's Parish, Prince Edward County, Va. Records, Vestry Book, 1755-1774. Accession 34422. Church records collection, Library of Virginia, Richmond.
[729] Meade, *Old Churches*, 2:31.

Henrico County (now Powhatan County).[730]

Abraham and Suzanne are commemorated on a plaque in the new Manakin
Church on the Huguenot Trail Byway, Route 711.[731]

---

[730] Cabell, *Turff and Twigg : the French Lands*, 280-3. Eggleston, "The Huguenot
Abraham Michaux and Descendants", VA Mag. Hist. 44:365-374, 45:102-107. This
contains transcriptions of wills.

[731] King William Parish, Va. *Vestry book*, xii.

BIBLIOGRAPHY

"A Beautiful Day on the Trace",
http://www.garringer.net/foam/archives/000171.html.

Aker, Mary Bullock, comp. *Bullocks of Virginia and Kentucky and their Descendants.* Parkville MO: 1952.

"Archibald Murphey Aiken." *Find a Grave.*
http://www.findagrave.com/cgi-bin/fg.cgi?page=gr&GSmid=46521264&GRid=8945617&pt=Archibald%.

Atkinson, Geo. W. *History of Kanawha County* .... Charleston: West Virginia Journal, 1876.

Avant, David A. *Some Southern Colonial Families.* 4 vols. Tallahassee FL: L'Avant Studios, 1983-91.

Barton, Jessie. *Index to Wills and Administration Recorded in Probate Records of Gregg County, Texas, 1873-1964.* Longview TX, 1965.

Bates, Onward. *Bates, et al of Virginia and Missouri.* Chicago: 1914.

Beale, Howard K., ed. *The Diary of Edward Bates 1859-1866.* Washington: Government Printing Office, 1933.

Beck, James, comp. Ancestral File accessed 1994, Family History Library, Salt Lake City UT.

Belton, Missouri Centennial 1872-1972, The First Hundred Years. Belton MO: Gen. Centennial Comm.

Benjamin Wilson Papers 1785-1916, 97MS439. Special Collections and Archives Department, Margaret I. King Library, University of Kentucky, Lexington KY.

Bivona, Brian. *Ancestors of Brian & Melissa Bivona.*
http://homepages.rootsweb.com/~bbivona/main.htm.

Blackwood, Samuel J. "Somerset" - Wilson Family Cemetery, Granville County North Carolina. Clearwater FL: 1990.

Blackwood, Samuel J. Tranquility Cemetery, Granville County North Carolina. Clearwater FL: 1999.

Blomquist, Ann Kicker. *The Vestry Book of Southam Parish, Cumberland County, Virginia, 1745-1792.* Westminster MD: Willow Bend Books, 2002.

Boddie, John Bennett and Mrs. John Bennett Boddie. *Historical Southern Families.* 23 vols. 1959-80. Reprint, Genealogical Pub. Co. 1993-95.

Bradford, Thomas Lindsley. *Homœopathy in Virginia.* Presented by Sylvain
Cazalet. http://www.homeoint.org/history/king/1-07.htm.

Bradshaw, Herbert Clarence. *History of Hampden-Sydney College.* Privately
printed. Durham NC: Fisher-Harrison, 1976.

"British Mercantile Claims 1775-1803". *The Virginia Genealogist* 7:112 (1963).

Broderbund Software's Family Archives (www.genealogy.com)/ Genealogical
Publishing Company, (www.genealogical.com). The following books reproduced
on Family Archive CD-ROM are listed also under the author or title heading:

> Boddie - CD #191 Southern Genealogies #1, 1600s-1800s
> Clift - CD#519 Early Kentucky Settlers, 1700s-1800s
> *Genealogies, Tyler's Quarterly* - CD #187 Virginia Genealogies, 1600s-1800s, #3
> *Genealogies, Virginia Magazine of History and Biography* - CD #162 Virginia
>   Genealogies, 1600s-1800s, #1
> *Virginia Biography.* - CD #205 Virginia Genealogies, 1600s-1800s #4
> Meade - CD#550 Virginia Genealogies and Biographies, 1500s-1600s
> Valentine. *The Edward Pleasants Valentine Papers* - CD #205 Virginia
>   Genealogies, 1600s-1800s #4

Brown, Elizabeth Trent Wight. *Genealogical notes concerning the Wight and
Wilson families.* Mss 6:1 W6395:2. Virginia Historical Society, Richmond.

Bryan, Wm. S. and Robert Rose. *A History of the Pioneer Families of Missouri* .....
St. Louis: Bryan, Brand & Co., 1876.

"Butler County, Missouri, Sparkman Cemetery".
http://www.rootsweb.com/~mobutle2/Cemmaps/sparkman/sparkman.htm.

Cabell, Priscilla Harriss. *Turff and Twigg : the French Lands* ...... Richmond VA:
P. H. Cabell, 1988.

Carlton, Nannie Page Trent. "Brief History of the Trent Family of Cumberland
County, Virginia." B. S., Longwood College, Prince Edward Co VA, 1938.

Chamberlain, Eric S. Family history records. Mt. Locust, Natchez Trace, MS.

Clift, G. Glenn. *Kentucky Obituaries 1787-1854.* Baltimore: Genealogical Pub. Co.,
1977.

"Col. Cy Wilson Remembered",
http://www.geocities.com/Pentagon/Quarters/6940/wilson.html.

Cumberland County, Virginia, Wills, Deeds, Orders, Marriage Records, Chancery
Records in the courthouse in Cumberland VA and on microfilm at the Library of

Virginia, Richmond.

"Cumberland County, Virginia, 1800 Tax List". *The Virginia Genealogist* 17:197, 243 (1973).

Cumberland County Virginia and Its People. Cumberland VA: Cumberland County Historical Society, 1983, (2nd supplement) 1991.

Cumberland County, Virginia Historical Bulletin. Cumberland VA: Cumberland County Historical Society.

Cumberland Presbyterian Church (Va.). *Records 1787-1900.* Accession 20080, Church Records Collection, Library of Virginia, Richmond.

Curry, Mabel Walters. *Colfax Cemetery, Van Zandt County, Texas.* 1974.

D'Aiutolo, Leila Eldridge, Warren L. Forsythe, William S. Hubard, and Mary Carolyn Mitton, comps. *Moseley Family History. The Descendants of William Moseley 1605/1606-1655 of Norfolk, Va.* Ellensburg WA: Warren Forsythe, 2000.

DAR. Daughters of the American Revolution, National Society. Washington DC. Willis Wilson Hobson Bible and Meredith Family Bible located in Benjamin Wilson Patriot File.

"Dardenne Prairie Fifty Years Ago", *St. Charles Cosmos,* November 25, 1891. (St. Charles MO).

Davis, Virginia Lee Hutcheson. *Tidewater Virginia Families.* Baltimore: Genealogical Pub. Co., 1989. A later edition has been published.

Dayton, Ruth Woods. *Pioneers and Their Homes on Upper Kanawha.* Charleston WV: WV Pub. Co., 1947.

Dorman, John Frederick, abs., ed. *Virginia Revolutionary Pension Applications, Abstracted.* Vol. 25. Washington: 1976.

Douglas, James W., comp. *A Manual of the Members of the Briery Presbyterian Church, Virginia.* Published by order of the session. Richmond, Printed by J. Macfarlan, 1828.

Douglas, William. *Douglas Register ... transcribed and edited by W. Mac. Jones.* Richmond VA: J. W. Ferguson, 1928.

DRT. Daughters of the Republic of Texas. Lineage Book Committee. *Founders and patriots of the Republic of Texas; the lineages of the members of the Daughters of the Republic of Texas.* Austin: Daughters of the Republic of Texas, 1963.

Drummond, Malcolm C. *Historic Sites in St. Charles County Missouri.* St. Charles County Historical Society. Harland Bartholomew and Associates, 1976.

Eggleston, J. D. *Historic Slate Hill Plantation in Virginia.* Bulletin of Hampden-Sydney College, 29, no. 2. Hampden-Sydney VA: The college, 1945.

Eggleston, J. D. "The Huguenot Abraham Michaux and Descendants", *Virginia Magazine of History and Biography* 44:365-374, 45:48, 102-9, ..., 411-419, 46:76-84, 165-6 (1937-8).

Elliott, Katherine B., comp. *Marriage Records 1749-1840, Cumberland County Virginia.* 1969. Reprint, Easley SC: Southern Historical Press, 1983.

Family Bible of Benjamin Wilson Jr. in possession of Ann Wilson of Lexington KY. Copy in 97MS439 in the Special Collections and Archives Department, Margaret I. King Library, University of Kentucky, Lexington.

Family Bible of Louis B. Chamberlain in possession of Eric S. Chamberlain, Natchez MS.

Family Bible of Willis and Mary Anna Wilson 1817-1919. Copy made by Maria Willis (Wilson) Finley in possession of John M. Finley, Austin TX. Original Bible in possession of William Gardiner Mitchell, Longview TX, Sep 1995.

Fayette Co. TX Cemeteries. http://www.angelfire.com/ab/oldplum/oplist2.html.

Finley, John Mallory. Family history research and letters. Austin TX.

Finley, Maria Willis (Wilson). Family history memories. Notes made by her, then copied by her son Willis Wilson Finley. (Transcription in Appendix.)

Fleming, Walter L. *Louisiana State University 1860-1896.* Baton Rouge LA: Louisiana State University Press, 1936.

Geddie, Jack, ed. *Colfax.* Colfax TX: Colfax Homecoming Committee, 1963.

Genealogies of Virginia Families from Tyler's Quarterly Historical and Genealogical Magazine. 4 vols. Baltimore: Genealogical Pub. Co., 1981.

Genealogies of Virginia Families from William and Mary College Quarterly Historical Magazine. 5 vols. Baltimore: Genealogical Pub. Co., 1982.

Germany Family Bible, in possession of Richard F. Thomas Jr. of Arlington TX.

"Great St. Louis Fire of 1849", http://www.ezl.com/~fireball/Disaster07.htm.

Gregg County Cemeteries, TXGenWeb project,

http://txgenes.com/TxGregg/CemIndex.html.

Gregg County Genealogy Society. *Gregg County, Texas Cemeteries.* Longview TX: Gregg County Genealogy Society, [1984]-1991.

Grundset, Eric G., ed. *Buckingham County, Virginia, Surveyor's Plat Book 1762-1858.* 2d edition. Reprint, Baltimore: Genealogical Pub. Co., 1996.

Hale, John P. *History of the Great Kanawha Valley ......* 2 vols. Madison WI: Brant, Fuller & Co., 1891.

Hall, Jean P. and Kathryn P. Hall, contributors, "Legislative Petitions: Cumberland County 1776-1786", *Magazine of Virginia Genealogy,* Vol. 30, No.2, p. 88-89.

Hall, William B. "Payne Data", *Genealogies, Virginia Magazine of History and Biography,* 4:252.

Hampden-Sidney College. *General Catalogue of the Officers and Students of Hampden-Sidney College, Virginia, 1776-1906.*

Handbook of Texas Online, "WILSON, WILLIAM REID", http://www.tsha.utexas.edu/handbook/online/articles/WW/fwigx.html.

Hanks, Betty and Terry McLean. *Cemeteries of Butler County Missouri,* "Wilson/ Rose Hill" .
http://www.rootsweb.com/~mobutle2/Cemmaps/Hanks/Volume4/wilson.htm.

Hanks, Betty and Terry McLean. *Sparkman Cemetery.*
http://ftp.rootsweb.com/pub/usgenweb/mo/butler/cemeteries/sparkman.txt.

Hening, William Waller, ed. *The Statutes at Large; Being a Collection of All the Laws of Virginia.* 13 vols. 1809-23.

Henneman, J. B., comp. "Trustees of Hampden-Sidney College." *Virginia Magazine of History and Biography* 6:174-184, 288-296 (1898), 7:30-38(1899).

Herndon, John Goodwin. "Thomas Wingfield (1670-1720) of York River, Va: .....".*Virginia Magazine of History and Biography* 60:305-322 (1952).

History of St. Charles, Montgomery and Warren Counties, Missouri, Written and Compiled from the Most Authentic Official and Private Sources. St. Louis: National Historic Co., 1885.

History of Virginia. 6 vols. Chicago: The American Historical Society, 1924.

Holcomb, Brent H, comp. *Marriages of Bute and Warren Counties North Carolina 1764-1868.* Reprint, Baltimore: Genealogical Pub. Co., 2004.

Hopkins, Garland Evans. *The Story of Cumberland County Virginia.* Privately Issued, 1942.

Hotten, John Camden. *The Original Lists of Persons of Quality ..... 1600-1700.* New York: G. A. Baker & Co. Inc., 1931.

Howell County, Missouri, Cemeteries, 1795-1987. West Plains MO: South Central Missouri Genealogical Society, 1988.

Hume, Edgar Erskine. *Sesquicentennial History and Roster of the Society of the Cincinnati in the State of Virginia 1783-1933.* Richmond VA: The Society, 1934.

Hurst, Melvin E. *Versailles Cemetery, Woodford Co., Kentucky.* Lexington KY: Fayette County Genealogical Society, 1999.

Ingmire, Frances. *Marriage Records of Rusk County, Texas, 1843-1877.* St Louis MO: 1979.

Ingmire, Frances T. *Rockingham County North Carolina Marriage Records 1785-1868.* St Louis MO: Ingmire Pub., 1984.

Ingmire, Frances. *San Augustine County Texas TX Marriages 1837-1880.* Signal Mountain TN: Mountain Press, 1985.

Johnson, Gertrude Pfeiffer, comp. *Obituaries, St. Charles County Missouri.* 1980.

Kanawha Co WV Marriage Records. Genealogical Society of Utah Microfilm Reel 521719. West Virginia Archives and History Library, Charleston WV. See "Kanawha County Marriages Microfilm Problems" by Susan Scouras, *WV Archives & History News*, Vol VI, no. 11, January 2006.

Kentucky Secretary of State, Land Office, http://apps.sos.ky.gov/land/military/revwar/Revdetail.asp?Type=w&warrant=0002.0

Kidd, Randy & Jeanne Stinson, comps. *Lost Marriages of Buckingham County Virginia.* Athens GA: Iberian, 1992.

King William Parish, Va. Vestry book of King William Parish, Virginia, 1707-1750. Midlothian VA: Manakin Episcopal Church, 1966.

Knight, Glenn B. "Brief History of the Grand Army of the Republic", Sons of Union Veterans of the Civil War, http://suvcw.org/gar.htm.

Knorr, Catherine Lindsay, comp. *Marriage Bonds and Ministers' Returns of Chesterfield County, Virginia, 1771-1815.* 1950. Pine Bluff AR: 1958.

Knorr, Catherine Lindsay, comp. *Marriage Bonds and Ministers' Returns of Prince*

Edward County, Virginia, 1754-1810. 1950. Reprint, Easley SC: Southern Historical Press, 1982.

Lee Family. *Papers, 1638-1867.* Section 161, Frames 610, 614. 1672 Lease for 200 acres at Passebehayes in James City Co. Virginia Historical Society, Richmond.

Ligon, William D, Jr. *The Ligon Family and Connections.* Hartford: printed by Bond Press, 1947.

"List of the American Graduates in Medicine in the University of Edinburgh". *New England Historical & Genealogical Register* 42:159-162 (1888).

Littleton Parish (Cumberland County, Va.). *Records, 1840-1899.* Accession 29330, Church Records Collection, Library of Virginia, Richmond.

Look, Karen (Crites). Family history records and letters.

Martin, Jimmye Maxwell and Martha Witten Johnson. *Carolyn Brooks' Manuscript, The Descendants of John Edwards.* Reproduced with permission by Jimmye Maxwell Martin and Martha Witten Johnson, 2005. Jimmye Martin, 180 PR 3311, Big Sandy, TX 75755

McClendon, Margaret Hobson. Application National number 564990. Daughters of the American Revolution, National Society. Washington DC.

McCrary, Patti Sue. *Cumberland County Virginia, Historical Inventory, Subject and Owner Indexes.* Westminster MD: Heritage Books, 2006.

McCrary, Patti Sue. *Wilson Families in Cumberland County Virginia and Woodford County Kentucky with Correspondence and Other papers 1785-1849.* Westminster MD: Heritage Books, 2005.

McElhiney, Mary Johnson. *Gone But Not Forgotten, ...Inscriptions ....St. Charles Co......* Missouri: A. M. Olson, 1970.

McIlwaine, H R, ed. *Proceedings of the Committees of Safety of Cumberland and Isle of Wight Counties Virginia 1775-1776.* Richmond: Davis Bottom, Superintendent of Public Printing, 1919.

McLean, Harry Herndon. *The Wilson Family - Somerset and Barter Hill Branch.* Charlotte NC: Observer Printing House, 1950.

Meade, William. *Old Churches, Ministers, and Families of Virginia.* 2 vols. 1857. Reprint, Baltimore: Genealogical Pub. Co., 1966.

Meyer, Virginia M. and John Frederick Dorman, eds. *Adventurers of Purse and Person Virginia 1607-1624/25.* 3rd edition. Richmond: Order of First Families of

Virginia, 1987. Volumes 1 and 2 of the new edition have been published.

Mills, W. S. *History of Van Zandt County*. Canton TX: 1950.

Mitchell, Mary Anna (Wilson). "Trent Family" (Written by the second Mrs. John P. Wilson, Elizabeth Woodson Trent). 1929.

Mount Locust on the Old Natchez Trace. Eastern National Park and Monument Assn., n. d.

Nash family. *Papers, 1734-1889*. Mssl N1786 a. Virginia Historical Society, Richmond.

Nethery, Loyal. Genealogy of Nethery, Neathery, and Netherly. http://www.loyalnethery.com:8180/loyalnethery/williamnethery.html.

Notes on Peter Field Trent. Microfiche 6019060. Family History Library, Salt Lake City UT.

Obernuefemann, Kelly and Lynnell Thomas. *Travel, Trade, and Travail: Slavery on the Old Natchez Trace*. Eastern National Park and Monument Assn., 2001.

Official Register of the Officers and Cadets of the La. State Seminary of Learning and Military Academy near Alexandria, Louisiana. New Orleans: Crescent Job Print, 1866-.

Passmore, John Andrew Moore. *Ancestors and Descendants of Andrew Moore (1612-1891)*. 3 vols. Philadelphia: 1897.

Phillips, Edward W. and Murle K. Phillips Rhodes. *Gregg and Pre-Gregg County Postoffices and Postmasters through the Year 1900*.

Portrait and Biographical Record of St. Charles Co. MO. Chapman Pub. Co., 1895.

Presbyterian Church. Histories of Roanoke Presbytery and Her Churches. Presbytery of Appomattox, VA Reel 2. Department of History, Montreat NC.

Putman, Wyvonne, comp. *Navarro County History*. 5 vols. Quanah TX: Nortex, 1975-84.

Railey, William E. *History of Woodford County, Kentucky*. 1938. Reprinted by Salem MA: Higginson Book Co., 1992.

Reynolds, Katherine, abs. *Abstracts of Cumberland County, Virginia, Will Books 1 and 2 1749-1782*. Easley SC: Southern Historical Press, 1985.

Richardson, Douglas . *Plantagenet Ancestry: A Study In Colonial and Medieval*

Families. Baltimore: Genealogical Pub. Co., 2004.

Robert A. Siegel Auction Galleries, Inc., Item 1145,
http://siegelauctions.com/2001/841/y84117.htm.

Rosen, Carl Coleman Sr. *History of Maysville Presbyterian Church, Buckingham Court House, Virginia 1824-1996*. Buckingham VA: Maysville Presbyterian Church, 1997.

Rosen, Carl C. *The Papers of Col. Richard H. Gilliam of Buckingham County, Virginia*. Westminister MD: Family Line Pub., 1992.

Ruff, Nancy Blakeley, comp. *Gregg County, Texas Marriage License Index: Books A, B, C & D, 1873-1895*. Longview TX: 1980.

Sanders, John Barnette, comp. *Index to the Marriage Records of Shelby County, Texas 1882-1936 (Vol 1 pg 1 to Vol 14 pg 638)*. Center TX: J. B. Sanders, 1967.

Sanders, John Barnette, comp. *Our Dead, Shelby County, Texas, 1836-1964*. Center TX: J. B. Sanders, 1966.

Schreiner-Yantis, Netti and Florence Speakman Love. *The 1787 census of Virginia: An Accounting of the Name of Every White Male Tithable over 21 years .... . 3 vols.* Springfield VA: Genealogical Books in Print, 1987.

Solomon, Alan. "Off the Beaten Trace".
http://www.chicagotribune.com/travel/chi-010522drives-natchez,0,6262737.story.

Southwest Corner: a Collection of Historical Articles of Early Southwest Virginia by Goodridge Wilson, 1887-1976 (in the Roanoke VA Times). 1981.

Stutesman, John Hale. *Some Watkins Families of Virginia and their Kin*. Baltimore: Gateway Press, 1989.

Swango, Maxine, ed. *Early Kanawha County Marriage Records*, 3 pts. in 1 vol. South Charleston WV: Kanawha Valley Genealogical Society, 1981.

Texas State-wide Records Program. *Index to Probate Cases of Texas, No. 201, Rusk County June 18, 1843 - December 29, 1939*. San Antonio TX: The State-wide Records Indexing and Inventory Program, 1942.

Today and Yesterday in the Heart of Virginia. Farmville VA: Farmville Herald, 1935.

Trent Family Bible Record, 1749-1903. Accession 25300. Archives & Manuscripts, Library of Virginia, Richmond VA.

Trotter, Margret G. "A Glimpse of Charleston in the 1890s from a Contemporary Diary", *West Virginia History*, 35:131-3 (1974).

Trout, W. E. *The Slate & Willis's Rivers Atlas: Rediscovering Historic Waterways in the Heart of Virginia*. Virginia Canals and Navigation Society, 1994.

United States, Dept. of the Interior. *Rejected or Suspended Applications for Revolutionary War Pensions: with an added Index to States*. Baltimore: reprinted for Clearfield Co. by Genealogical Pub. Co., 1998.

University of Pennsylvania.University Archives and Records Center. Philadelphia PA.
http://www.archives.upenn.edu/histy/students/med/az1806to1852/medmatric_m.pdf
http://www.archives.upenn.edu/histy/students/med/az1806to1852/medmatric_t.pdf
http://www.archives.upenn.edu/histy/students/med/az1806to1852/medmatric_w.pdf
http://www.archives.upenn.edu/histy/students/med/catalogs/catmedmat1831.html
http://www.archives.upenn.edu/histy/students/med/catalogs/catmedmat1845.html

Valentine, Edward Pleasants. *The Edward Pleasants Valentine Papers*, 4 vols. Richmond VA: Valentine Museum [1927].

Venable, Elizabeth Marshall. *Venables of Virginia …. Samuel Woodson Venable of "Springfield" and his brother William Lewis Venable of "Haymarket"*. Privately printed. New York: J. J. Little and Ives Co., 1925. (Available as book or on cd from Quintin Publications, PO Box 65546, Orange Park, FL 32065-7605, 904-375-1113 - http://www.quintinpublications.com/).

Virginia Biography, vols. 4-6. *History of Virginia*. Chicago, New York: American Historical Society, 1924.

Virginia Council of State. *Journals of the Council of the State of Virginia*. Richmond: Division of Purchasing and Printing, 1931-1982.

Virginia Gazette, 4 Dec 1766. October 3, 1751 - Mar 31, 1768, Miscellaneous Reel 162. Library of Virginia, Richmond.

Virginia Gazette, 25 Mar 1775. July 7, 1774-June 29, 1776, Film 11 Reel 5. Library of Virginia, Richmond.

Virginia Magazine of History and Biography. Richmond: Virginia Historical Society.

Virginia Revolutionary War State Pensions. Special Publication 7. Richmond: Virginia Genealogical Society, 1980.

Vogt, John and T William Kethley, Jr. *Powhatan County Marriages, 1777-1850*. Athens GA: Iberian Publishing Co., 1985.

Ward, Roger G. *Buckingham County Virginia Records, Land Tax Summaries & Implied Deeds 1782-1814, Vol 1.* Athens GA: Iberian Publishing Co., 1993.

Washington and Lee University. *Catalogue of the Officers and Alumni of Washington and Lee University, Lexington, Virginia, 1749-1888.* Baltimore: John Murphy & Co., 1888.

Watson, Elizabeth Audrain. *Heritage And Promise, A History of Dardenne Presbyterian Church and Its Community.* Chicago: Adams Press, 1977.

Watkins, Francis N. *A Catalogue of the Descendants of Thomas Watkins of Chickahominy.* Privately printed. New York: J. F. Trow, 1852.

Watkins, Marie Oliver and Helen (Hamacher) Watkins. *Tearin' Through the Wilderness : Missouri Pioneer Episodes, 1822-1885, and Genealogy of the Watkins Family of Virginia and Missouri.* Charleston WV: Mathews Ptg., 1957.

Webster, Irene B. *Rockingham County, North Carolina, Will Abstracts, Vol. I 1785-1865.* Madison NC: Mrs. S. F. Webster, 1973.

Weisiger, Benjamin B. "Powhatan County, Virginia Tombstone Inscriptions". *The Southside Virginian* 3:158-9, (1985).

West Virginia History, A Quarterly Magazine. State Dept. Of Archives and History. Charleston WV.

Whitehouse, Arch. "The Loco Boys Go Wild", *True, the Man's Magazine*, Nov. 1944.

Wiechens, Lucille Wittenborn and Carrol Geerling. *Cemeteries of St. Charles County, Missouri.* Bridgeton MO: Lineage Press, 1988.

Wilkins, John W. *Gregg County, Texas, South of the Sabine, Volume I, Kinfolk and Neighbors in Justice Precincts 4, 5, and 6, Based on the 1910 United States Census.* Gladewater TX: 1983.

Will of Benjamin Wilson, 1812-1814. Cumberland County VA Lodged Wills, Box 1, 1790-1825, Feb. 1814. Archives & Information Services Division, Library of Virginia, Richmond.

Will of James Seay 1752, King William Co VA. Burned County Records Collection, Library of Virginia, Richmond.

Wilson, Cornelia McLaurine. "Family History", transcribed by Philip Austin Lawless of Durham NC. ftp://ftp.rootsweb.com/pub/usgenweb/tx/sanaugustine/history/w4250001.txt.

Wilson, Cornelia Williamson McLaurine, comp. *Genealogical notes on the Harris, McLaurine, St. Clair, Stegar, Williamson, and Wilson families.* Mss6:1 W691:1. Virginia Historical Society, Richmond.

Wilson, Eloise. Papers of Eloise Wilson (1912-2003) concerning Wilson, Butts Families Primarily in East Texas. Vertical Files, Family History Room, Longview Public Library, Longview TX.

Wilson, Eugene V. "The Ninth Air Force from the Beginning". B-26 Marauder Historical Society WWII Air War Archive. http://b-26marauderarchive.org/DA/PA472/PA472.htm.

"Wilson Family of Princess Anne, Norfolk, &c." *Virginia Magazine of History and Biography* 25:199-200 (1917).

Wilson, Henry Harrison. *Papers, 1922-1925.* Mss2 W6938 b. Virginia Historical Society, Richmond.

Wilson, Henry Harrison. John Park Wilson family history notes. Copies in possession of John M. Finley, Austin TX.

Wilson, Nathaniel Venable, b. 1814. *Papers, 1834-1878.* Mss1 W6957 a. Virginia Historical Society, Richmond.

Wilson, Virginia. Family group sheets copies from Ann Wilson of Lexington KY in 2003.

Wiltshire, Betty C. *Mississippi Newspaper Obituaries 1862-1875.* Carrollton MS: Pioneer Pub. Co., 1994.

Wise, Bel Hubbard, abs. *Amelia County, Virginia Will Book 4 1786-1792.* Signal Mountain TN: Mountain Press, 1991.

Woodson Family. *Papers, 1740-1945.* Accession 29437-41, Prayer book of Anne (Seay) Wilson. Personal Papers Collection, Archives Branch, Library of Virginia, Richmond.

Woodson Family. *Papers, 1778-1908* Section 7. Mss1 W8687a 33-36. Virginia Historical Society, Richmond.

Woodson Family Bible. Accession 30316, Archives and Manuscripts, Library of Virginia, Richmond. Photocopies of original Bible, Accession 29437-43.

Woodson, Henry Morton, comp. *Historical Genealogy of the Woodsons and Their Connections.* [Memphis] the author, 1915.

WPA. Works Progress Administration Surveys.
  Buckingham Co. VA, Clay Bank #288, Maysville Presbyterian Church #70.
Maysville Presbyterian Church Cemetery #71.
  Cumberland Co. VA, Bonbrook #121, Bonbrook Cemetery #86, Barter Hill #114.
  Prince Edward Co. VA, Slate Hill #10, History of Early Private Schools in Prince
  Edward County (no number assigned).
These reports can be downloaded from the web site for the Library of Virginia,
Virginia Historical Inventory.

INDEX OF NAMES

(Some details given to me in recent correspondence may not be reflected in the index. PSM)

aft 1924] 220
William Willis [1815-1875]
. . . . 14, 305, 307
Williams [1928-] . 225, 226
Willis 308
Willis [1758-1822] . 1, 7, 12,
13, 307, 310
Willis [1795-aft 1840] . . 34
Willis [1817-1865] . . 14, 15,
17, 18, 21, 31, 144, 174,
305, 307
Willis [1858-1862] 101,
260
Willis [abt 1707-abt 1740]
. . . . 1
Willis Alexander [1825-
1866] 113
Willis Alexander [1870-
1932] 142
Willis Park [1815-1816]
. . . . 13
Willis Sherrard [1867-]
. . . . 304
Willis Trent [1902-1980]
. . . . 156, 160
Willis Trent, Jr [1941-1996]
. . . . 160
Willis, Jr [1850-1869] . . 15,
174
Woodville Bates [1894-1958]
. . . 259, 270, 273, 274
Zula (Anderson) 249
Windish
Helen 212-214
Wingfield
Rebecca [-bef 1773] 34
Winston?
Sarah [1600-1660] 314
Witten
Alice Evelyn (Edwards)
[1896-1983] . 121, 122
Ann Ruth (Claunch) [1925-]
. . . . 121, 122
Cynthia Ann [1949-] . . 121
Lucy (Clement) 121
Martha Alice [1950-] . . 121,
122

Patrick 121
Patrick Wilson [1922-1961]
. . . . 121, 122
Sidney Gipson [1892-1958]
. . . . 121, 122
Sydney Ann [1930-] . . . 117,
121, 122
Wittkuhns
Rose Marie 239
Wolters
Mildred Marie [1921-] . . 87,
88
Womack
Betsey 287
Wood
_____ 131
Chalmers Barbour . 148, 149
Christopher 131
Edward Chalmers [1923-]
. . . . 148
Edward Chalmers, Jr [1944-]
. . . . 149
Effie (Davey) 148
Eleanora (Wilson) [1875-]
. . . . 148, 149
Eva Marie (Ryan) [1960-
1997] 131
Helen West [1902-] . . . 148,
149
Kathleen Marie [1930-]
. . . . 148
Kimberly Elizabeth 131
Leslie Teresa [1948-] . . 149
Mary Adele [1901-] . . . 148
Shulamith (Appel) 148
Thomas Davey [1826-]
. . . . 148
Victoria (Doan) 149
Wilson Barbour [1898-]
. . . . 148
Woods
Elizabeth Jane "Bettie"
(Collins) [1858-1922]
. . . . 41
Lewis Richard [1849-1923]
. . . . 41
Sarah Eleanor "Sallie" [1892-

689839

Made in the USA